IA

R WORKED

RIC AND
SURVEY

C SURVEY

(LUCKNOW)

INDIAN ANTHROPOLOGY

DHIRENDRA NATH MAJUMDAR

Indian Anthropology

ESSAYS IN MEMORY OF D. N. MAJUMDAR

Edited by

T. N. MADAN and GOPĀLA ŚARANA

ASIA PUBLISHING HOUSE

NEW YORK

PRINTED IN INDIA

By Z. T. Bandukwala at Leaders Press Private Limited, Bombay
and Published by P. S. Jayasinghe, Asia Publishing House, 119
West 57th Street, New York

CONTRIBUTORS

BRIDGET ALLCHIN

FRANK RAYMOND ALLCHIN

F. G. BAILEY

GEORGE WILLIAM GREGORY BIRD

KSHITISH PRASAD CHATTOPADHYAY

SHYAMA CHARAN DUBE

CRISTOPH VON FÜRER-HAIMENDORF

REGINALD RUGGLES GATES

ELIZABETH W. IKIN

IRAWATI KARVÉ

HERMAN LEHMANN

DAVID G. MANDELBAUM

ADRIAN C. MAYER

ARTHUR ERNEST MOURANT

RAMKRISHNA MUKHERJEE

CALYAMPUDI RADHAKRISHNA RAO

HASMUKH DHIRAJLAL SANKALIA

SASANKA SHEKHAR SARKAR

DHARANI SEN

DILIP KUMAR SEN

POPATLAL GOVINDLAL SHAH

BENDAPUDI SUBBARAO

PREFACE

Anthropological studies in India have today reached a stage when the reorganization of research and the clarification of its aims and methods are being actively debated. There is a widespread feeling among anthropologists that what was good enough in the past is no longer always so. This is a happy sign, indicative of coming of age.

At such a time nothing could be more useful than a volume of essays covering the major divisions of anthropology, and dealing with past achievements and failures, present trends, and future possibilities. Further, there could be no better memorial, than such a volume, to the memory of D. N. Majumdar who had much more than a hand in the shaping of anthropology as an academic discipline in India.

The decision to bring out the present Volume of essays was taken by the undersigned, after consultations with several colleagues and friends, in March 1960. It was proposed that the Volume should be presented to Majumdar on his sixtieth birthday on June 3, 1962.

Invitations were sent to a number of scholars, some of whom could not contribute papers owing to previous commitments. The first letters of invitation were despatched on May 24, 1960, exactly eight days before Majumdar's tragic and unexpected death. Ironically enough, the first letter of acceptance, from Professor von Fürer-Haimendorf, was dated May 31, the very day of Majumdar's death; and the second, from Professor Mandelbaum, was dated June 1, the day of Majumdar's cremation.

With the consent of the authors and the publishers we decided to bring out the proposed Volume as a memorial to Majumdar.

We express our grateful thanks to all the scholars who have written for this book. There is, however, one contributor who is no more—alas! Professor D. P. Mukerji wrote a brief introductory note for the Volume in August 1961 when he was physically ill and mentally in anguish. He was dissatisfied with what he had written, in spite of our assurances that it was just what we had wanted. He died on December 5, 1961, at the age of sixty-seven. We take this opportunity to pay our tribute to him. "D.P." is dead. There is nobody like him who can fill the gap or put us in mind of him.

We received valuable suggestions and advice from our colleague Dilip K. Sen in planning and editing the Volume, and hereby acknowledge our indebtedness to him.

Lucknow, 31st March, 1962

T. N. MADAN
GOPĀLA ŚARANA

CONTENTS

PART ONE—DHIRENDRA NATH MAJUMDAR: IN MEMORIAM

PART TWO—ANTHROPOLOGY IN INDIA

PREHISTORIC ARCHAEOLOGY

PHYSICAL ANTHROPOLOGY

SOCIAL-CULTURAL ANTHROPOLOGY

The Map, showing areas in which Majumdar conducted
ethnographic fieldwork and/or anthropometric and serological surveys, has been prepared by Mrs. Uma T. Madan,
a former pupil of Professor Majumdar.

INDIAN ANTHROPOLOGY

PART ONE

Dhirendra Nath Majumdar: In Memoriam

I

INTRODUCTION

IN RECENT years several scholars have drawn pointed attention to and emphasized the interdependence of the social anthropology of India and Indology. Anthropological studies in India may, in fact, be said to have had their beginning in the investigations of Indologists. Sir William Jones (1746-94), judge, linguistic genius and Indologist, founded the Asiatic Society of Bengal in 1784. In his inaugural address he proposed that the Society undertake inquiries concerned with 'man' and 'nature' in India. The major interest was, of course, to reveal the past of India through the study of Sanskrit texts; however, the collection of ethnographic and ethnological data also was contemplated and encouraged. Throughout the nineteenth century a large number of missionaries, civil servants and travellers added to our knowledge of the tribal societies and the rural peoples of India. One of the earliest known studies was that of Francis Buchanon, who was appointed in 1807 by the Governor General-in-Council to undertake an ethnographic survey of the people of Bengal and their religion. Other names come readily to one's mind when thinking of the pioneers of anthropology in India—names like those of Hamilton, Thornton, Campbell, Latham, Ibbetson and, of course, Maine, Baden-Powell and Risley. During the early years of the present century others joined the ranks of pioneers: prominent among them were Thurston, Rangachari, L. K. Anathakrishna Iyer, Russell, Hiralal, Crooke, Hodson, Gurdon, and Sarat Chandra Roy. Rivers' visit to the Toda took place during this period and his famous monograph was published in 1906. An impetus was given to physical anthropological and archaeological studies by the work of Risley, Keith, Turner, Morant, Foote and Stein. Grierson's linguistic survey of India was a monument to painstaking research.

Anthropology as a scholarly discipline received formal recognition in 1920 when the University of Calcutta included the subject in its curricula. Among the earliest persons to receive their Master's degree in anthropology from this University was Dhirendra Nath Majumdar. He used to recall, in his later life, the acute disappointment of his parents when he decided to study an unknown and somewhat 'shady' subject instead of seeking a place in the civil services of the country.

Majumdar came to anthropology with more than an antiquarian interest; he was a formally trained scientist. From the beginning he combined anthropometric surveys with his ethnographic investigations. In later years he was to add serology, demography, growth, study of culture change, village studies and urban surveys to his already wide interests. Cultural anthropology and physical anthropology had a coordinate place in his work, neither occupying a position which was in any sense preferred. Although he did not engage in any investigations in prehistoric archaeology, he kept abreast of the major developments in the field and occasionally lectured on the subject. One of the editors recalls having attended a course on the 'Stone Age Cultures of Europe' which Majumdar gave at Lucknow in the summer of 1950.

Majumdar died on the 31st of May, 1960. Two of his books, *Race Elements in Bengal* (co-author: C. R. Rao) and *Social Contours of an Industrial City* (assisted by N. S. Reddy and S. Bahadur), had been published earlier in the year. At the time of his death a monograph on the Khasa of Jaunsar Bawar (Uttar Pradesh) entitled *Himalayan Polyandry* was already in the hands of the publisher and the manuscript of a village study called *A Village on the Fringe* was receiving final touches. A revised edition of his *Races and Cultures of India* was also in the press. Several other manuscripts were in various stages of completion. It will be sometime before all his works are published. We may, therefore, do here no more than indicate in outline the nature of his contributions in various fields of research.

In the field of physical anthropology Majumdar's contribution consists mainly in the extensive anthropometric and serological surveys which he carried out among the tribes and castes of Bihar, Madhya Pradesh, Uttar Pradesh, Gujarat and Bengal. He took measurements of 10,000 people and in Uttar Pradesh alone blood grouped about 5,000 individuals.

Quite early in his career he emphasized the importance of statistical techniques in the analysis of anthropometric and serological data. His collaboration with Professors P. C. Mahalanobis and C. Radhakrishna Rao resulted in the formulation of D^2 or the 'generalised distance statistic'. The distinguished French anthropologist

Henri V. Vallois has classed D^2 with Fisher's 'discriminant function' as an advanced and highly favoured statistico-taxonomic method in biometrical anthropology (*Anthropology Today* ed. by A. L. Kroeber, Chicago 1953, pp. 152-3).

In Uttar Pradesh, Majumdar tried to show that the caste hierarchy had a 'biometric basis'. The castes which constitute 'clusters', being close to each other in the hierarchical organisation, were shown to be also within a close range of biometric variation. A similar correlation between the order of social precedence and ethnic characteristics in a region was detected by him in undivided Bengal and in Gujarat. Although his investigations led him to draw attention to the racial factor in the formation of the caste structure, yet he was strongly and firmly opposed to both 'racism' as well as single-factor explanations of caste in India.

Majumdar did not confine his attention to distribution studies of racial characters; he was also interested in the ontogenetic development of Indian children. His study of school children in the city of Lucknow is a landmark in Indian physical anthropology.

In the field of cultural anthropology Majumdar's best work was ethnographic in character. He carried out extensive fieldwork among the Ho of Kolhan (Bihar) and the Khasa (Uttar Pradesh) and also made first-hand studies of the Korwa and the Tharu (both of Uttar Pradesh), the Gond of Bastar (Madhya Pradesh) and the Bhil (Gujarat). His knowledge of the Ho and the Khasa was unrivalled. Deeply influenced by Roy and Malinowski, he was a painstaking and patient fieldworker. He spread out his fieldwork in a tribe or village over several years, making his observations during short and long trips. He attached great importance to the learning of tribal and folk dialects. In ethnography he covered all the major aspects of a culture—economics, kinship, religion etc. He studied cultures rather than problems. An abiding interest, however, was culture change, in the study of which he underlined the importance of taking into consideration the psychological dimension of human behaviour.

With his early interest in culture change, he welcomed the emergence of rural studies and played a notable part in spelling out the problems involved in this new field of research. He also brought out one of the first village studies in India, viz. *Caste and Communication in an Indian Village* (Bombay, 1958).

Majumdar was a firm believer in applied anthropology. He

emphasized that although the findings of cultural anthropologists may not be of obvious practical value, as the findings of physical anthropologists are, yet the former could provide government and society with knowledge indispensable in the conscious shaping of the future. As a member of the Research Programmes Committee of the Planning Commission (Government of India) he underscored the role which the anthropologist could play in helping the administration by studying the problems of socially and economically backward peoples, and properly assessing them as well as administrative action.

Majumdar's contributions to anthropology in India were many and various. Not only did he himself engage in investigations, but he also initiated a large number of students into the various branches of anthropological research. They are today spread all over India, teaching in colleges and universities, working in research institutions or employed in the specialized departments of the Government. One of his students is teaching anthropology in the University of Bagdad (Iraq). His interest in and love for his students was unbounded. Mrs. Madhuri Majumdar writes (in a letter to the editors) that her husband used to tell her that his students were his sons (his only child was a daughter). In a country in which the chasm between the proximate generations is a marked one, and the relations between teacher and student characterized by reserve and mutual aloofness, the warm relations of Majumdar with his students were something out of the usual. And the love and loyalty which his students gave him also were extraordinary.

Although Majumdar succeeded only rather late in life in persuading the University of Lucknow to create an independent Department of Anthropology, he more than made up for the lost time by his incredible capacity for hard work and by his enthusiasm and devotion. Professor Fürer-Haimendorf writes in an excellent tribute: "His vision, wide experience of all branches of anthropology, and remarkable energy had made him a focal point of anthropological studies in India, and his department in the University of Lucknow, the foundation and development of which he always regarded as the core of his life work, has for many years been the most active department of anthropology in the whole of south Asia." (*Man*, Vol. LX, No. 212, 1960.....)

Majumdar was born of Bengali parents in Bihar. He received his education in Bengal and did his first fieldwork in Bihar among the Ho of Kolhan. But it was in Uttar Pradesh that he spent the greater part of his life, from 1928 till his death in 1960. It was, therefore, only to be expected that he should have taken a particular interest in the peoples and cultures of this State. In 1945 he founded the Ethnographic and Folk-Culture Society of U.P. The principal aim of this Society is to collect ethnographic data on the folk-cultures of Uttar Pradesh. Two years later the Society brought out a journal called *The Eastern Anthropologist*, largely at his initiative and with him as editor. This journal has since attained an international circulation and a high reputation.

Majumdar was a man who loved adventure and regarded obstacles as opportunities for hard endeavour. He was an optimist with a firm faith in his vocation. He was a genial, warm hearted and sociable person whose greatest virtue was his tolerance. He loved the good things of life including travel, company, conversation and good food. He was ever willing to learn and retained a youthfulness of body and mind till the very end. He was, in fact, at the height of his creative powers when a cerebral haemorrhage put an end to his remarkable life. Touching tributes on his death were paid him by his many friends in India, Great Britain and the U.S.A. A British colleague wrote with feeling (in a letter to one of the editors) that it was difficult to think of Indian anthropology without Majumdar, for he had so long been Indian anthropology.

II

MAJUMDAR : SCHOLAR AND FRIEND

D. P. MUKERJI

WE CAME to know each other in 1928 when D. N. Majumdar was selected as a lecturer in the Department of Economics and Sociology, of the University of Lucknow, at the age of twenty five. He had become a Premchand Roychand Scholar of the Calcutta University at a still younger age. Professor Radhakamal Mukerjee, the head of our Department, brought him in when he had sensed the talents of this young man. With the late B. Mukerjee, Dr. H. L. De and Majumdar, we formed a group of scholars in the making. There were differences no doubt, but somehow we managed to live and live in the midst of fairly scholarly habits and surrondings. My personal relations with him were extremely cordial. The fighting qualities which noted him as marked traits did not brush against me. He looked up to me as his elder brother and I also looked at him as my younger brother. The reason of my affection, if affection had reason at all, was simple: I recognized him to be a budding scholar. In fact, he became one soon. His was the rare example of an Indian scholar who loved scholarship to the depths of his being. He was certainly interested in the politics of the University, but he did not become a politician. His abiding interest was Anthropology. Did he not lead two expeditions to the 18,000 feet above-sea-level Rupkund Lake in 1956, when he was 53, to investigate the large litter of human bones and skulls discovered there?

His scholarship is a fairly long story. He first published a treatise on the Ho. I got it published from Calcutta and helped him in re-conditioning a thesis into a book. He then took up one by one the Korwa, the Tharu and the Khasa of Northern India (U.P.), the Gonds of Bastar and the Bhils of Gujarat, and produced two books and many papers.

But he began to change his views a little; his interest became cultural as different from its being purely ethnographical. When he went to Cambridge and London, in the mid-thirtees, he came under the influence of Malinowski even though he was primarily influenced by the veteran Indian ethnographer, Sarat Chandra Roy. Later on still the influence of Kroeber on him was very clear. He also escaped from ethnography through his interest in blood groups, in statistical surveys, in demography and in the study of growth among children. His anthropometric surveys in Uttar Pradesh and West Bengal with the help of Dr. C. R. Rao, and his demographic study of Kanpur with the assistance of Dr. Reddy are the models of their type and made him cast for new anthropological issues.

The Eastern Anthropologist, which he founded in 1947 and of which he was the editor upto the time of his death, claimed a great deal of his scholarly and organizational attention to become one of the leading anthropological journals of the world. It is good to know that the journal is being kept alive. It should be; it is probably the best memento he has bequeathed to future generations of Indian anthropologists.

I am not in a position to assess Majumdar's studies in physical anthropology, but I am in a slightly better position to estimate his contributions to "culturology". There, essentially, he did not distinguish between the terms of content and function *a la* Malinowski and the formal integration of Ruth Benedict. He was, I think, fundamentally a field anthropologist who had strayed into general anthropology. If I am not wrong again, he was not primarily interested in the theoretical implications of the science, as Nadel was. But, during his ultimate talks with me, he was veering round theory. He said, "Give me a chance. I shall try to build up some kind of theory after I have established a firm base," that is, of the field. It was, however, too late in the day.

I do not want to describe and examine Dr. Majumdar's research work. I would like to mention his other academic qualities. He was a very hardworking man, working for ten to twelve hours a day. In the late evenings he would go to the Hazratganj shopping centre in Lucknow and meet his publishers, students and friends in the bookshops. Some of the bookshops, thanks to him, were stacked with books on anthropology. The Coffee House he would religiously attend. His students also congregated there. From nine in the morning till seven in the evening he would work and then felt himself free. In that period also he discussed all the varied problems with his students and research scholars, their projects and schemes, and helped them seriously. He collected around himself a team of workers for research. In fact, he succeeded in enlisting them for the different colleges and universities of India, and also for his journal. I think very few men in India have produced a better set of research workers than he had done. He was a friendly man, and his students were devoted to him. There was no misunderstanding with them. I have hinted above that he was a fighter, but he fought for causes, for the principles he cared for. He excused people and hoped soon to be excused. A definite mellowness was developed in later years. He had become very mature, thanks to his intimacies with his students and with European, British and American scholars. I was expecting him to be ripe, and he had got into his stride. The best was yet to be; he was only fifty seven.

Dr. Majumdar was a good conversationalist and a lovable host. At first he was shy, but he soon conquered his shyness and became a good talker. He never monopolized the talk as most professors do. His wife and young daughter, their only child, collaborated with him in hostship.

One incident in the last days of his life struck me. I was with him for a week just a month before his tragic death. We talked about all manner of things, his research work and personal life in particular. He was an incorrigible optimist, but when he was elected Dean of the Faculty of Arts, at the University of Lucknow, in April 1960, he began to feel sorry. He was mindful of the honour but said he was going to lose his grip and unless he recovered it, he would be lost. At the same time he loved the life of action, notionally. But taking all into consideration he did not like the Deanship at all. The last thing he said was, "This Deanship will kill me." My reply was, "You will survive. If you don't like it, give it up." "Yes, I will soon." He died on the 31st of May from a cerebral haemorrhage. I have seen more than one man crumbling under the burdens of administration. And Majumdar was essentially a scholar.

I will remember him as a scholar and a friend who was as dear to me as a brother. He should not have died so young !

Dehradun (U.P.)
2nd August, 1961

III

DHIRENDRA NATH MAJUMDAR: VITA

1903 Born in Patna (Bihar), India, June 3. The eldest son of Mrs. Kusum Kumari and the late Mr. Rebati Mohan Majumdar.

1922 Graduated from the Arts Faculty of the University of Calcutta.

1924 Received M.A. degree in Anthropology from the University of Calcutta. Was placed in the first division and secured the first place among successful candidates.

1924 Made his first field trip, visiting the Ho of Kolkan (Bihar) in the company of the veteran Indian ethnographer the late Sarat Chandra Roy.

1926 Awarded the Premchand Roychand Scholarship by the University of Calcutta. The Scholarship, awarded on the merit of original research, was those days coveted as a great honour.

1927 Married Madhuri Guha, daughter of the late Mr. and Mrs. Prafulla Chandra Guha.

1928 Selected by Professor Radhakamal Mukerjee to become lecturer in primitive economics in the Department of Economics and Sociology at the University of Lucknow.

1929 Awarded the Mouat Gold Medal by the University of Calcutta.

1933 Went to Cambridge. Studied social anthropology with Professor T. C. Hodson and physical anthropology with Professor G. M. Morant. Attended Malinowski's Seminar at the London School of Economics. Also studied serology with Professor R. Ruggles Gates and worked in the Galton Laboratory (London).

1935 Received Ph.D. degree from Cambridge. The subject of his dissertation was culture change among the Ho.

1936 Elected a Fellow of the Royal Anthropological Institute of Great Britain and Ireland.

1936-37 Gave a series of lectures on Indian Culture at Vienna. Had given a similar series of lectures while at Cambridge.

1939 Presided over the Anthropology and Archaeology Section of the 26th Session of the Indian Science Congress held at Lahore.

1941 Elected a Fellow of the National Institute of Sciences (India).

1941 Invited by the Census Commissioner of the United Provinces (now Uttar Pradesh) to undertake an anthropometric and serological survey of the Provinces.

1942 Promilla-Kumkum born. She is the only child of Mrs. Madhuri Majumdar and the late Professor Majumdar.

1942 Invited by Sir Theodore Tusker, Supervisor of the Indian Civil Service Training Centre at Dehradun, to deliver a course of lectures on Indian anthropology. These lectures were later published in 1944 under the title *Races and Cultures of India*. The book has since been revised and reprinted three times. It is probably Majumdar's best known published work.

1945 Founded the Ethnographic and Folk-Culture Society (U.P.).

1945 Invited by Professor P. C. Mahalanobis, F.R.S., Director of the Indian Statistical Institute, Calcutta, to undertake an anthropometric and serological servey of Bengal.

1946 Invited by the University of Nagpur to deliver Sri Mahadeo Hari Wathodkar Memorial lectures. These lectures were published in 1947 under the title *The Matrix of Indian Culture*.

1946 Selected as Reader in Anthropology in the Department of Economics and Sociology at the University of Lucknow.

1946-47 Invited by Shri P. G. Shah, on behalf of the Gujerat Research Society, to undertake an anthropometric and serological survey of Gujerat.

1947 Founded *The Eastern Anthropologist*. Appointed its editor.

1949 Appointed as one of the Hon. editors of *Man In India*. Resigned in 1955.

1950 Awarded the Gujerat Research Society Medal for outstanding contribution to Indian physical anthropology.

1950 Appointed as Professor of Anthropology in the Department of Economics and Sociology at the University of Lucknow.

1951 Appointed Head of the newly created Department of Anthropology at the University of Lucknow.

1952 Represented India, Pakistan and Ceylon at the International Symposium on Anthropology organised by the Wenner-Gren Foundation and held in New York. Was co-chairman with Julian H. Steward of one of the of the sections.

1952-53 Appointed Visiting Professor of Far Eastern Studies at the Cornell University, Ithcaca, N.Y.

1953 Started the Lucknow-Cornell Research Centre in collaboration with the Cornell University (represented by Professor M.E. Opler) and the Ford Foundation in India.

1953 Elected a Fellow of the American Association of Physical Anthropologists.

1953 Invited by the Planning Commission, Government of India, to become a member of its Research Programmes Committee.

1954 Appointed a delegate by the U.N. to the World Conference on Population held in Rome. Elected a member of the International Union for the Scientific Study of Population.

1954 Attended as a delegate the International Sociological Congress at Paris.

1955 Presided over the Anthropology Section of the First All-India Sociological Conference held at Dehradun.

1955 Appointed member of the Standing Committee of the Research Programmes Committee (Planning Commission) Government of India.

1956 Elected General President of the Second All-India Sociological Conference held at Patna.

1957-58 Appointed Visiting Lecturer in Asian Anthropology in the School of Oriental and African Studies at the University of London.

1958 Awarded the Annandale Gold Medal by the Asiatic Society for contributions to Asian anthropology.

1958 Invited by the Government of India to become a member of the Central Advisory Board for Anthropology.

1958   Invited by the Indian Council of Medical Research to become a member of its governing body.

1959   Visited Britain and the Continent. Lectured at the Institute of Social Sciences at the Hague.

1960   Appointed Dean of the Faculty of Arts at the University of Lucknow.

1960   Died May 31 at Lucknow, from a cerebral haemorrhage.

IV

BIBLIOGRAPHY OF D. N. MAJUMDAR*

The following abbrevations have been used:

AAT—*An Appraisal of Anthropology Today*, Sol Tax et al (eds.), Chicago: The University of Chicago Press.

EA *The Eastern Anthropologist*, Lucknow,

HV—*Hindi Vishva-Bharati*, Shrinarayan Chaturvedi (chief ed.), Lucknow: Educational Publishing Company Limited.

JGRS—*Journal of the Gujerat Research Society*, Bombay.

JPASB—*Journal and Proceedings of the Asiatic Society of Bengal*, Calcutta.

JRASB—*The Journal of the Royal Asiatic Society of Bengal*, Calcutta.

MII—*Man in India*, Ranchi.

PISC—*The Proceedings of the Indian Science Congress*, Calcutta.

1923a 'The custom of burning human effigies', MII, vol. 3:97-103.

1923b 'Notes on Kali-nauch in the district of Dacca', MII, Vol. 3:202-16.

1923c 'Customs and taboos observed by an East Bengal woman from pregnancy to childbirth', MII, Vol. 3:232-42.

1924a 'Physical characteristics of the Hos of Kolhan', JPASB, Vol. 20:171-80; also MII, Vol. 5:83-114.

1924b 'Some of the characteristics of Kolarian songs', JPASB, Vol. 20: 181-92; also (Abstract) P, (Twelfth) ISC, p. 265.

1924c 'The traditional origin of the Hos: together with a brief description of the chief Bongas (Gods) of the Hos', JPASB, Vol. 20: 193-98.

1924d 'On the terminology of relationships of the Hos of Kohan', JPASB, Vol. 20:199-204.

1924e 'A few remarks on the Sema Naga kinship terms', MII, Vol. 4:193-208.

1925a 'The birth ceremonies of the Hos of Kolhan', MII, Vol. 5:175-82.

1925b 'Some ethnographic notes on the Hos of Kolhan', MII, Vol. 5:183-89,

1925c 'Some out-door and sedentary games of the Hos of Kolhan', MII. Vol. 5:190-98.

1925d 'The Hargari and its origin', MII, Vol. 5:199-204.

1925e 'Religion of the Kols' (Abstract), P (Twelfth) ISC, p. 263.

1925f 'The significance of totemism' (Abstract), P (Twelfth) ISC, p. 265.

1925g 'The physical characteristics of the Kols' (Abstract), P (Twelfth) ISC, p. 266.

1926a 'The Polias, Babupolias, Palias or Rajbansis: An instance of the conversion of tribes into castes in Bengal', (Abstract), P (Thirteenth) ISC, p. 326.

1926b 'The kinship terms of the Polias, Babupolias and Rajbansis in north Bengal' (Abstract), P (Thirteenth) ISC, p. 326.

* An effort has been made to make this bibliography complete, but we are not sure that we have succeeded in this task—Eds.

1926c 'A few types of dramatic and sedentary games of the Hos of Kolhan in Singhbhum' (Abstract), P (Thirteenth) ISC, p. 326.

1926d 'Marriage customs of the Hos of Kolhan' (Abstract), P (Thirteenth) ISC, p. 327.

1926e 'The beliefs about disease, death and after' (Abstract), P (Thirteenth) ISC, p. 327.

1926f 'Ethnographic notes on the ideas about eclipses, excommunication, adoption, rain-making, hoarfrosts, and hail-stones, dreams, earthquakes, etc. of the Hos' (Abstract), P (Thirteenth) ISC, p. 327.

1926g 'Ho life in Ho riddles' (Abstract), P Thirteenth) ISC, p. 327.

1926h 'Pseudo-Rajputs: The Polias, Palias, Babupolias or Rajbansis of north Bengal. An instance of the formation of tribes into castes', MII, Vol. 6: 155-73.

1926i 'The biogonial breadths of some of the Hos of Kolhan', JPASB, Vol. 22:347-49.

1927a 'A few types of Ho songs', JPASB, Vol. 23:27-36.

1927b 'Death and connected ceremonies among the Hos of Kolhan', JPASB, Vol. 23:37-44.

1927c 'Some of the worship festivals of the Hos of Kolhan', JPASB, Vol. 23:277-85.

1928a 'Some norms of Ho culture', (Abstract), P (Fifteenth) ISC, p. 317.

1928b 'The cult of the dead among the Hos', (Abstract), P (Fifteenth) ISC, p. 318.

1929a 'Race and adaptability', JPASB, Vol. 25:149-56.

1929b 'Maternity and couvade in primitive society', MII, Vol. 9:66-71.

1929c 'The Korwas of the United Provinces', MII, Vol. 9:237-50.

1929d 'Sex and sex-control in primitive society', MII, Vol. 9:251-66.

1929e 'The cult of the dead among the Hos', (Abstract), P (Sixtteenth), ISC, p. 318.

1930a 'Social organisation among the Korwas', MII, Vol. 10:104-15.

1930b 'The economic background of social institutions in primitive society', MII, Vol. 10:150-66.

1930c 'Totemism and origin of clans', *Journal of the American Oriental Society* Vol. 50:221-32; also (Abstract), P (Seventeenth) ISC,.

1930d 'The Korwas and their country', (Abstract), P (Seventeenth) ISC, p. 395.

1930e 'The cycle of life amongst the Korwas', (Abstract) P (Seventeenth) ISC, p. 396.

1931a 'The clash and fusion of cultures in perganah Dudhi, district Mirzapur, U.P.', MII, Vol. 11:54-55.

1931b 'The Darlung Kukis of the Lushai Hills', MII, Vol. 11:55-56.

1931c 'The position of woman in Ho society', MII, Vol. 11:56.

1931d 'Sorcery and divination in primitive society', MII, Vol. 11:65-57.

1931e 'The economic life of the Hos', MII, Vol. 11:57.

1931f 'Economic background of social institutions' (Abstract), P (Eighteenth) ISC, p. 414.

1931g 'Economic life in primitive society', (Abstract), P. (Eighteenth) ISC, p. 414.

1931h 'Economic life of the Korwas', (Abstract), P (Eighteenth) ISC, p. 415.

1931i 'Forms and functions of primitive religion', (Abstract), P (Eighteenth) ISC, p. 415.

1931j 'Marriage and marital life among the Rawaltas' (co-author: S. D. Bahuguna), (Abstract), P (Eighteenth) ISC, p. 415.

1931k 'Religious life among the Rawaltas' (co-author: S. D. Bahuguna), (Abstract), P (Eighteenth) ISC, p. 416.

19311 'Festivals among the Rawaltas', (co-author: S. D. Bahuguna), (Abstract), P (Eighteenth) ISC, p. 416.

1932a 'Marital problem: a new orientation', MII, Vol. 12:161-74.

1932b 'The cycle of life amongst the Korwas', MII, Vol. 12:255-75.

1933 'Disease, death and divination in certain primitive societies in India', MII, Vol. 13:115-49.

1936a 'The decline of the primitive tribes in India', *The Journal of the United Provinces Historical Society*, April.

1936b 'A plea for better treatment of the aboriginal population in India' *Calcutta Review*, October, pp. 67-75.

1936c 'Food and feeding among the Austric tribes', (Abstract), P (Twenty-third) ISC, p. 395.

1936d 'The concept of disease in Austric culture' (Abstract), P (Twenty-third) ISC, p. 396.

1936e 'The spirit of Bongaism' (Abstract), P (Twenty-third) ISC, p. 397.

1937a *A Tribe in Transition: A Study in Culture Pattern*, Calcutta and London, Longmans, Green & Co., vii + xii + 216 pp., Illustrations, Bibliography.

1937b 'Comparative anthropometry of a group of Saoras of both sexes', MII, Vol. 17:17; also (Abstract) P (Twenty-fourth) ISC, p. 336.

1937c 'Some aspects of the economic life of the Bhokasas and Tharus of Nainital Tarai', *Journal of the Anthropological Society of Bombay*, Jubilee Volume: 133-35.

1937d 'The cultural pattern of the Tharus' (Abstract), P (Twenty-fourth) ISC, p. 335.

1937e 'The material culture of the Rawaltas of Rawain' (co-author: S. D. Bahuguna), (Abstract), P (Twenty-fourth) ISC, p. 338.

1938a 'Racial admixture in the United Provinces', MII, Vol. 18:9-18.

1938b 'Modern trends in social anthropology', *Calcutta Review*, February: pp. 162-76.

1938c 'The marriage and nishpat customs of the Rishis' (Abstract), MII, Vol. 18:59.

1938d 'The tribal population and Christianity', *Modern Review*, May.

1938e 'Race and language in India', (Abstract), *Nature*, Vol. 141:1019.

1938f 'The relationships of the Austric speaking tribes of India, with special reference to the measurements of Hos and Saoras'. *Proceedings of the Indian Academy of Sciences*, Vol. 7:1-21; also (Abstract), P (Twenty-fifth) ISC, p. 1.

1939a 'The Murias of Narayanpur, Bastar state' (co-author: Kr. Indrajit Singh), MII, Vol. 19:68.

1939b 'Sex and marriage in the Doon district', *Calcutta Review*, March: 309-18.

1939c 'Tribal cultures and acculturation', Presidential Address, Section of

Anthropology and Archaeology, Twenty-sixth Indian Science Congress, 46 pp.; also in MII, Vol. 19:99-173.

1939d 'Primitive society and its discomforts', *Proceedings of Second Population and Family Conference*, 1939.

1940a 'The culture pattern of a polyandrous society', MII, Vol. 20:82-83.

1940b 'The racial composition of the polyandrous people of Jaunsar Bawar in the Dehradun district, United Provinces', *Journal of the United Provinces Historical Society*, Vol. 13:35-50.

1940c 'Blood groups and their distribution in certain castes in the United Provinces', *Science and Culture*, Vol. 5:519-22.

1940d 'Preface' in *Essays in Anthropology presented to Rai Bahadur Sarat Chandra Roy*, J. P. Mills, D. N. Majumdar, et. al., (eds.) Lucknow, Maxwell Co., pp. V-VIII.

1940e 'Bongaism' in *Essays in Authropology presented to Rai Bahadur Sarat Chandra Roy*, J. P. Mills, D. N. Majumdar, et. al., (eds.) Lucknow, Maxwell Co., pp. 60-79.

1940f 'Some aspects of the life of the Khasas of the cis-Himalayan region', JRASB, Vol. 6:1-44.

1941a 'Racial affiliation of the Gonds of the Central Provinces', JRASB, Vol. 7:35-56.

1941b Book notices of *How to make a little speech* by G. M. Allen and *Essays in Anthropology presented to R. B. Sarat Chandra Roy*, MII, Vol. 21:255-56.

1941-42 'Blood groups of criminal tribes', *Science and Culture*, Vol. 7:334-37.

1942a 'The Tharus and their blood groups', JRASB, Vol. 8:25-38.

1942b 'Blood groups of criminal tribes' ,MII, Vol. 22: 65-66.

1942c 'Blood groups of the Doms', MII, Vol. 22:239-44.

1942d 'Anthropometric measurements of the Bhils', JGRS, Vol. 4:220-37.

1942e 'The blood groups of the Doms', *Current Science*, Vol. 11:153-54.

1943 'Blood groups of tribes and castes of the U.P. with special reference to the Korwas', JRASB, Vol. 11:81-94.

1944a *Fortunes of Primitive Tribes*, Luckhow, Universal Publishers Ltd.

1944b *Races and Cultures of India*, Allahabad, Kitabistan, 285pp. Bibliography.

1944c 'Racial affiliation of the Bhils of Gujarat: of the Panch Mahal district and the Rajpipla state', JGRS, Vol. 6:172-86.

1944d Review of Verrier Elwin's *Maria Murder and Suicide*, MII, Vol. 24: 88-94.

1944e 'What is Frazerism?', MII, Vol. 24:269-70.

1946a *Race Elements in Gujarat*, Gujarat Research Society Publication, Bombay.

1946b 'The malaise of culture', in *Snowballs of Garhwal* (Folk Culture Series) edited by D. N. Majumdar, Lucknow, The Universal Publishers Limited pp. i-xiv.

1946c 'Biometric analasis of anthropological measurements on castes and tribes of the United Provinces', (Co-authors: P. C. Mahalanobis and C. R. Rao), P (Thirty-third) ISC, p-138.

1947a *The Matrix of Indian Culture*, Lucknow, The Universal Publishers, Ltd., VII—242 pp. Bibliography.

1947b 'Anthropology during the war', *American Anthropologist*, Vol. 49: 159-64.

1947c 'The United Provinces—A Cultural mosaic', in S. C. Dube's *Field Songs of Chhattisgarh*, Lucknow, The Universal Publishers Ltd., pp. III —XVIII.

1947d Racial Problems in Asia', Indian Council of World Affairs, New Delhi, (paper submitted to the Asian Relations Conference).

1947e *Progress of Anthropology in India* (1911-46): *A Brief Review*, Jointly Published by The Indian Science Congress Association and The Council of Scientific and Industrial Research, pp. 31.

1947f 'Blood group distribution in the United Provinces', (Co-author, Kunwar Kishen), EA, Vol. 1:1-8.

1947g 'Some Folk Tales of Kolhan', in S. C. Dube's *Field Songs of Chhattisgarh*, Lucknow: The Universal Publishers Ltd., pp. 66-95.

1947h 'Report on the serological survey of the United Provinces, 1941 Census', EA, Vol. 1:8-15.

1947i 'The criminal tribes of northern India', EA, Vol. 1:33-40.

1947j Review of W. G. Archers's *The Vertical Man*, EA, Vol. 1:66-69.

1947k Review of W. V. Grigson's *The Challenge of Backwardness*, EA, Vol. 1:69-70.

1948a 'Rh frequency in the people of Lucknow', *Heredity*, Vol. 2:399-401.

1948b 'Blood groups in the Gujarat Population', (Co-author: K. Kishen) JGRS, Vol. 10:161 ff.

1948c Review of Verrier Elwin's *The Muria and Their Ghotul*, EA, Vol. 1: 42-47.

1948d Review of *Marriage Magazine*, EA, Vol. 1:47-48.

1948e Review of Fürer-Haimendorf's *The Reddis of the Bison Hills*, EA, Vol. 1:48-49.

1948f Review of Swami Akhilananda's *Hindu Psychology*, EA, Vol. 1: 49-50

1948g Review of Mrs. I. Karve's *Anthropometric Measurements of the Mara thas*, EA, Vol. 1:50-51.

1948-49 'Serological status of castes and tribes of cultural Gujarat' (Co-author: Kunwar Kishen), EA, Vol. 2:92-97.

1949a 'Anthropometric survey of the United Provinces: A Statistical Study' (Co-authors: P. C. Mahalanobis and C. R. Rao), with a Foreword by M. W. M. Yeatts, *Sankhya*, Vol. 9:89-304.

1949b 'Report of the racial, serological and health survey of Gujarat; Part II Anthropometric status of castes and tribes of Gujarat' (Co-author A. R. Sen), JGRS, Vol. 11: 118ff.

1949c 'The racial basis of Indian social structure', EA, Vol. 2:145-52.

1949d Review of C. Von Fürer-Haimendorf's *The Raj Gonds of Adilabad*, EA, Vol. 2:171-73.

1949e 'Racial elements in Gujarat', JGRS, Vol. 11:188ff.

1949f 'Anthropometry and crime', MII, Vol. 29:46-58.

1949g 'A study of height and weight of the castes and tribes of Gujarat', MII, Vol. 29:110-123.

1949h 'Growth trends among aboriginal boys of Kolhan, Singhbhum, Bihar', EA, Vol. 2:201-4.

1949i 'The changing canvas of tribal life', EA, Vol. 3:40-47.

1949j 'Hamari sanskriti ka vikas' (Hindi), *Parchya Manav-Vaigyanik*, Vol. 1:21-35.

1949k 'The social economy of the Bhotiyas' in K. S. Pangtey's *Lonely Furrows of the Borderland*, Lucknow, The Universal Publishers, Ltd., pp. 1-XI.

1949-50a 'The racial status of the Nuniya, Nunera, Gola, Agaria, Shorgar, Kharkar, and similar castes of Etah, Mainpuri, and Farrukhabad, U.P.', EA, Vol. 3:101-9

1949-50b Review of R. Ruggles Gates, *Pedigrees of Negro Families*, EA, Vol. 3:113.

1949-50c Review of C. Kluckhohn and Henry A. Murray (eds.) *Personality in Nature, Society and Culture*, EA, Vol. 3:113-14.

1950a *The Affairs of a Tribe: A Study in Tribal Dynamics*, Lucknow, The Universal Publishers Ltd., IV-XXVI + 376pp., 20 Plates, Text Illustrations, Map, Bibliography.

1950b *Race Realities in Cultural Gujarat*, Bombay, Gujarat Research Society, p. 24.

1950c 'ABO blood among the Garos of Eastern Pakistan', MII, Vol. 30: 32-35.

1950d 'Anthropology under glass', *The Journal of the Anthropological Society of Bombay*, pp. 1-16.

1950-51a 'The Sankha Banik of Dacca', EA, Vol. 4:98-103.

1950-51b 'Review of Stephen Fuchs', *The Children of Hari*, EA, Vol. 4:112-15.

1950-51c Review of A. V. Thakker's *Tribes of India*, EA, Vol. 4:116-17.

1951a *Races nnd Cultures of India*, Second edition, Lucknow, The Universal Publishers Ltd., VII-XIV + 215 pp.

1951b 'Tribal rehabilitation in India', *International Social Science Bulletin*, Vol. 3:802-13.

1951c Review of Cora Du Bois', *The People of Alor: A Social-Psychological Study of An Eastern Indian Island*, EA, Vol. 4:189-91.

1951e 'Manav riti-vigyan tatha jan-sanskriti samiti Uttar Pradesh', (Hindi), *Prachya Manav Vaigyanik*, Vol. 2:1-3.

1951f 'Luniya, Nunera, Gola, Agaria, Shorgar, Kharwal, tatha, Mainpuri, Farrukhabad ki saman jatiyon ki jatiya-isthiti', (Hindi), *Prachya Manav Vaigyanik*, Vol. 2:29-41.

1951g 'Adim jatiya jivan men prayog', (Hindi), *Prachya Manav Vaigyanik*, Vol. 2:72-93.

1951-52a 'ABO blood in India' (Co-author: S. Bahadur), EA, Vol. 5:101-22.

1951-52b Review of *The International Journal of Sexology*, EA, Vol. 5:139.

1952a Review of Laura Thompson's *Culture in Crisis: A Study of the Hopi Indians*, EA, Vol. 6:90-92.

1952b 'Adivasi jivan ki chunauti' (Hindi) *Aj-Kal*, Vol. 8:15-18 and 61.

1953a 'Children in a polyandrous society', EA, Vol. 6:177-89.

1953b Review of Gordon Hamilton's *Theory and Practice of Social Case Work* EA, Vol. 6:211-12.

1953c On 'Acculturation', AAT: 125-26.

1953d On 'National character', AAT: 139.

1953e On 'Prestige and food', AAT: 146.

1953f   On 'Anthropology and medicine', AAT: 175.

1953g   On 'Anthropology in government', AAT: 183-84.

1953h   On 'Cultural-social anthropology', AAT: 222.

1953i   On 'Genetics and social selection', AAT: 272.

1953j   On 'Anthropology as a field of study', AAT: 343-45.

1953k   'Tribal economy of the cis-Himalayas', *The Indian Journal of Social Work*, Vol. 14:1-13.

1953l   'The aboriginal tribes of Orissa', *March of India*, Vol. 6:54-56.

1953m   'Modern trends and anthropological research—Lucknow Orientation', (40th session) *Indian Science Congress Souvenir*: 23-37.

1953n   'Racial survey of Uttar Pradesh', Ibid,: 94-106.

1953p   'India, Pakistan and Ceylon', *International Directory of Anthropological Institutions*, Williams L. Thomas, Jr. and Anna M. Pikelis, (eds.) New York: Winner-Gren Foundation for Anthropological Research, Inc., 67-77pp.

1954a   'Status of women in patrilocal societies in South Asia', A Appadorai (ed.), *The Status of Women in South Asia*, Bombay, Oriental Longmans Ltd., 99-115pp.

1954b   'Religious life of the Ho', MII, Vol. 34:346-50.

1954c   'Ethnic frontiers and caste distance in Uttar Pradesh', *The 31st All India Medical Conference Souvenir* Vol.:19-33.

1954d   'Caste and race', in *Professor Ghurye Felicitation Volume*, K. M. Kapadia (ed.), Bombay, Popular Book Depot., pp. 205-25.

1954-55   'Family and marriage in a polyandrous society', EA, Vol. 8:85-110.

1955a   'Introduction', *Rural Profiles* Vol. I, D. N. Majumdar (ed.) Lucknow, Ram Advani, pp. III-XV.

1955b   'Demographic structure in a polyandrous village', *Rural Profiles*, Vol. 1:32-44; also in EA, Vol. 8:161-72.

1955c   'Inter-caste relations in Gohana-Kalan', (Co-authors: M. C. Pradhan, C. Sen, and S. Misra), *Rural Profiles*, Vol. 1:63-86; also in EA, Vol. 8:191-214.

1955d   Review of J. J. Honigmann's *Culture and Personality*, EA, Vol. 9:63-67.

1955e   'The dynamics of social change', Address of the Sectional President (Anthropology), First Indian Sociological Conference, Dehradun, 19 pp.; also in *Agra University Journal of Research* (Letters), Vol. 3:28-40.

1955f   'The Chero tribe of Bihar', *The March of India*, Vol. 7:39-43.

1955g   'The eye and the anthropologist', *Journal of the Gandhi Eye Hospital and Aligarh Muslim University Institute of Ophthalmology*, Aligarh (Silver Jubilee), Special number: 65-69.

1955h   'Samajik parivartan ka gatishastra' (Hindi), *Samaj*, Vol. 1:166-80.

1955-56   'Rural analysis—problems and prospects', EA, Vol. 9:92-103; also in A. Aiyappan and L. K. Ratnam (eds.) *Society in India* (1956), Madras: S.S.A., pp. 134-48.

1956a   *An Introduction to Social Anthropology* (co-author: T. N. Madan), Bombay, Asia publishing House, V-x + 304pp.

1956b   'What the Sociologists Can Do, What They Must Do, How They Can Do and How They Should Do It? Presidential Address, Second Indian Sociological Conference, Patna; also in EA, Vol. 10:130-43; also in R. N.

Saxena (ed.), 1961, *Sociology, Social Research and Social Problems*, Bombay: Asia Publishing House

1956c 'Educated unemployment: nature and extent of unemployment among university students', (Co-author: S. K. Anand), EA, Vol. 10-43-51. Also published by the Massachusetts Inst. of Tech. as a monograph.

1956d 'Avadh ke ek gram men parivarik jivan' (Hindi), *Samaj*, Vol. 2:525-36.

1956-57a 'A Little Community: A polyandrous village Jadi in the Chakrata Tehsil, Dehradun District', *Sociologist*: Journal of the Sociology Association, Christ Church College, Kanpur, pp. 1-4.

1956-57b 'Anthropology and premitive medicine', *Manava*: The Organ of the Anthropology Club, Lucknow University, pp. 1-4.

1957a 'The functioning of school system in a polyandrous society in Jaunsar Bawar, Dehradun District, U.P.', (Co-author: S. K. Anand), EA, Vol. 10:182-210.

1957b 'Rapkund in oral literature', EA, Vol. 11:36-41.

1957c 'Bharat ke vikas men samaj-vaigyanikon ka dayitva', (Hindi), *Samaj*, Vol. 2:703-16.

1957-58 'Caste as a process', *Manava-Darpana*: Organ of the Anthropology Club, Lucknow University, Vol. 2:1-5.

1958a *Races and Cultures of India*, Third edition, Bombay: Asia Publishing House.

1958b *Caste and Communication in an Indian Village*, Bombay, Asia Publishing House.

1958c *Bharatiya Sanskriti ke Upadan* (Hindi), Bombay: Asia Publishing House.

1958d 'Rural life and communication', EA, Vol. 11:175-88.

1958e 'Jati parivartan ke prakram men', (Hindi), *Samaj*, Vol. 3:297-203 & 338.

1958f 'Rupkund rahasya', (Hindi), *Parchya Manav Vaigyanik*, Vol. 3:94-106.

1958g 'Notes and comments', EA, Vol. 12:1-4.

1958-59 'A Village school in the context of tribal education in Jaunsar Bawar', *Manava-Darpana*, Vol. 3:1-8.

1959a 'Rupkund in prospect and retrospect', *Uttar Pradesh*, March 1959:1-12.

1959b 'Shramdan: An aspect of action anthropology', *Indian Sociologist*, Vol. 1:1-12.

1959c 'Indian anthropologists in action', *Journal of Social Research*, Vol. 2: 10-15.

1959d 'The light that failed?' *Journal of Social Research*, Vol. 2: 90-97.

1960a *Race elements in Bengal*, (Co-author: C. R. Rao),Bombay, Asia, Publishing House.

1960b *Social Contours of an Industrial City* (assisted by N. S. Reddy and S. Bahadur), Bombay, Asia Publishing House.

1960c *An Introduction to Social Anthropology* (Co-author: T. N. Madan) Third impression, Bombay, Asia Publishing House.

1960d 'Shramdan: An aspect of action anthropology', in *Rural Profiles* II, Lucknow, Ram Advani, pp. 103-16.

1960e Review of Thomas O. Beidelman's *A Comparative Analysis of the Jajmani System*, *Man*, Vol. 60:80 (No. 117).

1960f 'Angrez' (Hindi), *Hindi Vishvakosh*, Vol. 1, Varanasi: Nagari Pracharini Sabha, pp. 13-14.

1960g 'Ho' (Hindi) in *Bihar Ke Adivasi*, edited by L. P. Vidyarthi, Patna: College Centre, pp. 111-125.

1960h 'Adivasi aur unki smasyayen', (Hindi), in *Bihar Ke Adivasi*, edited by L. P. Vidyarti, Patna: College Centre, pp. 180-96.

1960i 'Lineage structure in a Himalayan society, Himalayan district', International Journal of Comparative Sociology, Vol. 1, No. 1, pp. 17-42.

1961a 'Foreword' in L. P. Vidyarthi's *The Sacred Complex of Hindu Gaya*, Bombay: Asia Publishing House.

1961b *Races and Cultures of India* (4th edition), Bombay, Asia Publishing House.

N.D.(a) 'Vartaman Dharat ki adhm-jatiyon ki ek Jahalak', (Hindi), HV, Vol. 1:239-43.

N.D.(b) 'Madhya-Prant ke Gond' (Hindi), HV, Vol. 1: 363-70.

N.D.(c) 'Assam ke kuki log', (Hindi), HV, Vol. 1:639-47.

N.D.(d) 'Singhbhum (ya Sinhabhumi) ki Ho jati', (Hindi), HV. Vol. 2:773-80.

N.D.(e) 'Chota Nagput ki Kharia jati', (Hindi), HV. Vol. 2:901-6.

N.D.(f) 'Yukta Prant ki Korwa jati', (Hindi), HV, Vol. 2:1043-48.

N.D.(g) 'Jaunsar Bawar ki Khasa jati', (Hindi), HV, Vol. 2:1155-62.

N.D.(h) 'Orissa ki riyasaton men basanewali Juang jati', (Hindi). HV, Vol. 2:1177-82.

N.D.(i) 'Assam ki Garo jati', (Hindi) HV, Vol. 3:1393-1403.

N.D.(j) 'Karwal' (Hindi), HV, Vol. 3:1725-31.

N.D.(k) 'Dom—Sanyukta Prant ki ek aur jarayam-pesha jati', (Hindij), HV. Vol. 4:1949-55.

N.D.(1) 'Bhil-Jati (1)' (Hindi), HV. Vol. 4:2155-60.

N.D.(m) 'Bhil-jati (2)', (Hindi), HV, Vol. 4:2155-60.

FORTHCOMING PUBLICATIONS

Himalyan Polyandry. Bombay, Asia Publishing House.

A Village on the Fringe. Bombay, Asia Publishing House.

Chhor ka ek Gaon (Hindi). Bombay, Asia Publishing House.

Pragithas (Hindi) (Co-author: Gopal Sarana). Bombay, Asia Publishing House.

V

A SELECT BIBLIOGRAPHY OF BOOKS AND PAPERS WHICH DEAL, *INTER ALIA*, WITH MAJUMDAR'S WORKS

DUBE, S. C., 1952, *Anthropology: The Study of Man*. Hyderabad, Chetna.

ELWIN, V. E., 1947, *The Muria and Their Ghotul*. Bombay, Oxford.

GATES, R. R., 1946, *Human Genetics*, Vol. I. New York, Macmillan.

GHURYE, G. S., 1943, *The Aborigines—"So-called"—and Their Future*. Poona Gokhale Institute of Economics and Politics.

1959, *The Scheduled Tribes*. Bombay, Popular Book Depot.

GUHA, B. S., 1939, 'Progress of Anthropology in India during the past twenty-five years' in *Progress of Science in India*, General Editor, B. Prasad. Calcutta, Indian Science Congress Association.

MADAN, T. N., 1956, 'Social-Cultural Anthropology in India during the last three decades.' Seminar paper presented in the Department of Anthropology, Australian National University. (Mimeo.)

1961, 'Majumdar's contributions to Anthropology in Uttar Pradesh: A Note' in *Research Bulletin of the Faculty of Arts*, University of Lucknow, No. I.

MOURANT, A. E., 1958, *The ABO Blood Groups: Comprehensive Tables and Maps of World Distribution*. London, Blackwell.

1954, *The Distribution of Human Blood Groups*. London, Blackwell.

SARANA, Gopala, 1961, 'Professor Majumdar and Anthropology of Indian Religion' in *Aspects of Religion in Indian Society*, Editor, L. P. Vidyarthi, Meerut.

SRINIVAS, M. N. et al. 1959, 'Caste: A Trend Report and Bibliography' in *Current Sociology*, Vol. VIII, No. 1.

WEINER, J. S., 1958, 'Physical Anthropology since 1935: A Study of Developments' in *A Hundred Years of Anthropology*. London, Duckworth.

OBITUARIES

FÜRER-HAIMENDORF, C. von, 1960, 'Dhirendra Nath Majumdar; 1903-1960' in *Man* (London), Vol. LX, No. 212, pp.

MADAN, T. N., 1960, 'Dhirendra Nath Majumdar: 1903-1960' in *International Journal of Comparative Sociology* (Dharwar and Leiden), Vol. I, No. 2, pp. 262-64.

1961, "Dhirendra Nath Majumdar: 1903-1960' in *American Anthropologist* (Menasha, Winscosin), Vol. 63, No. 2, Part 1, pp. 369-74.

SARANA, Gopala, 1961, 'Dhirendra Nath Majumdar: 1903-1960' (with extensive bibliography) in *The Eastern Anthropologist* (Lucknow), Vol. XIV, No. 2, pp. 105-21.

TRIPATHI, Chandra Bhal, 1961, 'D. N. Majumdar, Doyen of Indian Anthropologists' in *The Pioneer*: *Sunday Magazine Section* (Lucknow), 28th May, 1961, p. 3.

VIDYARTHI, L. P., 1960, 'D. N. Majumdar: 1903-1960' in *Journal of Social Research* (Ranchi), Vol. III, No. 2, p. 146.

1960, 'Dhirendra Nath Majumdar' in *Man in India* (Ranchi), Vol. XL, No. 4, pp. 220-21.

COMMEMORATION VOLUME

VIDYARTHI, L. P. (ed.) et al., 1961, *Aspects of Religion in Indian Society*: *Majumdar Memorial Volume*. Meerut.

PART TWO

Anthropology in India

INTRODUCTION

A N T H R O P O L O G Y in India, as indeed elsewhere, has been a grouping of several more or less interdependent studies, rather than a single subject, embracing within itself prehistory, archaeology, physical anthropology, and social and cultural anthropology. The study of linguistics by anthropologists has not so far made much headway in this country. Archaeology has more often been allied to ancient Indian history than to anthropology; in university curricula the former two subjects are usually combined together. However, there is nowadays a growing realization of the need for closer ties between archaeologists, pre-historians and physical anthropologists.

Social anthropology has been, in the past, closely allied to pre-history and physical anthropology with good reasons. As it has progressed from the description of particulars to analysis, explanation and general descriptions, social anthropology has forged new ties with other social sciences, such as sociology and political science, often at the cost of the earlier loyalties. The scientific study of Man and his Works is a stupendous undertaking; it stands midway between the natural sciences and the humanities and consequently it will be always subject to an internal polarity.

We have included in this Volume papers on prehistory, archaeology, physical anthropology and social anthropology, so as to give as comprehensive a view of anthropological research today in India as possible. Its past history warrants such a presentation of the subject, although we do not presume to know what may happen in future. Majumdar, who played such a notable part in building up anthropology as an academic discipline in India, always pleaded for a broad-based view of the subject. In his lectures he used to emphasize that acquaintance with the fundamentals of all branches of anthropology should precede specialization in any particular branch of it.

I

Scientific interest in the prehistory of India started almost simultaneously with studies into European prehistory. Robert Bruce Foote collected the first Indian palaeoliths from the South in 1863. He had been preceded by Le Mesurier who had collected neoliths in 1860. The Archaeological Survey of India was founded in 1862, a year before Foote's discoveries. Although numerous palaeolithic and neolithic tools were obtained in the next fifty years by Foote, Wynne, Blanford, King, Hackett, and others, from various parts of the country, yet these were only stray surface collections and scientific prehistory did not make much progress.

It was in the early nineteen-thirtees that Burkitt and Cammiade threw 'Fresh Light on the Stone Ages of (South) India' by working out a cycle of pluvial and interpluvial stages for peninsular India. The greatest impetus to scientific work in prehistory came from the Yale-Cambridge Expedition, of 1935, led by H. de Terra and T. T. Paterson. The researches in the late Cenozoic of north-west India by the Expedition are the only baseline data we have for India and South Asia. Since then considerable work has been done by the University of Calcutta, the Archaeological Survey of India and the Deccan College Post-Graduate and Research Institute.

Another landmark in the study of Pleistocene and Holocene stratigraphy was the Geochronological Expedition, of 1949, under the leadership of Professor F. E. Zeuner. The relative chronology of Gujarat, which Zeuner has worked out, on the basis of palaeoclimatological evidence is a great contribution in the right direction.

The impressive and splendid work done by Sir John Marshall and Sir Mortimer Wheeler on Indian protohistory is too well-known to be referred to here in detail.

The papers included in the section on Prehistoric Archaeology, of the present Volume, represent a cross-section of the researches now being done in the prehistory and the early culture history of India. Shri Dharani Sen has given a synoptic picture of the stone tools and the environmental conditions in which they were fashioned by palaeolithic Man in India. He is of the opinion that the earliest Indian lithicultural tradition was a pebble chopping-tool one, like the east African Oldowan industry. The other four palaeolithic traditions were: Hand-axe and cleaver; Early Sohan pebble flake; Late Sohan consisting of evolved pebble tools and flakes showing Levalloisio-Mousterian features; and the blade tradition tending to microlithism.

Drs Raymond and Bridget Allchin have attempted to 'demonstrate

the use of archaeological field observation and historical context
to produce culture history' of the Raichur Doāb in south India.
Middle palaeolithic (according to the authors, Middle Stone Age)
tools, closely comparable to those found in Pleistocene deposits
on the Narmada river, are the earliest obtained from the Raichur
Doāb. Scrapers and other wood-cutting tools seem to have been
made by 'a technique parallel to the Lavallois of Europe'. The
authors expect to find Early Palaeolithic tools in the nearby
banks and gravel beds. The transition from the Middle to the Late
Palaeolithic, and even post-Palaeolithic is indicated by unpatinated
blades, blade cores and geometric forms which occur not very far
from the Middle Palaeolithic sites. To complete the picture, a
gradual transition to the Neolithic and to the Megalithic (the Iron
Age) is also postulated.

In India the same stages of transition, from savagery through
barbarism to urbanization, are observable which Childe worked out
for the whole of the Old World. But such a picture does not
emerge at any one site. Dr H. D. Sankalia divides India into thirteen
physico-cultural regions. He does not think any of the Lower
Palaeolithic industries to be of indigenous origin. Further, he
shows that as there is a change from flake industries to microliths,
the 'primitive to advanced food collecting stage changes to '(incipient) food production'. A few probable sources of external influence
on the early village cultures of India, such as that of Iran on the
early peasant villages of Amri and Sind, are indicated by the author.
He points out that owing to the paucity of data, it is difficult to
state definitively whether India was the eastern periphery of a
vast prehistoric cultural region extending westwards to Syria
and Egypt, or an independent cultural region.

Dr B. Subbarao has pleaded for closer ties between archaeology
and physical anthropology. The archaeologist has to come to
'the door of the anthropologist for the study of skeletal remains
and for the identification of the authors of the material relics'.
The two main goals of archaeology in India, according to him, are
'to reconstruct the cultural sequence of the various cultures in time
and space' and 'to bring into relief the main features of and the
stages of the evolution of Indian culture'. Of the racial classifications of Indian peoples given by Risley, Guha, Sarkar and von
Eickstedt, Dr Subbarao finds the last as being the most satisfactory.
Eickstedt, he writes, 'reveals a greater geographical and ecological

awareness than most other writers and takes the dynamic factors into consideration'.

The time seems to have come when an effort will have to be made to work out a comparable relative chronology of the Pleistocene period for the whole of the Indian sub-continent. It need not be stressed here that the necessary starting point for such a classification will be available from the work of Burkitt, Dainelli, de Terra and Zeuner. More organized and concerted efforts will have to be made to find out the skeletal remains of Early Man in India, particularly in the Narmada valley. One of the most urgent needs of the day in Indian prehistory is to give more serious thought to the problems of nomenclature and taxonomy, especially so far as the palaeolithic industries are concerned. Of late great divergences in the use of terms have been noticed.

The results of excavations at Lothal and recent reports regarding the probability of the extensions of the Harappan culture in Madhya Pradesh are bound to pose new problems of classification and will keep the prehistorians and the archaeologists engaged for quite some time. Of particular interest will be the correlation, which may be worked out, between these Harappan extensions and the excavated chalcolithic 'neolithic' sites of central, western and southern India.

II

The major interest in physical anthropological research in India has been two-fold: The determination, as precisely as possible, of the racial history of the country, and somatological-serological studies of present day populations. Physical anthropology has thus been mostly confined to ethnological research and studies in comparative racial anatomy. However, many subsidiary interests also have attracted the attention of research workers. Thus, Risely gave not only a classification of the peoples of India, at the turn of the century, but also tried to inquire into a possible correlation between 'race' and 'caste'. He discovered a rather striking correlation between caste hierarchy and nasal index, especially in northern India.

Risley envisaged a seven-fold division of the peoples of India which was altered, during the 'thirtees, by Guha who considered some of the former's categories or 'races' as wrongly constructed on the basis of erroneous interpretations of social and physical data. Guha himself divided the Indian people into seven racial categories but gave them different names. The basic difference lay in that while Risley considered the various races as having originated in India, Guha sought to show all of them to be of foreign origin. Other authors also have offered classifications which vary from each other. Thus, Haddon found fifteen 'races', Giufrida-Ruggeri six and von Eickstedt thought seven to be an adequate number to explain racial differences within the country. Though the names given to the various racial elements vary from author to author, yet, interestingly enough, six or seven appears to be the modal number.

As is well-known, Majumdar was interested in both the physical anthropology of the peoples of India, as well as in their social and cultural conditions. His extensive surveys in Bengal, Uttar Pradesh and Gujarat covered large numbers of castes and tribes. His major interests were to unravel the problem of 'racial composition' in these regions, and to inquire into a possible correlation between ethnic composition and social stratification. In this he followed in the footsteps of earlier workers, but the extent of documentation which be managed to achieve was truly impressive. He also collaborated with statisticians in the analysis of his data with excellent results and thus focussed attention on the desirability of closer ties between physical anthropologists and statisticians.

Dr C. R. Rao, one of the late Professor Majumdar's collaborators, writes of the scope of such collaboration. In his paper in the present Volume, and in other publications, he has shown how this collaboration has led not only to an improvement of the analysis of anthropometric and serological data, but also to advances in statistical multivariate analysis. Dr Rao spells out, in the present paper, the prerequisite conditions which must be met before statisticians may be called upon to render help in the analysis of anthropometric data.

Shri P. G. Shah, at whose invitation Majumdar conducted the Gujarat Survey, has summarized the findings of this survey and of later work conducted in the region under the auspices of the Gujarat Research Society. Shri Shah, who is the President of this Society, points out that psychological investigations have now been added to anthropometric and serological studies. He concludes his paper with a plea for examining the effect of nutrition, standards of living, and other 'environmental factors' on the body form and changes in it.

Dr R. Ruggles Gates, in his paper on the Asur and the Birhor, points out that no significant statistical difference exists between these tribes. He adds that they do not reveal any Australoid features. This means that they should be regarded as distinct from the neighbouring tribes, such as the Oraon and the Munda, who belong to the Proto-Australoid categary. Gates is here concerned with taxonomic similarities or differences, rather than with the process involved.

The serological approach is comparatively new in Indian 'racial' studies. Serologists in India are not much interested in taxonomic problems as are the anthropometrists. Although attempts have been made elsewhere to classify the peoples of the world into broad 'serological races', this interest has not developed much in India. Consequently, we generally find serologists describing populations (castes or tribes) with reference to their gene frequencies. A large number of such studies have been made and Dr Mourant has summarised these in his paper 'Notes on Blood Groups in India', in the present Volume, and elsewhere.

Dr D. K. Sen gives details of the available serological data on the Bengali speaking people. Basing himself on serological data, collected by him and other invetigators, he examines the relationship between the upper caste Bengali and compares them with the lower caste Hindus of Bengal. He also undertakes a brief comparison between the Bengalis on the one hand and some other populations in India and outside India on the other hand. He refers to the anthropometric studies of the Bengalis and points out that anthropometric data by themselves have been interpreted variously to suggest a western, or a northern and eastern origin of the Bengalis. Dr Sen concludes: 'Our conclusion, arrived on the basis of serology alone, ... is that the Bengalis are largely of western extraction with the Mongoloid element forming a minor factor in the population.'

In their study of blood groups and haemoglobins among the Malayalis, Drs. Bird, Ikin, Mourant and Lehman employed a number of antisera to identify blood groups and paper electrophoresis to identify the frequencies of abnormal haemoglobins. These were, however, found absent among the people investigated. The authors also point out, in their paper, that the Malayalis 'resemble, in their blood group frequencies, the other peoples of south India', especially the Tamils and the Sinhalese.

Very little work has so far been done on the study of the variations of dermatoglyphic patterns in the various populations of India. Most authors have concentrated upon the finger ball or palm pattern frequencies among selected populations, particularly the tribal peoples. Dr S. S. Sarkar has been one of the pioneers in this area of research in India. In the brief paper he has contributed to this Volume he deals with some methods of identifying and recording the relevant data.

We have already pointed out that a major interest in physical anthropological research in India has been, in past, taxonomic exactitude with reference to the peoples of India. When one considers the modern genetic definition of race, one wonders whether the question "How many races?" can ever be answered to the satisfaction of all. There is today unanimity on the changeability of 'race'. It may, therefore, be expected that future research will concentrate on the study of process and change rather than endeavour to fix labels to physical types which are slowly changing their form.

III

In the years following the end of the Second World War, a significant shift took place in social anthropological research in India: The peasant village (or community) displaced the tribe as a favoured unit of study and factual descriptions gradually and increasingly yielded place to analysis and theoretical interpretation. Whereas this development is to be unreservedly welcomed, it is also important to point out that, consequent upon it the study of tribal cultures has receded, more than somewhat, into the background. Today social anthropologists in India are looking beyond even the mud walls of the Indian village: Urban India, with its industries, institutions and politics, conservatism and change, is emerging as a new focus of interest. In such circumstances, the study of Indian tribal societies, or whatever is left of their traditional cultures, may seem old-fashioned. Nevertheless, this neglect is unfortunate.

Dr S. C. Dube has surveyed, in his contribution to the present Volume, the growth of social anthropology in India, Although written in the form of what may, at the first blush, appear to be a personal statement, there will be general agreement with most of his observations. We would like to draw particular attention to his reference to group and individual research—their advantages and limitations—and to his reaffirmation of the need to continue fieldwork among the so-called tribal groups. His remarks on the need for a clear definition of the relations between social anthropology and sociology, the development of an adequate and refined conceptual apparatus, and the reorganization of university syllabi and teaching all merit careful consideration.

Dr F. G. Bailey refers, in his paper, to the value which has currently come to be placed upon the kind of information which the social anthropologist can furnish to the administrator, 'to provide a hard core in the shaky foundations of social engineering.' But, the author asks, 'what special competence our techniques and our theoretical equipment provide for us, what types of problems in Indian society are tractable, and what are our limitations.'

Dr Bailey then proceeds to discuss the growth of social anthropology in India from 'the study of isolable wholes such as the village or the tribe' in states of 'equilibrium', through 'the study of change in these societies, following on the intrusion of factors from the complex society outside', to 'studies within the complex society itself.' He rightly emphasizes that the three types of study should proceed side by side, and that the third type of study has as yet scarcely begun. We are not equipped with the necessary concepts which would be required in this endeavour. The structural approach and concepts like 'structure' and 'system' are inadequate for this purpose. This does not mean, however, that the old techniques and methods have to be discarded; they can still be employed effectively and usefully, after necessary adjustments are made. The continuity in the development of the subject will thus be maintained.

It is interesting, and indeed symptomatic of the present position of anthropological studies in India, that Dr A. C. Mayer also should have concerned himself, in his essay, with the latest developments in the subject. He poses the question as to 'the way in which anthropological techniques can be used in the study of peasant and urban India'. He points out that the adoption of the peasant village as the unit of study has necessitated that the anthropologist reckon with the world outside the village, for the village is not 'a complete social isolate', and the 'outside influences are really 'external factors impinging on the village' within 'a wider system'. This development has led to 'the study of problems, rather than of village systems'. And, adds Dr Mayer, 'Ideally the village enters such studies merely as one of several contexts of research.'

To tackle the complex situation which confronts us, the author mentions 'teamwork', as a possible approach, 'in which several workers can deal with the same problem over a large area.' Alternatively, he recommends 'the technique of the 'village-outward' type of study. 'This consists of studying the population of a single village in its intra-village *and* inter-village activities, and in then trying to abstract the structure of those activities reaching outside the village.' In this connexion Dr Mayer refers to the concepts of 'region' and 'field'. (The latter is mentioned by Dr Bailey also.) However, the techniques and methods which prove useful at the level of the 'village-outward' study would not be so in a 'town-outward' study. Here the investigator may be forced, by his subject matter, 'to focus research on a relatively small area of activity.' As an illustration, Dr Mayer employs the notions of 'system' and 'network' 'to study political process in Dewas.'

While Drs. Dube, Bailey and Mayer point out what need be done and what can be done in extending the scope of social anthropological research in India and improving its conceptual apparatus, Dr C. von Fürer-Haimendorf draws our attention to one of several inadequacies in our study of traditional societies. 'The study of value systems and ethical concepts', he observes, 'has so far received less emphasis in anthropological research than the analysis of social and political structures. This is all the more regrettable as... an understanding of the ideology of a society is one of the most important keys to the interpretation of social conduct, and a description of a social system remains incomplete unless it accounts for the motives which determine the actions and moral choices of individuals.'

The author has, in his contribution to this Volume, described, analysed and compared the moral concepts ('descriptive ethics') of three Himalayan societies, namely the pre-literate Dafla society of Assam, the Chetri caste among the Nepalese Hindus and the Buddhist Sherpas of the Tibeto-Nepalese border.

Dr David G. Mandelbaum makes a contribution to our understanding of the working of caste rules in India by showing that in intra- and inter-caste relations various taboos and restrictions on behaviour do not always apply with equal force. There is a certain variability, arising out of a degree of liniency, of freedom of action permitted within prescribed limits. The author gives several examples to illustrate this point. Thus, he discusses hypergamy at some length, to show the existence of differing expectations from men and women with regard to marital restrictions. Similarly, he points out, children are not expected to observe all the restrictions on behaviour following from the notions of ritual purity and pollution.

He concludes: '. . . In certain matters, the *jati* role-definitions are specific and apply to all *jati* members alike; . . . But in other areas of social relations, the villager's definition of *jati*-role is a broad directive which allows for the kinds of variation we have mentioned—those of age and sex, of situation and occasion, of special bonds and considerations.'

Dr Irawati Karvé addresses herself to the task of delineating the characteristics of India as a cultural region. This is a favourite theme with her and her well-known study of kinship organization in India is a consequence of this quest. In the paper included here she chooses to concentrate attention on the tribal peoples of India. She begins with a discussion of the geographical features of the subcontinent and points out that 'Indian frontiers have never been impenetrable but they have afforded a certain type of isolation to people. When people came to India they could not keep up easy communications with the land they came from. They became isolated and became natives of the new land.' She then writes of the early immigrations into India. In this connexion she considers prehistoric industries and their affinities with similar industries outside India, as also racial and linguistic evidence and internal migrations, to conclude:

'The picture that I have in mind is of land-wandering hordes from the north coming into India and maritime people coming a little earlier or later from the south-eastern tip. They met in India two types of people: (i) hunters and gatherers who apparently were spread from the southwest upto the western part of central India and (ii) a more advanced people doing a little agriculture without the help of cattle in the south-east, north-east and westwards, perhaps right upto the Punjab. Most of these people were absorbed by the new comers but some remained isolated or escaped into the more inaccessible jungle tracts. These are the tribal people of today.'

Dr Karvé proceeds to divide India into 'two broad cultural regions, very roughly on two sides of a line drawn from Bengal to Karnatak', one on its north and the other on its south. The author's interest in culturology, her reliance on data drawn from all the fields of anthropology, and her ethnological approach are reminiscent of the catholicity of the anthropology of yester year.

Shri K. P. Chattopadhyay's essay also deals with one of the earliest, abiding and truly distinctive interests in social anthropology, namely the study of kinship terms. Like Dr Karvé, and indeed most anthropologists of the senior generation, he has devoted considerable attention to this field of research. In the present paper he writes of the influence of social factors like marriage and change in marriage rules on kinship terms, and of their extension into terms of social relationship, in the context of social groups, other than the family, such as the local settlement. Shri Chattopadhyay uses symbols to indicate the relation between the terms used and the kinds of groups involved (the family, clan, tribe etc.).

From Shri Chattopadhyay's use of symbols to Dr Ramkrishna Mukherjee's use of statistical principles in the classification of family structures is a long way indeed, and social anthropology in India has traversed all this way to modern techniques. Dr Mukherjee's intention is obviously not to 'analyse' or 'synthesize' the family as a social institution. His purpose is to attempt a comprehensive classification of 'family units' from the point of view of their 'structure.' As Dr Mukherjee sees it, any scheme of classification deals with a system or systems of variation, qualitatively and/or quantitatively characterized. Therefore, statistical principles and methods become essential to any classificatory procedure.

The author says that recent research and conceptual refinement are leading to the conclusion that the present classifications of 'family structures' are largely inadequate, and, therefore, a fresh effort is called for in this direction. He undertakes this task, in the paper included in this Volume, using data collected during a sample survey recently conducted in West Bengal.

The future of social anthropology in India is immense. As the subject develops into maturity it will face many problems, not only of subject matter, methods and techniques but also of its own office and nature. Is social anthropology in India going to be a regional specialization? Or is it going to be a study in its own right, not only with its specific factual content, but also with its distinctive concepts and canons of intelligibility and explanation?

It need hardly be said that an answer to this question ultimately ties up with the broader question of the nature and scope of social science *per se*.

Social anthropology in India has benefitted immensely by its close association with theoretical developments which have been the result of fieldwork in other parts of the world, such as Africa and America. If it has to make further progress it must stay in active touch with fieldwork and theoretical research outside India. If it becomes insular it shall have to pay too high a price for it. But social anthropology in India must also pay sufficient heed to the specificity of its subject matter in terms of which it can discover its own inner dynamic. It can ignore to do this only at its peril. We can hardly do better than recall Kroeber's statement on the organization of anthropology in India and ponder over it: 'India has listened both to Britain and to the United States and—wisely— to herself' (*An Appraisal of Anthropology Today*, ed. by Sol. Tax et al., Chicago 1953, p. 364).

Prehistoric Archaeology

1

ENVIRONMENT AND TOOLS OF EARLY MAN IN INDIA

DHARANI SEN

THE ANTIQUITY of Man goes back to the beginning of the last million years of geological history. As a tool-maker, Early Man emerged during the Pleistocene, which is the last epoch of the geological era Cainozoic (age of mammals). The Pleistocene was an epoch of great climatic change characterised by phases of repeated cooling and warming. This was mainly due to the fluctuations in the amount of heat received by the earth from the sun. Pleistocene glaciation was thus a universal phenomenon, directly affecting, as it did, about 30 per cent of the earth's surface. In the high and middle latitudes and in the high mountainous regions, there were phases of extreme cold when glaciers advanced and warm phases when glaciers retreated. The advance and retreat of the glaciers were thus cyclic in nature. Correspondingly, in the tropical and sub-tropical regions of the earth, there was a pluvial-interpluvial age characterised by alternate phases of intense precipitation and comparative aridity. Thus, during the Pleistocene epoch there were long phases of glaciations, inundations, warm-dry phases, descications and dust-storms affecting large tracts of the earth and their inhabitants. Repeated migrations of entire flora and fauna were characteristic of this last million years of geological history.

This critical period witnessed the evolution of Man and his cultural traditions. It was during this environmentally changing times, that Man became bipedal and tool-maker. In fact, he is often distinguished from the anthropoid apes by his tool-making capacity. According to recent authorities, most of the obvious differences that distinguish Man from the apes arose after he learnt to make artifacts. These artifacts along with the development of the brain, bones, teeth and other characters made him a *human being*, distinct from other primates. His tools were not only implements of his response and adjustments to his environment and of his survival. They were also the instruments of his *humanisation* and his emancipation from the simian way of life. Gradually he fabricated a large variety of artifacts revealing his great labours, his technical skill and adaptibility.

As an artificer, Early Man appeared in India (including Pakistan) about the middle of the Pleistocene epoch, roughly about four to five thousand centuries before the present. His first artifacts date in the Punjab from the Boulder Conglomerate of the Middle Pleistocene age (second glacial phase of the Ice Age). In peninsular India, the earliest tools came from the Boulder Conglomerate deposits which underlie the laterite near Madras. In the Narmada Valley in Madhya Pradesh and elsewhere, the earliest tools are found in the Basal Boulder Conglomerate associated with the Mid-Pleistocene fossil mammals.

Glaciological evidence in the Indian Himalayas shows that there were in the main four glacial phases and three interglacial phases in the Pleistocene. The relative duration of these climatic phases was not uniform. The second glacial phase was longer than the first, which was longer than the third. The last glacial phase was the shortest. Compared generally with the glacial phases, the interglacial phases were longer. The second interglacial phase was the longest like that in Europe. The first interglacial phase was longer than the third or the last interglacial phase. Correspondingly in the adjacent periglacial region, there were cyclic or alternate phases of aggradation and degradation, resulting in the formation of river-terraces as in the Punjab plains. There were generally four main phases of sedimentation and three main phases of erosion in the plains, one each in the Early and Middle Pleistocene and the last two in the Upper Pleistocene. The fact that the artifacts of Early Man are not found in the Kashmir valley shows that he avoided the cold Alpine heights and preferred the open river plains of the Punjab for his habitat.

During the first glacial phase in early Pleistocene times, the Kashmir valley was less elevated and was a faulted inter-montane basin. The climate was then very cold and the mammalian life was somewhat impoverished, perhaps due to the first impact of glaciation, as is exemplified in the Upper Siwalik *Tatrot* stage in the Punjab plains. During the following warm interglacial phase, when the Pirpanjal was still a low ridge, the Siwalik mammals from the north Indian plains like the ancient elephant, deer and other mammals migrated to the Kashmir valley. It was then a lake teaming with wild animal life. Near Gulmarg in Kashmir, interglacial fossiliferous clays have yielded Pine, Oak, Birch and shells of fresh-water molluses. The *Pinjor* stage in the Punjab likewise revealed rich Siwalik mammal life. About hundred species of fossil mammals have been found in the *Pinjor* beds, which include monkeys, tigers, elephants, horses, hippopotami and pigs. Pirpanjal being then a low ridge, there was a two-way traffic of mammalian movements. The Upper Gangetic plain now almost treeless, then supported extensive forest which was thorny towards the south and west, but luxuriant near the Himalayas. Buffaloes, rhinos, deer, tigers and other animals roamed about the plains and the foot-hills. The steppes supported horses and lions. Further south in the Narmada valley, the Pleistocene deposits reveal rich mammalian fauna including elephants, rhinos, hippopotami, horses, and wild cattle etc. Man had perhaps not entered the scene yet, since neither his tools nor his bones had so far been found. However, all the favourable ecological factors were here present and it is rather intriguing that artifactual remains of Man are lacking. It is however probable that Man was present during this first interglacial phase of the Ice Age.

It was during the next climatic phase, viz., the second glacial in Kashmir and the corresponding Boulder Conglomerate stage in the plains, that Man's presence is testified to by his tools. It was a period of intense glaciation in Kashmir and pluviation in the plains, forming in the latter wide flood-plains and abundant grazing ground for animal life. From this time onward till the end of the Ice Age, the northern plains were in continuous occupation of Early Man, migrating far and wide along favourable natural routes. The southern plains were also wide and open, and in the gravels and laterites was found definite evidence of human artifacts.

During the long second inter-glacial phase (constituting about one-third of the whole Pleistocene epoch) in the Punjab plains, when the climate was once again warm and dry and the first river terrace (T_1) was being formed, Man made farther technological progress and developed his lithic industries. During the following third glacial phase, it was again cold and humid but Early Man adjusted himself to this new change by elaboration of his lithic equipments. There was plenty of vegetation and game and Early Man was prolific in manufacturing new tools and weapons. After an initial pluvial phase, there was a short phase of wind-blown loessic deposit. Early Man must have witnessed in this periglacial region great dust-storms during this time. Many workshop sites containing highly evolved types of tools have been found in the terrace (T_2) deposits.

During the third warm-dry interglacial phase, there was redeposition of the so-called *loessic loam* (redeposited Potwar). Everywhere in the plains, the *loam* occupies the lower terraces (T_3) and here are found more evolved tool-types of Early Man.

During the last glacial phase, it was again extremely cold and humid and there was a deposition of loessic soil and of the low terrace (T_4), constituting the late Pleistocene times. Here we observe a late Palaeolithic industry of Early Man.

The problem of the age and environment of Early Man in Peninsular India is intimately connected with the detrital laterite which is a characteristic tropical deposit. It requires for its formation a succession of wet and dry phases. Generally fossil laterite suggests humid tropical or sub-tropical clmate, and lateritic crust suggests comparatively dry climate. The makers of the biface in peninsular India must have witnessed periods of dry and humid climatic change. Exact geological and climatic dating of the implementiferous laterite is yet an open question. In Mayurbhanj, however, such laterite has been geologically dated as within the Pleistocene. Pleistocene studies in the coastal areas have not yet been attempted in any detail.

Early Men were generally groundlings of open country, suggesting carnivorous habit and nomadic hunting life. They were nomads not by choice but by the prevailing natural environment. Their open habitats are generally located in broad river valleys, in terraces or peneplains or loessic stations which provided appropriate natural camps and where plenty of game for their sustenance and raw materials for their tools were available. They preferred flat and open lands as these gave them necessary open view of their natural enemies. Such a topography would also facilitate free movement. The proximity of water and forest together with the necessary raw material provided ample ecological opportunities to their ways and means of living. These early hunters generally followed the trail of bison and deer over the grasslands, the wild cattle, hippopotami and rhinos in forest glades and savannas, horses in the steppe and other contemporary mammals gradually shifting with the change of climate and vegetation. The raw materials were amply provided by the river-borne gravels and pebbles or by conglomerates along alluvial tracts. Factory sites have been located where there is ample supply of suitable raw materials. Although we do not have much evidence in India, Early Men must have occupied caves and rock-shelters where these naturally occur and used them as temporary sojourn during cold and rainy phases. The Kurnool caves in South India have yielded some evidence of human occupation.

Without fire and tools, Early Man could not have adjusted himself to the changing environment and survived in the struggle for exist-ence. Unlike other mammals, Man is ill-equipped by nature; having no specialised corporeal organ to procure food or fight for survival. It is his early knowledge of technology, based on wood, stone, bone and antler, in a word his *culture*, that stood him in good stead in his hunting and collecting economy. He was not yet a producer of food since he had no knowledge of agriculture and domestication of animals. His kit of tools reveals his flexibility and his roving life. Gradually he elaborated his technology and improved his methods of hunting, fishing and fowling. Not only could he make more and more efficient tools to suit his increasing needs, but also he could communicate his technical knowledge to his fellow men. And this useful and practical knowledge was handed down to successive generations. Thus the implements were made collectively according to accepted prevailing social traditions. Hunting then was a collective affair and certain traditional methods were pres-cribed according to the exigencies of environmental situations. Naturally many artifices were employed, such as camouflaging and trenching in order to capture large mammals which were their favourites.

Although we have rare evidence, Early Man must have used wooden implements, which have perished under natural forces of decay. Since he was a hunter, he must have used some sort of wooden spears and clubs, shaped by stone knives and scrapers like the Australian aborigines. A specimen of a wooden spear has been found in an early palaeolithic site in England and another specimen in a French site together with the bones of an extinct animal. One of the Mount Carmel cave-men in Palestine was killed by a wooden spear. It was perhaps a case of tribal feud.

Fire should be considered as a *tool par excellence* of Early Man. Although we do not have definite evidence of the use of fire here, as is found in Europe, Africa, West Asia and Far East, we can presume its early use in this country also. As fire provides natural warmth from the cold and protection from the wild animals, Early Man here as elsewhere must have used it or else he would have perished in dire cold during the glacial phases. Cave exploration in this country may reveal traces of ash or burnt animal bones as have been found in Choukoutienean caves in China.

The earliest fabricated stone tools found in India as in Africa are chipped pebbles. One end or one side of a handy river-worn pebble was flaked to a zigzag or rugged working edge, suitable for chopping, cutting and scraping. At first the technique was simple, being one-directional flaking, later it was replaced by two-directional alternate flaking, producing a more effective chopping edge. Archaeologists have named these tools as choppers and chopping-tools. This primitive tool-making tradition has been observed in a large number of palaeolithic sites both in peninsular India and in the northern plains. But like the *Kafuan* pebble-tool industries in Africa, these are not yet found exclusively in any particular bed or geological horizon in India. These chopper-chopping tools, made on river-worn pebbles, reflect warm forest and swampy environment. In Africa, the *Kafuan* pebble tools constitute the oldest lithic industry of Early Man. In peninsular India, however, the pebble tools are found associated with the handaxe. The evidence in Olduvai Gorge shows that the handaxe has evolved from the pebble chopper-chopping tool. From the field-data so far observed in peninsular India, it is probable that the pebble tools of the chopper-chopping variety were also more primitive than the handaxe.

The most widespread and standardised tool of Early Man in India is the handaxe, seemingly a multi-purpose tool used for cutting, digging, thrusting and such other purposes. The hand axe suggests tropical forest and wood-land environment. In India this is the most common and characteristic tool in the tropical peninsular region. Technologically, it is more evolved than the pebble tools described earlier and shows multi-directional flakings and symmetry of form. It is standardised into four or five main types and occurs over a large area of the Old World—extending from India to Western Europe and Africa. The African Abbevellio-Acheulian artifacts are typologically very similar to their Indian counterparts. In both the countries, the main raw material is quartzite. In technique and form the Indian Abbevellio-Acheulian tools are also generally similar to the West European proto-types

(Abbevellio-Acheulian), although the latter are made on flint, which is softer, easily flakable and commonly found in that country. Here it may be mentioned that India is the home of quartzites, and flint is comparatively rare. Credit therefore must be given to the early tool-makers in India, for their technical capacity to make as effective tools from such a hard refractory rock as quartzite. In Asia, the hand axe so far has been found in India and Pakistan, Arabia, Palestine, Uzbekistan, Armenia and in Java[1] in South-East Asia. The handaxe in India, as in Europe and Africa, shows a gradual refinement of form and technique. We have in India very good examples of Acheulian and Micoquian types. Handaxes occur both on core and flake as in Africa and show integration of core-flake techniques.

The tool called cleaver with a true axe-edge appeared a little later. In peninsular India, the cleaver is found often associated with the Acheulian type of handaxe. This tool is also standardised into four or five main types with some variations in technique. The Indian cleaver is generally similar to the African proto-type in form and technique. The cleaver generally suggests a tropical woodland environment, and was perhaps mainly used for cutting and shaping wood and for skinning and flaying animal carcass. It may be mentioned here that the handaxe and cleaver in India constitute elements of the same tradition described as the Indian Abbevellio-Acheulian tradition (*Madrasian*) and is characteristic of tropical peninsular India.

Besides these characteristic heavy implements, Early Man in India, as elsewhere, also fabricated lighter and smaller tools which he made on flake. At first the flakes were detached and worked by a simple technique (Clactonian) and later by a more refined technique of core-preparation. These latter types are made by what is known as the Levalloisean technique reflecting an increase in technical knowledge and adjustment. The Levalloisean in N. India is an element of the Late Soan tradition. It is likely that the tools made by this superior technique were marked for specialised functions. Characteristic tools such as knife, point, scraper, awl etc. were made by this technique. The triangular points probably used as arrow-heads, suitably hafted, were hunter's tool *par excellence*. Scrapers, knives, awls etc. were used as carpenter's tool for scraping, cutting etc. This technique and the range of typology suggest new human adjustments to the prevailing environment.

The idea of hafting and composite tools and the idea of a weapon used as a missile, arose with the invention and development of this new technique. The Levalloisean technique and its development in India as in Europe and Africa was an event of great significance. The core-preparation, before the flake was detached, suggests imagination and foresight of the artificer. It also involves less human labour and less wastage in the materials. This technique arose in peninsular India with the Acheulian and lasted much longer than any other technique man could devise during this age. Elaboration of this technique later gave rise to further ideas of tool-making and adaptations as are observed in many latter human cultures in India. The blade cultures in India, as in Africa, were influenced by this technique. Unfortunately very few serious studies have been attempted on the evolution of this technique in India. Levalloisean techniques have been so for observed in north-west India in the Late Soan Culture, in Gujrat, in Narmada valley, M.P. and also further south in the Deccan and Madras.

With the march of time, the core and flake cultures in India were gradually replaced by blade cultures heralding a new lithic tradition in India towards the close of the Pleistocene. New raw materials were tapped for making the blade industry. In the Deccan we find the extensive use of cryptocrystalline colloidal silica, such as agate, jasper, chert, chalcedony, flint etc. The blades were detached in such a way from prepared cores that the former were roughly parallel sided and often tabular is aspect. The flake scars are usually parallel and longitudinal. This is a developed Levalloisean technique. Thus a new range of tools reveals a new and superior technique of manufacture. Characteristic implements made on blade include various types of knives, scrapers, burins etc. Burins, rare in India, are made by a special notch technique. This blade typology and technique reveal finer adjustment to the environment with the adoption of improved methods of hunting and fishing. The multipurpose tools like the cleaver and the hand-axe are no longer in vogue. Their place is taken over by a variety of delicate implements serving specific purposes in their economy. The repertoire of tool types also suggests extension and varieties of human actions. Technical progress was certainly more rapid than before.

It is interesting to observe that all the blade industries in India so far reported are generally located in the Deccan Trap area.

The blade factory sites have been reported from Gujrat, coastal Bombay, Madhya Pradesh and Andhra Pradesh. It has been already stated that the material for the so-called blade industry in India is cryptocrystalline colloidal silica like jasper, agate, flint, chert, chalcedony etc. These naturally occur in great abundance as secondary minerals that are found as kernels in the amygdoloidal basalts or in the cavities of the Deccan Trap. The Deccan Trap of India provides flat plateau topography, generally devoid of thick forest growth. It is generally characterised by open vegetation like scrub jungle and park-lands where small game was once abundant. The blade tools are found in the Trap area in decomposed ferruginous and other soils, such as the *regur* underlain by trap rocks. Most of the sites are located on the slopes and lower reaches generally. Thus the Deccan Trap provided an appropriate natural habitat for the blade industry, where the ecological opportunities were present for its localization. The blade tradition thus reveals light equipments consisting of delicate tools adapted to specific regional environment unlike the biface tradition. The distribution of the blade industry in India is limited by the occurrence of raw material in the Deccan Trap area. It would not be out of place to mention here that in Kutch, Kathiawar and Cambay, an ancient tradition of making beads and other artifacts by a percussion technique out of agate and such other material is still in vogue. The proto-neolithic blade industry of Rohri and Sukkur may also be mentioned in this connection.

The reported blade and burin industry from the Upper gravels at Khandivli, Bombay, suggests a western extension of the blade industry towards the west coast of the peninsula. Here a texturally similar raw material like the colloidal silica, viz., the indurated shale[2] has been employed.

Taking the whole of the sub-continent of India (including Pakistan), we observe in the main five broad lithicultural traditions. The most primitive lithic tradition of India appears to be that of crude pebble chopper-chopping tools, which have a very wide geographical distribution in India, particularly in the peninsular region. This tradition appears in India as a *complex* associated with the Abbevellian type of handaxes and Clacton-like flakes. Typologically it recalls the *Oldowan* pebble-tool culture of east Africa.

A second tradition, which is more conspicuous in the subcontinent, is that of the hand axe and the cleaver, and it has also a wide distribution in peninsular India and extending as it does further north. This tradition recalls the biface tradition of Africa.

A third tradition, which is conspicuous in the northern plains in the Punjab, is that of the Early Soan pebble-flake tradition which is generally devoid of the true biface. This tradition recalls the Anyathian and Patjitanian cultures of southeast Asia.

A fourth tradition, also conspicuous in the same region, is the Late Soan tradition consisting of evolved pebble-tools and flakes, showing Levalloisio-Mousterian techniques. The Late Soan has evolved from the Early Soan tradition. It is significant that the Levalloisian technique is common both in the biface and in the Late Soan traditions. In the biface tradition, however, this technique is applied in the manufacture of the biface, whereas in the Late Soan tradition, it is observed among the flakes. This may suggest a diffusion of the Levalloisian technique over a wider area.

The last of the lithic traditions of Early Man in India is that of the blades with its characteristic developed Levalloisian and related techniques. The blade tradition tends to microlithism towards the end, extending to post-Pleistocene times, when it is replaced by full-fledged microlithic industries.

In many Palaeolithic sites in Gujarat and Madhya Pradesh, particularly in the Narmada valley alluvial tracts, we observed "mixed" cultures consisting of both the northern Soan element and southern biface.

To correlate individual lithic traits with particular elements in the Pleistocene environment is a difficult task. Broad cultural traditions, however, can be correlated with the general structure of the environment. We have stated that the primitive chopper-chopping pebble-tool tradition reflects warmer forest and swampy lowland environment. The handaxe tradition suggests a wider peninsular tropical forest and woodland environment. The two environmental conditions in certain regions somewhat overlap one with the other.

The biface tradition in its evolved stages shows a greater range of environmental adaptability extending as it did beyond its original habitat. The cleaver element of the biface tradition, suggesting open wood-land environment, illustrates geographical adjustment. The Early Soan tradition in its homeland reveals adaptation to a dry environment in the periglacial Punjab plains, whereas the Late Soan tradition shows an adaptation to a cold humid environment. With its greater range of tool-types, it flourished over a dry period in the Punjab for sometime. The blade tradition shows further regional specialization and adjustment with a new type of raw material in the Deccan Trap area reflecting new social needs of Early Man.

NOTES

[1] Movius, Jr., describes the Javanese specimens as recalling crude Abbevallian type, which has no relation to the classic bifaces of Europe, India and Africa.

[2] Indurated shale has a compact flinty structure and breaks with conchoidal fracture.

THE ARCHAEOLOGY OF A RIVER CROSSING

· F. R. ALLCHIN AND B. ALLCHIN

T H E R E A R E some geographical features which seem by their very natures predestined to play a leading role in controlling the routes men have followed through the ages,—the Quetta valley is one such; there are others which have acquired, perhaps by some quirk of fortune, an importance which—once gained—they have retained. An example of this kind is the Khyber pass. The crossing points of rivers, be they fords or be they ferry stations, are naturally more widespread and more flexible than are mountain passes. But some of them acquire almost incomprehensibly a significance which clings to them, so that age after age men, at very different stages of evolution and engaged upon quite different missions, have gone to them and used them. Thus they become established and fixed and in this way they have played their parts in the making of history. The countless lesser ferry points and crossings between villages are dwarfed by them; and often temples and sacred bathing places, tīrthas and places of pilgrimage have been established and enhanced their fame. Instances of crossings of antiquity and repute may be found on all the great rivers of India. One has only to recall the crossing of the Godavari at Nasik and of the Narmada at Maheshwar, or of the same river at Bheraghāt and Jabalpur, to see how interesting complexes of ancient sites are found clustered around such spots: in each case closely linked with ancient routes of importance. In the present paper we propose to discuss the evidence afforded by a smaller and less spectacular crossing which shows great antiquity and continuity. A subsidiary aim is to demonstrate the use of archaeological field observation and historical fact from a given geographical context to produce culture history.

The plateau of the North Karnataka once reached presents few obstacles to the traveller in any direction. Part of one of the most ancient land masses in the world, its surface has been reduced by time and weather to a gently undulating plain, dry, dusty and much cultivated; mainly covered by a 'sea' of black cotton soil from which rise occasional islands of residual granite boulders, small and widespread enough to be easily circumnavigated. The river valleys have also become wide and shallow with time and only the rivers themselves, the Krishna and its tributaries the Tunga- bhadra and the Bhima, remain to be negotiated. These like their counterparts of the Godavari system to the north rise in the Western Ghats and flow right across the plateau from west to east; conse- sequently they are of considerable size before they leave it. The Krishna, with which we are here mainly concerned, has in its central course sheer banks of 15 ft.—20 ft., cut chiefly through the accu- mulated black cotton soil. In places the valley approaches a gorge, but in general it is broad and with gentle slopes, with a fall of only some 60 ft. within two miles of the river upon either bank. Here and there on the slope are deposits of gravels of undetermined age, the remnants of ancient deposition before the river had cut down to its present bed. But there are no marked terraces, although gravels of this kind occur up to 100 ft. above the modern level. The gravels are important as they have served as sources of raw material for Stone Age man whenever they were exposed.

The area known as the Raichur Doāb, the triangle of land between the Krishna and the Tungabhadra, is crossed historically by three main lines of communication. In the west is the very ancient road from Surapur to Lingsugur, Mudgal and Vijayanagar, which crosses the Krishna at the still unbridged ford near the ancient settlement site and village of Tathni. In the east of the Doāb another less well defined line ran from Hyderabad southwards, via Gadwal and Alampur, to Karnul. In the centre of the Doāb is the crossing which is the subject of this paper.[1] It is situated where the road and railway line from Raichur to Gulbarga cross the river Krishna, some 75 miles west of its junction with the Tungabhadra and almost immediately below its junction with the Bhima. The latter *sangam* is characteristically a place of cult importance, and at certain times of the year people still gather there for religious and recreational purposes. The river is already of considerable size at this point, and though fordable in the dry season for those with local knowledge and physical strength, it presents none the less a considerable barrier at all times and an almost insuperable one during the wet season of the year.

That the crossing is older than the road- or the rail-bridge is shown by the presence of a disused causeway (what in Hindī is called a *rapaṭ*) and a large ruined travellers' bungalow on the southern bank, where travellers could stay and wait for the water to go down. That it was a centre of human activity and therefore also probably a crossing place of very much greater antiquity is shown by the presence of a Middle Stone Age factory site on a small outcrop of granite on the south bank, west of the modern road and about 3 furlongs from the river.[2] This yielded a considerable collection of tools closely comparable to those found in Pleistocene deposits on the Narmada river and in many other parts of India. That it was a factory with tools and by-products of their manufacture *in situ* is shown by the high proportion of the latter, and the unrolled condition of all the finds. They had clearly not been brought there by the flood waters of the river, but lay near where they fell from their makers' hands.

These tools which have been more fully described elsewhere include scrapers and other wood-working tools, struck from carefully prepared cores by a technique parallel to the Levallois of Europe, and numerous by-products and factory debris resulting from their manufacture (Fig. 1, Nos. 1-7). About 50 yards distant on another slope of the same hillock is a second factory site which yielded a number of blades, blade cores and geometric forms typical of the Indian Late Stone Age, together with characteristic factory debris. This site was first discovered by us in 1951 and in a single visit of less than an hour we collected 150 specimens. On a subsequent visit in 1957 we made a further collection of Late Stone Age materials and discovered the Middle Stone Age site which we had overlooked on our earlier visit. As the collection of Late Stone Age tools has not yet been published in full elsewhere,[3] the following list of tools and by-products collected from the site during both visits is included here.

140 Flakes and pieces of raw material	Of these 68 are unretouched with some slight signs of utilisation; 52 have definite use marks, in some cases suggesting retouch, but more often suggesting systematic use in one direction, possibly as small adze or knife blades (Fig. 2, No. 16).
39 Blades	17 complete, the remainder broken (Fig. 2, Nos. 3, 6 and 11).

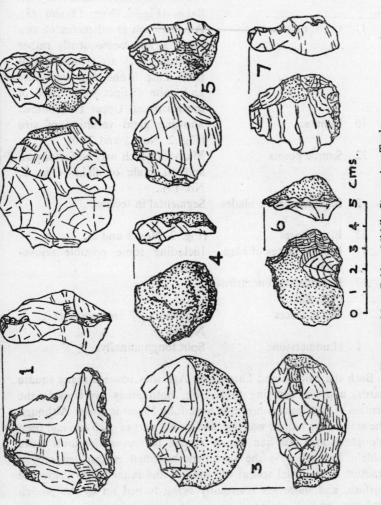

Fig. 1. Krishna Bridge, Middle Stone Age Tools.

5	Truncated blades	2 of which are also backed (Fig. 2, No. 14).
5	Concave scrapers	1 on the end of a short blade, 1 on the side of a short blade and 3 on flakes (Fig. 2, Nos. 12 and 13).
11	(?) Burins	All made on small pieces of raw material and consequently rather formless. They are typical of tropical Late Stone Age industries and quite distinct from those of the European Upper Palaeolithic.
16	Lunates	Showing great variation of size (Fig. 2, Nos. 5 and 7-10).
32	Simple points	Many of which may be fortuitous, and all made on flakes (Fig. 2, No. 15).
2	Segmental adze blades	Segmental in section.
33	Blade cores	(Fig. 2, Nos. 1 and 2).
11	Broken pieces of blade cores	Including some possible rejuvenators.
17	Longitudinal core trimming flakes	
9	Guide flakes	2 primary, 7 secondary (Fig. 2, No. 4).
1	Hammerstone	Split longitudinally.

Both the Middle and Late Stone Age sites covered many square yards, and the outlying tools from both areas overlapped: the centres of distribution however were fully 50 yards apart. Although the soil on the hillock was thin and stony, part of each site had been ploughed, and this had clearly tended to spread the tools more widely. In each case the specimens collected represented only a fraction of the total still at the site, on and immediately below the surface, and more are constantly being turned up by the plough and exposed by the rains. Both groups are made from stones brought from the nearby river gravels. These are generally some kind of crypto-crystalline silica, such as agate, or extremely fine-grained quartzite, worn by the action of the water into typical river pebbles. Many of the tools retain traces of the original pebble cortex. Many

View of the alignment looking east from the factory site

Stone circle grave in foreground. The factory site is on the rocky area in the left middle distance

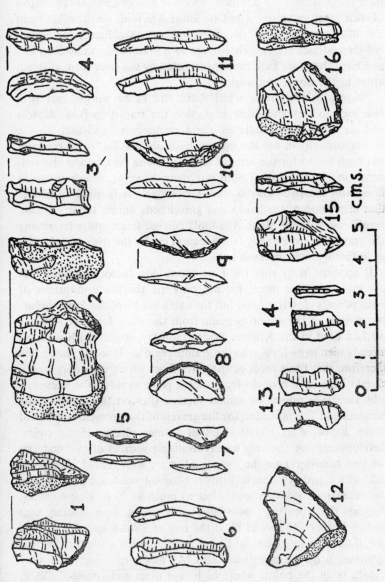

Fig. 2. Krishna Bridge, Late Stone Age Tools.

of the Middle Stone Age tools have a heavy ochreous patina on their outer surfaces in addition, which is almost certainly indicative of their great antiquity. The Late Stone Age tools on the other hand are often entirely free of patination or only lightly patinated. All these stones are entirely foreign to a granite region such as this and must therefore have been transported by the river from adjacent areas to the north and west.

There are indications, which have still to be worked out with reference to this and other sites, that the transition from Middle to Late Stone Age techniques was a gradual one, and that the site was continually in use throughout both phases. So far no evidence has been found for the activity of Early Stone Age man in the vicinity. On the occasion of both our visits, however, the river was in flood and the river gravels were submerged. It is highly probable that inspection of the banks and gravel beds during the dry season would reveal Early Stone Age tools derived from upstream among the gravels, if not actually in the section cut by the river in its banks, or at factory sites on those banks.

It appears likely that the Late Stone Age factory continued in use into Neolithic times, for not only are the blade industries of both periods closely related but the extensive Neolithic blade industry of sites of the region is made from the same kinds of stone as we find used in the Krishna Bridge industry, stone which we have already seen to be foreign to the granite regions. It seems reasonable therefore that these tools or the cores from which they were struck should have been brought from such a place as this. Not unexpectedly there are numerous similar factory sites on the banks of the Krishna and Tungabhadra, for the gravels of their present beds, or of those deposited at higher levels at former phases of the rivers' development, are the only locally available sources of raw material for tool making. That the river-bed factory sites should often coincide with crossing places or fords is a logical extension as their very distance from the settlements, often as much as 20 or even 40 miles, suggests that they were associated with routes. It is unlikely that such a factory site should be at the end of a road leading nowhere else, if only because a similar line of roads to other settlements would approach it on the other bank also. All analogies suggest that they should be at the points where highways meet and routes coalesce, in just the sort of position which a major river crossing provides. A similar pattern of factory sites is suggested at the Tathni crossing, for Dr. Krishna Murthi of the Hyderabad Geological survey discovered such a factory near the village of Honhalli on the road a few miles south of the crossing itself.

About 4,000 years ago a group of pastoral tribes in a Neolithic-Chalcolithic technological stage moved slowly southwards through the western parts of the Deccan plateau and occupied the Raichur Doāb and districts to the south. The hall-mark of their activities is their distinctive pottery, particularly grey and buff ware sometimes with unburnt ochre paint, and their ground stone axes. Another regular feature of their settlements is the Neolithic blade industry, with its large proportion of blades and smaller number of lunates and geometric forms. These people chose for their settlements the foot or side of the granite hills and made there levelled terraces on which they lived. The presence of the Neolithic folk at the Krishna bridge site, which has already been hinted at, is further confirmed by the discovery of the butt end of a worn and broken axe of basalt on the northern slope of the hillock, about a furlong from the factory area, and nearby of another butt of a large broken basalt axe.

Across the river there are further signs of Neolithic activities. The nearest hill of any size is near the village of Gudabelur, about 3 miles north-east of the crossing. Examination revealed there numerous terraces on the hill and fragments of a typical Neolithic blade industry. There can be no reasonable doubt that at some time there existed at this point a small Neolithic settlement. There are other confirmatory sites nearby. Munn and his associates discovered east of Hindupur village, near the bund on the track leading to Gudabelur, barely two miles from the crossing, a collection of well shaped ground stone axes, and here too their age cannot be in dispute (Munn 1944, p. 88). Another site was found near Kottapalli, some 7 miles away to the north, where there is a largish hill and again axes were discovered. It is reasonable to expect that exploration would reveal there a Neolithic settlement. Thus on the north bank there are manifold signs of activity at this period, while on the south two axes were discovered.

Of the ensuing S. Indian Iron Age, which we infer to have begun about the middle of the first millennium B.C., the most obvious traces are the Megalithic monuments. In this part of the Krishna valley these are of two principal forms, cairn-circle graves and stone alignments. So prominent are these megalithic features that the settlements of the period have been largely ignored by archaeologists. They appear on present showing to occur in clusters: probably in the areas of denser settlement at that time. The intervals, at least in some cases, may be inferred to be areas of forest which were then still unsettled. One cluster of grave sites occurs around Gadwal, about 30 miles east of the Krishna bridge crossing, where . in about 150 sq. mi. there are no less than 17 separate grave sites, containing upwards of 1,000 graves in all.[4] The same area today includes some 27 villages and about 20 smaller hamlets, so that there is surviving and so far discovered one Iron Age grave site for every three modern settlements. In addition there is near Gadwal a remarkable group of stone alignments which we have referred to elsewhere.[5] The next cluster of grave sites, moving westwards, is that immediately north of the Krishna bridge crossing. Here along a 14 mile stretch of the river's bank there are 7 grave sites. The same area includes no more than 7 modern settlements, and in addition 4 separate stone alignments. In other words in both these areas there is a suggestion that the number of settlements was already considerable and some features of the modern pattern were already established. We now return to consider those remains which are most nearly associated with the crossing place.

On the south bank, within 200 yards of the factory site, are the remains of a stone alignment (PL. 1a). Only about 20 stones remain standing of which the tallest are not more than 6 ft. in height. The stones are of grey granite, doubtless locally derived. Their original plan cannot be determined, but we infer that it was of the class which we named 'square alignments.' In one line there are still 5 stones standing with an orientation of 5° East of North. The function and purpose of these alignments remains mysterious, but what evidence was then available was collected in our paper in *Man*. About a furlong north of the factory site, and just under half way to the river bank, are the remains of a cairn-circle grave site (PL. 1b). The graves are in poor condition and much mutilated, but when visited in 1952 at least six were more or less complete. These were of the common dimensions of graves in this area, the largest being 35 ft. in diameter, the smallest 20 ft. One of the graves had a circle composed of flat slabs of granite set up on edge and standing to a height of 2 ft. 6 ins. This grave had been robbed at some date and fragments of typical black-and-red B1 ware scattered around. None of the graves contained any sign of a central cist but these may have been buried. North of the crossing similar evidence is available. About a mile and a half from the crossing, east of Hindupur village there is a stone alignment (see Munn 1941, p. 86), and another lies just by the Neolithic site at Gudabelur. At the latter there are 4 rows of 4 stones, set at intervals of 36 ft. and made of pink granite. The orientation in 10° East of North. The stones are of comparable dimensions to those of the Krishna bridge site. About 4 miles east, on the banks of the Krishna, about a mile south-east of Murardoddi village is another remarkable alignment. It stands by a mound studded with gneissic boulders and flanked by stone circle graves. East of the mound is a square alignment of standing stones of 14 ft.-16 ft. in height. There are 6 stones in each row and the intervals are 40 ft. in either direction (See Munn *ibid*). The whole area is dotted with grave sites, but we only visited one of them. This was situated about 4 furlongs north of Gudabelur. By the roadside there are 3 graves of unusual size, each being in the region of 180 ft.-190 ft. in diameter, and there are traces of many smaller graves of the common dimensions on both sides of the road. The large graves have double, if not treble circles of boulders around them and cairns of smaller stones in the centre. The unusual juxtaposition of large and common graves is echoed again in one of the Gadwal sites (so far unpublished) and in numerous other Deccan sites. It may well be taken to indicate the graves of persons of some sort of social eminence.

The transformation from the Iron Age to the Early Historic period in this region we infer to have taken place around the beginning of the Christian era. What the change entailed is a complex matter which we cannot discuss here at length.[6] It involved a radical change in the settlement pattern. The hill villages of the Neolithic and, we infer, Iron age were scattered upon the terraced slopes and shoulders of the granite hills. Now there was a move to consolidate the settlement in one place, usually in a suitable valley or at a corner of the hill. Another and more important change was that new villages now began to appear on the open plain. Indeed from this date a continued process begins which sets the pattern through the centuries up to the present of the expansion of settlements from the earlier centres into the hitherto unsettled areas. A detailed survey of the villages of any part of the Karnataka, backed up by historical records would make clear the process. Also at the opening of the Christian era Raichur town comes into prominence. Hitherto the only settlement of any size appears to have been at Kallur, the other larger Neolithic settlements all lying to the west around Mudgal and Maski. But it was perhaps during the Iron Age that a new settlement sprang up 10 miles east of Kallur at Raichur which afterwards grew into the great fortified town of the Middle Ages. Surface observation is not easy at Raichur as later fortification and dam building have so disturbed the ground, but in the field below the great bund north-east of the railway station and also near the station itself plentiful finds of black-and-red B1 ware and red B3 ware attest a settlement of some size. Here too a hoard of punch-marked coins was discovered some years ago. The settlement at Raichur, as it were, pinned down the Krishna crossing. This process of change may be also inferred to have happened at other sites. At Gudabelur it was probable that at this date the village shifted to its present site, south of the line of hillocks which had hitherto contained it. This change is linked with a matter of more than usual interest. On the rocks at the south-west extremity of the Gudabelur site we observed a number of thin short strokes cut on the face of the rock. We did not record the number of such marks but it was probably more than 50. Similar marks occur at other places in the Raichur Doab. Particularly Munn (1934, p. 124) recorded a large flat boulder at Kurkundi, just east of the Hutti gold bands where similar 'Ogham like' markings were cut. From the photograph which he published I have counted about 200 marks. Munn also mentioned that similar marks are found upon the rocks near the Kolar goldfields in Mysore. We take it that these marks are not as Munn thought a form of script, but rather some form of numerical check or count. Near the goldfields they indicated the number of loads (of whatever description) removed, and here at the crossing they seem to indicate a similar check upon the number of loads carried over. Their age is undetermined. Although they must have been made with a steel chisel they are more rough and weathered than chisel marks on the great blocks of masonry in the walls of Raichur fort. Further being as they are near the old settlement we are inclined to associate them with the period when it was still occupied, that is to say the Iron Age or Early Historic period.

The siting of Raichur fort barely 12 miles from the crossing assured it of its place in the wars of the Middle Ages. It need not be a matter of surprise that no forts were built at the crossing place; situated as it is and the ground being as it is they would have served little useful function. There is indeed an area marked on certain editions of the Survey maps as of about a mile along each face and apparently fortified, which Sewell remarks as lying just below the Bhima river junction with the Krishna, on the north bank about 2 miles west of the railway station, with its base on the river. This he took to be the remains of an entrenched camp, and well it may be for neither Sewell himself nor, to my knowledge, any other historians or archaeologists have commented upon it. It is certainly tempting to speculate upon its connection with the struggles of the Adil Shah and Krishna Deva Raya for control of Raichur fort, for it would seem to belong to campaigns of the size recorded by Nuniz and Ferishta. Be this so or be it otherwise at least it may be accepted that the Adil Shah did encamp upon the north bank of the river and that the dramatic attack which Ferishta describes, led by the king himself and followed by other elephants and men on rafts took place. The account is pregnant with meaning, for we learn that the Adil Shah was forced to build rafts because all the ferries of the Krishna were held by the enemy, and that the attack took place in the month of May, 1520, when the river might be expected to be at its lowest.[7] We learn more of the ferries of the Krishna and Tungabhadra at this period from the accounts of the Portuguese traveller Paes (c. 1520) who gives a vivid picture of the sorts of craft employed in the ferrying when the river was too deep to ford (quoted in Sarkar 1925, p. 18). As the craft is to this day in use we may have no hesitation in accepting the evidence, and indeed we may do much more. The craft are in actuality like the coracles of Ireland, Wales and North Europe generally. They are known by the name 'baskets' as their central feature is a hemispherical cane basket of large size over which a waterproof cover of skins is stretched and sewn. The size of the basket varies with the load it is to carry. The smaller sized vessel is barely 4 ft. in diameter and flattened at the base. The bottom is reinforced and the skin is sewn around the rim. In the larger examples which we have seen the size is up to 10 ft. in diameter and the basket is considerably deeper. In the smaller craft a single paddle is used but in the largest two men row each with a paddle. We have also seen large vessels of the same shape made of sheets of thin wrought iron, rivetted together. A basket of about 7 ft. in diameter will carry up to twenty passengers. There is no reason why the baskets with their skin coverings need not go back, unaltered into the remote past, to Neolithic times if not to Late Stone Age times, for they compare with the craft of primitive peoples in other parts of the world. The only monument of the Middle Ages which need concern us is a temple, of probably the 16th century, constructed at Gudabelur behind the stone alignments and near to the ancient settlement. This situation provides a suggestive emphasis upon the continuity of cult spots, even when the actual village had moved away.

The end of our story is soon told. In the 19th century the importance of the road increased and a causeway was eventually constructed, probably linked with an Irish bridge. The point of departure of this causeway was visible in 1957 when we visited the crossing, but the river was in flood and we could not find out how much survives. On the south bank by the road a handsome rest house was built. We did not specially notice its age but it probably belonged to the first half of the 19th century. When we visited it , it was already in an advanced state of decay: much of the roof had gone and the shutters flapped in the breeze. In 1871 the Great Indian Peninsular Railway extension from Sholapur to Raichur was carried acoss by a fine metal bridge. The railway passes about one mile west of the road, between it and the Bhima *sangam*, and thus is another example of the way in which Indian railways have followed the lines of ancient routes. Likewise the Nizam's State Railway extension from Hyderabad to Karnul crosses at Gadwal on the eastern line of communication. Finally just before the outbreak of World War II the beautiful concrete road bridge was constructed by the Nizam's government a few furlongs east of the old causeway.

From the Krishna bridge one can see the railway bridge and the old rest house by the causeway. Looking north one can make out the hillocks at Gudabelur behind which lies the Medieval temple and the stone alignment; one can see too the Hindupur alignment and the approximate position of the Neolithic axe site. Looking southwards one can see the little hillock below which are the cairn-circle graves and beyond which is the other alignment. The hillock marks the spot where in Late Stone Age and Middle Stone Age times men came to make their tools. Thus at this apparently unexciting spot there is evidence of human activity throughout the ages in all its variety.

NOTES

[1] This site which we named Krishna Bridge was discovered by us in 1951 while we were doing field work in Raichur District. An account of our dis-

coveries at that time were included in F. R. Allchin (1954, pp. 216-19). In 1957 we revisited the site and made further discoveries and collections.

[2] The Middle Stone Age assemblage has been described in detail in B. Allchin (1959, pp. 21-7).

[3] An account of the collection of 1951 was included in B. Allchin (1956, pp. 190-1), and a fuller study will appear in her forthcoming book on the Late Stone Age of the tropical regions of the Old World.

[4] This estimate is based upon our explorations in 1952 at sites noticed by Munn (1936) and others discovered by us at that time and reported in F.R. Allchin (1954).

[5] The Gadwal sites were described in F. R. Allchin (1954). The alignments were specifically referred to in F. R. Allchin (1956, pp. 135-6).

[6] This question was discussed in a paper read by F. R. Allchin at the International Orientalists Congress at Cambridge in 1954, but only a short abstract has been published. See F. R. Allchin (1957, pp. 226-7).

[7] Based upon Sewell (1900, pp. 136-60, particularly 151). We have not entered into discussion of the various details of the narrative challenged by Father Heras, Dr. Ramchandraiya in his *Studies of Krsnadevaraya*, and others, as they do not seriously affect our story. The fortified area we have mentioned is clearly of great interest as it is unlike anything else known in the Raichur Doāb. Its age must remain uncertain until it is explored, but a possibility exists that it is far older than the sixteenth century.

REFERENCES

ALLCHIN, Bridget, 1956, *The Blade and Geometric Industries of Australia, Southern Africa and India*. Ph.D. Thesis, London University.

1959, 'The Indian Middle Stone Age', *Bull. of Inst. of Arch.*, 2.

ALLCHIN, F. Raymond, 1954, *The Development of early Cultures in the Raichur District of Hyderabad*. Ph.D. Thesis, London University.

1956, 'The stone alignments of Southern Hyderabad', *Man*, No. 150.

1957, *Proceed. of 23rd Cong. of Orientalists*, abstracts of papers presented.

MUNN, 1934, *J. Hyderabad Geological Survey*, Vol. II, Pt. 1.

1936, *ibid.*, Vol. III, Pt. 1.

1941, *ibid.*, Vol. IV, Pt. 1.

SARKAR, B. K., 1925, *Inland Transport and Communication in Medieval India*.

SEWELL, 1900, *Forgotten Empire*.

3

FROM FOOD COLLECTION TO URBANISATION IN INDIA

H. D. SANKALIA

I. Introduction

ARCHAEOLOGY, in its origin and development, has been by and large a search for and study of old objects or antiquities. Until very recently it thought little of trying to understand the various stages by which man had developed or progressed to the highly advanced material (and spiritual) culture of the present day—what Braidwood[1] calls an "idea archaeology" aimed at broad culture-historical problems, or as Margaret Murray[2] puts it "an understanding of the human being in all his aspects, physical, mental and spiritual as manifested in the past." While the physical and cultural anthropologist concerned themselves with the study of the origin of man and the primitive tribes respectively, the full study of man—his physical, mental and material development— remained neglected.

This all-sided or comprehensive study cannot be made by archaeologists or anthropologists alone. It needs the co-operation of collateral sciences like physics, chemistry, botany, geology, zoology and several branches of medicine, such as dentistry, surgery and urology.[3] It is thus only that some idea can be had of the past climatic conditions, the flora and fauna of the region and man's utilisation of it. Environmental archaeology has thus become a prime need.

As usual, we in India have still to orient our archaeological efforts towards such an ideal. In the absence of such an attempt and the resultant evidence,

"the tracing of man's history from latest Pleistocene times upto the threshold of the urban civilisations, the archaeological evidence which reveal the varying degrees of intensification of food-collecting, the transitions from food-collecting to partial or to fully effective food-production and the eventual emergence of city life and civilisation, the cultural consequences and accompaniments of these transitions; environmental adaptations under differing conditions; shifts in adaptations either before or following the appearance of food production; the relative roles of environmental factors and migration and/or diffusion in the conversion of hunter-collector cultures to those of food production; the qualities and quantities of cultural intensifications immediately antecedent to the appearance of urban civilisations, analysing the evidences for such things as settlement patterns, population sizes and groupings, long range trade, incipient 'priesthoods', 'kingships' and the institution of warfare" is indeed impossible. So when a prehistoric archaeologist in India is called upon to contribute to the understanding of why urban civilisations came about when and where they did, he finds himself thoroughly ill-prepared to do so.

But this had to be done when the writer was invited to participate in a symposium[4] on "From 15,000 B.C. to the thresholds of urban civilisation—A world-wide consideration of the cultural alternatives". While presenting the essay—which has been fully revised and brought uptodate—it was realised that the evidence was inadequate in several respects.

Of course, traditionally it is believed that the centres of early civilisations in India were the Gangetic Valley, Sind, Sauvira, Saurashtra and Vidarbha, south of the Narmada. It is in these regions only, covering most of northern India and northern Deccan, that cities like Rajagriha, Pataliputra, Kosambi, Hastinapur, Ujjain, Kushasthali and Kundinapura existed. Ancient literature describes also very briefly how these centres developed. But we have had no idea of the actual stage of their development: were they really urban centres or merely peasant villages, though called *puras* and *nagaras*?

Having accepted to write, the most important question was the method or approach to the subject. Should it be based on a broad division of India as Eastern India (EI), Western India (WI) etc. or river-valley-wise as the Indus or Ganges basin or physio-culturally as done by Spate[5] and after him Subbarao.[6] Further, should we start with the assumption that the beginnings of civilisation took place in certain regions earlier than in others (in India as well as elsewhere). Both these questions are inter-related and have a direct bearing on our subject. Hence some detailed discussion is necessary before the discussion of the main topic is taken up.

Let us first define the areas or regions.[7]

Physio-cultural Regions of India

1. The Indus basin which drains central Himalayas is framed by the Aravallis and the desert of Rajputana in the east and the Sulaiman and Kirthar ranges on the north-west and west respectively. It is further divided by the junction of the hills from the west and the desert in the east into Lower Indus (Sind) and the Upper Indus (Punjab) basins.

2. The Ganges basin is likewise divisible into (a) Indo-Gangetic Divide or the Upper Ganges Plain, (b) the Middle Ganges Plain and the Deltaic region. These respectively constitute the Delhi, S. Punjab, U.P., Bihar and Bengal.

3. Further eastwards the Brahmaputra Valley forms Assam. But geomorphologically Assam consists of three entirely different regions belonging to three structural formations, the Himalayan frontier; the main Assam or Brahmaputra Valley which is an extension of the Indo-Gangetic trough and the Shillong Plateau which essentially belongs to the older Peninsula.

4. Bounded by the Aravallis in the west, the athwart lying Vindhyas in the south and the Ganga-Yamuna doab in the east-north-east is the Malwa Plateau and Bundelkhand. Its southern portion is built up by the Deccan Lavas; but the north has a varied composition. On the west and north it is drained by the Banas, Chambal, Sipra and their tributaries; in the south by the Narmada, in the east by the Son and south-east the upper courses of the Ken and the Betwa.

5. South of the Vindhyas is Maharashtra, its limits almost coextensive with the Deccan Lavas. It includes three or four former cultural units, viz. Khandesh, Vidarbha and Konkan. The most important drainages are the Tapi-Purna, Wardha-Vainganga and the upper Krishna-Godavari, whereas the Konkan which is a narrow strip of coastal plain is drained by numerous fast-flowing streams.

6. Andhra is mostly constituted by the middle and lower basins of the Krishna and Godavari, which flow through some of the oldest rock formations in India.

7. Karnatak or Mysore Plateau. This is a sort of triangle formed

by the Eastern and Western Ghats. Through the upper flow the Krishna and its tributaries; the Tungabhadra, Hageri, upper Pennar and Kaveri constitute the main drainage of the lower.

8. Kerala. Likewise, the still narrower coastal plain on either side of the Palghat gap in the Western Ghat is Malabar or Kerala. It is drained principally by the Periyar and the Pampa.

9. Tamilnad. This is believed to be a simple coastal belt, but as Spate has shown, it is not as simple as that. It is a great quadrant, lying between the sea and the Deccan plateau. The coastal plain proper extends from the Krishna to the Cape.But this is broken by the Kaveri delta. Inland are the discontinuous Tamilnad hills. In fact, the whole region is capable of six sub-divisions, though here it is treated as one. Its major rivers are the Pennar, Palar, Ponnaiyar, Kaveri and the Vaigai.

10. Orissa. Orissa, ancient Utkal, is also regarded as an emergent low-land, but like the Tamilnad consists of the deltas of the Mahanadi, Brahmani and Vaitarni, a zone of older alluvium, and laterite plateaus and hills on the west.

11. Gujarat. Gujarat consists of three distinct units—Kuccha, Saurashtra and Gujarat. While the first is mostly marshy and sandy, but having a rocky core, the great mass of Saurashtra is formed by the Deccan Lavas, the rest by earlier sandstone rocks, while the coast is made by the recent alluvium.

The major rivers of Saurashtra are the Bhadar and the Shetrunji. The basin of the former is considered the richest agricultural area, the other favoured regions being the Gohilwad low-land along the Nal depression and Sorath, a portion of south-west Saurashtra.

Gujarat proper has three zones: the purely coastal belt of southern and central Gujarat, then the large tract formed by the eolian sand and alluvium (old and new) formed by the Sabarmati, Mahi and other smaller, parallel flowing streams and the eastern most hilly and jungle country which forms, as it were, a bridge between Malwa, Gujarat and Rajputana.

12. Rajputana is made up of two natural divisions: Mewar and Marwar. The country to the west of the Aravallis is mostly sandy and covered by scrubby, stunted accacias, while the eastern part is more hilly, much less sandy and fertile. The latter as well as the eastern part of Bikaner drained by the ancient Sarasvati and Drishadvati is built up by the Gangetic-like alluvium. The Banas is the major river of Mewar. It later joins the Chambal which falls into

the Gangetic basin. The Luni is the only river of some consequence in Marwar.

13. The above mentioned areas are interspersed or intersected by three or four hilly and forest regions viz. (i) the great Central Indian belt where several rock formations, the Satpuras, Vindhyas, Maikal, Chota Nagpur and Orissan meet; primaeval forests still flourish in parts of Malwa, Khandesh, Central Provinces (M.P.), Chattisgarh, Chota Nagpur, Andhra and Orissa. This almost forms a solid continuous block in the heart of India. Here reside the Bhils, Dangs, Gonds, Santhals, Uraons, Gadabas, Marias, Savaras and many others. (ii) Likewise the Aravallis still harbour the Bhils, (iii) while along the Western Ghats we have the Warlis, Thakurs, Dhanagars and further south in the Nilgiris Todas, Kurumbars and others. (iv) The discontinuous Eastern Ghats in the present Andhra State are the home of the Baigas, Chenchus, Reddis, Savaras and others.

Among the physio-cultural regions, Subbarao regards (1) the Punjab, the Indo-Gangetic Divide, Gangetic Basin, Bengal, Malwa, Maharashtra, Karnatak, Tamilnad as "Areas of Attraction or Nuclear Regions"; (2) Sind, Marwar, Gujarat, Saurashtra, Konkan, Kerala, Assam, as "Areas of Relative Isolation" and (3) the Aravallis, the Central Indian highlands and forests, as well as similar areas in Andhra as "Areas of Isolation or *cul de sac*".

While there is no difficulty in fully accepting[8] the last category or group, there is considerable difference of opinion about the first two groups. For Spate includes among the nuclear regions Gujarat and Saurashtra, and Kerala or Malabar, among others in the south.

The main grounds of difference between Spate and Subbarao are that whereas to the former the nuclear regions represent the major agricultural areas which have been "perennially significant in Indian historical geography", to the latter, following Richards,[9] besides the agricultural potential, relation of the region to the main continental highways is also a major consideration. Since, from Subbarao's point of view, Sind, Saurashtra, Gujarat and even Kerala are situated away from the highways, these are areas of semi-isolation.

This may be. However, these areas are not truly isolated or even semi-isolated. The Indus Valley (besides being more fertile) and the entire west coast are open to direct contact with Western Asia and beyond with the Mediterranean countries. Hence throughout (even during the Early Stone Ages according to Wheeler) the protohistoric and historic times, developments in Western Asia have sooner or later reached India. And in fact, as will be seen in the sequel, Sind, Saurashtra, Gujarat and even Rajputana show the earliest traces of civilisation, including urbanisation.

We are thus up against the exact role of geography and environmental factors in the development of civilisation. Without going into much details, it is necessary to point out that even in the west, where formerly the "Fertile Crescent" was regarded as the cradle of civilisation, now the hilly flanks characterised by the foothills and intermontane valleys at an elevation of 1250 to 3000 ft. above sea level in Iraqi Kurdistan are regarded as such. Here it appears that transition took place from the earlier food gathering pattern of life to that of food production. For here more than anywhere else "the wild wheats and barley, the wild sheep, goats, pigs, cattle and horses were to be found in a single natural environment."

However, after this was written, investigations are being continued in Iran. And it was found[10] that such a zone of grassy and open oakland ran from Shiraz in Iran through highland Iraq and southern flanks of Turkey—a distance of some 1,200 miles. Hence Braidwood concluded, "It continues to appear that the more important generative factors in the appearance of effective plant and animal domestication are not to be sought in the facile explanation of environmental determinism."

He further said that Jarmo or any other site examined by them was not in any way a unique instance in time and place wherein food production began. These were sites which happened to be those which the accident of archaeological discovery had brought forth.

These revised views of an author who believed only a few years ago in a particular site in a particular area as the birth place of civilisation are quite relevant to the problem we are discussing.[11]

India appears to be on the periphery of the culture spread in relation to Western Asia. Within India itself we may note the present distribution of forests and the gradual removal of forest cover from Sind, the Punjab, Saurashtra, Malwa and U.P. It is even attested by literary evidence, for instance the burning of Khāndavavana, the home of Nagas, for building the new capital of the Pandavas—Indraprastha—is vividly described in the *Mahabhārata*. The concentration of primitive tribes in certain inaccessible forests and hills, and above all the increasing archaeological evidence including that of

ancient plant remains, such as wheat, lentil and linseed. Though all
this points to the spread of civilisation from west to east, *still it
cannot be over-emphasised that our knowledge is relative, based on insufficient evidence* (*in some cases no evidence at all*) and the fact that
there is no unanimously accepted opinion among the archaeologists
themselves whether the various Chalcolithic cultures which appear
in the wake of the destruction or disappearance or gradual transformation of the Indus civilisation are purely indigenous or introduced, (again) by movements and ideas from Western Asia.

Thus the question of the exact origin of the food production and
the subsequent steps which first led to the urbanisation in the
Indus Valley might be kept open.[12] For even Braidwood, who
has "no reason to suspect from the evidence available that traces
of the transition (from food gathering to food production)should be
sought outside Western Asia" is prepared to see independent
beginnings in food production based on other plants and sometimes
animals, in other parts of the world". Whether these should be
necessarily "later experiments than the Near Eastern instance"
only fuller research elsewhere would prove (or disprove).[13]

Under these circumstances the archaeological data are suc-
cinctly reviewed, without going much into the ecological background. The resultant inferences are therefore minimum.

II

Review of Archaeological Evidence
Primitive to Advanced Food Collecting Stages:
Flake Industries

A regional review is therefore desirable. Almost all parts or
divisions of India have now yielded Lower Paleolithic industries.
They are of two types (1) Soanian and (2) Handaxe-Cleaver type.
The former is primarily confined to the Punjab, though tools
resembling some of its types—e.g. Choppers and Chopping-tools
—do occur in the latter.

The handaxe or the biface industry has an all-India distribution,
though, owing to perhaps inadequate explorations, it has not
been reported so far from Sind, Saurashtra and Western Rajputana
in Western India, Assam in Eastern India and extreme south.[14]
Everywhere it can be placed typologically and/or stratigraphic-

ally in the Middle Pleistocene Period. In the Punjab this is related to the Second inter-Glacial period while in the rest of India, it may be placed in the first pluvial or a period of heavy rain. So far, however, nowhere its earlier antecedents are clearly visible. It may have been introduced from Africa,[15] where a well-marked development is available.

Until recently, the next cultural stage was not clearly discernible, except in the Punjab, and to some extent in Kurnool in South India. Work during the last six years has shown that the Handaxe Culture was followed by a culture in which scrapers, points, blade-like flakes, some of definite Levallois type, but others of non-descript nature, occur.

This culture has a wide distribution, almost co-extensive with the Handaxe Culture.

Since stratigraphically it succeeds the former—particularly at Nevasa etc., in Western India and Maheshwar etc., in Central India—and assignable in both to Terrace II it has been called "Middle Palaeolithic", or "Middle Stone Age" or after the type site "Nevasa", *Nevasian*. A Middle Pleistocene fauna like *Bos namadicus Falconer* has been associated with it at Kalegaon etc., on the Godavari in Western India, but since the culture is typologically so dissimilar from the handaxe culture and also uses a completely different raw material in Western, Central and Eastern India, it is advisable to place it in the Late Pleistocene. Moreover, it seems to bear a genetic relationship with the later blade cultures, though so far no undisputable stratigraphical evidence is available anywhere. For all these reasons, this culture has been discussed in some detail here, (though if it is indeed Late Middle Pleistocene, it would fall outside the scope of this subject.)

Observations by the writer in Western India, Central India, and Karnatak and Kurnool in South India and reports from Orissa, U.P., Central India and Rajputana definitely indicate that stratigraphically this culture succeeds the Lower Palaeolithic or the Handaxe Culture.

The raw material, except in Kurnool and Karnatak to some extent, is fine-grained stone-like jasper and agate or flint in Southern Rajputana.[16]

The tools indicate a peculiar combination of "free", "controlled", "soft hammer" and "pressure" techniques as well as the (occasional) preparation of the core as in the Levallois techneque. But by and large the makers preferred to use any flat or flattish flake or a suitable nodule and turned them into "Side" or "Hollow scraper" and a "Point". A recurrent type is a "Point-cum-Hollow Scraper". The retouch, sometimes very fine, but often nothing but nibbling is generally on one side, the upper or the under, but at times on both. Carefully finished specimens are a thing of beauty—perfectly symmetrical with retouches, and exhibiting an innate sense of the selection of the material. Points, for instance, are of a multi-coloured stone (jasper, Kalegaon, D.C., Poona).

Some of the points also indicate an incipient tang, and the use of hafting. Recently this feature was noticed in small hand-axes and cleavers of a Late Lower Paleolithic character from Gangapur, near Nasik, Western India.

There is also a blade element in this culture, the flakes being thin, and narrow, and at times quite long, as for example from the Tapi basin in Khandesh, and from Central India. These are also at times retouched, thus resembling the classical Upper Palaeolithic blades of Western Europe though prepared by a different technique.

Thus this new culture called here "Middle Paleolithic" or the "Nevasian" has some elements which recall those of Europe and Africa. Two of its most characteristic tool types—scrapers and points—definitely indicate a change in the hunting method of the people who made them. Bows and arrows, and spokeshaves had come into use, in addition to the earlier methods of snaring and capturing the prey. These included *Bos namadicus Falconer*, and probably the *Elephas anticuus*, *Equus*, Rhinoceros and the Hippopotamus, besides deer etc. (A fuller list will be available when Mr. C. Tripathi of the Geological Survey of India and Dr. Khatri working on behalf of the C.S.I.R. submit their reports).

The climate was decidedly wetter than when the silt of the first conglomerate phase was deposited owing to increasing dryness, but not so wet as to enable the streams to transport large and heavier material. Consequently the gravels everywhere are smaller in size, and often markedly contain different material. For instance, in the Deccan there are medium-sized chunks and occasional pebbles of agate, chalcedony, carnelian and jasper, and sometimes olive-green pebbles of basalt or olivine doletrite. This feature also indicates that the rivers could break the thin veins of the fine-grained rocks which appear in the trap hills.

Another notable feature is that the gravels almost everywhere covered the old conglomerate, but did not reach upto the silt, and thus form a kind of ledge or low terrace against the older formation. This is clearly visible at Maheshwar on the Narmada in Central India and Nandur Madhmeshwar on the Godavari in Western India. Probably it is for this reason that these gravels are found eroded at a large number of places, wherever these have been examined in India. However, some of the best exposures of this gravel are seen on the Godavari.

Briefly then the Middle Palaeolithic Culture characterized by scrapers and points and incipient blades may be assigned to the Late Pleistocene, when the climate was comparatively less wet than in the Middle Pleistocene when the Handaxe Culture flourished. The fauna and probably the flora (of which we have no remains) remained the same.

Of course, a wooded landscape might be inferred from the nature of the tools, and from the *present* ecology of the regions in which the tools occur. For all these lie within the tropical or semi-tropical belt in India, which do not seem to have undergone much vital climatic changes, though for a proper environmental appreciation we must have geological and other data. Pollen analysis is unlikely to be helpful, for the sandy calcareous alluvium does not preserve any trace of it.

Probably contemporary and perhaps related to this are the Late Soan Industries of the Punjab. The earlier, Late Soan A, belongs to the Third Glacial period, when T2, was being formed. It is placed in the Upper Pleistocene and contains a good deal of Levallois element along with the earlier Choppers (which are now smaller and neater) and a small percentage of blades. This last feature definitely indicates a change in the life of the people, and occupies a prominent place in Late Soan B industries. Thus for our purpose this phase in the Punjab is important. It is associated with the basal portion of the Potwar loessic silt on T2 and placed tentatively in late Third Interglacial.

Thus both the tools and the climatic conditions—a dry phase as in the rest of India—suggest different environment for men and his activities.

While thus recent work in India has been able to fill up the gap between the Middle Pleistocene and the earliest Holocene, there is no clear, undisputed stratigraphical evidence for a culture or

cultures as in Europe, Palestine and Africa (?) which can be assigned
to the latest Pleistocene times (unless of course future research
brings down the date of the culture just discussed above, or the
cultures which are about to be mentioned are relegated to this
phase of the Pleistocene from the Holocene).

III   Transition from Food Collection to (Incipient) Food Production: Microlithic Industries

As in Europe, Africa and several parts of Asia, towards the end
of the Palaeolithic period, great climatic changes had taken place
in India as well. These must have had bearing upon the environment of man and his mode of living.

Though there was widespread archaeological evidence for this
in the shape of microliths, it was not supported by stratigraphical,
geo-chronological and palaeo-biological data. Hence the microliths had little cultural significance. This deficiency is being slowly
filled up, though not so quickly and in such a planned manner as
one would wish.

Within the last 20 years, three or four other regions, besides the
classic sites of Cammiade in Kurnool District, have yielded microliths in a geological context. We may say that the whole of India
is thus represented. Todd's Khandivli microliths come from the
Western coast near Bombay, and that from Karachi in Sind may
be regarded as its continuation.

The evidence from Langhnaj is fully representative of the whole
of Northern and Central Gujarat which lies a little away from the
western coast.

In Eastern India the evidence is provided by Birbhanpur, Chakra-
dharpur and Mirzapur, while in South India we have evidence
from the Teri sites and from suface microliths of Mysore.

Of these, the oldest microlithic industry seems to be that from
the Teri in the Tinnevelly district in South India. The sites are
mostly along the eastern coast of the tip of the Peninsula and
though exposed, they are believed to be "derived from a soil profile,
now in the process of denudation and forming part of a series of
aeolian sands". The sites seem to be associated with a sea level
somewhat higher than at present.

On the basis of the available collection a sequence of three industries is postulated.

i. An earlier Teri industry consisting of flakes and core tools.
ii. A later—the main Teri industry, similar to the former, but including blades and geometric forms.
iii. A Neolithic blade industry, often accompanied by stone axes.

In fact nothing much is known about the last, and so it be better left out of consideration.

The first two are generally made on quartz and chert (though why these should be preferred when finer silicate material is locally available, is a mystery) and are heavily stained with red-hydrated ferric oxide. The tools comprise a large number of indeterminate flakes, blades, burins, geometric forms like the lunates, trapezes and triangles, scrapers and discoids, and small chopping tools, and points of various types, including a few pressure flaked bifacial ones.

These tools must have been made by hunting and/or fishing people living in temporary camps on or near the coast. The geological context and the presence of certain tool-types might make the industry Upper Palaeolithic and might be placed towards the close of the Late Pleistocene, but provisionally it has been given a date of 4,000 B.C. which is certainly very conservative.

The second, and perhaps equally ancient is the Birbhanpur microlithic industry. Because of the non-occurrence of the trapeze and the triangle it is regarded as non-geometric and includes—

i. Irregular, free flaked cores
ii. Fluted cores
iii. Blades
iv. Lunates
v. Points
vi. Borers
vii. Scrapers
viii. Burins

The material is mostly milky quartz, though occasionally crystal, chert, chalcedony, quartzite and fossil wood are used. Dr. Lal's geochronologic studies[17] indicate that the climate when the microlithic people occupied the site must have been comparatively dry and mild, after the last wet phase during which the laterite weathered, and dense forest existed in the region. This mild climatic phase was followed by a period of increasing aridity, and violent wind activity, so that the habitation layers were covered with wind-blown sand.

The evidence from Mysore is mostly surface. The only important site is at Jalahalli, near Bangalore. Here, Todd found in a reddish soil horizon, beneath the black soil, microliths of quartz, rock crystal and one of red jasper. Dr. Seshadri goups the collection on typological basis into:

i. Jalahalli microlithic industry with a preponderance of crescents, points and arrowheads, indicating a hunting economy and environment.

ii. Brahmagiri microlithic industry consisting primarily of parallel-sided flakes, and Gravettian-like pen-knife blades, implying a semi-urban culture in which arrowhead, crescent etc. are absent.

There is also a third group, formed by Kibbanahalli in which there are three or four types of scrapers, blades, and highly finished lunates.

Subsequent work elsewhere in India has shown that Brahmagiri microlithic industry indeed forms a part of the vast Chalcolithic culture-complex, which was mostly of a peasant village type, but had attained an urban stage in Sind, the Punjab and Saurashtra. Further, while this peasant stage can be approximately dated to 1,000 B.C., the purely geometric industry cannot be brought to that date. Probably it is early, and truly Mesolithic.

The Mirzapur (Singrauli basin) microliths occur about four feet below the Upper Alluvium along the southern bank of Bālia Nadi near Kotā. It is predominantly of limpid quartz which is easily available in the vicinity. "It is non-geometric denoted by parallel-sided blades, lunates and points. Only a few tools are either finished or retouched." It may be a degenerate, late Upper Palaeolithic blade industry, ascribable to an early Mesolithic period, when a gradual dryness came over the area after the end of the Palaeolithic period.

This brings us to Langhnaj. It is not a solitary site, an oasis, but one of the hundreds (Subbarao lists over 80) in the sandy undulating alluvial plain of Northern and Central Gujarat. The topography is

certainly different from what one sees in Kurnool, in the heart of
the old land mass. Here are miles and miles of flat sandy stretches,
where suddenly one finds two or three small hillocks, of the same
material, enclose an inundation lake, which keeps water for almost
ten months in a year. The tops and slopes of these small hillocks
are strewn with microliths. These, as well as the river banks, were
the resorts of the microlithic people. A series of small excavations
and examination of the soil by Professor Zeuner suggest that the
dunes were formed when at the end of the dry phase (U) a slightly
damper phase had followed, which in its turn was succeeded by a
drier phase. It was at this phase—sometime in the Late Pleistocene
—that "more or less isolated dunes were blown over the land
surface." A soil developed on these dunes.

The climate was slightly wetter so that large inundation lakes
were formed between the hollows of the dunes. A nomadic, hunting
people lived on these mounds and along the river banks. The
industry consisting of blades, lunates, trapezes, triangles, scrapers,
points and a few burins and fluted as well as amorphous cores—
may be described as geometric, but is on the whole coarse and
crude, though the material is chert, agate, carnelian and only occasionally quartz. Heavy tools so far are very few—only one
mace-head or weight of digging stick of quartzite was excavated.
With these, the men hunted rhinoceros (*Rhinoceros unicornis L*),
hog deer (*Hyelaphus porcimus Zimm*), Indian buffalo, antelope
(*Boselaphus tragocamelus Pall*), black buck (*Antelope Cervicapra Linn*)
and dog. All these, including the dog and the buffalo, according to
Professor Zeuner's study, seem to be wild. The fauna is thus of
games, and the people, primarily, hunters and fishers (as besides
animal bones remains of fish vertebra and tortoise shell have been
found).

Along with microliths and a large number of bones and a negligible quantity of pottery about 12 human skeletons have so far been
found. These are of a fairly tall, thin, dolicocephalic people with a
slight prognathism. Their cranial capacity compares well with that
of the modern Europoid, whereas other skull features suggest
Negroid affinities.[18]

Since a majority of microliths, animal remains and human
skeletons were found below four feet from the surface, which
represents a buried soil phase, the Langhnaj Culture is likely to be
considerably old, and may, by further tests and work, turn

FROM FOOD GATHERING STAGE TO THE THRESHOLD OF PASTORAL STAGE

	N.W.INDIA & KASHMIR	RAJASTHAN	CENTRAL INDIA	WESTERN INDIA	SOUTHERN INDIA	EASTERN INDIA
HOLOCENE	ROHRI-SUKKUR	DHANERI (W.R.) BICHRI (E.R) DABOK (E.R)	PANCHMARI MAHADEO HILLS ADAMGARH	RANGPUR-A WAI PANCHGANI LANGHNAJ-B KANDIVLI LANGHNAJ-A	MYSORE BELLARY NELLORE GIDDALUR KURNOOL TERI NANDI KANAMA	SINGHBHUM ORISSA SINGRAULI BIRBHANPUR
LATE PLEISTO-CENE	LATE SOAN-B LATE SOAN-A	(LUNI) NEVASIAN-A	NEVASIAN-B [SR.III] (SIVNA, BETWA, DHASAN) NEVASIAN-A	NEVASIAN-B [SR.III] (PRWARA-GODAVARI) NEVASIAN-A	NEVASIAN-B [SR.III] (GHATAPRABHA) NEVASIAN-A	NEVASIAN-B [SR.III] (KHADKI & TRIBUTARIES) NEVASIAN-A
MIDDLE PLEISTO-CENE	EARLY SOAN	HAND-AXE CLEAVER	HAND-AXE CLEAVER	HAND-AXE CLEAVER	HAND-AXE CLEAVER	HAND-AXE CLEAVER

out to be towards the closing phase of the Pleistocene.

Cammiade's Kurnool sites do not stand isolated now. Extensive explorations by Dr. Isaac of the Deccan College have brought to light numerous sites, some even extending into the limestone cave region of the district. This field will be further enlarged when the adjacent regions are similarly explored thus bringing in our purview those districts of Andhra, Madras and Mysore states which have similar geo-morphological features, implying similar or identical climatic conditions in the past.

The Kurnool microliths may fall into two series:—Non-Geometric and Geometric, though as yet a rigid stratigraphical correlation eludes us. The industry comprises parallel-sided blades, lunates, triangles, trapezes, scrapers, backed blades and burins.

Khandivali microlithic industry was supposed to mark the end of a rich cultural sequence beginning with the Early Palaeolithic. But the very recent study of the area by the writer, which was also visited by Professor Zeuner, shows that probably we have two main cultures only; the first belonging to the earlier deposition of the gravel by the hill streams, which formed a high terrace; the second to the lower terrace formed by the re-deposit of the eroded earlier gravel. The earliest culture is of the Nevasian type with a small percentage of the handaxes (if Todd's collection is included). This was followed by the blade and burin culture, and was later succeeded by the microlithic.

However, the sites like Marve, along the coast and the Thana creek and along the banks of the rivers like the Ulhas in the north and the Amba in the south of Bombay definitely suggest that the people inhabited these areas, on slightly higher elevated grounds— usually rocks or hillocks and avoided the thicker jungle in the interior. It is likely that they preferred the region because it grows abundance of bananas and coconuts and abounds in fish and fowl. Hitherto no remains of their temporary camps have been discovered, except microliths. These also contain a few heavier tools like the mace-head or digging weight, chopper, besides a purely geometric microlithic industry. It may, therefore, be divided into an earlier and a later series. The former may be derived from the blade and burin industry, dependent primarily on hunting, while the latter along with geometric forms and heavier tools like the "mace-head" may point towards a food producing stage.

Todd lists the following groups of tools. Microliths (obliquely and wholly blunted, lunates, triangles, trapezes, trapezoids, drills), five types of cores and scrapers, maceheads and axes.

This review shows that in a few areas in India the microliths claim a fairly good antiquity. This in Tinnevelley or at Birbhanpur might mean the latest Pleistocene times or the beginning of Holocene. The exact age in years is difficult to guess, but may be placed between 10,000—4,000 B.C.

In all the regions, an environmental change was definitely there, though differing in intensity and nature from region to region. But on the whole a climate drier than in the preceeding phase may be generally postulated. Except in Northern and Central Gujarat no idea can be had of the contemporary fauna or flora[19] (though even in Gujarat, the evidence for the flora is almost nil). In Gujarat, the man was practically a hunter, and almost all the animals on whom he subsisted were wild (or of hunting type) except perhaps the dog. It is argued from the presence of small flat querns (found so far in numerous fragments which cannot be put together and hence no idea can be had of its size) that man probably pounded (wild) grains and might thus be placed in the higher rung of the ladder between a food collecting and food producing stage. This view does not seem to be justified. Firstly the querns seem to have been too small to pound anything on them; these are more like stones used today for preparing sandalwood and other pastes. Secondly, the writer, so far, has not come across a single grain in any one of the numerous excavations on the site or elsewhere in the region. The pottery evidence is also negligible. Not more than 10 to 20 sherds, not one indicating the probable shape of the vessel, have so far been recovered. Thus the Langhnaj Culture has got to be regarded as a Food Collecting one, whatever be its exact antiquity.

With regard to the microliths—whether they contain geometric element or not—they might have evolved from the earlier "blade and burin" industry. But nowhere such an evolution is available stratigraphically. The Kurnool evidence is not from one stratified site, but a typological grouping of the collection from a number of sites.

So we may end this section with the observation that the microlithic industries are associated with an environmental change; that they do indicate a change in the mode of life of man in India; but it is not exactly clear whether the microliths developed out of the earlier "blade and burin" industries or due to the influence of some external stimuli.

IV *From the Semi-Nomadic and Pastoral Stage to Urbanisation Through a Peasant-Village Stage*

Just as we do not get well-documented data for the evolution of man, his environment and cultural equipment in the early period, from one single site in India, so also for his further march towards civilisation, the evidence is scattered and hence inadequate for understanding the steps by which this was achieved.

On the one hand, we find several cultures in the foothills of Baluchistan which from the existence of painted pottery—some of which is definitely wheel-made—is an index of a food producing stage, though among their other equipment are microliths and occasionally figurines of animals, "mother goddess", and rarely burials. However, none of this is fully or even partially excavated, so that we may have a clear image of the size of settlement, or even one of its houses. Fortunately some sites are now dated by Carbon-14, while their pottery definitely indicates Iranian influence. So we know the age of a few of these cultures and how they might have come about.

Immediately east of these peasant cultures, in the fertile valleys of the Indus and others in Sind and the Punjab, we meet suddenly face to face with a mature urban civilisation. Its antecedents are hitherto not known, though Wheeler's work at Harappa and Khan's at Kot Diji show that there were earlier stages. The civilisation had a much wider extension than originally realised; its offshoots are being found as far south as the coast of Gujarat in Western India and as far east as Delhi, and in the west beyond the borders of Sind proper.

But this was not the only culture in Western and Northern India. In the Punjab, as well as in Rajputana, Saurashtra, Central India, in the Deccan and Andhra and Mysore and probably in the Uttar Pradesh in the Gangetic valley, traces of peasant or early agricultural communities are being found every year, since 1947. The antecedents of these also remain unknown, as well as their relationship with the Harappan. It is probable that most of the Central India, Saurashtra and the Upper Deccan, painted pottery cultures are later than the original, mature, Harappa civilisation in the Punjab and Sind and that they were perhaps responsible for its destruction. But the same is not true of the purely Polished Axe Cultures of South-Eastern India. These were in a Neolithic stage, practising primitive agriculture and rearing animals, and dependant partly on hunting and fishing. Carbon-14 dates of two of these—Piklihal and Utnoor in Andhra State—give a date of 2,100 B.C. (4120 ± 150). They were definitely contemporary with —though far removed from—the Indus civilisation.

Thus four different cultures intervene between the Mesolithic cultures of the Latest Pleistocene or Early Holocene and the advent of iron and the second phase of urbanisation in about 500 B.C. With this brief introduction, we shall review in detail the size of the settlement, food economy and industry and affinities of some of the more important and well-documented sites of each of the four cultures mentioned above.

Early Food-Producing Cultures of Baluchistan or Indo-Pakistan Border

This account is mainly based on the recent work of Fairservis. Prior to it we had only studies of pottery collected by Stein, Piggott and others. The formers' work was confined to small excavations in the Quetta valley, and the adjoining eastern area viz. surveys in the Zhob and Loralai districts of Baluchistan.

Baluchistan lying between the higher inland plateau of Central Asia and the low flat plains of Sind is indeed a transitional zone. The region is mostly mountanious. The Quetta valley itself is very narrow, not more than six miles in width and running north-south. Since its physiographical features shut out the monsoon winds from the south and east, and admit, on the other hand, the winds from the north-west, the climate is more akin to that of southern Afghanistan and .eastern Iran than to that of Sind and the Punjab. This has had an important bearing upon the growth, development, decay and affinities of prehistoric cultures of Baluchistan.

The District of Quetta was extensively inhabited in prehistoric times. The earliest of the inhabitants, some 5,500 years ago [Kili Ghul Mohammad I (C-14 date 31,00—35,00 B.C.)] lived in small huts, at first, perhaps of mud and later of mud bricks. They had no pottery, but probably used skin bags and had basketry. They had bone and stone tools. It was thus an extremely primitive pastoral society which depended upon plentiful forage and water for their flocks in the central portion of the valley. During the next phase, Kili Ghul Mohammad II, probably because of the fertility of the soil, abundant water supply and arrival of people and ideas from Iran, we find a fine wheel-made pottery, implying the beginning of agriculture and even increase in population. This pottery, black-on-red, might have been locally made or brought in by traders from Iran. This stimulus from the west is also seen in a fine buff wheel-made ware having decorative styles of the Halaf type.

Probably these influences also introduced copper to the inhabitants with the help of which the drainage was improved, in the southern part of the Valley to enable its settlement.

From the size of the sites, it is estimated that the villages were large, the houses small and the passages between them irregular; doors moved on stone sockets, hearths were sunken and pottery bread ovens were utilized in every home. Flat stones and pebbles were employed as foundations for the mud walls. The predominant economy was agriculture (probably wheat and barley were cultivated though so far no actual grains have been found). Herds of sheep, goats and cattle must have been kept as before. The emphasis on the former is perhaps indicated by small Mother Goddess figurines, which are regarded as symbols of a fertility cult.

In the third and the last phase, owing to the increasing contact with the Indus valley, the original Baluchi Culture, inspired by Irani migrations and influences, underwent a radical change. Both the pottery and houses exhibit this in no uncertain way. The former now display typical Indian designs such as the Brahmi bull and the pipal leaf, whereas the latter are equipped with bricks and drains. But the Iranian influence persists, as instanced by the ibex and the desert antelope. Agriculture naturally must have received a great impetus.

However, instead of producing a large homogeneous culture or civilisation in the valley, a number of localized cultures came into existence, probably because of regional politics, economic outlets, and social affinities as it has happened so often in India and the East.

At present in the absence of other evidence we only see the different ceramic traditions, but there might have been probably minor variations in ritual, and crafts from region to region.

Indus Civilisation—First Urbanisation

This study of Baluchi cultures seems to explain the growth of the typical Indus, Sindhi or the so-called Harappa Culture. At first it appears there were a number of local cultures, for instance, the Amri, Kot Diji I and Harappa I, originally perhaps inspired by Iranian sources. But these cultures, being based on a different ecological background than that existing either in Iran or in Baluchistan, took a further step towards urbanisation. The fertile alluvial plains under efficient management could promise agricultural surplus—the main source of wealth and rise in population. Some genius, it is believed, under Mesopotamian influence[20] where earlier cities existed, turned these rich agricultural villages into fine brick-built towns and cities. This implies also great organising and unifying factors—whether it be a simple political figure or a religious-cum-political personality—something like a priest-king of Iraq and Egypt. Whatever it be, the indigenous character of the civilisation stands unchallanged. Once having established itself it affected in turn the Baluchi on the west—e.g. Mehi and Kulli and Sutkagen-dor in the south and Dabar Kot in the north, and soon encompassed on the east almost the whole of North India upto Delhi and the Simla foothills and Western India, as far as Surat.

But for some explanation like this, we cannot understand the rise and expansion of the Indus civilisation.

About the civilisation itself, much has been written. It is too well known. However, little is known about the method of ploughing and irrigation. The traces of the latter might have disappeared in the frequent Indus floods and ploughs, if of wood, might have perished. However, there is one terracotta toy-like specimen, mentioned by Mackay, which is now exhibited in the Prince of Wales Museum, Bombay. Both Dr. Motichandra and the writer have examined it and think that it is a model of a plough.

So far no remains of ploughs are found in any of the cities, so the exact method by which the agriculture was practised is not known. Whatever be the methods for ploughing and irrigation, it is suggested by some scholars that bunding was extensively prevalent, and it is these which were broken by the Aryans under Indra. It is the traces of these which were noted by Sir Aurel Stein in Baluchistan. The surplus grain was so much that it was

stored in large well built granaries. In fact, it was a special feature
of the Indus civilisation and has been noticed so far away at Lothal
on the Gujarat-Saurashtra border.

This civilisation was destroyed by invasion, floods or drought.
In Sind and the Punjab there is a hiatus so far, and we do not know
which culture replaced it. The Cemetery H culture at Harappa does
not exactly overlie it at Harappa; secondly, it has a localised distribution which may be due to want of field-work. At Chanhu-daro
the new people—Jhukar—are believed to have come after the
Harappan was deserted. So it is doubtful whether Aryans could
be held responsible for the destruction. In Rupar, another culture
succeeds it after a clean break indicated by a thick layer of sand.
At Alamgirpur (Ukhliana, District Meerut) a break is indicated
by a weathered surface.

Only at Rangpur in Saurashtra does it appear that the original
Harappan Culture gradually change into another.

Peasant Cultures

And this change was not for a better, still more highly organized
urban culture, but probably for a pastoral, or at most a Village
Culture.[21]. Rangpur illustrates what happened in the Punjab and
Sind. One cultural cycle ended with the Harappan. Another began,
and it was to take nearly a thousand or more years to reach urbanisation—a city civilisation once again.

Large parts of India, about 2,000 B.C., outside Sind, the Punjab,
Uttar Pradesh, Saurashtra, and even in these regions were enjoying
a peasant-cum-pastoral culture. This has been sufficiently demonstrated by explorations, followed by small excavations in the Punjab,
Uttar Pradesh (that is the Gangetic valley as far as Bihar), in Rajputana (the valleys of the Sarasvati, Drishadvati, Beas, Chambal
etc.), in Central India (the valleys of the Narmada, Chambal,
Ksiprā), in Northern Deccan (the valleys of the Godavari, Pravarā,
Mula), in Southern Deccan (the valleys of the Krishna), in Karna-
tak-Andhra (the valleys of the Krishna and Tungabhadra).

All these are riverine cultures. Except at two sites, viz., Nāv-
dāṭoli in Central India and the other at Nevāsā in Northern Deccan,
nowhere were excavations large enough to provide an answer
for their rise and growth or give a definite idea of the size and form
of the houses, and the food economy of the people. One does, how-

ever, notice a broad relationship between the riverine cultures of
Central India and Southeastern Rajputana on one side, and those
of Central India and Khandesh and Northern Deccan on the other.
At the same time, the tendency to develop a highly localized culture, evidenced so far by ceramic features, differing not only from
valley to valley, but within one river valley itself, has to be mentioned. This may be but a shadow of what was to happen throughout the historic times—small and large states dotted over the
length and breadth of India. Two exceptions to this may be cited
—one is the existence of Jorwe-Nevasa Culture which by 1,000
B.C. had spread over a large area, and the other is Malwa or Navdatoli culture which had covered an equally large area.

What gave birth to these riverine cultures? Was it a slow development from the earlier foodgathering-cum-food collecting stage?
or an external stimulus, such as colonisation by outsiders?

The evidence is so inadequate that no satisfactory answer can
be given. It appears however probable that

i.   in Andhra-Karnatak a purely Neolithic culture flourished
     around 25,00 B.C. This had possibly extended upto Nor-
     thern Deccan; Its one feature—Polished Stone axe—might
     have been derived from the east or alternatively from the
     west (?).

ii. Saurashtra, Rajputana, Central India, came under Iranian
     or Central Asian influences either because of the actual
     migration of peoples or because of ideas and contacts.
     This led to the colonisation or development of village
     cultures.

iii. that these—or some of their branches—migrated further
     down and impinged upon the Neolithic cultures of the
     Northern Deccan and Karnatak.

iv. the refugees of the Indus culture after its destruction spread
     out, and gave birth to another pottery tradition, bearing a
     vague affinity with the Indus.

Such is the most tentative explanation of the birth of these early
village communities. We shall now have a glimpse of their life.

This can be had in some detail from one or two sites in India.
Elsewhere the excavations were small, and nothing but pottery,
microlithic blades, beads and some animal bones have been found.

Moreover, the reports of these are not yet published, and hence nothing more than a brief reference to them is possible. Something about the food economy of the inhabitants is possible to guess because the excavators have kindly supplied to me the identification of the animal bones.

Presumably, all these settlements—in Sind, the Punjab, Rajputana, Uttar Pradesh, Bihar, Saurashtra, Central India, Khandesh, North and South Maharashtra, and even in the granitic regions of Andhra-Karnatak were clusters of mud huts. But barring Saurashtra (Rangpur), Rajputana and the Punjab where the settlements seem to rest on sandy alluvium, elsewhere they are on a black soil. This may imply a clearance of the jungle, the black soil itself being a weathering *in situ* of the brownish alluvium, owing to thick vegetation. This is clearly demonstrated at Navdatoli and Nevasa, the two sites which have so far been horizontally excavated and of which the writer has first-hand knowledge. Navdatoli is situated opposite Maheshwar on the Narmada, about 60 miles south of Indore. They stand on an old crossing of the river, which itself is a great commercial artery dividing India into two parts: Northern and Southern.

This blacksoil at Navdatoli, a small hamlet *now* occupied by boatmen, (*nāvḍas*), covers a fairly large area, about 2 furlong by 2 furlong, and caps the top of four mounds which some 4,000 years ago probably formed a single unit, but which was later cut up by erosion. This single mound represented the topmost terrace of the Narmada; the river itself presumably was flowing at the foot of its northern extremity, though now it flows at a distance of about three furlongs to the north.

The present village of the *nāvḍas* is situated on a still younger terrace.

Excavations on all the four mounds indicate that the entire pre-historic mound was occupied, but that some of its parts might have been occupied later than others. For instance, it was revealed in 1958-59 season that the north-eastern extremity of Mound IV was not inhabited before the end of Period II within the Chalcolithic.

From the very beginning the inhabitants built round and square or rectangular huts. These houses were raised on thick wooden posts. Around these were put bamboo screens, which were then plastered with clay from outside and inside. The floor was also made of clay mixed with cowdung. Both were then given a thin coating of lime, so that the house when first built must have looked spick and span. The size of the largest rectangular room was 20 feet by 40 feet. But sometimes, a circular hut was only three to four feet in diameter, the largest being of 8 feet in diameter. So it is doubtful, if the small one was meant for habitation. Such small huts might have been used for storing grain, hay, etc., as the writer recently saw in Kurnool, Andhra State. But normally in Period II, the size of a room was 10 ft. × 8 ft. How many persons lived in a room or a house can only be guessed. But possibly not more than four in a room of 8 feet × 10 feet. Secondly, the settlement was so often rebuilt as evidenced by house floors that it is difficult to distinguish the house plans by mere occurrences of postholes. But judging from the modern village of Navdatoli, one may guess that the prehistoric village might have had 50 to 75 huts, supporting a population of about 200 persons.

In one house was found a well-made rectangular pit, in the midst of it. Its sides are slightly bevelled; all round there are postholes; on either side at some distance is a pot-rest made into the ground, and possibly the remains of a single-mouthed hearth. Inside the pit were found two charred logs of wood, placed almost at right angles and the remains of two unique pots. These have a high corrugated neck with everted rim, a ribbed ovalish body with one or two incised bands, filled in with lime and a high hollow base (which looks similar to the mouth, so that until we could reconstruct the pots from this pit we were not certain which was the mouth and which the base).

These houses were built very close to each other. But between a row of 4 or 5 houses, it appears, there was an open space, like a Chowk (square).

These houses were furnished, as can be expected of those days and as we find in a farmer's house even today, with small and large earthen pots for storing, cooking and drinking. The large storage jars were strong and sturdy but generally decorated with an engraving along the neck. But what surprises us and delights our eye is their "table service", or dinner set. It is this which distinguishes these Early Navdatolians from the modern primitives like Santals and other tribes in Chota Nagpur, for instance. The Navdatolians had a large number of pottery vessels which according to their fabric, shapes and designs fall into four distinctive groups, each having certain shapes and designs associated with a particular period. The most common is a pale red slipped fabric with paintings in black over it. Since this occurs throughout Malwa (and old geographical name for parts of Central India), it is called the "Malwa Ware". This occurs as a major pottery fabric right from the first occupation and runs through the entire Chalcolithic habitation. However, in the earliest period only certain shapes and designs figure, both becoming more varied later.

Then there is a sprinkling of black-and-red ware, with paintings in white, comprising generally bowls with gracefully inturned sides and cups. This fabric is confined only to Period I, and seems definitely to be an import from the adjoining region of Rajputana, where at Ahar it occurs in profusion.

The third important fabric is the white-slipped one. It is associated with the first two periods only, but died out later. It has several gradations in slip and texture, but the finest is smooth, lustrous and slightly greenish-white.

Though it copies some of the shapes of the Malwa Ware, its own distinctive shapes are a shallow dish with broad, flat rim and stand, and a high concave-walled cup with bulging bottom. An almost complete bowl of the latter in fine white slip recalls a similar vessel from the earliest period at Sialk, in Iran (Ghirshman, "*Fouilles de Sialk*", Vol. I, Frontispiece, 4). A band of running antelopes and dancing human figures seem to be characteristic designs in this fabric.

In Period III occurs, for the first time, a new fabric called "Jorwe" after the "type site" in the Deccan. This has a well-baked core with a metallic ring and a matted surface. Comparatively limited numbers of shapes and designs figure in this ware. It is also at this time that the most distinctive form of a vessel occurs. This is the teapot-like bowl. It is in Malwa fabric. During 1958-59 we were lucky in getting a complete bowl, which leaves no doubt about its shape and function. It seems to have been a vessel with which ablutions were performed. Since it is without a handle, it has got to be held in the palms of both the hands, and the contents (liquid) poured slowly, as in a sacrifice or some such ritual. In order to control the flow of the liquid, a hole was sometimes made at the junction of the spout and the body of the vessel. A similar contrivance may be noticed in the channel-shaped bowls from Western Asia. A vessel identical in size and shape but in copper or bronze was found at Parbatsar Tehsil, Dist: Nagaur in Jodhpur some years ago, and it is exhibited in the Museum at Jodhpur.

Besides this important change in pottery, there was another very significant change in the life of the people. For the first couple of hundred years or so, the inhabitants ate principally among the cereal grains, two types of wheat *Triticum vulgare-compactum* and *Triticum* sp. The former, which is small with small blunt ends, was extremely common, while the latter is larger and has pointed ends. They also consumed from the beginning five kinds of legumes, viz., (i) Masur or Lentil (*Lens culinaris* Medicus), (ii) Urd or Black Gram (*Phaseolus mungo* L.), (iii) Mung or Green Gram (*Phaseolus radiatus* L.), (iv) Vatana or Mutter or Green Peas (*Lathyrus sativus* L.), and (v) *Lathyrus* sp. besides four other leguminous weeds, the identification of which is not certain. The food was probably cooked with linseed (*Linum usitatissinum*) oil, the grains of which are found from the earliest phase.

However, it is in Phase II and onwards that rice enters the dietary of the inhabitants though throughout—(from the quantity and distribution)—the life of the occupation, it seems to be scarce and in short supply.[22]

These are the grains which are grown and eaten in the Nimad District today. Our discovery, the first of its kind in India, shows that the food habits of a section of the people of Madhya Pradesh are at least 3,000 years old. Though wheat was known before from Mohenjodaro, these are the earliest examples of rice,[23] two kinds of grain, masur, (lentil), kulathi and beans, and oil seeds like linseed. Further the distribution and antiquity[24] of wheat, lentil and linseed suggests Western Asiatic contacts, whereas rice is believed by most authorities as indigenous to India. Thus two cultural and ethnic(?) strains seem to have met at Navdatoli. And though we do not know how these grains were cultivated, for no plough has been found, a number of heavy stone rings, which have been discovered might have been used as weights for digging sticks, as some primitive people still do in Orissa. Still it is obvious that a people who ate so many types of grains, and had such a variety of pots and pans, indicating varied needs and uses, were not so primitive as some tribes today are.

The stocks of the grains were probably cut with sickles set with stone teeth,[25] as thousands of such stone tools have been found. The grain might not have been ground into flour, but merely crushed[26] either dry or wet in deep, basin-shaped stone *patas*, called querns in English, with the help of a pounder or rubber. The resultant bread will be unleavened, as it is even today done in several parts of India. A number of these querns were found, as they were left by their users, right on the kitchen floor, near *chulhas* or hearths. These again were quite large, made with clay and thinly plastered with lime. It is however not to be presumed that the inhabitants were strictly vegetarians. In the debris of their houses have been found remains of cattle, pig, sheep-goat, and deer. Except for last, all must have been domesticated and eaten. But since the grains were varied and plentiful they relied less on animal food, and hence their remains are comparatively few in number as compared to those from Nevasa.

Economically, thus, the early inhabitants of Navdatoli were fairly well off. They were essentially farmers or peasants, though a section might be living by hunting and fishing. They did not yet know iron; copper they used, but sparingly in the shape of simple, flat axes, fish-hooks, pins and rings. In a later phase possibly they used daggers[27] or swords with a midrib, as suggested by a fragment found in 1958-59. So for their daily needs of cutting vegetables, scraping leather and piercing stone, they had to rely upon stone tools; their blades are so small that we call them "microliths".[28] These were hafted in bone and wooden handles, as we nowadays fix an iron blade into a pen-knife. Among ornaments, we have thousands of beads of sand coated with a glaze and called "faience", or chalk and a few of semi-precious stone such as agate, and carnelian. These must have been strung into necklaces. Bangles and rings were also worn. These were of clay and copper.

These earliest farmers in Madhya Pradesh lived, as we know from Carbon-14 dates kindly supplied by the Pennsylvania University, about 2,000 B.C. and continued to live on with three major destructions by fire at least upto 7,00 B.C., when an iron-using people from Ujjain and possibly further North wiped out their existence and laid the foundation of a new economy in which iron, minted money, houses of bricks and altogether a new pottery played a dominant part.

The question who the first dwellers were, whose remains are found all over Malwa, is not yet resolved. Probably they were a people from Iran, as their pottery shows. This is a very important and interesting clue. In that case, they might be a branch of the Aryans. This trail is to be followed up by further detective work across India and Pakistan upto Eastern Iran.

While Navdatoli illustrates the settlement pattern in Central India, Nevasa helps to understand the burial practices and their relation to the habitation in Northern Maharashtra.

Nevasa is the headquarters of a taluka of the same name in Ahmednagar District. It is situated on both the banks of the river Pravara, a tributary of the Godavari, and is about 110 miles north-east of Poona.

A large mound, perhaps originally one but later bisected by river and giving birth to Nevasa Khurd (small) and Nevasa Budruk (big), overlooks the river. The portion lying on the southern side (or on the left bank) is nearly 1½ furlong long and ½ furlong wide. It is now called "Lādmod", and cut up into three smaller mounds by erosion and man. From the water-level it is nearly 70 feet high, the top 30 feet or so containing the debris of four cultural periods from 15,00 A.D. to 1,000 B.C.—15,00 B.C. It is the first period from the bottom upwards which concerns us here.

The earliest occupants settled on a thick layer of black soil by affecting an opening in the jungle with the help of copper and polished stone axes. For the rest of the cutting and clearing activities they used short parallel-sided and Gravette-like blades and points of a limpid chalcedony. Of the earlier microlithic tradition, we find a sparing use of lunates and trapeze. True saws also occur in this assemblage. The technique by which blades were removed has been studied in great detail by Dr. Subbarao. It has been described as a "Crested Ridge and Fluted core" technique and is a common feature of all the Chalcolithic cultures mentioned above. Among the heavier tools, we have occasionally mace-head or weight for digging stick, small querns, mullers, rubbers and large querns are comparatively very few. This is possibly because agriculture was in its infancy. Negatively, this is confirmed by the absence of any grains, so far, whereas a large amount of animal bones, among which those of cow/ox predominates, underlines the predominance of beef in the diet. Not only their food habits, but their pottery is strikingly different from that of Navdatoli. It is generally matt, having geometric paintings in black over a red surface. Wheel-made, it is so well-baked that it gives a metallic ring when struck. The shapes are again comparatively limited; carinated bowls of various sizes; vessels with tubular spout and flaring mouth and carinated belly, and vessels with globular body and high neck. Dishes are rare. Among the unpainted group there are sturdy storage jars, with finger-tip decoration, basins or troughs and fine black slipped ware with red coating which vanishes on touch.

So far the existence of spinning was inferred from the occurrence of small baked clay spindel whorls. Last year, however, a copper bead necklace in a child's burial preserved the threads. These on very careful study by Dr. A. N. Gulati turned out to be strands of silk with a nep of cotton. We may thus say that cotton clothes were worn and necklaces were strung with silk threads, as they are done today. It appears that this is the earliest well recorded occurrence of silk which was probably wild.

The people who enjoyed such a material culture lived in mud huts which were generally square or rectangular. These were built with the help of uncut thick wooden posts. The floors were made with lime and clay but at times with a bedding of sand or gravel. The size of the rooms so far found is 9 feet × 7 feet.

A more detailed picture of the alignment of the houses has not yet emerged. But what is remarkable is that the inhabitants buried the dead right in the floor of the houses. Three or four different burial methods were followed:

    (i)   the adults were at times laid right on the black soil which was smeared with lime;

    (ii) or put in a long, large earthen jar, the outlines of the pit being marked with lime;

   (iii) or several jars (five) were used to cover the dead body;

   (iv) or children, as a rule, were interned in a double or single, at times treble, wide mouthed urns, after the remains were probably exposed. For in two cases, the skull is in two parts, and kept separately.

So far an area of 80 ft. × 40 ft. and 250 feet × 200 feet has yielded over 90 skeletons,[29] of which six are of adults. Thus little doubt remains about the burial practices of this people. Since similar pottery and remains of urns are found over a large area from Khandesh in the north to Brahmagiri in Northern Mysore in the south, a distance of over 500 miles, the extent of this culture known as "Brahmagiri-Jorwe-Nevasa Culture" was certainly wide. Its east-west extension is not yet known.

The origins of this culture are not known. Partly it is derived from the Neolithic cultures of Andhra and Karnatak. These seem to have been the substratum over which the copper-knowing, painted-pottery people using a wheel, from the north slowly impinged in about 15,00 B.C. Who they could be, we shall discuss later on. Before that an idea of the Neolithic cultures of Andhra-Karnatak is necessary.

The region, which these cultures flourished in, is now shared by the states of Andhra and Karnatak. Since the raw material was a consideration the remains of these cultures are found in areas with granitoid hills, with dykes, of fine grained basalt, the latter being most suitable for polished axes. So far only two or three sites are very partially excavated. None of these gives an idea of the houses at present. But it is inferred that the people lived under overhanging rocks and carried on a primitive agriculture in the plains below. By and large they were pastoral people and hunters. This has been now proved by the identification of the remains of large cinerary mounds, as accumulated heaps of cow-dung. Both short-horned cattle and long-horned variety (Indian buffalo), besides sheep/goat, were domesticated.

The principal tools of this people were pointed-butt polished stone axes, adzes, chisels, hammerstones, fabricators and microliths. Carbon-14 dates from two sites, Piklihal and Utnoor, would place their culture around 2,100 B.C.

Towards Second Urbanisation

None of these cultures—whether the Chalcolithic of Saurashtra, Rajputana, Central India or Northern Deccan or the purely Neolithic of Southern Deccan—gradually developed into an urban civilisation. Around 800 B.C., another copper-using culture, with an altogether different pottery tradition—called the Painted Grey Ware—spread over the entire Gangetic valley. Traces of it are found in Rajputana and Central India. Since it occupies the same position as some of the traditional cities of the *Mahābhārata*, like Hastināpura, Ahichchhatra and later Kausambi—it should be, at least in its chief cities, of an urban character. But owing to the smallness of the excavations, nothing can be said about the character of the Culture.

Within two or three centuries, however, possibly due to Iranian influence, from the Achaeminian empire, iron came to be introduced. Along with this the pottery changed into a fine polished lustrous black, grey, gold or silvery. Its principal centre is the Gangetic valley. And here[30] the first cities of the historical period arose, very soon to be followed at Ujjain and Maheshwar in Central India and at Nasik and Paithan in Northern Deccan, and possibly Brahmagiri in Mysore. This happened in the wake of iron, and a pottery, which is called "black-and-red", but may better be described as "black-topped", according to the late Professor Childe.

None of these early cities is excavated so that we can have an idea of its size. Mauryan Taxila was irregularly laid with very narrow streets. It is only with the Indo-Greeks that the chess-board like cities appeared at Charsadda and Taxila in the Punjab, and possibly later at Mathura, Kausambi, Pataliputra and Ujjain. Thus it took nearly 2,500 years for an old concept to re-assert itself in India.

Conclusions

In India thus we witness almost the same stages of development from food gathering stage to urbanisation through the intermediate stages of food producing-cum-food gathering stage and early peasant economy. At no one site or in one region are all the stages of development discernible. The picture is built from a scene here and a scene there. This unequal development might be due to geographical factors. But how was each particular stage of culture reached?

Even the earliest—Handaxe Culture—is believed to be introduced from Africa, where a well attested development from a crude pebble-culture is available. Looking to the geographical position of Africa and India, and the absence of a stratigraphically earlier stage of Handaxe Culture, one has to accept the present hypothesis. The Soan, as is well known, has a limited distribution and connected with South-East Asia.

The next Palaeolithic culture characterised by points and scrapers and called "Nevasian" or Middle Palaeolithic or Middle Stone Age has also a great affinity with some of the African cultures. But unless actual tools are available for a comparitive study, further comments are unnecessary. From what the writer has seen, the tools seem to evolve after the Late Acheulian. This was first marked by my pupil and now colleague, Dr. K. D. Banerjee, in Karnatak. It is now being confirmed by our collections from North Deccan, Kurnool and Central India. So, for the advanced food collecting stage, now witnessed almost all over India, no external influences are at present postulated, though one will have to account for the man's rejection of the old raw material. A different man and/or new ideas should have been on the scene. But whether he or the ideas belonged to India or came from outside requires much deeper studies based on planned explorations.

The same is true of the various microlithic industries. They are believed to have evolved from the earlier blade and burin industries. The classical, well documented, regions are however known from outside India, e.g. Palestine, and it has been said by writers that the stimulus might have been received from the peripheral area through Palestine. But without further research this remains a mere suggestion.

This position dogs us when we enter the early pastoral and peasant village stage. The early peasant villages of Sind, like Amri, are believed to have originated under Iranian influence, and later under Sumerian or Mesopotamian impetus achieved a still better, and highly efficient, urban civilisation.

While this may be true, what happened to the early village cultures in the rest of India? Are they all indigenous or owe their birth to outside forces? According to one theory based on ceramic evidence from Rangpur in Saurashtra and Navdatoli in Central India we may postulate the existence of these cultures to the arrival of Aryan or Western Asiatic tribes from Iran. This explains the appearance of almost identical vessels—such as goblets, channel-spouted cups, and fine white-slipped ware in such profusion at Navdatoli. While the shapes are very much similar, the Indian fabrics are inferior. This may be due to the non-availability of the kind of clay found in Iran and elsewhere in Central Asia. Further, the occurrence of lentil and linseed at Navdatoli points to the same conclusion. In fact De Candolle goes as far as to suggest that lentil was unknown in India before the invasion of Sanskrit-speaking people.

Some of the tribes with highly specialised pottery penetrated further south in the Deccan and brought about the Daimabad-Jorwe-Nevasa-Chandoli-Brahmagiri Culture.[31] Similar thing seems to have occurred in Saurashtra and Rajputana, where several local cultures came into being.

While all these—Saurashtra, Central Indian and the Deccan tribes—might be thought to stem out from one common stock, another Aryan tribe bearing the Grey Ware entered the Punjab and spread into the Gangetic valley. This pottery with typical Svastika design is traced in the West to Shahitump in Southern Baluchistan, while the fabric and colour reveals similar pattern in Thessaly.

This theory of Aryan migration in two principal waves may accord with the once held view of Grierson and others of an "Outer" and an "Inner" band of Aryans; the "Grey Ware" people being the latter, and the various painted pottery groups representing the "Outer". There are, however, two serious weaknesses in this theory. First, if the "Aryans", or, whoever the immigrants were, brought the pottery tradition with them, why even one of them could not transplant the advanced metallurgical technology of the West? This argument also holds good against the Sumerian theory, which seeks to explain the urbanisation in Sind and the Punjab. For some reason[32] the tools and weapons of the Indus as well as the latter village communities in India remain of a simple, unsocketed, type. It is only when they came into contact with the Indo-Greeks and the Romans in the early centuries of the Christian era and a little before, that socketed axes, arrow-heads, spear-heads etc. were manufactured.

Secondly, in the absence of well-marked links between Central India and Iran, the theory lacks confirmation. While we are trying to fill up the gap[33] in India, it is the work in Pakistan and Indo-Pakistan-Iranian border that may help elucidate the problem.

If we do not accept this Aryan or outside emigration theory for the birth of certain cultures in the Gangetic Valley and Central India as well as the Deccan, we must credit the known indigenous tribes—such a Kolis, Bhils, Nagas, Andhras, Pulindas,[34] Nishadas —for their authorship.

This will to some extent nullify the view that India is a peripheral region. For we are postulating an independent origination of cultures. Much of this dilemma, I believe, is due to our ignorance. With planned work in Rajputana, Saurashtra and Indo-Pakistan-Iranian border, it is probable that a more definite solution can be found.

NOTES

[1] Braidwood and Howe, 1960.
[2] Murray, 1961, p. 12.
[3] Braidwood and Howe, 1960, p. 46.

[4] By the Wenner-Gren Foundation at Burg Wartenstein, in July 1960. Originally only 25 copies of the essay were photo copied for distribution. It is being published here for the first time.

[5] Spate, 1954.

He gives a very detailed regional division, (pp. 352-61) and fig. 62 which for the present purpose is unnecessary. Spate's remarks on the difficulties of a proper division are worth reading.

[6] Subbarao, 1958, 16; fig. 6.

[7] Subbarao's picture is here amplified and changed wherever necessary.

[8] Though even here it is necessary to prove by archaeological excavations, as Furer-Haimendorf suggested over 10 years ago, that these primitive tribes are comparatively recent arrivals in the area, and not residing from time immemorial.

[9] Richards, 1933.

[10] Braidwood, in *Illustrated London News*, October 22, (1960), pp. 695-97.

[11] Cf. also Wright in Braidwood and Howe, 1960, p. 73: "Speculation about the effects of climatic change on the inception of agriculture is justified only after the fact of climatic change has been established" and this must be based on geological evidence.

[12] Significant in this context is the discovery of "town" wall of undressed stone at Jericho going back to 6,000 B.C. Whether this is regarded as indicating "civilisation" or urbanisation as the discussion in *Antiquity* shows is indeed immaterial. What is certain is that given favourable circumstances, such as perennial water supply, one may witness the various steps in the development of civilisation as at Jericho in Palestine. For the final position see the latest review of the question by Kathleen M. Kenyon in *JRAI*, Vol. 89 (1959), pp. 35-42. Another equally old site is found near Petra in Jordan.

[13] As if in immediate answer to Braidwood, James Mellaart discovered at Hacilar in Turkey (or Anatolia) nine building levels ranging from Acermaic (or pre-pottery) phase C. 6,000 B.C. to a late Chalcolithic C. 4750 B.C. of which the late Neolithic (Level VI-IX) are dated by radiocarbon to $5590\pm$ 180 B.C. See *Illustrated London News*, April 8, 1961, p. 588.

[14] Of course, the absence may be genuine, due to several factors, such as the existence of thick, almost impenetrable forest in Assam; or nonavailability of suitable raw material, or the nonexistence of the land itself!! Thus recent work by Misra of the Deccan College in the Luni Valley in South Rajputana brought to light a palaelothic industry in which small bifaces, besides scrapers and points occur, but larger handaxes are absent. And it appears that this industry belongs to the second aggradation phase in the rest of India, but the first in south-west Rajputana, the earlier phase being non-existent., as this part of Rajputana was under a sea.

[15] Where not only tools but recently teeth of a child and skull of an adult associated with the earliest tools were discovered by Leakey in the Olduvai Gorge, Tanganyika. *ILN.*, March, 4, 1961 p. 346. These are now dated by Potassium-Argon method to 17,50,000 years.

[16] In Kurnool, however, where quartzite is plentiful, the tools continue to be made of this material. And it appeared to the writer when he recently examined the sites there, that this region might provide a clue to the development

or evolution of a Middle Paleolithic and Late Paleolithic cultures from the Lower Paleolithic. Elsewhere there appears superficially to b , clean break between the techniques as well as the raw material of the two cultures. But it must however, be mentioned that a tendency towards smaller and neater bifaces, very nearly like points, is visible at a number of sites in Western and Central India.

Further evidence was provided this season (1960-61) by Gangapur, near Nasik and a number of sites on the Betwa and its tributaries in Central India.

[17] Lal, 1958, p. 47 and A. I., No. 17, 1961, p. 37.

[18] This is based on a preliminary study by my colleague Dr. (Mrs.) I. Karve as far back as 1948. Since then the human remains have been more fully studied by Dr. (Mrs.) Erhardt of Tübingen University. It is hoped to publish her report very soon.

[19] This might mean a scrubby desert-like landscape in Northern Gujarat and Rajputana or a scrubby jungle with an occasional water-fall during a part of the years in the limestone area of Kurnool, as well as in the similar hill-ranges in Mirzapur, though at present it receives much more rainfall than Kurnool.

[20] So far this is merely a guess. Real Mesopotamian cities are or will be almost contemporary with the earliest city levels at Mohenjodaro. Still none of these can boast of a fine sense of town-planning in burnt brick houses for the entire population as witnessed with such a uniformity in the Indus cities (barring, of course, some sites in Bikaner where mud-brick houses are turning up). It will not be surprising, therefore, if future work at Mohenjodaro—whenever its deeper levels are unearthed—proves the independent origination of the Indus cities. For, as Robert M. Adams says in Adams, 1960, p. 10: "There is not one origin of cities, but as many as there are cultural traditions with an urban way of life. Southern Mesopotamia merely provides the earliest example (which, as we have suggested, might not be the earliest) of a process ... "

Cf. also Kathleen M. Kenyon 1959, p. 42, where she has argued well for an independent sequence of cultures, leading to urbanization at Jericho in Palestine.

[21] Unfortunately all excavations, including that by the writer and Dr. M. G. Dikshit in 1947, were on a small scale, and those carried out by Shri S. R. Rao have not been fully reported.

[22] This is a revised account based on the final report by Dr. Vishnu-Mittre of the Birbal Sahni Institute of Paleobotany, Lucknow. It is being published by Deccan College as "Plant Economy in Ancient Navdatoli-Maheshwar", in *Technical Reports on Archaeological Remains.*

[23] The earliest well-dated occurrence of wheat, lentil, peas and barley is from Hacilar, near Danzli in Turkey. Here Level VI (from top), that is IV from botton upwards, is dated by radiocarbon to 5590, $\pm$ 180 B.C., *Illustrated London News,* April 8, 1961, p. 588.

[24] Since writing this rice has been reported from Lothal and Rangpur. See Ghosh, S. S., 1961, pp. 295-301.

[25] The earliest again comes from Hacilar, Level VI (or IV from botton). Here, no less than six antler sickles with chert blades set in a V-shaped groove were found. We have thus evidence from Egypt, Iraq, Palestine and Turkey.

[26] I am glad to note that Braidwood, *op. cit.* p. 45, also recognises this fact

and says that the querns might have been used for cracking of grains for porridge.

[27] This impression has been strengthened by the discovery of a small dagger head with antennae in the excavations at Chandoli, near Poona, in 1961.

[28] Though this is not the correct term. For these small blades are different from true microliths.

[29] This number has now gone over 110.

[30] Professor G. R. Sharma informs me that this season (1960-61) a huge palace of dressed stones was found below the NBP levels at Kausambi. It is attributed to king Udayana. If along with this palace, there were also brick-built houses for the citizens, then in one respect at least—monumentality—we can say that Kausambi had achieved urbanisation.

[31] The site at Chandoli is about 40 miles north of Poona in Poona District. Its excavation by the Deccan College in 1961 showed a mixture of Centra Indian and the Deccan Cultures.

[32] The facile explanation that we in India have not taken easily to technological advances should remember that well-aligned cities of the Indus Civilisation presupposed a good sense of architectural planning as well as engineering skill and geometrical tools. Some of the latter—a graduated scale, compass-like instrument and a drill—were found at Lothal during 1959-60. Thus some deeper, another, explanation is not unlikely. See *Indian Archaeology—A Review*, 1959-60 and *Illustrated London News*, February 25, and March 11, 1961.

[33] As mentioned earlier a channel-spouted bowl in copper was found some years ago in Jodhpur State and is presented in the local Museum. This may indicate the route to and fro from Maheshwar.

[34] One of my pupils, Shri Dhavalikar, tells me that in the Puranas, the Pulindas are credited to have spread from Malwa in the north to Maharashtra in the south. Thus the proto-historic Andhras and Pulindas might turn out to be the authors of the Jorwe-Malwa Cultures.

REFERENCES

ADAMS, Robert M., 1960, 'The Origin of the Cities', *Scientific American*, September, 1960.

ALLCHIN, Bridget., 1960, 'Middle Stone Age Culture in India', Institute of Archaeology, University of London.

BANERJEE, K. D., 1957, *Middle Palaeolithic Cultures of the Deccan*, Mimeographed, thesis, Poona University, 1957. Poona, Deccan College and Poona University Libraries.

BRAIDWOOD, Robert J. and HOWE, Bruce., 1960, *Prehistoric Investigations in Iraqi Kurdistan*, Studies in Ancient Oriental Civilization, No. 31, Chicago.

BURKITT, M. C. and CAMMIADE, L. A., 1930, 'Fresh Light on the Stone Age of South-East India', *Antiquity*, Vol. 4, pp. 327-39.

FAIRSERVIS, Jr., WALTER A., 'Excavations in the Quetta Valley, West Pakistan', *Anthropological Papers of the American Musem of Natural History*, Vol. 45, Part 2, pp. 165-402.

1958, 'Archaeological Surveys in the Zhob and Loralai Districts, West Pakistan', *Anthropological Papers of the American Museum of Natural History*, Vol. 47, Part 2, pp. 277-448.

GHOSH, A., (editor), 1953-60, *Indian Archaeology—A Review*, 1953-54, 1954-55, 1954-55, 1955-56, 1956-57, 1957-58, 1958-59 and 1959-60.

GHOSH, S.S., 1961, 'Further Records of Rice (*Oiryza* Spp.) from Ancient India', *Indian Forester*, Vol. 87, pp. 295-301.

GORDON, D. H., 1950, 'The Stone Industries of the holocene in India and Pakistan', *Ancient India*, No. 6, pp, 64-90.

ISSAC, N., 1960, *Stone Age Cultures of Kurnool*, Mimeographed, Ph.D. thesis, Deccan College and Poona University Libraries.

KENYON, Kathleen M., 1959, *Journal of the Royal Anthropological Institute*, Vol. 89, pp. 35-42.

LAL, B. B., 1954-55, 'Excavations at Hastinapur and other Explorations in the Upper Ganga and Sutlej Basins 1950-52', *Ancient India*, Nos. 10 and 11, pp. 5-151.

1958, 'Birbhanpur, A. Microlithic Site in the Damodar Valley, West Bengal', *Ancient India*, No. 14, pp. 4-48.

HARGREAVES, H., 1929, 'Excavations in Baluchistan, 1925, Sampur Mound, Mastung and Sohr Damb, Nal. *Mem. Archael. Surv. India*, No. 35.

KRISHNASWAMI, V. D., 1951, 'The Lithic tool-industries of the Singrauli basin', *Ancient India*, No. 7, pp. 40-65.

MACKAY, Ernst., 1937-38, *Futher Excavations at Mohen-jo-Daro*, Being an official account of archaeological excavations at Mohenjo-Daro carried out by the Government of India between 1927 and 1931, New Delhi, 2 volumes.

1943, *Chanhu-Daro Excavations*, American Oriental Series, Vol. 29, New Haven, American Oriental Society.

MARSHALL, John, 1931, *Mohenjo-Daro and the Indus Civilization*, Being an official account of archaeological excavations at Mohenjo-Daro carried out by the Government of India between the years 1922 and 1927, London, 3 volumes.

MISRA, V. N., 1961, *Stone Age Cultures of Rajputana*, Mimeographed, Ph.D. thesis, Deccan College and Poona University Libraries.

MOHAPATRA, G. C., 1960, *Stone Age Cultures of Orissa*, Mimeographed, Ph.D. thesis, Deccan College and Poona University Libraries.

MURRAY, Margaret., 1961, 'First Steps in Archaeology', *Antiquity*, Vol. XXXV, (No. 137, March 1961).

PIGGOT, Stuart., 1950, *Prehistoric India to 1000 B.C.*, Middlesex, Penguin Books.

RICHARDS, F. J., 1933, 'Geographical Factors in Indian Archaeology', *Indian Antiquary*, Vol. LXII.

ROSS, E. J., 1946, *Rana Ghundai*, in Ross, E., J., et al (eds.), 'A Chalcolithic site in northern Baluchistan', *Journal of Near Eastern Studies*, Vol. 5, No. 4, pp. 291-315.

SANKALIA, H. D., 1956, 'The microlithic industry of Langhnaj, Gujarat', *Journal of Gujarat Research Society*, Vol. XVII, No. 4, 275-84; and other earlier papers mentioned therein.

1956, 'Animal fossils and Palaeolithic industries from the Pravara Basin at Nevasa, District Ahmadnagar', *Ancient India*, No. 12, pp. 35-52.

1958, 'New Light on the Aryan "Invasion" of India: Links with Iran of 1000 B.C. Discovered in Central India', *Illustrated London News*, September 20, 1958, pp. 478-79.

1959, 'Four-Thousand-Year old Links with Iran and Central India: New Excavations at Navdatoli', September 5, 1959.

SANKALIA, H. D., SUBBARAO, B. and DEO, S. B., 1958, *Excavations at Maheshwar and Navdatoli*, Deccan College Monograph Series, Poona, Deccan College.

SANKALIA, H. D., DEO, S. B., ANSARI, Z. D., and EHRHARDT, S., 1960, *From History to Prehistory at Nevasa*, Deccan College Monograph Series, Poona, Deccan College.

SESHADRI, M., 1956, *The Stone-using Cultures of Prehistoric and Proto-historic Mysore*, London.

SOUNDARA, RAJAN, K. V., 1952, 'Stone Age Industries near Giddalur, District Kurnool', *Ancient India*, No. 8, pp. 64-92.

SPATE, O. H., K., 1954, India and Pakistan, London,

STEIN, Aurel., 1929, 'An Archaeological tour in Waziristan and northern Baluchistan', *Mem. Archaeol. Surv. India*, No. 37.

1931, 'An Archaeological tour in Gedrosia', *Mem. Archaeol. Surv. of India*, No. 43.

SUBBARAO, B., 1948, *Stone Age Cultures of Bellary*, Deccan College Dissertation Series, No. 7, Poona, Deccan College.

1952, 'Archaeological explorations in the Mahi Valley', *Journal of M.S. University of Baroda*, Vol. I, pp. 33-69.

1958, *The Personality of India*, M.S. University Archaeology Series No. 3 (2nd edition), Baroda, M.S. University.

THAPAR, B. K., 1957, 'Maski 1954: A chalcolithic site of the southern Deccan', *Ancient India*, No. 13, pp. 5-142.

TODD, K. R. U., 1948, 'A microlithic industry in eastern Mysore', *Man*, Vol. XLVII, N. 27, pp. 28-30.

VATS, Madho Swarup., 1940, *Excavations at Harappa*, Being an account of the archaeological excavations at Harappa carried out between the years 1920-21 and 1933-34, Delhi, 2 volumes.

VISHNU-MITTRE, 1961, Plant Economy in Ancient Navdatoli-Maheshwar, in *Technical Reports on Archaeological Objects*, Deccan College Monograph Series, Poona, Deccan College.

WHEELER, R. E. M., 1947, 'Harappa 1946: the Defences and Cemetery R.37', *Ancient India*, No. 3, pp. 58-130.

1959, *Early India and Pakistan*, London.

ZEUNER, F. E., 1950, *Stone Age and Pleistocene Chronology in Gujarat*, Deccan College Monograph Series No. 6, Poona, Deccan College.

ZEUNER, F. E., and ALLCHIN, Bridget., 1956, 'The microlithic sites of Tinnevelly District, Madras State', *Ancient India*, No. 12, pp. 4-20; and other earlier articles mentioned therein.

4

ARCHAEOLOGY AND ANTHROPOLOGY IN INDIA

B. SUBBARAO

I

"WHEN Sir Herbert Risley took the Census of India in 1901 he not only numbered the heads of the population, but also sought to determine what kind of heads they were . . . ." wrote Sir Arthur Keith (1936) reviewing Guha's report of the 1931 Census. Unfortunately, there have been too many experiments in our Census-ethnographic reports and the data have always been inadequate to permit any probable generalisation.

The purpose of the following paper is to show how an archaeologist, trespassing into one of his border disciplines gets stuck up in a welter of conjectures. While admitting that we too sometimes indulge in speculations on inadequate data, I propose to bring out some of the outstanding and urgent problems in Indian anthropology, in the light of the spectacular development in archaeological studies in the various focal regions of India within the last decade.

I take this opportunity to pay my tribute to the late Professor D. N. Majumdar. I had the privilege of knowing him and I was benefited from his great erudition. So here is an appeal for co-operation and helpful criticism so that both the allied disciplines can be concerted to solve some of the urgent problems in Indian archaeology.

We are all familiar with the fact that the Indian sub-continent, which comprises the two political units of India and Pakistan, is located at the margin of the Eurasian land mass. It was subjected to recurrent migrations of cultures and races across the land, as well as, by the sea. This physiographic contiguity had another greater impact on the development of civilisation in our sub-continent. Immediately to the west of it, lay the great focal region of the Near East, where by a remarkable coincidence of favourable factors, Man won his first battle against Nature by the great Neoli-

thic revolution. This led to a great accentuation of the pace of
change and very soon urban civilisation of a very high order appeared with all the technical and technological achievements.
The Indus Basin could not escape the impact of these advances.
Unfortunately, we are not in a position to visualise at present the
beginnings of the process that culminated in the cities of Mohenjodaro and Harappa. Yet, the Harappan culture is one of the most
important components of Indian Culture, before the Indo-Aryans
gave us a language and preserved an intellectual heritage that
moulded the entire Indian culture and thought. With this example
we take up a few general considerations.

After all, the primary agent of this great fusion is Man himself.
Here we come to the door of the anthropologist. Indian anthropologists have given us a number of systems of classification of the main
and sub-groups among the Indian races. How exactly these various
peoples moved in space and time is also a burning problem for the
archaeologist. Within the last fifteen years, great advances have
been made in Indian archaeology. New sites have been excavated
from different focal regions of India and also a rough outline of the
development of material culture in India is emerging. The archaeologist deals only with the shadows—the material relics of the past.
He may excavate a few graves or a cemetery and expose skeletal
remains. But it is only the anthropologist, and particularly the
human palaeontologist, who can study the skeletal remains and
help the archaeologist in his attempts to identify the authors of the
material relics.

II

The year 1961 marks the Centenary of the Archaeological Survey
of India and the last fifteen years of this century have witnessed very
great advances in Indian archaeology, as a result of the activities of
the century old Archaeological Survey of India, some of the State
Governments and a few Universities and learned Institutions. A
coordinated attempt is being successfully made to reconstruct the
cultural sequence of the various regions and to establish a comparative stratigraphy of the various cultures in time and space (Subbarao, 1958). Without going into any details of stratigraphy or of
individual sites, I will give the picture as it emerges in the Indo-Pakistan sub-continent. The object of this Survey is to bring into

relief the main features and the stages of the evolution of Indian culture. Incidentally it reveals the movements of peoples and cultures.

The story of man in India starts with the 'Palaeolithic' or the Early Stone Age somewhere in the Middle Pleistocene. The earliest definite occurrence of human tools is in the Sohan Valley in the terrace assigned to the II Glacial period. While the peri-glacial foot hills of the Himalayas show a predominance of pebble choppers, the Peninsular part of our ancient land shows a uniform and well developed industry of hand-axes, cleavers etc., belonging to the Abbevillo-Acheulean complex. The most striking feature of these 'food-gathering communities' is the widespread distribution of their industries in almost all the major river basins of the country.

In recent years, with the remarkable discoveries of Dr. H. D. Sankalia (1961) at Nevasa, a new industry characterised by the presence of small scrapers, blade flakes and an occasional burin (in a tradition reminiscent of Levallois and the Upper Palaeolithic of Europe), has been found. Again, this industry has a widespread distribution in space and it can be dated to the Upper Pleistocene and early Post-Pleistocene. Culturally, we can visualise a higher stage of food-collecting with specialised smaller tools and possibly a primitive arrow head. This has been termed, Middle Stone Age.

In this series of food-gathering cultures, we can bring in the third of the Late Stone Age Microlithic industries. These Microlithic people lived a life of hunting and selective food-gathering. If evidence from Langhnaj is to be taken, the dog had already been domesticated. As in Europe and Africa, these Microlithic cultures adopted themselves very well to the steppes of Europe or the wooded regions of North Africa, specially the harpoon and the arrowhead must have helped them to settle even in the wooded regions of Africa. They survived happily in Central and Southern Africa and also in India. A core of bottle glass was found at Mahabaleswar by S. C. Malik (see figure XXV in 1959).

This widespread uniformity, with an occasional variation, in the three main stages of Stone Age—Early, Middle and Late—within the broad food-gathering stage of culture in the sub-continent, is broken up when the country passes to the next stage, viz., the food-producing. Here the environment begins to exercise its influence. Unfortunately the Neolithic cultures of India are not very well clarified,

If we mean by Neolithic revolution, the emergence of agriculture, domestication of plants and animals, fixed settlements and polished stone tools, our picture is still incomplete. We have widespread use of polished tools in the Central Deccan (Andhra-Karnatak areas), Tamilnad north of the river Cauvery, along the foot hills of the Vindhyas, in the Mirzapur and Banda districts of Uttar Pradesh. Here they are confined to the deciduous and dry deciduous forest areas. In the Gangetic basin, we see a slow movement from the foot hills into the plains after the advent of metals, suggesting that the tropical river-basins could only be inhabited after the clearance of the forests with the heavy metals. Unfortunately, the more interesting and a focal region like the Gangetic basin is still a *terra incognita* as far as the Neolithic studies are concerned. A large collection made by Cunningham from Mirzapur and Banda districts is being studied by F. R. Allchin (1957, pp. 321-35).

However, the Central Deccan has been very systematically studied by Wheeler (1948), Subbarao (1948), Allchin (*op. cit*) and Thapar (1957). Here we have a fairly satisfactory picture of these early Neolithic communities. The earliest site is Utnoor in the Mehboobnagar district of Andhra Pradesh with a *C*-14 date of 4120 + 150 *B. P.* (Before Present). Here we have a cinder camp of the Neolithic period with coarse burnished grey ware with remains of cattle. Professor Zeuner studied the cinder from the various Neolithic sites of Bellary-Raichur region (Kuditini and Kupgal in the Bellary and Piklihal in the Raichur districts). He eliminated the possibility of the cinder being volcanic ash, travertine, cremation material, glass slag or metallurgical slag, and suggested that it consisted of large heaps of burnt cow-dung (Zeuner, 1960). We have large groups of cattle among the graffiti and paintings at Kupgal and a number of associated sites in the region. Finally, terracotta figures of long-horned cattle were also found at Piklihal by Allchin. Actual bones of cattle were recovered at Maski and Piklihal. They were using polished tools. We have no evidence as yet of any food grains. We are fairly safe in inferring from the nature of settlements, granatoid hills overlooking plains below, that these people were early agricultural and pastoral communities.

This picture is well corraborated by the excavations at Piklihal and Sangankallu (Subbarao, 1948 and 1958, pp. 79-80), where we have stratigraphic evidence for the intrusion of the Chalcolithic communities with painted pottery (black-on-red), a blade industry and a knowledge of metals. These elements can now be derived from the Chalcolithic cultures of Malwa and Maharashtra which have been dated again by C-14 to the 2nd half of the 2nd Millenium B.C. (1500-1,000 B.C. or later) (Ralph, 1959, pp. 45-58).

Unfortunately, the origin of this wide-spread Neolithic culture of Central Deccan eludes us. Yet the close typological relation of the Deccan and the Gangetic valley stone tools suggests that all this belongs to a single complex with the chipped and ground elliptical or ovoid section axe or celt as the type tool of the Indian Neolithic. Into this, what may be called the "Peninsular Neolithic Complex", intrude certain S. E. Asian types associated with shouldered adze with cut sides and square sections. Just now, the relations between these two typological series is not clear. There are three possible alternative hypotheses for the origin of the Indian Neolithic culture:

(1) It might have been derived from the West across the land through the Punjab and Sind. Unfortunately, there are large gaps in our evidence, specially in the absence of any excavation at Neolithic sites in the Gangetic basin or the Eastern India. The excavations at Burzhom may pave the way for such, but as yet there is no absolute chronology (see *Indian Archaeology* 1959-60: *A Review*). Secondly, the burnished grey ware of Burzhom is very tempting to think of parallels for it, very much down in the Deccan. The large unexplored and vast gap in space (nearly 1200 miles) is too evident and it will be a very rash hypothesis indeed. For this we need more evidence from the North and preferably in the Gangetic basin, where we have at least a very closely paralleled stone tool typology.

On the present evidence, if one has to derive from the West, we have to think of a fantastic hypothesis that the polished axe of Deccan represents the substitute for the metal axes, since we do not know of any pure Neolithic Culture in the Indus basin and Western India.

(2) The second hypothesis was put forward by Dr. Eugene Worman (1949). On a pure typological analysis of all the materials, he put forward a view that the Indian Neolithic complex is derived from Eastern Asia. Dr. A. H. Dani (1960) has made an analysis of all the known materials from South East Asia and compared them with those from Eastern India. He has put

forward the hypothesis that the chipped or pecked and ground axe with the lenticular section is the Indian in contrast with the shouldered adze. While the South East Asian specimens are generally sawn (being the copies in stone of the shouldered metal axes) the square section is achieved in Eastern India with chipping or pecking and grinding.

This hypothesis of an eastern origin of the entire Neolithic complex of India requires further study in view of the very early dates of the Peninsular series in Deccan (2000 B.C.). But this raises complicated problems of chronology and we are not in a position to solve the tangle in view of the very unsatisfactory nature of the excavations in the Far East. But this tendency to look West should be reconsidered since we have overwhelming evidence of anthropological and ethnological data to prove strong influences from the East, specially South East.

(3) The last hypothesis, when we exclude the Eastern and the Western is an independent origin in the South. This is almost fantastic, since it is impossible to visualise a neolithic revolution in Central Deccan, or Eastern India independently of Western Asia.

No final solution is available at the present stage of knowledge. But the Neolithic problem can be tackled only by a concerted effort in the southern U.P., Bihar, Bellary and Salem where we have recognisable elements. Once this is done, I am sure, it will fall into a pattern and will throw light on the sub-stratum that went into the make up of the Chalcolithic and higher communities in India, and throw further light on the Neolithic revolution in India.

III

When once we come to the more advanced stages of food production and the beginnings of the emergence of self-sufficient village economy, we witness the most interesting phase of Indian archaeology. More or less coinciding with it, we enter technologically into the Age of Copper and Bronze or Chalcolithic communities. Just as we had the problem of diffusion versus independent origin, we have an equally complex problem. This reminds me of the controversies about the Aryans among our historians in the early years of the 20th century. Some of our scholars were literally aghast at the possibility of deriving the most important component of our Indian culture—the Vedic Aryans—from outside. Slowly we have lived through this controversy and I may be pardoned for raising this problem of the development of higher technology and material culture and their indebtedness to Western Asia again. The broad facts may be stated as follows.

Looking at the historical geography of India, we have already stated that the Indus basin is one of the main foci in the "Afrasian dry-zone" that stretched across North Africa, Western Asia and India. The civilisations that sprang in the Nile, Euphrates and Tigris and the Indus Valleys constitute the results of the great Neolithic revolution that took place in the "Fertile Crescent". There were divergences or localisation of certain ideas. If one may say so, the differences are due to the mutation of some common ideas on different cultural *milieu* and their growth under different physical environments.

In the Indus basin this stage could not have been an independent development in isolation. Nor does the diffusionist hypothesis help us immediately as we have equally significant divergences to balance the affinities. For the present, let us satisfy ourselves with the concept advanced by Sir Mortimer Wheeler—"diffusion of ideas without goods."

The village communities along the eastern border of Iran with Pakistan show close affinities to the early Iranian sites and suggest a strong influence, if not a genetic relation. Similarly our technology is of Western origin. The wide-spread "Chalcolithic Blade Industry" of India had originated in Palestine about 8000 B.C. (Subbarao, 1955-56). Similarly the other traits can be studied. *We may say that the Indus Valley cultures resulted from local acceptance and development of generalized and/or specific traits which could be isolated in the neighbouring focal regions of Western Asia.* This is not the place to go into them.

"The alternative postulate, that in each of the three lands so accessible to one another the immensely complex idea of an evolved civilisation should, within the narrow space of five, six centuries, have emerged spontaneously and without cross reference is too absurd to merit argument." (Wheeler, 1959, pp. 104-5).

Due to historical accidents, the archaeological explorations in India were not directed to the solution of this important problem of the origin of the urban civilisation in the Indus basin. After the partition of the sub-continent, the crucial areas where these could be studied have gone over to Pakistan. Hence in the present stage of our knowledge, we have to wait to define the extent and nature of the traits which the Indus Valley cultures owed to Western Asia.

The most remarkable feature of the Harappan civilisation is the extent of the area over which it spread from the foot-hills of the Himalayas to the Gulf of Cambay and from the Baluchistan to the Gangetic Doab. Recent evidence from Saurashtra and the Sarasvati Valley and Baluchistan certainly point out that there was a great time lag in the development and decay of this great civilisation. In its later stages, it certainly co-existed and overlapped with the later cultures in Central and Eastern India. This inter-relation is one of the most important problems, which are being tackled in India today.

The Harappan civilisation based in the Indus Valley is one among the complex of Proto-historic cultures that emerged in the Indian sub-continent in the 2nd and 3rd millennia before Christ. For a clear understanding of this problem, we have to go into the dynamics of Indian culture. The chief factor is the existence of the areas of retardation of culture due to great physical and physiographic diversity within the sub-continent. With every advance in the technology and the emergence of the stage of food-production, these differences were accentuated to produce a complex pattern of areas of isolation or retardation (hills and forests of the country) in contrast to the fertile river basins with an optimal raintall. The other factor is that of communication, which is regulated again by the physical features. From the openings in the north-west, across the upper courses of the Indus (Punjab plains) to the delta of the Ganges is a constant line of communication. From the Central Gangetic basin (ancient Magadha) to the West coast along the foot of the Vindhyas and Sahyadris is the second recurrent line. Then from the West coast to the east coast along the valleys of the Krishna and Godavary is the third regular channel. Finally from the Krishna basin to the Cauvery basin through the opening of the Nallamalai, north of Madras, is the fourth channel that completes the famous Z-pattern line of communication for the migration of peoples and cultures within the sub-continent. F. J. Richards (1933) had very effectively demonstrated this pattern of national highways on the basis of archaeology and historical geography. This constant communication pattern isolated some more of the regions like Assam, Kashmir, Gujarat, Orissa and Kerala. This facilitated certain survivals and mutual culture relations in time and space. For example, Gujarat is very typical of what we may call areas of relative isolation. It received maritime influences early and continental influences later. So here, Harappan managed to survive in a relatively pure form well into the post-Harappan phases of Northern and Central India.

On account of these diversities of cultures in time and space, it is not possible to treat the entire sub-continent uniformly. Besides, I do not want to go into tedious details. So I propose to give a summary of the entire Proto-historic cultures. To serve as a background, I repeat the earlier phases also.

I. FOOD GATHERING. (Early Stone Age)

Basic semi-parasitic cconomy with no selectivity in food habits—Palaeolithic cultures. Hand-Axe, Cleaver, Chopper-chopping complex (Series I)

II. FOOD COLLECTING (A). (Middle Stone Age)

More skill and selectivity in food habits—appearance of smaller tools and a primitive arrowhead—an Upper Palaeolithic culture type in India—Middle Stone Age or Nevasian of Dr. Sankalia. (Series II)

FOOD COLLECTING (B). (Late Stone Age)

More advanced hunting and fishing stages and probable beginnings of domestication-dogs—collection of seeds and specialised food habits Langhnaj—with a predominantly hunting type of life. Similar cultures of a proven antiquity—Teri, Birbhanpur etc.

III. FOOD PRODUCTION.

In India, due to the problem of survivals and spread in time and space, it is not possible to draw any finer distinction on urbanisation etc. Hence here, "Food Production" is used primarily for the emergence of large-scale agricultural communities. For example C and D really represent urbanisation, but evidence of other concomitants is absent except in the Indus basin.

(1) *Indus Valley*

(a) *More transitional* type with C-14 date at Kili Gul Mohammed comparable to Hassuna-Jarmo technologically. Domesticated Bos etc. No trace of definite food production. (3500 B.C.).

(b) *Self-sufficient village economy* of the Indo-Iranian border village levels with rudiments of irrigation. Gadarbands-Zhob-Ranaghundai-Amri-Nal.

(c) *Incipient urbanisation*—Kot Diji.

(d) *Full fledged urban cultures* with a system of polity and city economy. Mohenjodaro and Harappa, Lothal, Kot Diji and other Harappan settlements of a larger type.

(2) *Central India*

(Malwa) Self-sufficient village economy of the type of III b in the Indus Valley. The knowledge of metals is present, but it is difficult to explain whether they were imported or made locally in view of the known scarcity of raw materials. An incipient urbanisation possible in larger settlements like Nagda, Manoti etc., and also centres of traditional kingdoms mentioned in the Puranas and accounts of Aryan kingdoms like Mahishmati, Tripuri etc.

(3) *Eastern India* (Gangetic Basin)

(a) Basically a neolithic economy with a system of agricultural and pastoral communities occupying the higher foot hills of the Vindhyas—probably like III a, but with Stone Axes indicating heavy forests of the Gangetic valley.

(b) Somewhere into this environment, copper and bronze come in and alter the vital pattern. We see the establishment of riverine sites throughout the Gangetic basin after the clearance of the tropical jungles (Hastinapur I and copper hoards). Probably a third element that went into the make up of the first settlers in the river basin is the surviving Harappan civilisation which overlaps with these in time and space (Kausambi, Alamgirpur).

(4) *Southern India*

(a) Here we have a better picture with Early Agricultural and pastoral communities of the type III (3) (a). C-14 date at Utnoor is 2000 B.C. in the valleys of the Krishna and Godavary (Middle and Lower reaches) more akin to Gangetic valley. (Sangankallu II a)

(b) An interesting junction and culture contact comes between these incipient agricultural communities and self-sufficient village economies of Central India and Maharashtra.

(c) We see this interaction resulting in a fusion with the dominance of the resident traits—Brahmagiri, Maski, Sangankallu IIb and Piklihal Neolithic B (technologically chalcolithic). Allchin (1960).

IV. *Iron Age and the rise of Empires*

(a) The concept of shifting focii of Indian cultures. An early *Primary Urban focus* in the Indus Basin.

(b) The *second shift* to the Indo-Gangetic divide coinciding with the Aryan advent and their self-sufficient village economy—Copper and bronze in technology.

(c) Gradual expansion into the Gangetic basin.

(d) Advent of Iron and consolidation leading to larger political units.—The emergence of Magadha in the 6th century B.C.—The Sixteen Janapadas of Buddhist India.

(e) Iron Age in India probably datable from about 700 B.C. introduces large scale urban economy (specially in the South) and specialisation of labour and craftsmen. A wide spread uniformity in normal pots and pans and other material relics emerges in the whole country—Megalithic cultures of the South. (General life remain the same with difference only in burials).

Thus we can now see the complexity of the development of material culture and growth of civilisation in India, with its problems of survivals and movements in time and space. It is only when we take the dynamic factor, created by differential ecology, that we can understand the differences in the cultural *milieu* of the first large-scale agricultural communities in each of the major river basins of the country. Accepting this fundamental concept of areas of attraction, relative isolation and isolation, the whole pattern of development of material culture in India, may be defined as one of horizontal expansion of the higher cultures, leading to displacement, contraction and isolation of the lower cultures in different parts of the country, at different periods and at different cultural levels. This is the picture as it emerges from recent studies in Indian archaeology (See Fig. on page 116). It is like a crossword puzzle with various interlockers and alternative solutions. But one great lacuna which we in Indian archaeology feel is this: What has the anthropologist got to say in identifying and studying the skeletal remains found in the excavations and their relations with the living people who carry forward the great traditions of our culture today?

IV

This dynamic factor, which recent studies in Indian archaeology are emphasising was conceived earlier by Baron von Eickstedt (1935) in dealing with the anthropological problems of this sub-continent. He envisaged a continuous struggle between the various racial

Development of large-scale agricultural economy in India and Pakistan—
Dotted line

groups, which did not permit any stability of racial conditions. He put it in economic terms when he said:

> "The higher agriculturists are bound by this very cultivation to the fertile alluvial soil; and the primitive hunters and mattock-cultivating people by their primitive economic methods to the poor soil of the woodlands. But when considering the distribution of Indian vegetation, one observes yet a third type of landscape, namely, grass and bush land. It belonged to one, and sometimes to another somatic group. Here lies therefore, the disputable uncertain area between the economic protagonists—the hunters of the woods and the farmers of the plains" (*ibid.*, p. 99).

It is this very instability and fusion of the various components of the people of the sub-continent that has vitiated all attempts at evolving a reasonably acceptable system of classification of the races of India. This cultural synthesis has also produced an ethnic conglomerate, which may be roughly called the Indian. As Bernard Cohn (1957) puts it, "in summary and to push the data to its furthest conclusion, we might say that, even though historically and contemporaneously there is a tremendous diversity physically in India, there is roughly speaking, a physical type which is Indian." Keith, Hooton, Coon and Boyd opined: "in classification of the world's population most recently developed, anthropologists see India's population as forming basically one race with varying sub-stocks, or at best two races (*ibid.*, p. 52).

This complex problem of racial composition of the Indian people has been complicated by the scarcity of studies based on modern and ineradicable traits which could be used to classify the Indian population. As regards the study of the racial composition through the historic and prehistoric past, the problem of the anthropologist is, to a certain extent, similar to that of the archaeologist in trying to differentiate the various elements that went into the make up of the Indian civilisation. So before enumerating the anthropological problems of an archaeologist in India, I wish to give a brief summary of the various systems of classification.

Sir Herbert Risley first gave us a system of classification in 1901 based on language, race and culture which he managed to confuse, ignoring the warning of Max Muller against "the unholy alliance of ethnology and comparative philology". He (1915) divided the Indian people into:

1) Turko-Iranian—Baluchistan, and the N.W.F. in Pakistan.
2) Indo-Aryan—Punjab, Rajputana, and Kashmir.
3) Scytho-Dravidian—Gujarat, S.W. Sind and Bombay.
4) Aryo-Dravidian—U.P., E. Rajputana and Bihar.
5) Mongolo-Dravidian—Bengal and Coastal Orissa.
6) Mongoloid type—Himalayas, Assam, Nepal.
7) Dravidian—Madras, Andhra, Kerala, Madhya Pradesh, Highland Orissa, Southern Bihar, Hyderabad.

This system was modified by Hutton with the Census of 1931. He gave in the order of their supposed arrival.

1) Negritos.
2) Proto-Australoid.
3) Early Mediterranean.
4) Advanced Mediterranean.
5) Armenoids.
6) Alpines.
7) Vedic Aryans.
8) Mongoloids.

His system postulated the movement of all the above racial groups into India at different periods.

This system was further modified by B. S. Guha (1944) who was associated with the Census of 1931. He postulated two types: Aboriginal races (Negrito, Proto-Australoid and Mongoloid and Progressive races (Palae-Mediterranean, Mediterranean, Oriental, Alpo-Dinaric and Nordic.) He examined geographic and cultural regions and on the basis of actual anthropometric data of 2511 individuals, enunciated a system of six races and sub-races distributed as follows:

1) The Negrito: Hills in Travancore, Cochin.
2) The Proto-Australoid: Tribal areas of Central and Southern India.
3) The Mongoloid: consisting of:
   (i) Palaeo-Mongoloids of   (a) long headed type
                                          (b) broad headed type

(ii) Tibeto-Mongoloids
(Himalayan fringes and Assam.)

4) Palae-Mediterranean: (Basic Dolico-cephalic) South India and lower classes in the North.

5) Mediterranean (Indus valley type) Dominant element in N. India.

6) Oriental type: Punjab, Sind, Rajputana and Western U.P.

7) Western Brachy-cephals: South Baluchistan, Sind, Gujarat and Maharashtra.

8) Nordic: North-western India.

Guha's system is the one generally and widely used today. An interesting factor, which Keith pointed out while reviewing the Census Report containing Guha's classification, raises certain important issues of interest to archaeologists as well. Keith questioned the basic assumption that all the racial strains in India moved into a veritable vacuum and he was fascinated by the "anthropological paradise of India" (Keith, 1936). The second criticism that is generally levelled is against the term Proto-Australoid, which took so many things for granted.

This revolt against the emigrant hypothesis of the earlier systems of classification was raised by S. S. Sarkar who in his latest work (1958) has proposed a classification based on the cephalic index and suggested that the people of India are predominantly Dolico-cephalic and consist of three ethnic strains:

I. Dolico-Cephalic:
1. Veddids—autochthenes of India.
2. The Dravidians of South India—evolved out of the hyperdolichocephalic veddids through various ecological changes.
3. Dolicocephalic Indo-Aryans.

II. Meso-cephalic:
Meso-cephalic element followed the Indo-Aryans and this ethnic strain is due to the Indo-Scythians.

III. Brachy-cephalic: from 4 different sources.
1. some-Indo-Scythians.
2. Brachy-cephalic elements from Central Asia.
3. Malayan-coastal regions of Chittagong and Tirunelveli.
4. Mongolian.

The great interest of this system, however, is an attempt to explain the autochthenes of India. But the analysis based on some of the unstable elements and eradicable traits has its pitfalls. Yet, it takes into consideration the inevitable changes that should occur in the vast movements and displacements that have taken place from times immemorial due to what Haddon calls "expulsion and attraction" within the tribal areas of India and on its periphery and also the broader movements within the sub-continent.

Finally, the system suggested by Baron von Eickstedt (1935, pp. 72-73) should be mentioned, since he reveals a greater geographic and ecological awareness than most other writers and takes the dynamic factors into consideration. His classification is also more attractive to the archaeologists. As Aurel Stein (1934) put it aptly "less liable to serious changes than any other factor, the ground can be studied here, as it were in broad day light."

I. Racially primitive people of the jungle region: Ancient Indian or Weddid group, divided into:

1. Dark brown curly (wide curls) haired people; totemistic mattock-using culture with matriarchal influences: Gondid.
2. Black-brown curly (narrow curls) haired people; originally ancient culture with foreign influences.

II. The Racially mixed and dislodged group: Black Indians or Malenids. It is divided into:

1. Black-brown progressive people in the most southern plains with strong foreign matriarchy (now strongly overstratified): South Melenids.
2. Black-brown primitive people of Northern Deccan forests with strong foreign (totemistic and matriarchal) influences: Kolid type.

III. The Racially progressive people of the open regions: New Indians or Indid group. It is divided into:

1. Gracile brown people with enforced patriarchy: Gracile Indid race.
2. Coarser light brown people with possible original patriarchal herdsmanship: North Indid type.

Thus all the systems of classification stated above are based on different criteria and there is a great need for a fresh concerted effort at evolving a system based on the latest techniques. Yet I would like to emphasize the need to bear in mind the dynamics of Indian culture and study the changes that would take place in the movement of a tribe from an adverse to a favourable environment and *vice versa*. The study of the Maler by Sarkar and others is very instructive. Finally, as a lay man, I get the impression that the diverse approaches of the anthropologists in India point again to the pattern based on human geography. The foot hills of the Himalayas including the valleys of Brahmaputra and the Central Indian forest zones serve as a refuge zone for the stagnant elements of the Indian population, while the more dynamic elements occupy the major river basins. In view of this, one feels impelled to ask, Is there any justification for the differentiation of the progressive and the backward races in this sub-continent (see Subbarao, 1958, p. 144). As the present writer has stated elsewhere, some of them missed the bus on the road to progress and have survived at different cultural and economic stages. After all, they may provide the clue to the racial history of India better than the mixed societies of the Plains.

V

The problems which an archaeologist faces in India are twofold as far as Indian anthropology is concerned. One is that of physical anthropology—the study of the fossil skeletal material (in a wider sense including those of recent historic communities). It is in this field, that there is scope for the maximum degree of co-operation between the two disciplines. The second is the problem of the more conventional ethnology, or study of the material culture of the various communities in an attempt to understand and correlate living and fossil communities. In spite of an unavoidable determinism behind the concepts of the *kulturkreise* school of thought, this type of approach is paying great dividends to the archaeologist in his quest for understanding the life of the various communities, whose material relics he unravels.

Coming to the problem of human palaeontology, we are in a very unfortunate plight. Inspite of the tons of Palaeoliths lying in the various museums of India, we have not yet succeeded in getting any human remains of any of our Stone Ages—Early (Lower Palaeolithic of Europe) or Middle (Middle and Upper Palaeolithic). This is supremely important in view of the vast development of studies in Africa. Here, Dart and his colleagues in South Africa and Leakey in East Africa have been producing fossil evidence for the evolution of Man on the African continent. With the closing of the gap between ape and the man (see Dart, 1959, p. 228), and the fine studies of Oakley on the evolution of the Human skull (*see* in Singer and Hall, 1954, pp. 1-38), the African evidence on the evolution of the Man and his Culture cannot be overlooked. How is the Indian related to the African? On top, we have the classic section of Leakey in the Olduvai Gorge in East Africa. In view of all this and the great affinities between the Indian and African Stone Ages, the problem of the origin of the Indian Stone Age is very urgent and calls for some cooperation. Now we know that the Early Stone Age man lived throughout the sub-continent in almost all the river basins.

Equally uncertain and vague is the problem of the second series of stone implements, which the present author has termed 'Middle Stone Age' to avoid the confusion by implication with the European Palaeolithic series. Archaeologically, we see a complete change of raw materials from the coarse grained quartzite to the fine grained series of cherts, jaspers etc. with a few exceptions in the Kurnool district of Andhra. Does this industry of flake, flake-blade, scraper, and borer etc. represent a new immigration? The evolution of tool typology is widely divergent in the Upper Palaeolithic all over the world. According to Prof. Zeuner, there is a non-descript industry of this type in the Jordan valley and in the interior of Palestine, inspite of the classic sequence of a Mediterranean series akin to Europe at Mt. Carmel. Similarly in East Africa we have allied industries. Does it all mean another migration or a local development from the Lower Palaeolithic series of India? This industry has an equally wide distribution. Here again, fossil human evidence is missing and requires a concerted effort of the archaeologist and the anthropologist.

We come to the next phase, the Late Stone Age, or the Mesolithic (microlithic series of Europe and Africa). I do not know whether our anthropologists have realised the implications of their classifications. According to Sarkar (1958, p. 22) the aboriginal races of India belong to the Veddid strain and on account of their resemblances to the Australian aboriginals, they have been described as the Australoid. The evidence from Australia in this connection is very interesting and calls for a fresh thinking on our part. According to

Keilor, *Homo Sapiens* reached Australia very early. According to Prof. Zeuner (1959, p. 281), "there is other evidence for even greater antiquity for the Australian aborigines and that they are contemporary with the extinct giant marsupials and the dingo (13,725 $+$ 350 *B.P.*). As Aiyappan (1945) puts it,"several of our cultural impulses have had enough time to travel round the world." There are very widespread microlithic industries in the old world—Africa, Asia and Australia which show great affinities in technique and typology, allowing for a few variations (*see* B. Allchin, 1957, pp. 115-36 and 1958). For example, East Africa, Ceylon and Australia show bi-facial points in their microlithic industries, while South Arabia (Hadhramouth) and the main Indian peninsula excluding the southernmost tip of the country (Teri region), have an asymmetrical point to compensate for it (*see* Zeuner, 1952). As the earliest cultures of Australia and of Ceylon are microlithic in character, what happens to the Pre-Australoid racial strains in India? Have they become extinct or have they merged with the Australoid and other later races?

In India, the only microlithic site that has produced skeletal material is Langhnaj in North Gujarat. Dr. Erhardt is now making a study of these remains and the preliminary studies of Mrs. Karve show that there is a primitive negroid strain in it.

The other complication which results from the problem of survival of the earlier cultures among our tribes, is serious enough. As already said we have a core of bottle glass from Mahableshwar and there are a chain of Microlithic sites on the fringes of the Aravallis and the Western Ghats right upto Calicut on the west coast. Since we have pottery using and non-pottery microlithic industries, it is not unreasonable to presume a survival of some of the microlithic industries in some of the backward areas of the country.

When we pass on from the Stone Ages into the Chalcolithic and other higher cultures, we have some skeletal material. For example, the skeletal material from Mohenjodaro already attests to the presence of the following elements:

1) Australoid.
2) the Mediterranean.
3) Mongolian branch of the Alpine stock and
4) Alpine.

This miscegenation is understandable, on account of the cultural and commercial contacts of the Indus Valley people. Besides, recent archaeological work has abundantly shown that the Harappan civilisation did not become extinct, but was co-existing (influencing and absorbing) with the non-Harappan elements. We hope the skeletal material lying with the Anthropological Survey of India from Harappa and other sites will see the light of the day and help us understand the various race movements.

Though chronologically later in time, the most interesting materials are the skeletal remains from Nevasa. Unfortunately Dr. Erhardt has simply catalogued the material without any comparative study, or even a suggestion of the racial stock (see Sankalia et. al., 1960, pp. 506-23). Hence this does not lead us anywhere. Still we await the publication of the chalcolitic skeletal material from the burials of Brahmagiri.

In this connection, I would like to state the problem of the Dravidians and the Megaliths, and the controversy started by Prof. Von Furer-Haimendorf. As in the previous cases, the key to the solution lies in the large number of human remains from the megalithic monuments at Brahmagiri, Sanur, and Nagarjunakonda, now with the Anthropological Survey of India. Professor Von Furer-Haimendorf sought to make a distinction between the megalithic monuments of South India, belonging to the Iron Age and the living megalithic and associated cults of Central and Eastern India. Since the known distribution of the historic megaliths coincides with that of the Dravidian speakers, he inferred that the megalithic builders of South India were the Dravidians. It is the same old error of linking of race with the language. The recent archaeological work in India takes us to the same position as that of Europe, where a burial complex or megalithic idea influenced various communities with different cultural assemblages giving rise to different grave goods in what looked like a single burial complex[1]. Now for the megaliths of South India, the two most essential components of the grave goods: black-and-red pottery and iron, infiltrated southwards from a non-megalithic context. Thus a typical Iron Age culture of Central and Western India and Northern Deccan manages to spread into South India and their burial system is the megalithic type.

The second difficulty is the great time lag between the megalithic monuments of Europe and the Mediterranean and those of South

India—a gap of 1000 to 1500 years. Only two possible alternatives are available. If the move is terrestrial and from the west, it has to be derived from the Cairn burials of Western Pakistan and Baluchistan and those from the Luristan region. In that case, by the time the megalithic idea penetrates into Central and Southern India, the Iron Age assemblage of Black-and-red Ware and Iron provide the grave goods.

The second hypothesis is based on the suggestion of Dr. Aiyappan (1945, p. 184) connecting the living megalithic cults and rituals of Eastern India with the older ones in and those of South-east Asia and Polynesia. I would quote here Dr. Sunitikumar Chatterjee (1951, p. 148):

"After the Melanesian and Polynesian types in ethnology and language came to be established, it would appear that there were back-washes of immigration of Malenesians and Polynesians into India, which brought in new cultural contributions from these peoples . . . . From the Melanesians, the custom of the disposal of the dead by exposure, communal houses, head-hunting and a canoe cult appear to have been introduced into India."

Alphonse Reisenfield (1952, p. 642) in his great work has given us full accounts of these megalithic cultures of Melanesia. According to him *Vierkentbeil* (Square Axe) is associated with the megalithic cultures. Dr. Aiyappan (1945, p. 181) has already given us parallels to the famous Ram Sarcophagus from Sankavaram, Dt. Cuddapa, Andhra Pradesh from Java and Bali. The typical tripod vessels of Porkalam (see Thapar, 1948, p. 146) suggested to the Late Gordon Childe a far eastern origin.[2]

It is here that the anthropologist can help the archaeologist. A suggestion has been made that the authors of the introduction of the Megalithic cult into India from the East, are the Palae-Mongoloid Gadabas, Bondos etc. Probably they are the communities referred to by Sunitikumar Chatterji in the passage quoted above, as the youth dormitories and community houses were introduced by the Palae-Mongoloid.[3] This is a field which cannot be left to any single discipline and co-operation of the anthropologist and the archaeologist is a great desideratum.

There are two more prominent migrations into this sub-continent which have been recognised by the anthropologists; the major movement of the Indo-Aryans and the minor movement of the Indo-Scythians, the element responsible for the Meso-cephalny in Western India. About the Aryans, I may state our problem. These were pastoral communities who moved into highly populated regions. They could only be distinguished by their languages and a literature as in India, but their distinctive material contribution is very difficult to dignose. The Saka-Kushana rule in Western India and the extension of the Sassanian rule into North-western and Western India provide the means and semi-arid Sind and Rajasthan gave the Indo-Scythians a chance to develop their distinctive artistic traditions. The recent discovery of the Rang-mahal culture with its highly artistic pottery and their terracottas, belonging to the early centuries of the Christian era is very significant and the continuity of their dress and ornaments makes it easy for us to recognise them.

These racial movements in time and space have produced a complicated pattern. Yet in terms of languages, they have left us in all four groups of languages: Indo-Aryan, Dravidian, Austro-Asiatic and Sino-Burman. It is now admitted on all hands that the Dravidian languages have exercised a strong influence on Sanskrit "from the Vedic downwards." This is very significant and speaks of the Pre-Aryan elements in the country. Similarly Dr. Schaffer has shown that the name *Ganga* for the Ganges is itself Sino-Burman.[4] Similarly he derives the names of the five kindred groups of Sudyumnas who are described as Mlechchas, from the Tibeto-Burman or Indo-Burman group:

Anga . . . An
Vanga . . . Wan or Van
Kalinga . . . Klin or Klin
Suhma . . . Suh-ma

This is very important, as the linguists tell us that from the earliest stages the Vedic Sanskrit shows foreign influences—Dravidian as well as Austric. The word Ganga occurs in the *Rigveda* itself. Does it not indicate that one of the earlier sub-strata in the Gangetic basin are an eastern people already in the 2nd millenium B.C. This is again an example of the value of linguistics and the need for concerted studies. In this connection, I quote below an extract from Gates (1948, p. 339):

"The full Neolithic is less known than this pre-Neolithic, but there is evidence that the Neolithic population of Java was relatively dense. Heine-Geldern believes that the southeastern Asiatics (Austronesians), already having considerable Mongoloid mixture which had come down into Assam and Burma, migrated westwards into India and introduced the tanged adze between 2500 and 1500 B.C. before the Aryan invasion. Percy Smith (1921) recognises a Gangetic race in northern India before the Aryan invasion. He believes that a Himalayo-Polynesian race, allied to the Chinese and Tibetan, formerly spread over the Gangetic basin from further India."

Rice is believed to have originated in the Far East. Hastinapur has provided the earliest dated specimens of rice in India (see Lal, 1955, p. 131).

VI

The other aspect of anthropology which concerns the archaeologist is methodology. Being an allied discipline dealing with Man as the theme, archaeology draws heavily on anthropology. While the anthropologist deals with the living communities, the archaeologist tries to study the extinct communities, represented by their material relics, which symbolise fossilised human behaviour. There exactly lies the limitation of archaeology, because the living centre of human activity, namely the mind is absent and hence he is left to guess. In this attempt, he draws heavily on ethnology and uses the knowledge gained by the study of the life and behaviour of living communities—particularly of people who are historically backward and in earlier stages of civilisation. For example, the tool techniques of the Stone Age Man could only be understood in relation to the stone-using communities of primitive Australian aboriginals and other tribal groups in the Pacific Ocean.

The basic concept is one of evolutionary patterns or culture stages. For example, Professor Von Furer-Haimendorf (1948) has drawn a picture of the aboriginal population of Deccan into what he called "Cultural Strata". This is very essential in India, as our pattern of culture development falls in between that of Europe and Australasia. While there were dynamic and continuous changes in culture development in the former, the latter had witnessed a cultural stagnation and isolation, till it was broken by the Colonial movements of the 18th and 19th centuries. In India, on the other hand, the great diversity in the physical and physiographic features from dense tropical and sub-tropical jungles to large fertile river basins, has enabled a hormonious co-existence of the different strata of cultures in different environments. Thus while we have the non-agricultural food-gathering communities in Chenchus and Kadars, a near Neolithic type of primitive agriculture is represented by the Reddis. We have tribes in Central India with high material culture, metallurgy, social institutions and rituals. At the other end of the scale, we have a continuous growth of higher cultures and technology in the major river basins of the country. Owing to the vast size of the sub-continent and fixed pattern of communication system, there was a slow eastward and southward movement of cultures based on large scale agriculture and technology. Thus we have vast developments in time and space of over 3000 years from the early farmers and city dwellers of the Indus basin in the 4th and 3rd millenium B.C. to the Iron Age village and town sites of the Cauvery basin associated usually with the Megalithic culture (about 500 B.C.). Yet even today there are environmentally backward areas of repulsion where primitive tribes live in different economic stages of life without the benefits of large scale agricultural production and its socio-economic impacts.

It is this complexity that calls for a concerted effort in India. The archaeologist has a unique opportunity to work in collaboration with the anthropologist in trying to understand the various strata or stages of the evolution of the Indian culture and find possibly in our tribal populations, living representatives of the earlier stages.

VII

Finally I would like to end this essay on Archaeology and Anthropology with a renewed plea for co-operation. Anthropologists find in India a paradise and a field for study of the large number of movements of races and sub-races which have contributed to the development of the Indian type. Similarly archaeology, specially during the last decade, has produced a story of a widely distributed and uniform cultures in the Pre-agricultural "food gathering phases". Significantly the differences emerge with the Neolithic and later phases, where we have an evidence of horizontal spread in time and space from two primary foci—an active and easily accessible one in Western Asia and the other but less known from the Far East. Only we seem to have neglected the Eastern influences. A close study of migrations and the historical events that surround these movements provide a set of subcultural historical continua for the various regions of India. What is needed in this great quest for discovery of our past is the willing cooperation of the archaeologist, the anthropologist, the linguist and the historian with the technical assistance of the natural and physical scientists in identifying the authors of the various cultures that moved into this subcontinent.

NOTES

[1] "On the coast of Atlantic, the North sea and the Baltic, megalithic tombs exhibit a continuous distribution in space. But they do not disclose a single culture in the usual sense of a complex of traits—similar pottery, tools, weapons and ornaments regularly recurring together in these tombs and not in other sepulchral associations. Only one class of pottery, the so-called Beakers, is at all often found in these tombs all over the province." Childe concludes his provocative summary with the remark that, "the quest for any megalithic circle culture is much less promising than for a tomb complex" (Childe, 1947-48, pp. 6 and 13).

[2] In a personal communication dated 27th January, 1957, during his visit to India before his tragic death, Childe wrote to me:

"These tripods from Porkalam look very Chinese. (I noticed this at Calcutta), and must I reflect sea-borne Chinese influence on S. India? I do not know off hand where you will most readily find pictures. Menghin—*Weltgeschte der Steingert* and many volumes of the *Bulletin*, Museum of Far Eastern Antiquities, Stocholm are full of them.'

[3] A casual suggestion has been given by Professor Furer-Haimendorf in a letter for which I am very grateful.

[4] "These geographical names lead to the conclusion that a Sino-Tibetan people or peoples had pushed west and had occupied the Gangetic Valley, the richest part of Madhyadesa . . . . ' (Schaffer 1955, p. 14).

REFERENCES

AIYAPPAN, A., 1945, "The Megalithic cultures of Southern India" in *Proceedings of the 32nd Indian Science Congress, pt.* 2. Nagpur, *Ancient India* 1959-60: A Review. New Delhi.

ALLCHIN, Bridget, 1957, 'Australian Stone Industries, Past and Present' in *J.R.A.I.*, Vol. 87, pt. 1.

1958, 'The Late Stone Age of Ceylon in *JRAI*, vol. 88, Pt. 2.

ALLCHIN, F. R., 1957, 'The Neolithic Stone Industry of the North Karnataka Region in *Bull. of the Sch. of oriental and African Studies*, Vol. XIX, No. 2.

ALLCHIN, F. R. 1960, Piklihal Excavations, Andhra Pradesh Government Archaeological Series. I. Hyderabad (Dn).

CHATTERJI, S. K., 1951, 'Race Movements and Prehistoric Culture in *The Vedic Age*. London.

CHILDE, V. G., 1947-48, 'Megaliths in *Ancient India* No. 4.

COHN, B., 1957, 'India as a Racial, Linguistic and Cultural Area' in *Introducing India in Liberal Education* ed. by Milton Singer. Proceeding of a conference held at Chicago in May 1957.

DANIC, A. H., 1960, *Prehistory and Protohistory of Eastern India*. Calcutta.

DART, Raymond A., 1959, *Adventures with the Missing Link*. London.

EICKSTEDT, Baron von, 1935, 'The Position of Mysore in India's Social History in the *Mysore Tribes and Castes*, Vol. I, Mysore.

FURER-HAIMENDORF, C. von., 1948, 'Culture Strata in Deccan in *Man*, Vol. 48, Art 96.

GATES, R. R., 1948, *Human Ancestry*. Harvard.

GUHA, B. S., 1944, *Racial Elements in the Population*. Oxford pamphlets Bombay.

HUTTON, J. H., 1935, *Census of India*, 1931. Vol. I.

KEITH, Arthur, 1936.

LAL, B. B., 1955, 'Excavations at Hastinapura and other Explorations in the Upper Ganga and Sutlej Basins 1950-52' in *Ancient India*, Nos. 10 and 11. New Delhi.

MALIK, S. C., 1959, *Stone Age Industries of Bombay and Satara Districts* Baroda.

RALPH, Elizabeth K., 1959, 'University of Pennsylvania Radio Dates III in *Amer. J. of Science, Radio Carbon Suplement*, Vol. I.

REISENFIELD, Alphonso, 1952, *The Megalithic Cultures of Melanesia*, Leiden.

RICHARDS, F. J., 1933, 'Geographical Factors in Indian Archaeology' in *Indian Antiquary*, Vol. LXII.

RISLEY, H. H., 1915, *People of India*. Calcutta.

SANKALIA, H. D., *et al.*, 1961, *From History to Prehistory at Nevasa*. Poona.

SARKAR, S. S., 1958, 'Race and Race Movements in India' in *Cultural Heritage of India*, vol. I, Calcutta.

SCHAFFER, Robert., 1955, *Ethnography of Ancient India*: Wiesbaden (Germany).

SINGER, HOLMYARD and HALL (Eds.), 1954, *A History of Technology*, Vol. I Oxford.

STEIN, Aurel., 1934, 'The Indo-Iranian Borderlands . Huxley Mem. Lect. Vol. 64.

SUBBARAO, B., 1948, *Stone Age Cultures of Bellary*. Poona.

1955-56, 'Chalcolithic Blade Industry of Maheshwar and a note on the history of the technique in *Bull. of the Deccan College Research Institute*, Vol. XVII.

SUBBARAO, B., 1958, *The Personality of India*: Pre and proto-historic Foundations of India and Pakistan, Second Ed. Baroda.

THAPER, B. K., 1948, 'Porkalam in *Ancient India*, No. 8.

1957, I Maski 1954—A Chaleolithic site of Central Deccan in *Ancient India*, No. 13.

WHEELER, R. E. M., 1947, 'Brahmagiri and Chandrawalli, 1947 in *Ancient India*, No. 4.

1959, *Early India and Pakistan*. London.

WARMAN, Eugene G., 1949, 'Neolithic Problem in the Prehistory of India' in *Jour. of the Wash. Acad. of Sciences*, Vol. XXXI.

ZEUNER, E. F., 1952, 'The Microlithic Industry of Langhnaj' in *Man*, Vol. 52, Art, 82.

1959, *Dating the Past*. Fourth Ed. London.

1960, 'On the origin of the Cinder mounds of Bellary District, India' in *Bull. of the Inst. of Archaeo.*, No. 2, 1959.

Physical Anthropology

5

SOME OBSERVATIONS ON ANTHROPOMETRIC SURVEYS

C. RADHAKRISHNA RAO

Introduction

HAVING collaborated with the late Dr. D. N. Majumdar in the analysis and interpretation of data collected by him in two large-scale anthropometric surveys (Mahalanobis, Majumdar and Rao 1949, Majumdar and Rao 1959 and 1960). I feel it is my duty to make some observations on a subject which was nearest to his heart. It is said that the scientific worker is reluctant to consult a statistician in planning his experiments for collection of data and/or for statistical analysis of data lest the latter may claim co-author-ship in the publication of the results. This problem was seriously raised and discussed in a scientific meeting during one of the sessions of the Indian Science Congress—a suspicion which may be genuine but a situation which is unfortunate. Dr. Majumdar set an example by inviting the collaboration of statisticians in the large-scale anthropometric projects undertaken by him and demonstrated that much fruitful work was possible by such collaboration.

Dr. Majumdar, by his untiring efforts, had provided comparable data on groups of people in a number of states in northern India and he had plans to cover the other states also. Unaware of the difficulties of field workers, his statistical collaborators were extremely critical of very minor errors in the recorded data, but Dr. Majumdar accepted these somewhat unfair criticisms in a true scientific spirit. His collaboration with the statisticians has also led to some research in statistical multivariate analysis. His untimely death is indeed a great blow to the future of anthropometry in India.

Standardisation of anthropometric technique

Physical anthropologists have, often, to study differences between groups of individuals measured by different observers, or by the same observer at different points of time. For this purpose, it is necessary to examine whether the measurements taken by different observers or at different points of time by the same observer are comparable or not. The importance of this was first pointed out by Mahalanobis in a remarkable paper, in 1928. It was shown how even leading anthropologists all over the world had differed in the definition and technique of measurements of important anthropological characters, with the result that about 80 per cent of the material was not comparable.

It is, indeed, unfortunate that a chaotic state of affairs exist even now, in spite of international agreements on the technique of measurements. Apart from the demands of scientific discipline, since public money is usually expended in the collection of material for comparative studies, anthropological investigators have an obligation to make serious attempts to remove this limitation. I shall give a few examples of differences between investigators from recent anthropometric surveys (Guha 1931, Majumdar 1950, Karve and Dandekar 1951, Karve 1954 and the reports cited in the opening sentence above), to show the confusion they have led to and how an excellent opportunity of comparing groups of people living in different parts of India has been lost.

For instance, Karve adopted the following definitions of Nasal height, Upper facial height and Facial height:

Nasal height—From the sellion to the sub nasal, the sellion being determined as the most depressed part at the root of the nose in the median sagittal plane.
Upper facial height—From sellion to prosthion.
Facial height—From sellion to gnathion.

Majumdar took these measurements from the nasion instead of sellion to the other points mentioned in the above definitions. The nasion is above the sellion and therefore Majumdar's measurements of these characters are expected to be larger than those of Karve. Not aware of such differences in the techniques followed by Majumdar and Karve, the authors of a report write, 'In the U.P. sample (measured by Majumdar) the Nasal length varies from 47 to 52 m.m. Thus the nasal length is somewhat larger than the Maharashtra sample (measured by Karve) with an effective range of 45 to 50 m.m.' The average difference between nasion and sellion is of the order of 2 m.m. and when an adjustment for differences in technique is made, it is seen that there is no difference between Maharashtra and U.P. samples so far as the Nasal length is concerned.

Again comparing the samples of Maharashtra and Gujarat (measured by Majumdar) the authors say, 'The nasal index here (Gujrat) is definitely lower than that for the Maharashtra sample'. Part of this difference could be explained by the larger Nasal length according to the technique followed by Majumdar. There are also differences in the definitions of Auricular height adopted by Karve and Majumdar.

Guha seems to have followed the technique advocated by the international agreement of 1909 *with a few modifications*, (perhaps his own). One point of difference between Guha and Majumdar seems to be that the former used *slight* amount of pressure in measurements like head length, breadth etc., whereas the latter in his definition of head length mentions that 'care was taken that no pressure was exerted'. In many reports and papers on anthropometric investigations, the authors have, unfortunately, made no mention of the technique of measurement followed. This practice should be seriously discouraged. Further, the authors should publish the original measurements along with their report, for this may be the only redeeming feature in case something has gone wrong with the author's summary of the data or his conclusions are drawn on the basis of incomplete or incorrect analysis.

There are some measurements like stature which are subject to diurnal variations. For instance, in an experiment conducted at the Indian Statistical Institute, it was found that, on the same individual, the morning stature is about 9.6 m.m. longer than the evening stature. Further experiments revealed that elongation takes place in the main trunk of the body when we sleep, but it is not known whether there is any period of the day when the stature is stable. If not, the situation is somewhat serious as the measurements of stature taken at two different times of the day may not be comparable. It may therefore be necessary to specify the time at which stature is taken.

Weight is another character which may not be suitable for comparative purposes. This is evident from the definition of weight given by Majumdar.

Weight of the subjects was taken in plain clothes, without the shoes, and an allowance of 2 lbs. was made for clothes. The dress of the various groups measured differed from caste to caste, some put on *pugris*, others like Khasas put on heavy woollen coats and trousers, but the subjects were persuaded to remove unnecessary apparels and thus with the deduction of 2 lbs., the weights were reduced to nude weights. There is no likelihood of arriving at precision with regard to this measurement as the effect of a heavy stomach could not be estimated and weights taken at different times of the day may not be comparable.

Age is difficult to ascertain in most cases and the ages recorded in published reports are probably what have been guessed by the investigator, and it may not be known to what extent they are in error. But age is not relevant if all the individuals measured have reached *adulthood*, a stage beyond which no appreciable change takes place in the characters under consideration. It may not be difficult to ascertain by some means, whether the individual selected is an adult or not for inclusion in the sample. Of course, in any case, there is some advantage in recording the age as reported by the subject or as inferred by the investigator based on some information supplied by the subject.

Some characters like weight may not reach stability but vary systematically with age even upto old age. In Europe it was found that the mean weight increases by about 4 k.g. between 20 and 40 years of age. In Japan the variation was found to be of a smaller order. We have no accurate information on weight changes during adulthood of Indians but, perhaps, it is not negligible. Mean weights of groups of individuals are, thus, strictly comparable only when the age composition of individuals in the different groups are the same. *In Race Elements of Bengal*, the authors found that even the Total face length (TFL) exhibits a similar phenomenon although the magnitude of variation is small, with respect to the *recorded age*. To what extent this is due to regression of TFL on *true age* has to be investigated.

Investigator bias

Even if the technique of measurements is standardised, differences between observers can arise in the interpretation of the definitions. Slight errors are bound to occur in the location of various points such as the gnathion, sellion etc. Two observers measuring the same individual or the same observer measuring an individual on two different occasions will generally provide observations differing to a certain extent depending on the complexity of the measurement. This is not, however, serious if errors contain no bias. On the other hand, errors may be of systematic types specific to observers, in which case measurements taken by different observers are not strictly comparable. Such systematic errors may be corrected to a large extent by a proper training of the investigators.

This is important specially when an anthropometric project employs more than one investigator. The differences between investigators and the sets of instruments they use have to be carefully examined before starting the field work by well-designed experiments in the laboratory. An example of such a laboratory experiment with reference to anthropometric measurements has been given in *Race Elements of Bengal* on page 296. The idea is similar to the investigation of differences between observers in large-scale sample surveys, numerous examples of which are contained in a paper by Mahalanobis (1946).

The ideal rule to be followed in such experiments (although more complicated designs have been used) is that the same subject should be measured by all the investigators preferably with all the duplicate sets of instruments intended to be used in the survey, at least twice allowing some time gap between repeated measurements. It is important that the investigator does not remember the previous value while repeating the measurement, which can be ensured to some extent by using a different person to record the values and allowing sufficient time between repeated measurements while keeping the investigator engaged in other measurements during the interval. The analysis of data may be undertaken on the lines indicated in appendix S. 3 of *Race Elements of Bengal*. Differences between observers which are not likely to affect the results of investigation may be ignored. But in the case of larger differences, it is necessary to examine the nature of discrepancies. It may be possible that by further training and practice, differences could be narrowed down to negligible limits.

Two anthropologists A, B, both trained in the same anthropometric technique, during the same period by a well-known anthropologist, and who had at least 2 years of field experience were asked to take a number of measurements independently on each of 23 students of a class, in the year 1957. The measurements were taken with the same set of instruments and the values were recorded by a third person. There were huge differences between A, B in a few cases (3 out of 300 recorded values); the individual values being 142, 121 for Bizygomatic breadth, 94, 114 for Bigonial breadth, and 804, 864 for Sitting height. These may be considered as recording or reading errors. Assuming the differences to be zero in these three cases, the distribution of the difference A-B (in m.m.) for each of the 12 characters considered is examined as in Table 1.

TABLE 1

CHARACTERISTICS OF THE DISTRIBUTION OF DIFFERENCE (A-B) in m.m. BASED ON n=23 VALUES

character	mean difference		max. diff.	min. difl.	distribution of 23 differences		
	actual $\pm$ s.e.	absolute			—ve	o	+ve
1. Max Head length (HL)	.4783 $\pm$ .2658	1.0000	2	—3	3	8	12
2. Max. Head breadth (HB)	.7826 $\pm$ .4072	1.3913	4	—5	3	8	12
3. Least Frontal bredth (FB)	—.3043 $\pm$ 1.2978	1.0000	2	—4	9	8	6
4. Bizygomatic breadth (BzB)	—.2609 $\pm$ .1689	.4348	1	—3	6	15	2
5. Bigonal breadth (BgB)	—1.4348 $\pm$ .2252	1.4348	0	—4	19	4	0
6. Total facial length (TFL)	—.7391 $\pm$ .3731	1.6087	2	—4	14	3	6
7. Upper facial length (UFL)	1.7391 $\pm$ .4499	2.0870	7	—3	2	6	15
8. Nasal length (NL)	.5652 $\pm$ .3004	1.2609	2	—3	4	4	15
9. Nasal breadth (NB)	—.6957 $\pm$ .2031	.9565	1	—2	14	6	3
10. Nasal depth (ND)	.6522 $\pm$ .2712	1.0000	4	—2	3	9	11
11. Sitting height (SH)	—10.78261 $\pm$ .8575	13.9130	5	—28	22	0	1
12. Stature (St)	—2.34781 $\pm$ .0828	4.3478	6	—17	17	0	6

It may be seen that A's values are generally smaller than B's for BgB, TFL, NB, SH and St, indicating statistically significant observer's bias. The actual discrepancies may not be considered serious except in the case of SH, where some further probe is necessary. Let us now examine the differences between the measurements taken by the same anthropologist on the same subjects at two different points of time.

Anthropologist A repeated his measurements on 4 subjects in 1961 after the lapse of 4 years, which are given in Table 2. The large differences between the 1957 and 1961 measurements on the

TABLE 2

DATA ON FOUR SUBJECTS MEASURED BY A IN 1957 AND AGAIN IN 1961

character	subject 1 1957	subject 1 1961	subject 2 1957	subject 2 1961	subject 3 1957	subject 3 1961	subject 4 1957	subject 4 1961
HL	193	194	193	196	181	183	171	173
HB	147	148	144	146	143	143	151	152
FB	111	111	103	104	105	105	100	101
BzB	140	140	133	135	130	130	132	135
BgB	101	101	100	104	93	95	100	100
TFL*	117	125	124	127	114	122	121	121
UFL*	71	78	72	74	70	77	74	79
NL*	56	60	52	55	56	58	56	61
NB	40	41	39	40	41	41	32	33
ND	18	18	19	18	16	16	14	14
SH	873	872	876	868	804	791	845	838
St.	1706	1705	1701	1706	1578	1574	1610	1619

* Indicates characters with a large difference between '57 and '61 measurements.

same individual in TFL, UFL and NL deserve our very serious attention. The differences are of a much larger order than those between A and B on the same individual in 1957. All the subjects were adults in 1957, about the age of 21 and to what extent the higher values for 1961 could be attributed to growth cannot be easily settled. An increase in musculature and fat content over the four-year period is likely to result in a small increase in TFL and BzB but not perhaps in UFL and NL.

Has A changed his technique of measuring these facial characters? If we were comparing two groups of people, one measured in 1957 and another in 1961 by the same anthropologist A the conclusions regarding the differences in facial characters might have been fallacious. I do not suggest that one should lose confidence in anthropometric work faced with situations such as the above. On the other hand, one should accept such discrepancies as a normal feature and take appropriate precautions. A solution would be to have some test subjects on whom the field anthropologist could periodically take measurements to examine and maintain his own consistency.

Recently, I had the opportunity of meeting two Indian anthropologists (to be designated as C and D) who are engaged on a project to study the differences between the measurements of Anglo Indians, Bengalis and Europeans resident in Bengal. At my request they independently measured subjects 3 and 4 with the same instruments used by A. The following figures relate to the measurements of sitting height and stature as observed by the anthropologists A, C, and D in 1961 and by A in 1957.

	Subject 3				Subject 4			
	A	A	C	D	A	A	C	D
	(1957)	(1961)	(1961)	(1961)	(1957)	(1961)	(1961)	(1961)
SH	804	791	820	815	845	838	845	868
ST	1578	1574	1590	1586	1610	1619	1624	1623

I imagine that stature will be one of the important characters which the anthropologists would like to examine in a study of race mixture. The differences between observers seem to be much larger than what may exist between communities under study. Some caution is needed if measurements taken by different anthropologists have to be used in such studies.

To sum up, the anthropometric technique, as followed now, involves considerable difficulties and, judged by the criteria of inter and intra observer consistency, its use in scientific investigations appears to be somewhat limited. An alternative is photogrammetry which is more convenient for field work; the subject has to be photographed on the field in a specified way and all measurements carried out on the photograph at leisure in the laboratory. This will eliminate the errors of measurement and recording and also the strain to which both the subject and the investigator are put. A large number of individuals can be included in the sample by following this technique, for the same cost or time. The photographs will create a more permanent record available for checking the previous observations and for further research. Several years ago this suggestion was put forward by Mahalanobis, (1943) who also designed a profiloscope for obtaining the facial profiles. Some more research is urgently needed in this direction and also in developing the photographic method for obtaining depth measurements.

Specification of the universe sampled

The inference drawn from a sample is strictly limited to the group of individuals from which the sample can be considered to be chosen at random. It is therefore necessary for an investigator to clearly define the group of individuals under study and lay down the rules adopted in choosing a sample. The analysis of Bengal anthropometric data and other available material has revealed regional differences within a state far more significant than caste, tribal or religious affilations. If so, descriptions of groups such as Brahmins of Bengal or Andhra without any reference to the regions from which the individuals are selected, as mentioned in many previous reports on anthropometric surveys, must be misleading. The physical characteristics may also depend on the economic condition of individuals, in which case it is necessary to specify the economic status. For instance, students of different communities, studying in a university may not show any marked difference in some physical characteristics like the stature, 'belonging as they do to rich and middle classes, commonly styled as Bhadraloks and not reflecting the conditions prevalent among the rest of the population'.

Often vital information is withheld from reports purporting to present a strictly scientific study and thus vitiate the usefulness of the conclusions drawn. It is, therefore, essential that investigators should put on record complete details of the localities visited and groups of individuals selected for measurement. The samples of individuals with the same caste or religious affinities but belonging to different localities and different economic classes may be pooled at the stage of statistical analysis if no significant differences are found.

The specification of the population sampled becomes particularly difficult in dealing with skeletal remains of fossils. Does the sample drawn from the preserved material represent the *general population* to which they belong? Or in other words, do the characteristics of the preserved material differ from those of the population to which they originally belonged? Unless this question is satisfactorily answered, any inference drawn should be restricted to the 'preserved population' only. It has been shown (Rao and Shaw 1948, p. 247 and Rao 1952, p. 111) that human skulls preserved in a complete form in deep graves are on the whole smaller than those partially or completely destroyed. A measurement like the cranial capacity on preserved skulls would then provide estimates somewhat smaller than what is true of the population to which they belong.

Bias in the selection of Individuals

As a rule any method of selection or rejection of individuals based on physical characteristics or any associated measurement should be avoided because the exact adjustment to be made on that account in the estimates of mean values and variances cannot be easily found. For instance, Karve and Dandekar mention in the Maharashtra report that too fat subjects were rejected, fatness being presumably judged by the amount of fat at the gonia. This affects the mean values of Bigonial breadth and also the other correlated characteristics. The same is true of Risley's material which is known to be defective from this point of view. In such attempts the anthropologists have been probably guided by the desire to consider proper *representatives* of a group under study, which, if it can be done without personal bias, perhaps gives better results. But careful experimental investigations have shown that attempts to select so-called representative samples were usually unsuccessful and had given wrong results due to the unconscious personal bias of the investigators making the selection.

To choose a random sample of individuals by the 'orthodox method' involving the prepartation of a suitable 'frame' and the use of random sampling numbers may be a difficult task. This could be achieved if anthropometric surveys are conducted in conjunction with large scale sample surveys like the National Sample Survey or the decennial census which use suitably built up frames for sampling or for purposes of complete enumeration. Of course, other problems like training a band of anthropologists for field work and ensuring the comparability of their measurements would arise.

Coverage and Sample

What groups of people in a state should be included in a survey? This is an important question both for studying intra-state as well as inter-state comparisons. It would be insufficient to measure only a few of the groups or only groups belonging to particular regions of the state, if some general and meaningful conclusions have to be drawn. Further, since the object of anthropometric surveys is to trace the ethnic composition of the people, it is necessary to define the groups in such a way that they are as homogeneous as possible within themselves, as for instance mutually distinct endogamous units. Since such a classification would result in a large number of groups it would be difficult to study all of them in a single survey. The initial attempt might be to obtain broad anthropometric differences between well defined social groups living in different parts of a state and then, in gradual stages, intensive studies could be undertaken of social groups within regions by further splitting the groups into smaller homogeneous units.

The next problem is to decide on the number of individuals to be measured from each group. It must be noted that the interest of an investigation does not simply consist in declaring by suitable statistical tests of significance that the observed samples have probably come from different groups. This, indeed, is no new knowledge because no two groups of people would have exactly identical distributions and with increase in the sample size even small differences could be detected. What is of interest is to examine the magnitude of differences in the physical characteristics between groups and obtain a classification of the groups based on such magnitudes.

The question of adequate sample size has also been discussed in *Race Elements of Bengal*. It was shown that between 200 and 300 samples for each group is a safe size for a proper study of the configuration of the mean positions of the groups. This would also allow us to examine the nature of the distributions within groups, with some precision. For instance, it has been the practice with anthropologists to obtain from the sample the percentages of

Dolicocephalic and Brachycephalic individuals. The errors in these percentages, when the sample size is small, will be quite large.

Genetic characters

Somatic characters which are affected by environment and/or subject to changes under natural selection may not be quite suitable for studying inter-relationships between groups living in widely separated regions. Very little is known about the effect of environment on the physical characteristics generally used in Anthropological investigations. It is worth exploring whether simple genetic factors such as blood groups provide more effective information on the inherent differences between groups. In the case of blood groups determinations the difficulties referred to such as observer's bias, selection of samples, etc., are present to an equal degree as in the measurement of physical characteristics.

The author had the opportunity of examining large bodies of data on ABO, MN and Rh blood group determinations made in the field and in well-equipped laboratories as well. The statistical analysis of the available data on ABO blood groups of the people in Bengal has revealed differences between investigators of a larger order than between caste groups. In one survey where Rh blood groups were determined on about 1000 individuals, 8 cases of a rare combination of the allelomorphs of the C, D, E were reported. When the investigator was asked to check these cases, he could contact only some of these individuals and in each case, the determination was wrong. This threw doubt on the entire data and, perhaps, the longest series on Rh blood groups of Indian people could not be published. In the case of MN blood group determinations similar discrepancies were found, and the investigator was advised not to publish his results.

All this suggests that blood groups study needs very careful work both in collecting samples and testing with reliable anti sera. Arrangements should be made in all blood group work to have at least every 10th sample checked by an independent investigator using a different source of supply of anti sera.

Scrutiny of field records

Field investigators in anthropology have often to work under very difficult circumstances and some 'inadvertence is natural' resulting in errors of measurement and recording. But if the magnitude and proportion of recording errors is large, the analysis based on such data may be misleading. Nothing is more frustrating to the investigator to discover at a later stage that his observations collected at a considerable expense of money and energy are worthless because of obvious inconsistencies and failure to furnish complete information.

In *Race Elements of Bengal,* an account was given of the types of errors found in the primary records in a number of large scale investigations and the complications involved in detecting them and making suitable adjustments at the stage of statistical analysis. Many of these errors could have been avoided or corrected if some scrutiny could be undertaken in the field itself immediately after measuring some individuals, a task which could be left to an independent member of the team with some experience in scrutiny of records. His job will be to check whether measurements are entered under proper headings, any information is missing and any entries look suspiciously high or low. This will give a chance to the investigator to supply the missing information and to obtain a second measurement if possible in the case of doubtful entries.

The preparation of a proper schedule for recording the observations must be emphasised. Perhaps the best way is to have registers with columns indicating the measurements and other particulars to be recorded. The observations on an individual could be entered in a row under different columns. Such records, providing measurements on a number individuals in a single page, are convenient for purposes of scrutiny, transferring the information to punched cards for computations, or for directly computing from the original records means, variances and correlations needed for statistical analysis.

Object of the Survey

Above all, it is important to formulate the object of a survey in precise terms. The number and nature of characters to be measured and the coverage of the survey will naturally depend on the purpose for which the investigation is undertaken. For instance, if standards are to be provided for readymade garments, certain length and breadth measurements of the body are more important, and the sample should ideally represent the whole population, i.e., covering all individuals for whose needs the readymade garments are to be designed. The sampling design must be so as to yield norms for the population as a whole, or for different subsections of the population. If an investigator is interested in ethnic studies, it may be necessary to choose some groups on the basis of caste or religious affiliations and economic status, and measure a suitable number of individuals from each group. In such a case, the average values for the population as a whole or for some combinations of groups are not of direct interest, and need not be ascertained. What is important is that the data collected should provide sufficiently precise estimates of the averages for each group selected for study. The measurements should preferably be large in number, and include both somatic and genetic characters. Designers of furniture and equipment to be used by mechanics and operators have to concentrate on numerous measurements restricted to particular portions of the body and cover only the effective group of individuals for whom the furniture or equipment is meant. Those interested in building up health indices, growth studies, etc. have to choose characters which are good indicators of health, and the survey must have a long-range view designed to provide estimates of changes taking place in the characters over time. One method of increasing the efficiency of such estimates is to have some common subjects for measuring at different points of time.

REFERENCES

GUHA, B. S., 1931, 'Ethnographical', *Census of India*, 1931, Vol. 1, Pt. III.

KARVE, I., 1954, 'Anthropometric Measurements in Karnatak and Orissa and a comparison of these two regions with Maharashtra', *Journal of Anthropological Society*.

KARVE, I. and DANDEKAR, V. M., 1951 *Anthropometric Measurements of Maharashtra*. Deccan College Monograph Series, No. 8.

MAHALANOBIS, P., C., 1928, 'Need for standardisation in measurements on the living', *Biometrika*, Vol. 20, pp. 1-31.

1937, 'On the accuracy of the profile measurements with a photographic profiloscope", *Sankhya*, Vol. 3, pp. 65-72.

1946 'Recent experiments in statistical sampling in the Indian Statistical Institute', *Journal of the Royal Statistical Society*, Vol. 109, pp. 326-370; also reprinted in Sankhya, Vol. 20, pts. III & IV, pp. 329-97.

MAHALANOBIS, P. C., MAJUMDAR, D. N. and RAO, C. R., 1949, 'Anthropometric survey of the United Provinces: A Statistical Study', *Sankhya*, Vol. 9., pp. 90-324.

MAJUMDAR, D. N., 1950, *Race Realities in Cultural Gugarat*, Bombay, Gujarat Research Society.

MAJUMDAR, D. N. and RAO, C. R., 1959, "Bengal Anthropometric Survey, 1945: 'A Statistical Study', *Sankhya*, Vol. 19, pp. 203-408.

1960, *Race Elements of Bengal*, Bombay, Asia Publishing House.

RAO, C.R., 1948, and SHAW, D.C., 'On a formula for the prediction of cranial capacity' Biometrics, Vol. 4, pp. 247-253.

RAO, C.R., 1952, *Advanced Statistical Methods in Biometric Research*, John Wiley & Sons, New York.

6

RACIAL SURVEYS IN GUJARAT

P. G. SHAH

Introductory

WHEN a comprehensive history of anthropology in India is written, and the evaluation of the work of various Indian anthropologists is made sometime in future, the contributions of Dr. Dhirendra Nath Majumdar will secure a priority which we cannot perhaps appreciate now, when the living memories of his life and that of other anthropologists are likely to blur our vision. But judging from the point of view of cultural anthropology, social anthropology, physical anthropology, ethnology or ethnography, his outstanding performance in the fields of teaching, research and writing give him a well-merited high place. I will, however, restrict my tribute to his labours in the field of physical anthropology and describe his personal efforts in conducting racial surveys of Uttar Pradesh, Bengal and Gujarat and how by careful statistical analysis, he brought about a new outlook in our field work techniques and methodology.

It is thought by at least some people in India that cultural studies are more useful and helpful in understanding the cultural and social changes that are taking place in a group than the dry-as-dust facts obtained by the elaborate techniques of measurement, calculations, and statistical analysis. Further, anthropometry is more time-consuming and it is assumed that it does not prove as much as is expected. Dr. Elwin thinks that elaborate academic enquiries and research into the racial characteristics of a tribe, important as they are, may be postponed in favour of ascertaining the evaluation of the cultural changes that are taking place. It has been, however, shown by the researches of the late Dr. D. N. Majumdar that all the three assumptions are, at least, only partially correct. By a suitable and appropriate combination of cultural and physical anthropology and by careful and painstaking research in the collection of facts, their collation and statistical analysis, he has given a modern turn to Indian anthropology which now occupies a high place in the map of anthropological studies in the world.

It is perhaps not sufficiently well known that the ground for the foundation of physical anthropology was prepared by the father of anthropology in India, Rai Bahadur S. C. Roy, who as early as in 1920, delivered before the Patna University, a course of lectures on physical anthropology. He made a spirited appeal that anthropology as the Science of Man aimed at the systematic study of mankind in the processes of its evolution and that physical anthropology demanded equal attention with cultural anthropology. He fore-sighted in many ways the modern definition of physical anthropology by declaring that the function of physical anthropology is "the study of man on his physical side to determine his place in the order of mammals, his origin and antiquity, primeval home and migrations to classify mankind on the basis of physical characteristics into races, tribes and other groups, and to study their genetic inter-relations, and the conditions affecting their physical evolutions and their distribution over the globe. Certain mental characteristics, such as temperament and intelligence in so far as they depend, on the bodily organism, may legitimately be within the scope of this subject" (1920, pp. 7-9).

This compares favourably with Ashley Montagu's description of physical anthropology given thirty years later. "Anthropology is the science of man, the science devoted to the comparative study of man as a physical and cultural being. The physical anthropologist studies man's physical characters, their origin, evolution and present state of development, while the cultural anthropologist studies man as a cultural being in all the varieties which his cultures take. Both physical and cultural anthropology are conveniently recognised as separate, though interested and interdependent sub-divisions of anthropology which should never be permitted to become too detached from one another" (1951, p. 5).

Anthropology as the most important and comprehensive of social sciences supplies a universal blend and synthesis of mor-phology and human genetics on the one hand, and psychology and sociology of individuals as well as groups on the other hand, while economics and statistics are invaluable adjuncts in field work, design and interpretation. The multipurpose and multiphasic activities of man in groups or as individual demand the co-operation in all branches of anthropology including physical anthropology.

It is physical anthropology that has helped in the discovery of the great truth that the same evolutionary principles have governed the development of all men, past and present, and that such differences as the existing varieties now exhibit are not of a kind which upon any scientific system of biological, or even social values would justify any one of them as being distinguished as biologically superior or inferior to any other.

I had the good fortune of meeting Dr. D. N. Majumdar at the Lahore Session of the Indian Science Congress in 1939. My interest in anthropology was aroused during my tour of Europe in 1935, and the Gujarat Research Society founded in 1936 at Bombay had the study of man in that region as one of its objectives. Dr. Majumdar was then the President of the Anthropology Section of the Indian Science Congress and also of the joint Session with the Indian Statistical Conference. I was deeply interested in the 'biometric plan' for India for determining physical norms of Indians as compared to Englishmen and Americans, which were considered as the standard. Meeting for the first time, we greeted each other as kindred souls with the spirit of research burning in both of us. He accepted my invitation to visit Bombay and Gujarat during the vacations and to make the first anthropometric investigations on behalf of the Society. I accompanied him and we visited the Panchmahals Bhils at Dohad, in 1941, where we met Shri Thakkar Bappa and conducted preliminary investigations among the Bhils of Panchmahals. He later came in 1946 for a racial survey of Gujarat, Kathiawar and Cutch.

I will always remember with pleasure the days I spent on fieldwork with him in 1941 and later in 1946. One could see that work was his religion and research a passion. He had come with his party of students, willing, enthusiastic and responsive, equipped with a travelling laboratory, consisting of measuring tools and standard solutions in big bottles, all carefully packed. We spent several days at the elaborate camp provided by the Rajpipla State authorities on the top of the Malsamot Hill eighty miles away from the railway station. The day was, of course, full of field work among the villages and huts, taking photographs, measurements and blood samples, but work would not stop till all the blood samples collected were tested even though we had to work in light provided by the Kitson lamps. Each person was examined by a group of three investigators, one taking height and weight, another taking anthropometric measurements and the third taking the sample of blood. It was a remarkable feat that all the anthropometric measurements were taken by Majumdar himself standing in a line with other investigators and so also each examination of blood grouping was checked over the microscope by him personally. A high degree of reliability in testing and measuring was thus achieved in the course of Majumdar's anthropometric and racial surveys in U.P., Bengal and Gujarat. Even his expedition to solve the Rupkund mystery was characterised by the same thoroughness and reliability.

His literary style added new strength and popularity to his books, which are in great demand. The chapters on "Race Elements in India" and "The Blood Map of India" in his book *Races and Cultures of India* will remain a monument to the genius of Dr. Majumdar as displayed in the field of physical anthropology.

I cannot end my tribute to Majumdar without mentioning three events that are still fresh in my mind. The first was the occasion when the Gujarat Research Society at its 10th Annual General Meeting presented him the Society's medal at the hands of the Governor Sir Maharaj Singh followed by a dinner at the Government House. The second was our stay in New York in June 1952 for the Wenner-Gren Foundation International Symposium on Anthropology when as President of the Anthropological Society of Bombay, I was the second delegate from India. We lived in the same hotel and had constant contact for nearly one month. The official Report of the Symposium, *An Appraisal of Anthropology Today* edited by Sol Tax contains a record of our contributions to the discussions. It was in New York that I appreciated fully the simplicity of his life, and also the humour and wit in the man and came to know his accomplished wife and daughter when they came to New York later on. The third event was the brilliant popular lecture he gave at Bombay in the Townhall about the Rupkund Mystery illustrated with films and photographs. He carried conviction about his theory of the mystery.

Physical Anthropology in Western India

The Anthropological Society of Bombay, since its inauguration in 1886 by the Founder President Mr. E. T. Leith, has concentrated on cultural anthropology, and the Society's *Journal* contains mainly papers on cultural anthropology. However, a valuable paper on the anthropometric measurements in Karnatak, Orissa and Maharashtra by Dr.(Mrs.)Irawati Karve was published in its March 1954 number.

When Sir Herbert Risley conducted his anthropometric survey for the Indian Census Report of 1891, Bombay supplied its share of anthropometric measurements through Mr. B. A. Gupte who was a Member of the Staff of the office of the Collector of Bombay. Risley's findings were summarised also in his classic work *People of India*. His anthropometric work was supplemented by Dr. B. S. Guha for the Census Report of 1931 but as the number actually measured from the Gujarat region was small, the Gujarat Research Society decided as early as in 1939 to conduct anthropometric surveys for the region of Maha Gujarat including Gujarat, Kathiawar and Cutch. No trained observer was available till 1941 when Dr. D. N. Majumdar agreed to conduct the survey as a labour of love.

The First Racial Survey of Gujarat

When the Racial Survey of Gujarat was undertaken by Majumdar he had already completed similar surveys for U.P. in 1941-43 and for Bengal in 1945. Guha's work for Gujarat during the 1931 Census had covered only 105 Nagar Brahmans, 99 Banias, 93 Audich Brahmins, 40 Kathis and 31 Brahmakshatris—a total of 368 persons. Against this, Majumdar took up the study of 24 tribes and groups, measured 3,600 persons and tested 3,000 blood samples belonging to these groups. He was then well-equipped with the experience necessary for such large scale surveys both with regard to the technique of field investigations and the methods of statistical analysis of the serological and anthropometric data. This racial survey was noteworthy as it covered most of the common caste groups of cultural Gujarat and one tribal group namely the Bhils. The title of the book *Race Realities in Cultural Gujarat*: *a report on the anthropometric, serological and health survey of Mahagujarat* is both descriptive and suggestive.

The results of the anthropometric measurements are summarised below in his words:

(i) 'Our measurements of the 24 tribes and castes, show the range of the cephalic index from 75.61 of the Bhils to 83.75 of the Bhadelas. The Parsi have a cephalic index of 82.47 the Bhatia 82.90 the Miana (Muslims) 82.44, the Khoja 79.95, the Memon 79.95 and Sunni

Bora 89.91. The Luhana who have provided the recruiting base for the Muslims have a cephalic index of 79.45, corresponding to the indices among the Khoja, Memon and Sunni Bora; it is only the Miana who have a very high cephalic index, affiliating them to the Parsi and the Bhatia for all these latter groups have a cephalic index above 80.

(ii) 'If we follow the standard grouping into the ethnic types, dolichocephalic, mesocephalic and brachycephalic, Maha Gujarat has an interesting distribution. The Bhil and the miscellaneous tribes, show dolichocephaly, the Bhatia, Parsi, Bhadela, Rabari, and Miana are brachycephalic, and the rest are mesocephalic. Considering the large number of groups falling in the intermediate rungs, Maha Gujarat is a Mesocephalic Province and not Brachycephalic. The Audich Brahmin have a cephalic index of 77.96, while the Nagar Brahmin have an index of 79.58. The Nagars are, therefore, more broadheaded than the Audich.

(iii) 'The tribal or the artisan groups who are also recruited from the tribal substratum, but mixed with other castes, are dolichocephalous or have a tendency towards dolichocephaly.

(iv) 'If Maha Gujarat is a mesocephalic region, as it appears to be, then this mesocephaly may be a result of an admixture between two racial strains, one a brachycephalous race, represented by the Parsi, the Nagar Brahmin, the Bhatia, the Bhadela, the Rabari and the Miana, the other a dolichocephalous strain represented by the tribal substratum, be the Bhil, and Bhangi, the miscellaneous artisans (Koli, Dubla and Nayaka and others) and the Macchi and the Kharwa. In between lie the rest of the groups we have included in our Survey. The higher castes in Gujarat including the Parsi and those who are known to be converted from the higher castes into Muslims, belong to an original brachycephalic race, the lower castes and tribes belong to a dolichocephalic one, but mixtures, large scale we think, have produced intermediate types who can be arranged in an order of racial distance from either of the two racial strains according to the degree of their blends. . . .

(v) 'Both from the definite and indefinite characters, the two racial strains in Gujarat, Kathiawar and Cutch are easily distinguished, but the intermediate rungs of the racial ladder follow imperceptably one after the other, producing a more or less homogeneous ethnic type. The Muslims of Gujarat unlike those of Bengal are more akin to the higher caste elements and the historical origin of the various Muslim groups of Maha Gujarat do not allow any scope for a different conclusion. The Khoja are similar to the Luhana, the Miana, and the Bhadela to the Bhatia and the Parsi, and the Rajput and Mehr have association with the Muslims. The Oswal of Cutch show occasional epicanthic folds in their eyes, and their origin would be an interesting study, the rest of the groups we have discussed in this report do not exhibit Mongoloid infusion. The Muslims of Cutch, and of Kathiawar and the Sunni Bora, show occasional traces of woolly hair and thick and inverted lips, but the Negroid affinities, are due to absorption and not to any substratum of a Negrite race. . . . .

(vi) 'From the serological study of the Gujarat castes and tribes we found a heterogeneity among the various social groups we sampled for blood group tests. This heterogeneity, we think, is due to the fact that there is a great deal of intermixture among the ethnic groups in Maha Gujarat. We found the Khoja and the Luhana to possess similar incidence of the blood groups and we found the Audich Brahmin, the Nagar Brahmin, the Bhatia, the Mehr, the Miana, and the Kunbi Pattidar forming a constellation with respect to their p-values. We found also the Parsi having a similar serological status as those of the higher castes, for they approach the latter with respect to their p-values. The Rabari and the Waghar are not yet permanently domiciled in Kathiawar or in Gujarat, and their isolation and that of the tribal groups explain their serological status vis-a-vis other ethnic groups. In a way, the serological evidence does not run counter to that provided by anthropometry and even if we have not established correlation between blood groups and anthropometric characters, we have not found our analysis devoid of significance. The scope for further inquiry is amply indicated by our survey, and we feel that in respect of inter-group and intra-group relationship, the racial and serological investigations have provided the anticipated results. It would be fruitful to study intra-group variations among the castes, high and low, for anthropometry has proved to be an efficient tool in determining race affiliation and distance and with the aid of serology may be expected to unfold further the tangle of race origins. A historcial study of race origins would be possible when we have complete data on inter-group and intra-group race relations' (1950, pp 55-8). (The break-up of the quotations into paragraphs marked (i), (ii), (iii), (iv), (v) and (vi) is mine—P.G.S.)

Further Anthropometric Work in Gujarat Region

Majumdar's work on the cultural groups of Gujarat included only one purely tribal group, namely, the Bhils. The Gujarat Research Society has since 1946 extended its study to other tribes of Gujarat and in virtue of a definite plan has divided its attention equally between cultural and physical anthropology including anthropometric, serological and psychological investigations.

The anthropometric measurements taken by Dr. Majumdar and his assistant Dr. D. Singh have been supplemented by the measurements taken by Dr. Stephen Fuchs, who had his training in Vienna. The results as summarised by Dr. S. Fuchs are given below. In the serological field he has taken the help of experts from the Human Variations Unit of the Indian Cancer Institute at Bombay. (The extract is from my new book on the Dhanka tribe which is being got ready for the press).

(i) The measurements taken of five Gujarat tribes, the Bhils, the Naikas, the Dublas, the Gamits and the Dhankas, show that all these five tribes have racially much in common and, as a group, differ from the non-tribal population of Gujarat more than from each other. It is probable that they all are merely sub-sections of the great Bhil tribe, going under different names and having separated from the original stock for various reasons, which may be geographical (isolation), social (various degrees of Hinduisation) or economic (various transitional stages to plough cultivation).

(ii) To mark their racial characteristics in clearer relief we shall compare them consistently with a representative group of non-tribal communities living in Gujarat. The six castes selected for this purpose were Bhatias, Sunni Bohras, Rajputs, Khojas, Parsis and Audich Brahmins; the measurements are those taken by Majumdar in 1946.

(iii) Significant is the difference in Stature and Sitting Height between the tribal and the non-tribal groups: the stature of the tribals varies between 158.7 (Naika) and 160.2 (Dhanka), while that of the non-tribal group ranges between 162.9 (Sunni Bohra) and 167.7 (Parsi).

The average stature of the Dhankas is 160.2. Of the 112 Dhanka males measured, only 2 were below 150 cm., 48 between 150 and 160, 56 between 160 and 170 cm. and only 5 individuals were above 170 cm. The Dhanka women proved to be much shorter: their average stature is 148.6 cm. Of the Dhanka women, 103 measured between 150 and 160, and 1 above 160 cm.

(iv) *The sitting height* of the tribal group varies between 80.4 (Naika and Dhanka) and 81.8 (Dubla), whereas that of the non-tribal group ranges between 84.5 (Khoja) and 87.8 (Rajput). In comparison to the limbs the trunk of the tribals is distinctly short, shorter than in the non-tribals. The average Sitting Height of the Dhanka Males is 80.48, that of the Dhanka women remarkably lower: 74.07 cm.

The forearms and legs of the tribals are usually slender and the calves poorly developed. But in spite of the fragility and delicacy of their frame the tribal physique is not weak; they are wiry and enduring.

(v) *Head measurements*: The skull of the Gujarat tribes is slightly smaller than that of the non-tribals. The range of the head-length is in the tribal group from 17.90 (Gamit) to 18.20 (Dubla), whereas that of the non-tribal group is between 18.27 (Sunni Bohra) and 18.50 (Bhatia).

The Dhankas, in particular, have an average head-length of 18.18 cm. the head-length of the Dhanka women is, however, only 17.64 cm.

(vi) Significant is that the *head-breadth* of the tribal group is comparatively low: from 13.67 (Bhil) to 14.00 (Dubla and Naika), whereas that of the non-tribal group is between 14.35 (Audich Brahmin) and 15.34 (Bhatia).

The Dhankas have an average head-breadth of 13.87, that of their women being only slightly less 13.85 cm.

(vii) *The Cephalic Index*[2] of the tribal group is markedly lower than that of the non-tribal group: it varies between 76.11 (Bhil) and 78.92 (Gamit), while that of the non-tribal group is between 77.96 (Audich Brahmin) and 82.90 (Bhatia). Though both groups are, as a whole, thus still mesocephalic, the tribal group approaches dolichocephaly, while the non-tribal group tends towards brachi-cephaly and, in fact, the Bhatias and the Parsis are in their average brachycephalic. The long-headedness of the tribals is, however, not due much to a greater head-length—it is in fact less than in the non-tribal group but to an extreme narrowness of the head. This narrowness of the skull shows itself also in a narrow forehead.

(viii) Our general statements about the *head-form* of the whole tribal group apply also fully to the head form of the Dhankas.

Of the 112 Dhankas measured, 64 (57.14 p.c) were mesocephalic, 39 (34.82 p.c.) dolichocephalic and only 9 brachycephalic, one of these was even hyper-brachycephalic. The cephalic index of the Dhanka women (103 in number) is 78.6 that of the males being 76.29. That means that the Dhanka women are more broadheaded than the men.

(ix) *The face of the tribals* appears shorter than that of the non-tribal group probably because of their less developed chin. The total *facial length* of the tribal group varies between 10.94 (Bhil) and 11.01 (Dhanka), whereas that of the non-tribal group is between 11.12 (Audich Brahman) and 11.48 (Khoja). The total Facial Length of the Dhanka males is 11.01, that of the Dhanka women 10.16 which is a considerable difference.

(x) The *upper facial length* of the tribals is between 5.96 (Bhil) and 6.80 (Gamit and Naika), whereas that of the non-tribal group varies only between 6.08 (Rajput) and 6.40 (Khoja). The fact that the average upper facial length is less in the non-tribal group proves that the lower portion of their face is more developed.

The Dhanka males have an average upper facial length of 6.28, while that of the Dhanka women is only 5.92 cm.

(xi) The more pronounced development of the *chin* portion in the face of the non-tribals is also revealed in the *lower Facial Index* of the non-tribals; it is only between 81.40 (Bhatia) and 84.50 (Sunni Bohra), while that of the tribals is between 83.96 (Dubla) and 85.20 (Bhil).

The tribals have in general moderately high to thick mucons lips, the males have a broad mouth while that of the women is much smaller.

(xii) (a) *The Nose*: As in the whole of India, so also in Gujarat the tribals have a shorter and broader nose than the non-tribals, the *average nose length* varies in the tribal group between 4.75 (Dhanka) and 5.00 (Naika and Gamit) whereas it is between 5.13 (Sunni Bohra) and 5.46 (Parsi) in the non-tribal group. The average nose-length of the Dhanka males is 4.75, that of the Dhanka women 4.52.

(b) *The Breadth of the Nose* is slightly larger in the tribal group: it ranges between 3.66 (Bhil) and 3.84 (Dhanka), while the nose-breadth in the non-tribal group varies between 3.56 (Rajput) and 3.81 (Bhatia). The average nose-breadth of Dhanka men is 3.84, that of Dhanka women 3.51.

(c) Consequently, the tribals have a higher *nasal index*. Their nasal index varies between 76.00 (Naika and Gamit) and 80.93 (Dhanka), while that of the non-tribal group is only between 67.67 (Parsi) and 73.58 (Bhatia). The nasal index of Dhanka women is 77.71. This considerable difference in the nasal indices of the Dhanka males and females is also found in the other tribes; it reveals the fact that the type with extremely distended nostrils is more frequent among the males, though individuals with high and narrow noses with steep lateral parts are not altogether absent. Of the 112 Dhanka males measured, 6 had such leptorrhine noses, while 73 had mesoleptorrhine, 28 chamaerrhine and 2 hyper-chamaerrhine noses. The latter 2 had a nasal index of 100.

The Serological study was entrusted to Mr. G. N. Vyas, M.Sc., who worked under the supervision and collaboration with Dr. Sanghvi of the Human Variations Unit of the Indian Cancer Institute. His results are published in my book on Naika-Naikdas. In all he investigated seven groups viz. the Naikas, the Dublas, the Gamits, the Dhankas, the Dhodias and the Kolis. Out of these the last two were not anthropometrically measured and are not comparable. It is an important and significant fact that the Kolis are not at all tribes as assumed originally by the investigator. The remaining six tribes have no large differences among them, even though they can be arranged in two clusters.

The seven tribes were investigated for A_1A_2 BO, MN, Rh (tested with anti-sera -C, -c, D, -E), Duffy and P Blood groups, secretion of ABH substances in saliva, threshold determination of p.t.c. taste reaction, colour-blindness, sickling and paper electrophoresis for other haemoglobin variants. The results show a closer affinity between the Dubla, the Bhil, the Dhanka and the Naika on one hand and the Gamit and Dhodia on the other hand, the two clusters themselves showing no remarkably large difference between them.

ABO blood group data for seven tribes do not show any highly significant[2] value to indicate internal heterogeneity. In case of the Naika group the Rh blood group data showed significant[2] value ([2] = 7.838 for 1 degree of freedom).

The genetical difference between Gamit and Dhodia is small and they cluster together with respect to the other five groups. Similarly the genetical differences between Dubla, Bhil, Dhanka and Naika are small and they cluster together with respect to the other three groups. These two clusters can be taken as situated at two ends of an axis representing the average difference between the two clusters.

This brings out an interesting fact that there are no remarkably large genetical differences between the various tribes studied. It is possible that all the six tribes of Gujarat are genetically allied and probably originated from one stock.

Conclusions

We may end this paper by pointing out that the study of ethnic groups in India will be facilitated by drawing up maps for the distribution of the various criteria of classification which have been described in the present paper. However, when one wants to draw such a map one is faced with the problem of paucity of data in all fields of physical anthropology. This is especially true with respect to the blood group and other genetic characters. It is needless to mention that samples for such studies should be carefully drawn, keeping in view the modern trend of population genetics. Thus, for example, subcaste samples are liable to give more information of a genetic nature than those drawn without such specification.

Race is a dynamic concept. The boundaries and the internal genetic materials are changing constantly. In addition to this kaleidoscopic change inherent in Mendelian population, we have to take into account that caused by nutrition and raised standards of living. This brings forth the immediate necessity of studies purporting to show the effect of nutrition and other environmental factors on the body form. Thus prepared, we shall be able to assess the physical changes that are taking place now and will take place in future as a consequence of economic and social changes resulting from the Five-Year Plans.

REFERENCES

DAVE, T. N., 1948, 'Bhili language', *Journal of Gujarat Research Society*, 10, 1, pp. 80-134.

ELWIN, V., 1960, Report of the Committee on Special Multipurpose Tribal Blocks. New Delhi, Govt. of India.

MAJUMDAR, D. N., 1942., 'Raciology of the Bhils', *Journal of Gujarat Research Society*, 4, 3, pp. 2-27.

1950, *Race Realities of Cultural Gujarat*. Bombay, Gujarat Research Society.

1958, *Race and Cultures of India*. Bombay, Asia Publishing House.

MONTAGU, Ashley, M. F., 1951, *Physical Anthropology*. Illinois, C. C. Thomas.

RAISLEY, H. H., 1912, *People of India*. Calcutta.

ROY, Sarat Chandra, 1920, *Principles and Methods of Physical Anthropology*. Patna, Patna University.

SHAH, P. G., 1958, *Dublas of Gujarat*. Delhi: Adimjati Sevak Sangh.

1960, *Naika-Naikadas*. Bombay: Gujarat Research Society. 1959.

TAX, Sol, et al. (ed.), 1953, *An Appraisal of Anthropology Today*. Chicago, University of Chicago Press.

7

THE ASURS AND BIRHORS OF CHOTA NAGPUR

R. Ruggles Gates

I am glad to be able to make this contribution to a memorial volume for the late Professor D. N. Majumdar of Lucknow University. I first knew him as a post-graduate student of anthropology in the University of London in the '30's. Indeed he said that I first interested him in the human blood groups. He afterwards became attached to the whole range of anthropological investigations, as his books and papers testify. His *Races and Cultures of India*, written from the modern point of view, summarises all the work on Indian blood groups up to the time of its publication. He shows that the B blood group in India decreases from East to West, and from South to North. The great energy he displayed made Lucknow an important centre for anthropological research. His untimely and unexpected death at the height of his activity is a serious loss to Indian anthropology. My visit to Lucknow and lectures in his Department were a pleasure which was unfortunately soon followed by his death.

No other country equals India in the range and variety of its native peoples. In culture they range from the lowest to the highest culture levels, and physically they are generally regarded as including Proto-Australoids, Mediterraneans, Nordics, Alpines, Dinarics and Mongoloids, as well as others with some Negroid characters, also Veddoids, Kadars, etc. To unravel these tangled strains after millennia of mixture will require the labours of many physical anthropologists. Mass measurements of groups is only one method of approaching this problem. A more fundamental method is by the genetic analysis of racial crosses, through the tracing of characters in the pedigrees of racial hybrids. By such studies of Anglo-Indians, for example, an analysis of the physical characters both of Dravidians and Europeans can be reached.

This method has scarcely as yet been used in the study of Indian populations, but the possibilities are great. My recent demonstration

(Gates 1960a and Gates and Bhaduri 1961) that hairy ear rims are relatively frequent in the Dravidian population of India, especially in the South, and that the gene is in the Y-chromosome, shows that many unexpected developments may occur in such studies. But special training is required before genetical methods of racial hybrid study can be successfully adopted.

This paper to the memory of Professor Majumdar records the results of a short expedition from Ranchi to study two formerly wild tribes in Bihar.

During the visit to the Institute for Tribal Research in November, 1959, my wife and I set out in a party in charge of Miss Uma Chowdhury to study the Asurs and Birhors, the arrangements being made by Dr. B. S. Guha.[1] We travelled in a jeep to Bishunpur, about 80 miles from Ranchi. After waiting there to pick up a man who is informed regarding the natives, we drove on for another 20 miles up the mountain through a rough and tortuous road in the forest, to Netarhat. Here we measured 20 Asurs belonging to the village of Jobhipat several miles away. They were brought to Netarhat in the jeep. I had intended to go to their village and study them on the spot. I could then have examined a larger number, which would also be free from any kind of selection. But this could not be done owing to unavoidable circumstances. However, those who came included all ages of both men and women, but some were a little below the age of full maturity.

Measurements were made of ten men and ten women, as shown in Table I. Mr. S. P. Malhotra, a student at the Institute, aided in making the measurements, and he also wrote down the names of all the Asurs examined. It will be noticed that three of the ten women bore essentially the same name, Atwari, and two others the name Sukhni.

It will be seen from Table I that the skin colour is close to No. 3 of the Gates colour chart, but some are more brownish, others nearer mahogany. The men's mean cephalic index is practically 74, but the range is from 69.95 to 83.52. The C.I. of No. I is brachycephalic and far removed from all the rest, which range from 70 to 75.62—a compact group. Probably No. I is an intruder into this mesocephalic group, as he has also narrower nostrils.

The range of ear-length is from 45.3 to 62.6 mm., and of ear-breadth from 27.1 to 33.1. a much narrower range, the ears as a whole being small. In stature the range is from 149.6 (just under the mean for dwarfs) to 164.8, the mean being 155.6 cm. which is decidedly short.

The men and women all have black hair, slightly wavy, except Mangra (No. 9) whose hair was strongly wavy to curly. The lips are thin, except that in numbers 6, 10, 12, 13, 15, 17, 19 and 20 they are slightly protruding. But in no case do they approach the markedly everted Negroid condition frequently found in the Muria Gonds (Gates 1961).

The nostrils are just under 40 mm. broad in the males and 36 in the females. The nasal root is generally about half-depressed, but in Nos. 6, 11, 14 and 20 was fully depressed and in others slightly or 1/4 depressed. Characters such as nasal depression, which show various degrees of development, are believed to be based on a small number of cumulative genes.

The ten women (Table I) have essentially the same eye and skin colour as the men. The last four young women in the table are not quite adult, which is shown perhaps by their narrower heads. This results in a mean C.I. of 74.3 for the women, which is scarcely greater than that of the men. The nostrils of the women are, as might be expected, narrower than for the men, though there is much overlapping. The mean stature of the women is, as usual, nearly 10 cm. less than for the men. Only one of the men is below 150 cm. and only one woman below 140 cm. in height. The tribe are clearly not dwarfs but decidedly short.

It will be seen that the Asurs are not now Australoid. None have heavy brow ridges, but many have a depressed nasal root. Sunken orbits scarcely appear except in small degree. The skin colour is nearly the same as that of the ordinary Indian population. Figs. 1-4 are photographs of individuals, three male and two female. The explanation of plates describes them. Fig. 5 shows a group of men and Fig. 6 a group of women.

After finishing the photography, in black and in colour each was given a rupee to facilitate their future co-operation. Then they engaged happily in a rhythmic group dance before being returned to their village. The sexes formed two separate parallel lines, which swung in unison to the beat of a native drum. The dance was symbolic of the harvest. In leaving Netarhat we passed through mesophytic forest, the main timber tree being *sal* (Shorea). We descended to the plain with many hairpin turns, through a wide zone of tall feathery bamboo.

TABLE I

Asurs Name	Age	Eyes	Skin	L	B	C.I.	Nostrils	Ears	Lobe	Height	Fig.
Males											
1. Paklu	35	4	—	176	147	83.52	35.9mm	61 ×33.1	—	—	1
2. Biphay	40	4	3	187	137	75.27	40.3	53.1×27.1	No lobe	158 cm	
3. Tejua	55	4	more brown	177	130	73.47	41.2	62.6×32	sm. lobe	150	
4. Birsai	25	4—5	+3	192	135	70.31	43.8	45.3×33.1	sl. lobe	151	2
5. Bridhua	22	4	+3	177	134	75.70	40.9	57.3×32	lobe	160	3
6. Sawana	28	4	3	178	131	73.59	36.0	56.2×37.1	no lobe	161	
7. Bhadvan	26	5	3	171	131	75.72	37.3	45.9×32.2	sm. lobe	149.6	
8. Dauritha	18	4	+3	182	130	71.43	40.2	48.0×27.4	—	151.8	
9. Mangra	22	4	+3	187	132	70.59	38.8	52 ×31.5	lobe	154.6	
10.	—	4	3	193	135	69.95	41.3	58.7×27.1	sm. lobe	164.8	
Means (10)				181.7 ±6.543	134.2 ±4.833	73.955 ±3.831	39.57 ±2.412	54.5 31.36 ±5.855±3.062		155.6 ±5.194	
Females											
11. Atwari	50	4	+3	174	132	75.86	44*	—	—	135.5	4
12. Sukhni	55	4	3	165	130	78.78	38.3	—	—	148.8	4
13. Jhario	40	4	3	175	130	74.28	35	—	—	148.3	
14. Arvari	40	4—5	+3	171	128	75.85	37	—	—	151.3	
15. Phagli	20	4	+3	180	126	70.00	35.3	—	—	140.3	
16. Atwari	20	3	3	177	136	73.44	40.2	—	—	148.3	
17. Budhui	16	4—5	3	170	125	73.53	32.4	—	—	148.2	
18. Agni	18	4	3	181	128	70.77	28	—	—	150.6	
19. Somri	17	4	+3	171	127	74.26	34.8	—	—	151	
20. Sukhni	13	4—5	3	168	129	76.91	34.0	—	—	140.5	
Means (10)				173.2 ±4.895	129.1 ±3.015	74.296 ±2.465	35.9 ±4.144			146.3 ±5.193	

* The ears of all the women were distorted by many rings in the rim, so that measurement was impossible. Some of the men also had one or more rings in the ear rim, but not enough to prevent measurement.

It is well to remember that the fringes at least of many Indian jungle tribes have been in contact with each other and with the Dravidian population for at least three millennia, and that there was early infiltration in North and Central India by settlers of Aryan origin. These long contacts have undoubtedly resulted in a toning down of the Australoid and other primitive characters of the southerly jungle tribes, as indicated in Gates (1960). The Oraons and Santals here have very marked Australoid features, but neither the Asurs nor the Birhors are Australoid in origin. They belong rather to the Mundari stock of Munda-speaking peoples (Sarkar 1954) whose origin is somewhat obscure.

That much assimilation of this kind has taken place through the centuries is shown, for example, by the fact that the only marked difference between the Asurs and Birhors is in ear size (see page 175) which is found to be due to the age factor although at first regarded as genetical. Datta (1939) has made an extensive inquiry into various correlations between anthropometric measurements, which show that caste-Hindus are not dissimilar to the depressed castes in various somatic characters, except that they have broader hands, longer middle finger and probably taller stature. The last at least can be referred to better nutrition. Datta gives statistics showing that students in Italy, France, England and Spain are taller than labourers in these respective countries, the mean differences being over 4 cm. except in England where it is only 2.6 cm. Datta also finds that caste-Hindus are taller than Mohammedans, having also longer hands and longer mid-finger, but there is no significant difference between the depressed castes and Mohammedans. This may have a historical basis. Among the Hindus, the non-manual classes have longer arms but are no taller, a condition the causes of which are not clear. But the manual class has broader hands and a higher hand-index, which could be a direct effect of usage.

Historical

The Asurs are now shifting cultivators, apparently but a remnant of a formerly great people. They grow rice, but shift the cultivation every three years or so. The name Asura is of ancient and distinguished vintage, being the Aryan name for the supreme God. References in Vedic literature indicate that they were in Aryan times "a distinct and mighty people" who contended with the Aryans

(Mazumdar 1927). Northern India was then known as Aryavarta. South of this is the belt of Central India, extending to Peninsular India, which was mainly of Dravidian culture, intermingled with pre-Dravidian (mainly Australoid) and Munda-speaking tribes.

Risley (1890) recognised three types in the Indian population: I. The Aryans, tall, fair, dolichocephalic and leptorrhine, with a high facial angle, who entered India from the N.W. and centred in the Punjab. They fought and drove into Central and Southern India a "black, snub-nosed" race which they called the noseless ones or Dasyus. Some of these were absorbed in the process of conquest. Risley recognised two general types of them; (a) Dravidians, autochthonous, who entered India prehistorically from the N.W. and are now regarded as essentially an eastward extension of the Mediterranean race; (b) Kolarians, who came from the N.E. with a different language and have been regarded as Mongoloid. They were really from Indo-Burmese stocks, retaining slight Mongoloid traces only at second hand.

It has recently been found (Vos and Kirk 1961) that the Diego blood group, which is confined to Mongoloids, is apparently not present in the Veddas of Ceylon nor in the Kurumbas and Irulas of Southern India. But it was present in 6 of 125 (4.8 per cent) Oraons in Chota Nagpur, thus indicating a small Mongoloid element in the ancestry of these people, which was probably introduced via Assam and Burma. Similarly 7.4 per cent Diego was found in Siamese and 1.2 per cent in Malaya. The Js blood group, which appears to be restricted to Negroes was not found in S. and SE Asia and has not been known in Caucasoids, Amerinds or Polynesians. These rarer blood groups are important in determining the primary racial relationships.

Risely finally characterised his Dravidians as platyrrhine, dolichocephalic, short, with dark skin and low facial angle, well represented by the types in Chota Nagpur. His Kolarians were characterised as mesorrhine, brachycephalic, short to medium in stature, with yellowish skin, broad face and low facial angle, found typically on the frontiers of Bengal. This classification still has much to recommend it, but is now superseded by Von Eickstedt (1935).

It is objected that language terms should not be used for races, even though it is now generally recognised that language cannot be equated with race. Eickstedt (1935) criticises the usage of Risley and substitutes a more natural classification of Indian races into

Veddids (primitives) and Indids, the latter of two types. There is some ground for preferring the term Australoid to Veddid.

The central zone of India, which includes Chota Nagpur (formerly Chutia Nagpore), extends from N. Lat. 24° on the northern side of the Vindhyan range, overlooking the narrow valley of the Ner-budda in the west, to 19° N. on the left bank of the Godavery, the northern boundary of Hyderabad, with its tributaries, the Indravati and Savari, in Bastar, the most southerly part of Bihar. Mazumdar (1927) offers the probable conjecture that these two rivers, which flow through Bastar, were the Tamasa and Murala, cited in Vedic literature. Indravati is a Sanskrit name although it is now the river of the Gonds, and it flows past the town of Jagdalpur. There were Aryan settlements on its banks, so it retained the Aryan name, whereas the name Savari of the river flowing farther east, shows that it remained within the influence of the Savara people. Although the aboriginal tribes were infiltrated by Aryan settlements, they remained an important element in the population.

This central zone of India extended from 87° E. long., on the western borders of Bengal, to Jubbulpur, 80° E. long. This region remained the home of various scattered aboriginal tribes, although many Aryan settlements took place there in early historic times.

The Savaras or Sabaras are described in the *Puranas*, which are of no later date than the 6th century A.D. Mazumdar (1927) gives good reasons for concluding that these aborigines originally occupied the Vindhya mountains in the forested districts of the modern Mirzapore and Allahabad, where they wore tree leaves as garments and offered human sacrifices to a goddess. This area now contains remnants of the Kol people, who still have a traditional memory of the name Sabara. The latter people had their home in the Chhatisgarh Division of the Central Provinces, which extended to the banks of the Godavery where it meets the Savari in eastern Bastar. Today Sabaras or Saharas are found further east, in western Orissa, and even as far as Visagapatam in Madras, where they are adepts at magical charms, witchcraft and snake veneration. In physical measurements they closely resemble the Kols, whose origin Mazumdar discusses at length.

Risley (1891) described the Asurs as a small non-Aryan tribe "who live almost entirely by iron-smelting." They may be a "rem-nant of a race of earlier settlers who were driven out by the Mun-das." Traces of a more civilised mining and temple-building people are found throughout Chota Nagpur. The Asurs were divided into 13 totemistic sections, the total population being 1578 in 1872 and 1204 in 1881.

The Asuras in eastern Chota Nagpur adopted the Kol language although apparently of different stock. S. C. Roy (1915), who has written so much on the native tribes and peoples of India, finds that the Asuras and Mundas must have once struggled for supremacy in the State of Kalhandi. The Asuras were originally a powerful and well-organised people with whom the Vedic fathers contended. It has even been suggested (*The Vedic Age*, p. 250) that they were immigrants from Assyria who preceded the Aryans in India and were the creators of the Indus Valley civilisation. At a later period the Vanaras, an aboriginal tribe, were allied to the Brahmanas, Asuras, Daityas, Danavas and Nagas, who were in various culture stages from aboriginal to semi-civilised and opposed the spread of Aryan culture, which ultimately reached even South India (1. c., p. 313).

The Kolarian speech of the Asurs is shared with the Mundas, Birhors, Hōs, Santals, Kodas, Korkus, etc. The Gonds, one of the largest aboriginal tribes (Gates 1961), came into power in the Central Provinces not later than the 9th Century A.D.

Roy (1917a) has studied totemism amongst the Asurs. He found them divided into three classes: Thania (settled Asurs), Soeka (nomadic), and Birjia, essentially a separate tribe, sub-divided into Thamas (settled) and Uthlus (migratory). Other subdivisions of the Asurs have been recognised. Among the Asurs in the Districts of Ranchi and Palamau and in the States of Surguja and Jashpur traces of early stages of totemism are found, but totemistic restrictions on marriage are no longer observed by the settled Asurs.

Banerji-Sastri (1926) gives an interesting but partly conjectural history of the Indo-Aryans and the Iranians. In prehistory, Ashur emerges as the city of the Assyrians, which "absorbed the culture of Egypt and Babylon and passed it on to Iran and India". Assyrian supremacy was in the 12th century B.C. During the 16th century B.C. they conquered the Mediterranean coast-lands from the Egyptians and the Hittites. In about the 10th century B.C. Ashur re-emerges. The Asura are regarded as a sea-faring people who advanced up the Indus and founded the Mohenjodaro-Harappa civilisation. In the long drawn out Arya-Asura conflict the Asura were finally conquered by the Aryans coming down from the steppes of Central

Asia. Roy (1926) shows how the Asura figure in Sanskrit writings from the *Rig Veda* onwards. He refers to the cinerary urns in Asura graves of Neolithic and Chalcolithic age in Chota Nagpur. But he concludes on good grounds that the present Asurs are a tribe of Munda or Kol-speaking stock who adopted the characteristic (iron-smelting)[2] occupation of the ancient Asura and with it the name. The Mundas and Hōs lived in contact with the ancient Asura and still bury a few bones of their dead under stone slabs. The modern Asurs are thus of the same stock as the Mundas, the ancient Asura belonging to a different ethnic stock and culture. Roy (1923) had earlier suggested that the Asurs of Chota Nagpur were a Caucasian race who moved into India before the Vedic Aryan period and gradually absorbed the native melanoderm Nisadas by miscegenation, thus producing the Asura civilisation of the *Rig Veda*. After defeat by the Aryans they retreated into East, Central and South India. There was thus an Asura period preceding the Aryan period. Dravidian culture is based on this period, and Bengalis as well as other parts of India received some Asura blood.

Chakladar (1936) concludes that the Caucasians spread into South East Asia in remote prehistoric times before the Mongoloid waves moved down from the Tibetan plateau and later from China. (See also Keane 1896, p. 297). The pre-Vedic stock of Caucasians which spread over North India included both brachycephalic and dolichocephalic elements. Roy (1938) found an Alpine race element in them. Chakladar finds that the Indonesians belong to a Caucasian stock which migrated from the Ganges Valley and reached the Indian Archipelago long after the pre-Dravidians, probably picking up some Mongolian mixture in passing through Assam and Burma. It is well recognised that the Polynesians also have some Caucasian ancestry.

Ruben (1939) gives a full ethnological account of the modern Asurs and the iron-smelting of Asurs and other tribes, which includes a history of tribal iron-smelting methods and their final decay. Elwin (1942) suggests that the Agaria and Asurs are both descendants of a tribe represented by the Asura of Sanskrit literature. This tribe may have invaded the Munda country of Chota Nagpur and been driven back by the Mundas. Elwin suggests that they then spread west and north, and down to Raipur where they found in the Maikal Hills a congenial home and a plentiful supply of iron ore.

As already pointed out, the modern Asurs are not Australoid in type, but the traditions of the present Asurs may connect them with the Asura of Hindu mythology. Elwin thinks the Asur-Agaria who are now regarded as a branch of a Munad tribe, came originally from a Proto-Australoid stock. They may be descended from stray survirors of the ancient Asura in Chota Nagpur. If so, they have entirely lost the physical features of the latter and are now the degenerate descendants of distinguished ancestors. He finds that the Asur-Agaria tribes of the Western Ranchi plateau have the same iron-smelting technique, with bellows and furnace, the same mythology and magic and the same worship. Photographs show that the Agaria frequently have thick lips, especially the lower lip, a condition which one often meets with in Indian jungle tribes.

Jain (1958) has recently studied the kinship system of the Asurs of Jobhiput, which is 98 miles west of Ranchi and now has a population of 172.

Among his many contributions to Indian anthropology and archaeology, Roy (1915, 1920) gives an account of a tour in the former land of the Asuras, in which he describes villages containing remains of very ancient brick buildings (Mohenjodaro[3] was built of large bricks), stone temples and sculptures, cinerary urns, huge slabs and columns of sepulchral stones, and large tanks mostly silted up. These were "all locally attributed to an ancient people called the Asuras", who occupied the Chota Nagpur plateau before the Munda advent. They were thought of by the Mundas as a tall, huge-limbed race of herculean strength, having a much higher civilisation than their own.

Roy (1915) describes the remains of brick buildings and traces of iron-smelting. Evidence, to be mentioned later, showed that these people passed from the Neolithic through the equivalent of the Copper, Bronze and Iron Ages, but not necessarily in strict succession. The Asuras of Sanskrit literature are sometimes represented as lingam worshippers. Many artifacts, including copper and bronze ornaments, gold coins and stone implements, are sometimes unearthed by the plow. Forts for defence were built on elevated tracts of land on the banks of rivers and commanding a wide view of the surrounding country.

In the Ranchi District (Roy 1920) are found Asur forts and cemeteries; also at Singhbhum, an administrative district southeast of Ranchi. Over a hundred villages scattered through this

region have Asur sites of this "long extinct ancient people." In
an Asur graveyard at Khuntitoli the graves are in irregular order
and are marked by slabs. The roof stones are generally 8' 11"
× 7' 0" × 6" and may be 10-12 feet long. Small ones occur down
to 1' × 1' × 3". These centuries-old structures represent the
megalithic culture formerly widespread in parts of India and further
East. The slabs were placed over pottery urns. They contain beads
and ornaments, with sometimes remnants of incinerated corpses.
Each roofstone is generally supported at the four corners by a piece
of stone, like a large but low stool. Under each slab were cinerary
urns (*gharas*) numbering 2-13 and presumably belonging to one
family in the extended sense. The urns were earthen, but copper
vessels were also found.

The building sites were in three stages, belonging to the Neolithic,
Copper and early Iron Ages. There were Neolithic stone celts, bronze and copper bracelets (52), anklets, bronze and copper finger rings,
toe rings, stone beads, iron rings and arrow-heads, bronze plates
and cowries. The swords and sickles were all of iron. Terra cotta
phallic figures and fragments of thin bricks were also found. The
latter are still made in Bengal. Thus the whole period from Neolithic
to Iron Age is in a sense represented. The historical age is as
yet unknown, but may be determined in some cases by the C_{14}
method.

Other artifacts include a copper axe and chain, bronze bells,
dishes, ear-rings as well as bracelets and anklets, occasionally
with a twisted pattern like a torque. The bricks found resemble in
size, shape and colour those of the Pre-Mauryan and Mauryan
period, 17" × 10" × 3". The bricks in the Asoka stupa at Sanchi
(3rd century B.C.) measured 16" × 10" × 3". The innumerable
potsherds were generally without paint or polish, but some were
coated with red paint and a few showed remains of a black
enamel.

If the modern Asurs are really descendants of the Asura, who
progressed through the Neolithic and Megalithic periods into the
Copper, Bronze and finally the early Iron Age and have since retro-
gressed to a remnant of shifting cultivators and gatherers, this would
be a remarkable instance of historic and prehistoric people dege-
nerating under defeat. But equating the modern Asurs with the
ancient Asura seems to depend mainly on the name, and names
have sometimes been transferred, so the basis of this conclusion

seems uncertain. However, Sarkar (1949) says that the Asuras and Birhors "Undoubtedly form a very old ethnic strain." He blood-grouped small numbers of Asurs, Birjias and Bhuiyas with the following results:

	N	O	A	B	AB
Asurs	21	38.1%	57.1%	0	4.76%
Birjias	45	11.1	28.9	48.9	11.1
Bhuiyas	35	25.7	34.3	25.7	14.3

It will be seen that the Asurs were extremely high in A, the Birjias in B, while the Bhuiyas were high in both A and B. The Asur population in 1941 numbered 2024. The Birjias are found in the districts of Ranchi and Palamau in Chota Nagpur and are said to be related to the Asurs, but in these small numbers the ABO blood groups are very different. Bhuiya signifies landlord (Roy 1935). They are a "better caste" with "better features" than the Bhumij, who are a depressed caste. Both are of aboriginal origin but the Bhuiya are more Hinduised. They claim to have been feudal landlords of Vishnapur State. Some have secured the social status of the Rajputs. Other are merged with the lower castes. The Bhuiyans (or Bhooyas) of Palamau District make baskets and are of low social status, but the Bhooyas of Gaya claim to be high-caste Hindus and are well-to-do agriculturists. This is an example of the way in which caste status may change with economic conditions. The Bhumij are another aboriginal tribe now being Hinduised.

The Birhors

We arrived at the colony of Beti Birhors too late in the day to make a long series of measurements. The records for six men and four women are shown in Table II. In comparing Tables I and II it will be seen that the mean values for all the measurements are closely similar, except that the Birhor men have larger ears. The ears of the Asur women could not be measured because the rims were distorted with many rings, but as the Birhor women had ears of the same size as their men (see Table II) their ears were evidently also larger than those of the Asur women. But, as shown (p. 175), this results from an age difference. Both tribes are meso-cephalic, with practically no difference in C.I. between the sexes.

The Birhor ear would rank as medium in size, while that of the Asurs was smaller owing to their younger ages.

My friend, Dr. Fraser Roberts, has kindly submitted the measurements in Tables I and II to statistical analysis, which fully confirms the conclusions reached above by inspection. There is no significant difference in head size, cephalic index, nostril width or stature. That the difference in ear length is statistically highly significant at the 1 per cent level is shown below.

Difference of means	Standard error	Diff./S E
8.623	3.25	2.65

It is now known that human ears continue to grow more or less throughout life. Lasker (1953) finds that in Mexicans the nose, mouth and ears are significantly larger in older than in younger adults. Not only facial measurements but the length and breadth of the head (L and B) tend to increase (especially in females) as well as the bizygomatic and bigonial measurements. However, after about 54 years of age these measurements as well as stature tend to decrease, but the ears keep on growing.

Kaneko, Sento and Takahashi (1954), in an extensive study of ear size in relation to age, involving 2897 measurements of persons from new born to age 24, find that at age 0 in Japanese the mean ear-length is 43.60 mm for 75 males and 43.27 mm for 86 females. In age groups numbering from 20 to 138 there is a steady yearly increment in mean ear length up to about 17 years for males and females. These authors find that the ears then nearly stop elongating until about 30 years of age in males and 40 in females. At about this age ear growth is resumed, and continues at a *faster* rate after after 60 years of age. (I measured an Indian woman in Cuba with ears over 80 mm long. She was 80 years old).

The average rate of growth in length of Japanese ears between birth and age 17 works out at 1.05 mm per year in males and 0.88 mm per year in females. However, in the whole period up to 24 years of age the mean yearly rate of increments in length is 0.75 mm for males and 0.67 mm for females, the growth being suspended in the last seven years.

As regards the ear index (length/breadth) it gradually diminishes in Japanese from 61.17 at birth to 51.39 at 24 years in males, and from 59.29 at birth to 51.35 at 24 in females. In Mexicans, Lasker

(1953) finds the ear-length to increase in males from 65.8 mm at 18.20 years to 71.0 at 50 + years; also in females from 60.1 mm to 66.0 during the same age period. Grouped in ten-year periods there was no evidence of suspension of ear-growth, as found in Japanese, but with a one-year grouping such a suspension of growth might be revealed.

From Table I it will be seen that the mean age of the 9 male Asurs measured was 40.4 years while that of the 5 male Birhors was 30.1 years. Thus the Birhors averaged 10.3 years older. With a mean growth of 1.05 mm per year the mean ear-length of the Birhors should be 10.3 mm greater, whereas it is actually 8.1 mm greater, or if the mean rate of 0.75 mm is taken it should be 7.5 mm greater. Thus in either case the whole difference in ear-length may be accounted for by the age difference in the two tribes.

One may conclude that for the interpretation of some measurements it is necessary to record age differences, which are "significant" until account is taken of the age factor. It is evident that in anthropometric measurements more attention should be paid to the ages of the individuals measured. The difference in ear-length of these two tribes was at first regarded as genetical, until it was seen that it could be accounted for purely on an age basis.

The eye-colour of the Birhors appears to have been a shade darker than that of the Asurs, although with variable light Nos. 3 and 4 in the Martin Augenfarbentafel are difficult to distinguish. In skin colour the Asurs, male and female, were a very uniform mahogany, sometimes more brownish. The Birhors, especially the women, were a shade darker, and some showed a difference between face and body, the body being a little darker than the face. Among the names of Birhor women, it will be noticed that Advari and Budhui are very similar to or identical with names of the Asurs. This indicates a close social connection.

The Birhors are described by Risley (1891) as a small Dravidian tribe of Chota Nagpur who live in the jungle in tiny huts made of branches and leaves of trees and eke out a miserable living by snaring hares and monkeys, and collecting jungle produce.

Among modern accounts of the Birhors, the earliest I have seen is that of Bradley-Birt (1903). He describes the Birhors of Hazaribagh as the wildest tribe in Chota Nagpur. He reckoned about 1000 woodmen (Birhor means wood-cutter or jungle folk) living far from the towns, in the depths of the jungle. Their huts were

FIG. 1. ASUR (Paklu)
(No. 1 in Table 1)

FIG. 2. ASUR (Tejua)
(No. 3 in Table 1)

FIG. 3. ASUR (Birsai)
(No. 4 in Table 1)

FIG. 4. ASURS
(No. 11 and 12 in Table 1)

FIG. 5. ASURS

FIG. 6. ASURS

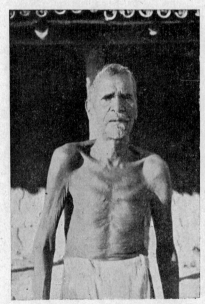

FIG. 7. BIRHOR (Jara)
(No. 4 in Table II)

FIG. 8. BIRHOR (Nauki)
(No. 7 in Table II)

FIG. 9. BIRHOR (Nauki)
(No. 8 in Table II)

FIG. 10. BIRHOR (Chota Budhui)
(No. 10 in Table II)

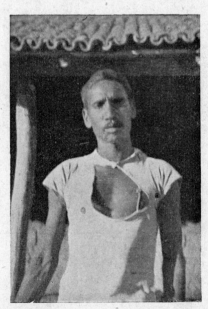

FIG. 11. BIRHOR

FIG. 12. BIRHORS

(From left to right): 1. Bandhwa 2. Konda 3. Jara 4. Birsu 5. Deonath

TABLE II

| Birhors | | | | | | | | | | | |
Name	Age	Eyes	Skin	L	B	C.I.	Nostrils	Ears	Lobe	Height	Fig.
Males											
1. —	—	3	3	182	132	72.52	44.2	63.8×36	sm. lobe	159 cm	
2. Bandhna	45	3	2	187	138	73.79	41.9	62 ×34.3	—	154	
3. Konda	17	3	F3 B2* more brown	178	131	73.59	37.4	53.5×29.8	—	161	
4. Jara	55	3	F3 B2 more brown	181	130	71.82	40.5	68.4×36.9	lobe	151	7
5. Birsu	35	3	3	183	131	17.58	41.2	70.4×32	lobe attached	154	
6. Deonath	50	4	F2 B2	178	137	76.96	38.5	57.7×31		152	
Means (6)				181.5	133.3	73.38	40.6	62.6×33.3		155.1	
Females											
7. Nauki	22	3	F3 A2	174	137	78.73	32.7	59 ×28	—	148	8
8. Nauki	38	3	2	174	125	71.83	35.6		ear lobe distorted	146	9
9. Atvari	55	4	2	187	129	68.98	42	64 ×35	lobe	154	
10. Chota Budhui	35	3	2	178	130	73.03	35.5	65.9×34.8		150	10
Means (4)				178.25	130.25	73.14	36.45	62.9×32.6		149.5	

F = face, B = body colour.

made from branches of trees covered with leaves fastened together so as to make a waterproof covering. Their umbrellas were also constructed of leaves. Few Birhors had at that time taken up cultivation. Roy (1917) wrote a preliminary account of the Birhors which was afterwards (1925) expanded into a large volume,—the third on the tribes of Chota Nagpur. He describes the Birhors as living on the hills and in the jungles which fringe the Chota Nagpur Plateau on the east and northeast, with an area of 70 × 20 miles. Here they wander, collecting rope-fibres and honey and camping in rude hovels of bamboo and leaves. They made string from the bark of *chob* (*Bauhinia scandens*) and collect berries of *Mahua* (*Bassia latifolia*) for fermentation, as well as yams and various roots and herbs. Their menu includes deer, porcupine, hare, rat and monkey. They also hunt the tiger, leopard, hyena, bear, wolf and nilgai, as well as peacock, pigeon, plover, partridge, snipe, teal and parrots.

The Birhors were scattered over an extensive area in small migratory bands, always on the move except in the rainy season when they camped in inaccessible places away from the villages. Col. Dalton (1865) in 1864 gives the earliest reference to them, including a circumstantial account of a peculiar form of cannibalism. When an old man was near death he invited his kin "to come and eat him", according to the Raja of Jashpur. Others were accused of hastening the end of their dying parents in order to feast on them. Before British rule, a human sacrifice was offered every third year before the shrine of *Kali*, supporting the theory that Hindus derived from aboriginal races the early practice of human sacrifice. At the time of Dalton's tour there was still strong sentiment in favour of suttee. Its prohibition had not long been enforced, and widows sometimes insisted still on mounting the funeral pyre. The Raja (p. 18) mentioned "a tribe called Birhors, whom he accused of a sort of interfraternal anthropophagy, of feeding literally on their blood relations." Some who were "captured", said they had given up the practice, but admitted that their ancestors had indulged in it. They declared that they never shortened life to provide such feats, and "shrunk with horror at the idea of any bodies but those of their own blood relations being served up to them." Col. Dalton seems to have been still doubtful about the practice, but he gave instructions to the Rajah to enquire into it; and he gave out that if it still existed it must be discontinued. The Birhors were said to speak "a jargon of

Hindu" but no other language. The Oraons in this region were significantly stated to "approach the Negro physiognomy".[4] The Kaurs in Oodeypore (Udaipur) were stated by Dalton (p. 19) to be the ugliest race after the Oraons, having "dark and coarse features, broad noses, wide mouths and thick lips." The Gours or Gonds were the most degraded in Bonai, but "holding a high position" in Oodeypore.

As a further picture of early conditions in Chota Nagpur, Dalton mentions an expedition into the princely State of Sirgoojah (now Surguja) which restored Burway as one of the Parganas of Chota-Nagpore and made Sirgoojah a British dependency in 1818. It is now a part of the State of Madhya Pradesh. Its area was *ca* 90 × 80 miles, with 1197 villages and a population of *ca* 1,30,000. About one-sixth of these belonged to the Gour tribe, the Kols numbering 5000—7000. Some 2000 Bhooyas or Bhuiyas (Hinduized tribes) were reported, the Rajpoots (rulers) numbering 505 and the Brahmins 369.

Reference is made to an earlier account by Col. Ouseley in *J. Asiatic Soc.* No. 186 for Jan. 1848, which I have not been able to see, as it is not in the Library of the Royal Anthropological Institute.

Some Birhors were already more advanced and semi-sedentary. In 1868 these began migrations to work in the tea gardens of Assam. In 1872 their language was described as a mixture of Mundari and Santali with a few words of either language.

The Birhors formerly spent years in the forest at one locality until its roots were exhausted, living also on monkeys, birds and other animals. As food, 13 kinds of leaves and 16 kinds of roots are mentioned. Their hunting was done without the bow and arrow. They were adepts at catching monkeys by means of nets in the trees. They also teach monkeys to dance. We saw a most diverting exhibition in Delhi of a monkey (Rhesus) whose keeper had taught it to dance most skilfully to an accompaniment of music.

The Bengal Census of 1901 reported 943 male and 890 female Birhors. In 1911 there were 927 in Ranchi (500 of them animists, the rest Hindu in religion) with a total of 2340 in the Province. The 1921 Census showed 1510 in Chota Nagpur. Deforestation has been a cause of the population decrease. In 1911, some were already taking up settled work as labourers, living on the outskirts of villages, making ropes and collecting wild honey, which is an occupation of various Indian jungle tribes. Well-to-do Birhor families built mud huts and had a shed for cattle.

The Santals, Birjias (in Ranchi and Palamau districts) and Birhors, who speak a mutually intelligible language (Sarkar 1954), are all very high in the B blood group, (Table III in Gates 1961 a) though the results are somewhat uneven. The Birjias on the Neterhat Plateau are now called Birjia Asurs and have taken to cultivation. In a recent account of the Birhors of Palamau, Bhattacharyya (1953) states that the Austric-speaking Birhors occupy three neighbouring districts of Chota Nagpur (Hazaribagh, Palamau and Ranchi) in dense jungle. Their customs are described, many of them borrowed from nearby tribes or from the Hindus.

Recently the Government has considerably transformed this tribe, or one group of them. The colony of Beti Birhors we visited had been provided with simple shed-like houses with a dirt floor arranged in a village on the plain at the foot of a mountain. The roofs were of tile, the houses of mud and the porch, which was supported by a row of posts, was used to shelter cattle and goats. These Birhors are assisted by Government workers in ways of farming with settled habitations closely grouped in a village.

By way of illustrations, fig. 7 represents Jara, age 55, No. 4 in Table II. The woman in Fig. 8 is No. 7 in Table II. Fig. 9, with child, is No. 8 in the Table. Fig. 10 is No. 10 in the Table. Fig. 11 is a Birhor man who was not measured. Fig. 12 is a group of five men in front of their houses.

Summary

Measurements taken of 20 Asurs and 16 Birhors show that there is no significant statistical difference between these tribes in head measurements, nostril width, or height, but the Asurs measured have definitely smaller ears because they are younger. The Asurs appear to have slightly lighter eyes and slightly lighter skin, but these differences are possibly not significant. The Asurs were very uniform in skin colour, close to No. 3 of the Gates colour chart. In both tribes there is little difference between the cephalic index of males and females. The women in both tribes have narrower nostrils than the men.

Neither tribe is now Australoid. None of the Asurs have heavy brow ridges but some have a depressed nasal root. The Birhors have slightly wider nostrils than the Asurs but this difference is not significant.

References to the Asuras in the Vedic literature show that they were a mighty people who contended with the Aryan invaders. The modern Asurs are a remnant in Chota Nagpur now living at the level of shifting cultivators. Archæological remains indicate that they passed through the Neolithic into the megalithic period when great numbers of cinerary urns under stone slabs in cemeteries, as well as forts, indicate a long megalithic period or a large population, with artifacts belonging to the Copper, Bronze and Iron Ages, as well as bricks of the type used at Mohenjodaro and in the Asoka period (3rd century B.C.). When and how the retrogression to tribal food-gatherers took place is not clear.

The Birhors appear to have been always at the jungle level of existence, with some evidence of a peculiar form of cannibalism when first contacts were made a century ago. Later, some became semi-sedentary and by 1868 migrations to the tea plantations of Assam began. They remain experts in catching monkeys in nets. The Government has now given them new habitations, part of which they use for sheltering their cattle and goats. Their farming is supervised and the children receive instruction in schools.

NOTES

[1] Reference must be made here to two important general summaries of the native tribes of India by Guha (1937, 1951). One can only deplore his recent tragic death in a railway accident.

[2] Burkitt and Gordon Childe both say that iron-smelting was discovered by the Hittites in Anatolia in the 14th century B.C.

[3] There is still difference of opinion as to whether the Indus valley civilization was pre-Aryan or post-Vedic (Majumdar and Pusalker 1951).

[4] One Oraon woman, measured by me in Ranchi, had a very Negroid appearance, with broad nostrils (42 mm.), nasal root 3/4—depressed and fully everted lips, but she was exceptional. These characters appear to be too widespread, especially in Oraons and Gonds, to be attributed to crosses with imported Negroes in modern times.

Acknowledgements

I am indebted to Dr. T. N. Madan of Lucknow University and to the Tribal Institute in Ranchi for various references. Mrs. Beverly Emery and other Librarians at the Royal Anthropological Institute have also aided me in the search for literature.

Explanation of Figures

Asurs Figs. 1-6

Fig. I. Paklu, No. I in Table I. Black wavy hair, slight black eyebrows and dark brown eyelashes. Nose depressed, orbits slightly sunken.

Fig. 2. Tejua, No. 3 in Table I. Brow ridges slight, no eyebrows. Nasal root half-depressed, nostrils broad.

Fig. 3. Birsai, No. 4 in Table I. He has smooth hair, black eyebrows and lashes, slight brow ridges and sunken orbits. Nasal root strongly depressed, lips full, scarcely everted.

Fig. 4. Atvari, No. 11 in Table I. Hair long, black, near straight. Eyebrows brown, lashes dark brown. No brow ridges, nasal root depressed, nostrils broad, lips thin. Ears distended with many rings in rim and a big coil in the earlobe. On right is Sukni, No. 12, with brown rather than mahogany skin colour. She has black eyebrows and brown lashes, no brow ridges. Nasal root slightly depressed, lower lip protruding. Her ears are similarly decorated with rings and plugs.

Fig. 5. Group of 9 men.

Fig. 6. Group of 9 women.

Figs. 7-12. *Birhors.*

Fig. 7. Jara, No. 4 in Table II.

Fig. 8. Nauki, No. 7 in Table II.

Fig. 9. Nauki, No. 8 in Table II.

Fig. 10. Chota Budhui, No. 10 in Table II.

Fig. 11. A Birhor man who was not measured.

Fig. 12. Five Birhor men at the entrance to one of the houses.

REFERENCES

BANERJI-SASTRI, A., 1926, 'The Asurs in Indo-Iranian Literature', *J. Bihar & Orissa Res. Soc.* 12, 110-39.

BHATTACHARYA, A., 1953, 'An Account of the Birhors of Palamau', *Bul. Deptt. Anthrop.*, v. 2, 2, 1-100.

BRADLEY-BIRT, F. B., 1903, *Chota Nagpore: A Little Known Province of the Empire*. London, 310 pp.

CHAKLADAR, H. C., 1936, 'Causasic Peoples between India and the Pacific', *Man In India*, 16, 183-89.

DALTON, LT. COL. T., 1865, 'Notes on a tour made in 1863-64 in the Tributary Mahals under the Commission of Chota-Nagpore, Bonai, Gangpore, Odeypore and Sirgooja', *J. Asiatic Soc. Bengal*, 34, II, 1-31.

1872, *Descriptive Ethnology of Bengal*, London.

DRIVER, W. H. P., 1888, 'Birhors', *J. Asiatic Soc. Bengal*, 57, 12-15.

DUTTA, B., 1939, 'An enquiry into correlations between stature and arm-length, stature and hand-length, stature and hand-index, also somatic differences between different social and occupational groups of the people of Bengal', *Man In India*, 19, 1-53.

EICKSTEDT, BARON von, 1935, 'The position of Mysore in India's racial history', L. K. A. Iyer's *The Mysore Tribes and Castes*, Vol. 1, Ch. 1, pp. 80.

ELWIN, V., 1942, *The Agaria*. Oxford, 292 pp.

GATES, R. R., 1960, 'Australoid tribes, India', in *Mankind Quarterly*, 1, 83-88.

1960a, 'The Y-chromosome inheritance of hairy ears', *Science*, 132, 145.

1961, 'The Muria Gonds of Bastar', *Mankind Quarterly*, 1, 176-88.

1961a, 'The Kurumbas in the Nilgiri Hills of South India', *Mankind Quarterly*. 1 : 258-276.

Gazetteer, District of Ranchi, Hazaribagh, 1907.

GATES, R. R. and BHADURI, S. N. 1961. 'The inheritance of hairy ear rims,' *Mankind Quarterly, Monograph* No. 1 : 24-38.

GUHA, B. S., 1937, 'An outline of the racial ethnology of India', *Proceed. Ind. Sci. Cong.* (Calcutta), 125-39.

1951, 'The Indian aborigines and their administration', *J. Asiatic Soc. Science*, 17, 19-44, 4 plates.

JAIN, R. K., 1958, 'Features of kinship in an Asur village', *East. Anthrop.*, 12, 25-40.

KANEKO, Y., C. SENTO and K. TAKAHASHI, 1954, 'Changes in the dimensions of the ear with age', *Anthrop. Reports Deptt. Anat., Niigata School Medicine*, (Japanese), 9, 1-10.

KEANE, A. H., 1896, *Ethnology*. Cambridge, 442 pp.

LASKER, G. W., 1953, 'The age factor in bodily measurements of adult male and female mexicans', *Hum. Biol.*, 25, 50-63.

MAJUMDAR, D. N., 1958, *Races and Cultures of India*. Bombay, 465 pp.

MAJUMDAR, R. C. and A. D. PUSALKER (eds.), 1951, *The Vedic Age*. London, 556 pp.

MALHOTRA, S. P., 1960, 'Birhor resettlement schemes', *J. Soc. Res.*, 3,2.

MAZUMDAR, B. C., 1927, *The Aborigines of the Highlands of Central India*. Calcutta, 84 pp.

RISLEY, H., 1890, 'The study of ethnology in India', *J. Anthrop. Inst.*, 20, 235-63.

1891, *The Tribes and Castes of Bengal*. Calcutta, 3 vols.

ROY, S. C., 1915, 'A note on some ancient remains of the ancient Asuras in the Ranchi District', *J. Bihar & Orissa Res. Soc.*, 1, 229-53.

1917, 'A general account of the Birhors', *J. Bihar & Orissa Res. Soc.*, 2, 2, 1-11.

1917a, 'A note on totemism amongst the Asurs', *J. B. & O. Res. Soc.*, 3, 567-71.

1917b, 'Social organization of the Birhors', *J. B. & O. Res., Soc.*, 3, 363-371, 7 plates.

1920, 'Distribution and nature of Asur sites in Chota Nagpur', *J. B. & O. Res. Soc.*, 6, 393, 423, 40 plates.

1923, 'A possible ethnic basis of the Sanskrit element in the Munda languages', *J. B. & O. Res. Soc.*, 9, 376-93.

1925, *The Birhors: A Little-Known Jungle Tribe of Chota Nagpur*. Ranchi, 608 pp. 36 plates.

1926 'The Assurs—ancient and modern', *J. B. & O. Res. Soc.*, 12, 147-52.

1935, 'Bhuiyas', *Man In India*, 15, 220.

1937, 'Caste, race and religion in India', *Man In India*, 17, 39-63, 147-76, 212-254. Also 18, 85-105.

1946, 'The aborigines of Chota Nagpur: their proper status in the reformed Constitution', *Man In India*, 26, 120-36.

RUBEN, W. 1939, 'Eisenschmiede und Damonen in Indien', *Inter. Arch. f. Ethnogr.*, 37 suppt., xx + 306 pp., 32 pls.

SARKAR, S. S., 1949, 'ABO blood groups from Palamau, Bihar' India', *Am. J. Phy. Anthrop.*, N. S., 7, 559-62.

1954, *The Aboriginal Races of India*. Calcutta, 151 pp.

SEN, B. K., 1955, 'Notes on the Birhors', *Man In India*, 35, 110-18.

SEN, B. K. and JYOTI Sen., 1955, 'Notes on the Birhors', *Man In India*, 35, 169-76.

SINHA, D. P., 1958, 'Cultural Ecology of the Birhors: a methodological illustration', *J. Soc. Res.*, 1.

1959a, 'World-view of a wandering tribe', *J.Tribal Res. Bureau (Bhubaneshwar)*.

1959b, 'Research and development in Anthropology: a case of Birhor resettlement', *J. Soc. Res.*, 2.

1960, 'Portrait of a Birhor chief', *J. Soc. Res.*, 3.

VIDYARTHI, L. P., 1959, 'Cultural types in tribal Bihar', *J. Soc Res.*, 1.

1960, 'The Birhors: a study in ecology, economy and wandering', *Selected Papers of the 5th International Congress of Anthropological and Ethnological Sciences, Philadelphia*.

VOS, G. H., and R. L., KIRK, 1961, 'Dia, Jsa and V blood groups in South and South-east Asia', *Nature*, 189, 321-2.

8

NOTES ON BLOOD GROUPS IN INDIA

A. E. Mourant

THE LATE Professor D. N. Majumdar was a pioneer in the application of blood group testing to anthropology in India, and he has left behind a very large amount of information on the blood groups of Indian populations. Many other workers have also contributed to our knowledge of the subject, knowledge which is continually increasing. Seven years ago (Mourant, 1954) I attempted to summarise what was then known. I wish that I could now have brought this account up to date and prepared a full summary of our present knowledge. The data are, however, now so numerous that I have found myself unable to complete the task in time for inclusion in this volume, and I have therefore limited myself in this paper to a brief account of recent advances in knowledge, and to a survey of those fields where more facts appear to be needed or where further work might be of particular interest. I hope that the paper will prove of value not only to those wishing to know the facts, but also to those who are planning further investigations in this almost limitless field.

ABO Groups

An exhaustive compilation of published ABO frequencies for the whole world, including the Indian Region, has fairly recently been prepared (Mourant, Kopeć and Domaniewska-Sobczak, 1958) and illustrated by maps. The few data since published affect the general distribution, and the lines on the map, only slightly. Two unexpected recent findings were the low frequency of A in Vizagapatam (gene frequency in Hindus only 12.4 per cent) (Dronamraju, Meerakhan and Narayana Murty, 1961) and the high frequency of the same gene in Baltistan (gene frequency 28.2 per cent) (Clegg, Ikin and Mourant, 1961).

In drawing up the map mentioned above, and in trying to revise it recently, it became evident that, despite the enormous numbers of tests carried out in India by Majumdar and others, there are exceedingly few observations available for the inland parts of Madras and southern India generally, and much more work is needed here.

MNS Groups

It has long been known that the frequency of the M gene in India, as in Asia generally, is higher than in Europe. In India, however, as in Europe, there is a relatively high frequency of the gene complex of MS, whereas in Eastern Asia the high frequencies of M are mainly accounted for by the Ms combination. In the tribal peoples of India, as in the settled population, there is in general a high frequency of M, but the range of variation is greater, and some of the tribes have quite low M frequencies.

P Groups

The few available data appear to show lower frequencies for the P_1 gene in the Indian Region than in Europe, though higher than in Eastern Asia. In view of the paucity of data, and of the possibility of obtaining false negative results when specimens are not quite fresh, further data are to be desired, from as many populations as possible and carefully tested with potent sera on fresh specimens.

Rh Groups

In the settled populations of the Indian Region the frequencies of the Rh groups (as tested with 4 or more antisera) show a close resemblance to those of the Mediterranean region of Europe and North Africa, with higher frequencies of CDe (R_1) and lower frequencies of cde (r) than are found in northern and central Europe. Since the ABO frequencies of India differ so greatly from those of all parts of Europe, full blood groups studies in the various countries of south-western Asia are much to be desired an order to bridge the gap between the two regions.

As in the case of the MN groups, many of the tribes show Rh frequencies similar to those of the settled peoples, but some tribes, especially in the south, are very different, and with CDE (R_z)

present, and cde (r) infrequent or absent, resemble rather the peoples of Southeast Asia and even Australia.

ABO Secretion and Lewis Blood Groups

The only available data on Lewis blood groups in the Indian Region show the Chenchu of South India to have 9.2 percent of Le^a - positives, and the Veddahs 28.8 per cent.

We now possess, however, very extensive data on the distribution of the secretor phenomenon. The frequency of the secretor gene in the settled people of India is in most cases between 50 and 60 per cent, as it is in most of the peoples of Europe who have been much more extensively studied. It exceeds 60 per cent in the Chenchu, in the Galong of Assam and in the Onges of Little Andaman. Much more interesting however, are the very low frequencies found, mainly by Buchi, in certain of the tribal peoples of South India. Such peoples, if reliable evidence of family relationships could be obtained from them, would form admirable subjects for a study of the serological and genetical interrelations of the Secretor and Lewis systems, and might yield information which would be difficult to obtain anywhere else in the world. The feasibility of such genetical studies is a matter upon which the advice of social anthropologists would be necessary, but, even in the absence of family data, a careful study of the Lewis and secretor factors in the red cells and saliva of random samples of a number of these peoples would be of considerable interest.

Other Blood Group Systems

The Kell (K) gene is probably rare in India but there are considerable frequency differences between some published series and others. In view of this variation, and of the paucity of data, further work is needed. When sera become available it is desirable that tests should also be done with anti-k, anti-Kp^a and anti-Kp^b.

The Lutheran (Lu^a) gene appears to be almost completely absent from India, but more data are needed.

The Duffy (Fy^a) gene, on the other hand, reaches much higher frequencies than in Europe. In most series, however, there are some Fy(a-) individuals, but there has never been any of the exceedingly rare anti-Fy^b serum available at the right place and time to test any Indian blood specimens with it, in order to see whether any of them are of the Fy (a-b-) phenotype, which is common in Africa but very rare or absent in Europe.

No tests appear ever to have been carried out on specimens from Indians with either of the Kidd antisera, anti-Jk^a and anti-Jk^b. These sera are both very rare but it is important that some tests should be done as soon as possible, at least with anti-Jk^a.

Tasting of Phenylthiocarbamide

Though the genetically controlled taster system for phenyl-thiocarbamide is not a blood group system, it is of wide interest to geneticists, including blood group workers. The frequency of tasters in Indian populations mostly varies around 70 per cent, a similar value to that found in Europe. Much higher frequencies are found in Eastern Asia and among the American Indians.

Other Genetical Factors

A very considerable amount of work has been done on the distri-bution of abnormal haemoglobins in India, summarised by Lehmann (1961). Such haemoglobins are much less rare in India than in Europe, and sickle-cell haemoglobin is not uncommon in the tribal peoples. Even if full electrophoresis tests cannot form part of every anthropological survey it may be worth while, therefore, to carry out tests for the sickle-cell trait.

The number of known genetically controlled characters expressed in the blood is growing almost monthly, but most of the tests have been done on persons of European and African descent, and there is a vast scope for surveys of Indian populations for such factors as the Gm groups, haptoglobins and transferrins. The great variety of physically distinct peoples still living and maintaining their separate identity in India renders it an ideal field labora-tory for the application of the new genetically-based methods of physical anthropology, of which Professor Majumdar was one of the initiators.

REFERENCES

I have already stressed the fact that very large numbers of papers have been published on the distribution in India of the blood groups and other genetically simple chararters. References to almost all papers published up to the end of 1957 are included in two previous books (Mourant, 1954; Mourant, Kopeó and Domaniewska-Sobczak, 1958). The present bibliography, like those just mentioned, has been prepared by Mrs. K. Domaniewska-Sobczak, of the Nuffield Blood Group Centre, Royal Anthropological Institute, London. An attempt has been made to include below references to all papers within the scope of this paper and not included in the previous lists. In addition, papers listed in the second-mentioned book are also listed here if they contain data, on blood groups systems other than ABO, which were not themselves tabulated in the book. While it is not to be expected that there are no accidental omissions whatsoever, the worker on Indian blood groups and population genetics can therefore hope to see all available data by consulting the tables in the two books and the papers listed below. No attempt has been made to list exhaustively the numerous papers which have been published on abnormal haemoglobins in India, but full references to these papers are given by Lehmann, Sharih and Robinson (1961). Papers on colour-blindness are also not listed here, but they are listed, and the results tabulated, by Kherumian and Pickford (1959).

ANAND, Swadesh, 1957, 'A genetic survey of ABO blood group among the Punjabis,' *Anthropologist*, v. 4, Nos. 1-2, pp. 28-34.

ANAND, Swadesh, 'Distribution of ABO blood group and the ABH secretion in saliva in the Banias of Delhi,' 47th *Indian Sci. Congr.*, iii, p. 502. (Not seen).

ANAND, Swadesh, 'A genetic survey of the Garhwalis,' 47th *Indian Sci. Congr.*, iii, p. 502. (Not seen).

BANKER, D. D. and G. N. VYAS, 1955, 'Determination of blood groups and other genetical characters in certain endogamous Gujerati groups in the city of Bombay,' *J. Gujarat Res. Soc.*, pp. 157-161.

BHATIA, M., J. TINN, H. DEBRAY, and J. CABANNES, 1955, 'Etude anthropologique et génétique de la population du nord de I'Inde,' *Bull. Soc. Anthrop.* Paris, x. s., v. 6. pp. 199-213.

BHATTACHARJEE, P. N., 1954, 'Blood group investigation in the Abor tribe,' *Bull. Dep. Anthrop. India* (publ. 1958), v. 3, no. 1, pp. 51-54.

BHATTACHARJEE, P. N., 1961, 'ABO blood groups in the Raj Gonds,' *Curr. Sci.*, v. 30, p. 181.

BHENDE, Y. M., 1959, 'ABO, MN and Rh blood group frequencies in two endogamous units of Gujarat," *Indian J. Path.*, v. 1, pp. 213-217.

BIRD, G. W. G., 1955, 'Hemolytic disease of the new born. The relative importance of ABO sensitisation in India,' *Indian J. med. Scie.*, v. 9, pp. 300-307.

BIRD, G. W. G., 1955, 'The P blood group in Indians,' *Curr. Sci.*, v. 24, p. 268.

BIRD, G. W. G., ELIZABETH W. IKIN, H. LEHMANN, and A. E. MOURANT, 1956, 'The blood groups and haemoglobins of the Sikhs,' *Heredity*, v. 10, pp. 425-429.

BIRD, G. W. G., T. K. JAYARAM, Elizabeth W. IKIN, A. E. MOURANT and H. LEHMANN, 1957, 'The blood groups and haemoglobin of the Gorkhas of Nepal,' *Amer. J. Phys. Anthrop.*, v. 15 n.s., pp. 163-169.

BOYD, W. C., and L. G. BOYD, 1954, 'The blood groups in Pakistan,' *Amer. J. Phys. Anthrop.*, v. 12 n.s., pp. 393-405.

BUCHI, E. C., 1953a, 'Frequency of ABO-blood groups and secretor facto in Bengal,' *Bull. Dep. Anthrop. India*, (publ. 1956) v. 2, no. 1, pp. 49-54.

1953b, 'ABO, MN, Rh blood groups and secretor factor in Kanikkar: a genetical survey in South Travancore and contribution to the race problem in India,' *Bull. Dep. Anthrop. India* (publ. 1958), v. 2, no. 2, pp. 83-98.

n.d. 'ABH secretion in India,' *Anthropologist*, vol. 1, no. 1, pp. 3-9.

1955a, 'Blood, secretion and taste among the Pallar, a South Indian community," *Anthropologist*, v. 2, no. 1, pp. 1-8.

1955b, 'A genetic survey among the Malapantaram, a hill tribe of Travancore,' *Anthropologist*, v. 2, no. 2. pp. 1-11.

BUCHI, E. C. and S. ROY, 1955, 'Taste, middle-phalangeal hair and colour vision of the Onge of Little Andaman,' *Bull. Dep. Anthrop. India* (publ. 1959), v. 4, no. 2, pp. 7-10.

BUCHI, E. C., 1956-57, 'Uber die Frequenz einger Erbmerkmale bei den Onge von Little Andaman', *Bull. schweiz., Ges. Anthrop.*, v. 33, pp. 20-21.

1957-58, 'Die Geruchsempfindilichkeit gegenuber Natriumcyanid bei den Bengali,' *Bull. schweiz. Ges. Anthrop.*, v. 34, pp. 4-5.

1957-58, 'Blut, Ausscheiderstatus und Geschmack bei den Ulladan, einem Dschungelvolk in Südindien,' *Bull. schweiz. Ges. Anthrop.*, v. 34, pp. 5-7.

1958-59, 'Genfrequenzen von Mala-Vedan (Südindien),' *Bull. schweiz. Ges. Anthrop.*, v. 35, pp. 6-9.

1959-60, 'Blut, Geschmack und Farbensinn bei den Kurumba (Nilgiri, Indien),' *Bul. schweiz. Ges. Anthrop.*, v. 36, p. 4.

1959-60, 'Uber Blut und Geschmack der Mala-Kuruvan (Kerala, Indien),' *Bull. schweiz. Ges. Anthrop.*, v. 36, pp. 5-6.

CLEGG, E. J., ELIZABETH IKIN, and A. E. MOURANT, 1961, 'The blood groups of the Baltis,' *Vox Dang.*, in press.

DAS, S. R., and LALITA GOSH, 1954, 'A genetic survey among the Paniyan —a South Indian aboriginal tribe,' *Bull. Dep. Anthrop. India* (publ. 1958), v. 3, no. 1, pp. 65-72.

DAS, S. R., 1958, 'Inheritance of the P.T.C. taste character in man: an analysis of 126 Rárhi Bráhmin families of West Bengal', *Ann. hum. Genet.*, v. 22, pp. 200-212.

DESAI, M. D., 1955, 'A report on health survey of middle class families in Ahmedabad,' *J. Gujarat Res. Soc.*, v. 16, pp. 109-156.

DRONAMRAJU, K. R., 1961, 'Frequences of hairy pinnae among Indian and Sinhalese Peoples,' *Nature*, v. 190, p. 653.

DRONAMRAJU, K. R., P. MEERAKHAN and V. V. NARAYANA MURTY 1961, *Man*, in press.

GHOSH, LALITA, 1956, 'Taste sensitivity to phenylthiocarbamide in the Padmaraj (Pod) and the Bagdi of West Bengal,' *Anthropologist*, v. 3, no. 1-2, pp. 56-63.

GHOSH, M. N., B. N. BISWAS, and M. L. CHATTERJEA, 1957, 'ABO blood groups and peptic ulcer in Indians,' *Bull. Calcutta Sch. trop. Med.*, v. 5, p. 169.

GUPTA, S. P., 1958, 'ABO blood groups in Tripura (North-East India), *J. R. Anthrop. Inst.*, v. 88, pp. 109-111.

HIRSCH, H., 1958, 'Blood group distribution in Natal: Preliminary note,' *Trans. R. Soc. trop. Med. Hyg.*, v. 52, pp. 408-410.

INDIA. BLOOD GROUP REFERENCE CENTRE. INDIAN CANCER RESEARCH CENTRE, BOMBAY. Report of the work done from Oct. 1958 to Sep. 1959 (stencilled).

KHERUMIAN, R., and R. W. PICKFORD, 1959, Hérédité et fréquence des dyschromatopsies. Paris: Vigot Freres.

KHERUMIAN, R., and NIOGUY, 1960, 'Note sur les groupes sanguins ABO des Brahmanes de Pondichery,' Bull. Soc. Anthrop. Paris, xi. s., v. 1, pp. 241-244.

KUMAR, N., 1954, 'Blood group and secretor frequency among the Galong,' Bull. Dep. Anthrop. India (publ. 1958), v. 3, no. 1, pp. 55-64.

KUMAR, N., 1958, 'ABO blood groups and secretor factor distribution among the Noatia,' Anthropologist (publ. 1960), v. 5, no. 1-2, pp. 1-3.

LEHMANN, H., A. SHARIH and G. L. ROBINSON, 1961, 'Sickle-cell haemoglobin in a Pathan,' Man, v. 61, pp. 108-110.

LODHI, M. A. K., 1960, 'A study of blood groups in Multan (West Pakistan)', Medicus, Karachi, v. 20, pp. 53-61.

MAJUMDAR, D. N., 1958, 'Blood groups of tribes and castes of Bengal,' Sankhya, v. 19, pp. 319-323.

MASTER, H. R., H. M. BHATIA, and L. D. SANGHVI, 1959, 'The rare Ry chromosome in two Parsi families,' Curr. Sci., v. 28, pp. 18-19.

MATHEW, N. T., 1959, 'Relation between stature and blood group among Indian Soldiers,' Sankhya, v. 21, pp. 1-12 in reprint.

MOTEN, A. N., and G. T. STEWART, 1956, 'Blood groups of Muslims and Parsees in Pakistan,' Brit. J. Haemat., v. 2, pp. 61-64.

MOURANT, A. E., 1954, The distribution of the human blood groups. Oxford, Blackwell Scientific Publications, Also: Springfield, Ill., C. C. Thomas.

MOURANT, A. E., Ada C. KOPEC and KAZIMIERA DOMANIEWSKA-SOBCZAK, 1958, The ABO blood groups: Comprehensive tables and maps of world distribution. Oxford, Blackwell Scientific Publications.

PATHAK, M. L., 1954, 'Rh incidence in the Punjab,' Indian J. Med. Res. v. 42, pp. 147-149.

RAO, C. R., 1958, 'A statistical assessment of some of the existing data on A-B.O. blood groups of Bengalese,' Sankhya, v. 19, pp. 323-330.

ROY, M. N., D. R. MAHASAYA, and P. C. MITRA, 1959, 'Incidence of Rh-negative rate and nature of phenotypes amongst the Bengalees,' J. Indian Med. Ass., v. 32, pp. 10-13.

ROY, S., 1955, 'Distribution of ABO, MN blood groups and the ABH secretor among the tribes of Central and Northern Travencore,' Man in India, v. 35, no. 1, pp. 57-65.

SANGHVI, L. D., P. K. SUKUMARAN, and H. M. BHATIA, 1954, 'The blood group distribution of the Marathas of Bombay,' 5th Int. Congr. Blood Transfus., Paris (pub. 1955), pp. 253-259.

SARKAR, S. S., G. RAY, M. R. CHAKRAVARTTI, A. R. BANERJEE, and P. BHATTACHARJEE, 1958, 'A preliminary note on the Kadars of Kerala', Sci. & Cult. v. 23, pp. 562-563.

SARKAR, S. S., 1959, 'Blood groups and colour blindness among the Kotas of the Nilgiris,' Sci. & Cult., v. 25, pp. 379-380.

SARKAR, S. S., A. R. BANERJEE, P. BHATTACHARJEE, and A. K. ROY

1960, 'Further studies on ABO blood groups from Orissa,' *Sci. & Cult.*, v. 25, pp. 694-695.

SEN, D. K., 1960, 'Blood groups and haemoglobin variants in some upper castes of Bengal,' *J. R. Anthrop. Inst.*, v. 90, pp. 161-172.

SEN, N. N., C. L. MUKHERJEE and B. K. AIKAT, 1959, 'Incidence of ABO and Rh (D) blood group amongst Bengalese,' *J. Indian Med. Ass.*, v. 33, pp. 210-213.

SHARMA, J. C., 1957, 'Inheritance of secretor factor and the frequency distribution of the secretor gene among the Punjabis,' *Anthropologist* (publ. 1959), v. 4, nos. 1-2, pp. 44-49.

SIRSAT, H., 1956, 'Effect of migration on some genetical characters in six endogamous groups in India,' *Ann. hum. Genet.* v. 21, pp. 145-154.

SOLANKI, B. R., R. N. SHUKLA, and J. J. SOOD, 1960, 'Study of blood groups of Mahars and Marathas showing presence of sickle cell trait at Nagpur,' *Indian J. Med. Res.*, v. 48, pp. 146-148.

SRIVASTAVA, R. P., 1959, 'Measurements of taste sensitivity to phenylthiourel (P.T.C.) in Uttar Pradesh,' *East. Anthrop.* v. 12, pp. 267-272.

TALWAR, C. L., and C. P. SAWHNEY, 1958, 'ABO and AB blood groups in Punjab,' *Indian J. Med. Sci.*, v. 12, pp. 942-944.

1959, 'Rh frequency in Punjab (India),' *Indian J. Med. Sci.*, v. 13, pp. 324-325.

VYAS, G. N., H. M. BHATIA, D. D. BANKER, and N. M. PURANDARE 1958, 'Study of blood groups and other genetical characters in six Gujarati endogamous groups in Western India,' *Ann. hum. Genet.*, v. 22, pp. 185-199.

9

THE RACIAL COMPOSITION OF BENGALIS

D. K. SEN

INDIA with its 1,176,864 sq. miles of land is inhabited by 356,879,394 people (Census of India, 1951). This population can be divided, on the basis of social structure into tribal and non-tribal communities. There are, however, many groupings which cannot be neatly placed in either of these categories. It is generally thought that these tribal populations are the descendants of the earliest settlers of India. They now live in the more inhospitable regions of South and Central India and in the hilly parts of Assam.

The non-tribal populations are divided into various religious groups, each of which is endogamous. Throughout the length and the breadth of the country they are broken up into several cultural groups with distinctive environments and historical backgrounds. Generally speaking, each of these isolates is distinguished by language, marriage customs, kinship systems and various other cultural factors. These prevent marriage alliances between the populations of distinctive cultural zones, which are usually named after the language used in the area. The States of India correspond to these cultural areas to a large extent.

One of the most characteristic features, of the Hindu social organisation, which has been at least partially retained by Muslim and Christian converts, is the remarkable system of dividing the community into a very large number of endogamous groups called 'Castes'. Risley (1912) defines the caste system as "a collection of families or groups of families, bearing a common name which usually denotes or is associated with a specific occupation; claiming common descent from a mythical ancestor, human or divine; professing to follow the same calling; and regarded by those who are competent to give an opinion as forming a single homogeneous community. A caste is almost invariably endogamous in the sense that the number of the large circle denoted by the common name may not marry outside that circle; but within this circle. There are usually a number of similar circles, each of which is also endogamous . . . ." These smaller circles may ultimately be formed of exogamous divisions called the 'gotras'.

Socially, the caste system is a hierarchical order, where every caste has a traditional and recognised position. The prestige of a caste depends on its distance from the top, which is always and everywhere occupied by the Brahmins. However, the positions in the hierarchy of other castes may vary from place to place. This paper deals primarily with the genetic relationship between the Hindu castes of Bengal. It is therefore necessary to give a short summary of the latter which follows.

According to Risley (1912) the entire Hindu community of Bengal may be divided horizontally into seven tiers, of which the highest position is occupied by the Brahmins. These have several more or less endogamous territorial sub-divisions of which two are most important. These are the Rarhi and the Barendra, occupying originally the western and northern parts of Bengal respectively. Besides these, there are other Brahmins, some of whom are considered to be degraded, for they officiate in the religious ceremonies of the low castes in which the higher caste Brahmins would not participate.

Second only to the Brahmins are placed the Vaidyas and the Kayasthas. The traditional profession of the former is the practice of medicine, of the latter the performance of tasks generally related to keeping of accounts and clerical duties. Members of the foregoing three castes are well educated, and only a minute fraction of them stick to their traditional professions. As will be shown most of the Bengali students, who were in the United Kingdom in 1957-59 pursuing higher studies, belong to one of these three castes.

Next in social status are the so-called Nabasakha, consisting of castes mostly occupational in nature. Some lower castes are also included in it, those who are considered as being 'clean'. The following are some of the castes included in the group: Modak (confectioners), Teli (oilmen), Mali (gardeners), Kumhar (potters), Napit (barbers), Kahar (servants), Dhobi (washermen) etc. The social position of these castes, though lower than that of the Brahmin-Vaidya-Kayastha group, is not degraded, and a Brahmin does not have to take a bath after touching them. The higher castes accept water from them without hesitation.

The Goala (milkman) and the Chasi Kaibarta (cultivator Kaibarta) are placed at the next lower level. The latter have now changed their name to Mahisya, and are known as such by other members of the community.

In the fifth group belong the Sundi (wine maker) and the Subarnabanik (gold merchant). They are low caste people even in the eyes of a barber who would not cut their toe nails, or attend the marriage festivities of these people.

Next in the caste hierarchy are a number of castes which are considered as degraded but not untouchable and the washerman will serve them. They abstain from eating beef. The Bagdi, the Pod, the Jalia Kaibarta (fisherman Kaibarta) and the Namasudra are some of the castes included in this group. Except the Jalia Kaibarta, none of these is occupational. They are usually village servants and small farmers or landless labourers.

The Dom, the Hari, the Chamar (tanner), the Muchi (shoemaker), the Bauri and such other castes, belong to the lowest class of castes. They eat everything that is abhorrent to the high caste Hindus, and their occupations of tanning and attending the crematorium are considered to be sufficient reason for making them the untouchables. They can live only on the outside of the village.

These are some of the thirty-six or forty castes traditionally recognised in Bengal. Some of the caste distinctions are not inviolable. In particular, castes influential in the wider community may rise in social status and avoidance patterns to a higher level. But this is not allowed to interfere with the strict endogamy of the castes.

The foregoing discussions reveal a number of factors that go into the formation of genetic isolates. These are, apart from geographical factors, religion, cultural differentiations, and lastly, caste. The latter is the smallest unit of the three and, therefore, ideal for population genetical studies.

I have made an attempt in this paper to utilise the existing blood group frequency data of the Bengalis with a view to elucidating some of the problems of physical anthropology of the Bengalis. The basic data are extensive though rather patchy and confined almost entirely to only one of the many systems of blood groups. Besides several blood group systems the relative trait of secretor factor has been considered as also the variants of the normal haemoglobin. As has been mentioned earlier the samples herein considered are from castes which are largely endogamous and are thus synonymous with the modern genetic concept of 'Race'.

The X^2 (the symbol 'X' will denote 'chi' throughout this paper) method has been applied throughout to test the statistically significant differences between samples and to test the heterogeneity of a number of samples.

PART I: *Relationship between the Upper Caste Bengalis*

In all 726 Brahmins were tested for their ABO frequencies. The ABO gene frequencies of these samples are shown in the following table:

TABLE NO. 1.16

Authors	No. Tested	Gene frequencies %		
		p	q	r
Greval & Chandra (1940)	201	14.48	24.03	61.49
Sen (1954)	100	26.16	18.99	54.85
Majumdar & Rao (1958)	237	16.51	25.57	57.92
Sen (1960)	188	15.60	22.18	62.23
Total	726	17.04	23.36	59.60

$$X^2 = 18.23; \quad \text{d.f.} = 9; \quad P = 0.05\text{---}0.02$$

We observe from the rather low value of the P, that the variation between the several authors' samples is just significant at the 0.05 level; and this is wholly due to the high frequency of A among a set of Brahmins tested in a restricted locality of South Bengal (Sen, 1954). This is in contrast to the other samples which were either tested in the city of Calcutta, where populations from all parts of Bengal congregate, or represented a pooled figure comprising observations from several districts (Majumdar). The heterogeneity goes to show that there is an isolated niche in South Bengal consisting of Brahmins whose origin might perhaps be different from that of the rest. But this needs further confirmation.

Because of the heterogeneity of the Brahmin samples it would not be advisable to pool the results of the several authors. We therefore, put down the weighted average gene frequencies of the various samples as shown in table 1. These are:

$$p = 17.04; \quad q = 23.36; \quad r = 59.60$$

The Kayastha samples are shown below:

TABLE NO. 2

Authors	No. Tested	Gene frequencies %		
		p	q	r
Chowdhury (1936)	154	15.43	22.64	61.93
Majumdar & Rao (1958)	364	19.03	23.57	57.40
Greval & Chandra (1940)	149	13.01	26.03	60.96
Sen (1954)	139	14.75	23.65	61.60
Sen (1960)	269	18.50	19.89	61.61
Total	1075	17.00	22.87	60.14

$$X^2 = 11.49; \quad d.f. = 12; \quad P = 0.5$$

The X^2 value points to a homogeneity among the Kayasthas of Bengal with respect to the ABO frequencies. It is to be noted that unlike the Brahmins of South Bengal, the Kayasthas belonging to the same region (Sen, 1954) do not show any distinguishing features in their ABO frequencies. The pooled gene frequencies of the total number of 1075 Kayasthas comes to:

$$p = 17.00; \quad q = 22.87; \quad r = 60.14$$

The size of the Vaidya caste is very much smaller than either that of Brahmins or that of Kayasthas. Probably because of the relatively small size, the Vaidya samples are also smaller than those of other castes. Besides that of Sen (1960) there are two other samples, one consisting of only 50 observations (Greval and Chandra, 1940) and the other by Majumdar and Rao consisting of only 95 tests. The total number of Vaidyas tested by all authors is only 233. The gene frequency data are shown below:

TABLE NO. 3

Authors	No. tested	Gene frequencies		
		p	q	r
Gravel & Chandra (1940)	50	9.45	10.56	80.00
Majumdar & Rao (1958)	95	21.75	21.08	57.17
Sen (1960)	88	24.51	20.13	55.35
Total	233	20.15	18.47	61.38

$$X^2 = 15.9; \quad d.f. = 6; \quad P = 0.01$$

A test of X^2 on three samples give a P value of 0.01 showing that the samples are differentiated. The weighted average gene frequencies would be:

$$p = 20.15, \qquad q = 18.47, \qquad r = 61.38$$

This heterogeneity is largely due to the small sample of Greval and Chandra which shows an usual pattern of the ABO gene frequencies for the Bengali upper castes. The data were collected from hospital patients.

In the following table all the samples from the three upper castes are compared.

TABLE NO. 4

Caste samples	No. tested	Gene frequencies		
		p	q	r
Brahmin	726	17.04	23.36	59.60
Kayastha	1075	17.00	22.87	60.14
Vaidya	233	20.15	18.47	61.38
Total	2034	17.36	22.54	60.09

$$X^2 = 7.89; \qquad d.f. = 6; \qquad p = 0.3 - 0.2$$

It will be noticed that the Vaidyas show somewhat different gene frequencies from those of the Brahmins and the Kayasthas. This difference is particularly noticed in the lowered B gene incidence and a raised O gene frequency of the Vaidyas as compared to those of the other two castes. However, as the P value shows (between 0.3 and 0.2), the gene frequency differences are not statistically significant. We conclude from this that the Bengali upper castes cannot be differentiated from one another with respect to the available ABO data. The pooled gene frequencies of the upper caste samples are:

$$p = 17.36, \qquad q = 22.54, \qquad r = 60.09$$

Part II: *Comparison between upper caste and lower caste Hindus of Bengal*

ABO data of the following lower caste groups are available; Bagdi, Pod, Rishi, Namsudra, Kaora ani Mahisya. Besides these specific caste groups, several other samples which are not so definite as regards caste affiliation of the subjects were tested. These have been variously called Depressed Classes, low castes or Hindu non castes by the authors.

We shall first compare the upper caste samples with those of the lower castes that have definite caste affiliations. The number of persons tested and the gene frequencies of the latter are given in the following table:

TABLE NO. 5

Vaste samples	No. tested	Gene frequencies %		
		p	q	r
Bagdi (Macfarlene and Sarkar, 1941)	107	19.10	26.35	54.55
Bagdi (Sen, 1954)	38	23.69	29.02	47.29
Pod (Sen 1954)	133	14.86	36.42	48.72
Rishi (Majumdar & Rao, 1958)	72	20.20	30.43	49.35
Namasudra (Majumdar & Rao, 1958)	383	17.95	23.86	58.19
Kaora (Sen, 1954)	78	19.28	27.70	53.01
Mahisya (Macfarlane, 1958)	160	15.24	27.57	57.19
Mahisya (Sen, 1954)	277	16.36	24.55	59.09
Total	1248	17.49	26.82	55.77

$$X^2 = 43.6, \quad d.f. = 21, \quad P = 0.01$$

X^2 test applied to the values presented in the above table shows that the variation observed between the samples is statistically significant (P = less than 0.01). This is in contrast to the homogeneous nature of the upper castes with respect to the ABO frequencies. The weighted average gene frequencies of the total lower castes are compared with the pooled gene frequencies of the total upper castes as follows:

	p	q	r
Lower Castes	17.49	26.82	55.77
Upper Castes	17.36	22.54	60.09

It will be seen that the lower castes differ from the upper castes chiefly in their raised q. Moreover, they also show a relatively lower O gene frequency. The A gene frequency is similar in both groups. In this connection it is interesting to note the close similarities between the lower castes mentioned above and the santals, the largest tribe in India, which occupies the eastern parts of Bihar and the western and the northern parts of Bengal at the present time. It is said that the distribution of tribe in former times was much more widespread than at present. There are altogether three samples from the Santals which are homogeneous with regard to the ABO frequencies. The total number of Santals tested was 746. The pooled gene frequencies of the Santals are compared with those of the lower castes in the following table.

TABLE NO. 6

Caste samples	No. tested	Gene frequencies %		
		p	q	r
Lower Castes	1248	17.49	26.82	55.77
Santals	746	17.80	26.89	56.84

Although we have said that the upper castes and the lower castes are distinct with respect to the BO frequencies, it must be borne in mind that the value taken to represent the lower castes, is the average of the several values, having a wide range of dispersal. When we examine table No. 5 we notice that the values of the samples Namasudra and Mahisya, overlap those of the upper castes and are therefore, different from those of the lower castes. The former two castes form two large populations in Bengal, the Namsudras being considered as particularly low in the caste hierarchy in Bengal. Their separation from the other lower castes and approach to the upper castes raise the problem of their genetic status *vis-a-vis* the upper and lower castes. Could it be that they were an earlier branch of the western people settled in Bengal followed by the earlier representatives of the modern higher castes, who finally subjugated them and forced them to accept a lower position in Hindu society? The difficulty in accepting such a view is that there is no definite historical evidence of such a migration, though it is obvious that the western invaders did not reach Bengal in a single wave. Secondly, we do not really possess enough data for this type of generalisation, for all we know, the similarity of the ABO data might be fortuitous, and the evidence of the other genetic systems might point to quite a different direction. In any case, further investigations on these lines might show fruitful results of the composition of the Bengali people.

Part III: *Comparison of Bengal castes with respect to the blood groups other than ABO, the secretor status and the haemoglobin variants*

At present no data on the distribution of the blood groups other than the ABO in Bengal are available for comparison with the present study, except some undifferentiated samples whose caste affiliations are not given. In fact, Sen's (1960) study is the only one of its kind which given some information about A_2 MN, ABH secretion, P. Kell and Rhesus blood groups, based on the castes of the subjects.

Besides that of Sen (1960) there are two other samples both from Calcutta hospitals, where MN tests were carried out. In both these castes, caste affiliation of the subjects are not given. In one (Gravel et al. 1939) even the linguistic affiliation is not shown. These are compared with the present data of the Bengalis in the following table.

TABLE NO. 7

Authors	No. tested	Gene frequencies %	
		M	N
Greval et al (1939)	300	66.00	34.00
Macfarlane (1940)	130	60.77	39.23
Sen (1960)	594	64.57	35.43
Total	1024	64.51	35.49

$$X^2 = 3.4, \quad d.f. = 4, \quad P = 0.3$$

It will be seen that the values of Sen's sample come very close to those of Macfarlane (1940-6), but differs somewhat from the 'Hindu' sample of Greval et al. However, the three samples are found not to differ significantly from one another (P = 0.3). We may then pool the three samples together and characterise the MN frequencies of the Bengalis as: m = 64.51, n = 35.49.

The non-secretor frequency of the Bengalis tested by Sen (1960) varies considerably, the range of variation being between 27.22 per cent among the Miscellaneous castes and 50 per cent among the Vaidyas. This difference among the caste groups was found to be statistically significant. There are two other undifferentiated samples from Calcutta. Buchi (1953) tested 414 Bengalis and found 33.09 per cent of non-secretors, similar to the average of the non-secretor frequency of the castes of the present samples. Gravel's sample (1951) of 50 Indians is not comparable, because he does not even mention the linguistic affiliation of the subjects. However, the value of 30 per cent non-secretors in this example is not very different from that of the present series.

In the Rh system Sen (1960) has found 6.01 per cent and 4.1 per cent of D-negatives respectively in two sets of data, one tested by anti-D only and the other tested with the four usual anti-Rh sera. The pooled frequency was 5.05 per cent. Greval and Chowdhury (1946) tested two sets of Indians of Calcutta (undifferentiated). Sen's sample (1960) therefore, contains less D-negatives than those of Greval and Chowdhury. However, the difference is not statistically significant (P = between 0.3 and 0.2).

Besides Sen's series (1960), there is only one other sample from Bengal in which 200 'Indians' were tested with anti. C,-D,-E by Venkataraman (1950). His calculated chromosome frequencies are compared below with those of Sen of 171 Bengalis:

	Chromosome frequencies %				
	CDe	*Cde*	*cDE*	*cDe*	*cde*
Sen (1960)	67.06	3.41	7.92	5.50	16.11
Indians (Venkataraman, 1950)	63.72	1.74	1.16	4.60	27.88

It would appear from the comparison that Sen's sample shows somewhat different frequencies of the chromosomes cDE and cde, as compared to those of Venkataraman's. It is obvious that the two samples are not strictly comparable, the latter being an undifferentiated one. We are, therefore, not in a position to assess the significance of the sample differences.

Of the 564 persons whose blood samples were tested electrophoretically for abnormal haemoglobins (Sen, 1960) a total of 14 or 2.5 per cent were found to carry abnormal haemoglobins of one kind or another. Ten of these or 1.8 per cent of the total tested were carrying HbE as well as the normal HbA. One of the two remaining was probably heterozygous for HbE and thalassaemia. The phenotype of the remaining one is rather uncertain but it could have been homozygous for HbE.

Distributed according to the castes, it was found that 12 out of the 14 affected persons or about 85 per cent belonged to the higher castes, the remaining 15 per cent belonged to the Miscellaneous castes (1 Muslim and one Vaisya). Of the 564 persons, 507 or about 90 per cent belonged to the upper castes and 57 or about 10 per cent belonged to the various lower castes and Muslims. We thus find that the distribution of the haemoglobin variants between the higher and lower castes is proportional to their numerical strength in the total sample. We may perhaps conclude from this that the upper and the lower castes in Bengal do not differ as regards the frequency of the haemoglobin variants.

The finding of J. B. Chatterjee et al. (1957) of 3.6 per cent of Hbe is comparable to the 1.8 per cent of the same character among the Bengalis of the present sample. He also found two instances of homozygous HbE as against one among the castes of the present study. On the other hand HbD was absent from their sample of 700 Bengalis, whereas at least two were detected in the present series of tests.

The Bengalis can then be characterised as possessing a moderate amount of HbE at a rate of about 27 per 1000 of the population (the mean between the two samples being 2.7 per cent). HbD is also found among them as a much lower rate, while cases of thalassaemia minor are found at a rate of 37 per 100 persons. Lastly, the Bengalis most certainly lack the haemoglobin S responsible for the sickle cell trait.

The present information about the genetic characteristics of the Bengalis has been given in the foregoing pages of this paper. On the basis of this information certain inter-relationships between the Bengali castes have been postulated. It remains for us to see whether these inter-relationships correspond to the socially accepted relations prevailing in Bengal at present or in the past. Thus, we wish to know whether the genetic inter-relationships between the upper castes shown in the foregoing pages reflect a similar social relationship. Sen (1960) has shown that while in most genetic characters (ABO, MN, Rh, P and Kell) the upper castes form a homogeneous unit, with respect to one character (secretor status) the Vaidyas stand apart from the rest i.e., Brahmin and Kayastha. This shows that the three upper castes largely share a common gene pool: which means that they never formed complete isolates. This is particularly so for the Brahmin and the Kayastha which reveal close similarity with each other, while the Vaidyas are somewhat less mixed with the other two. Theoretically each caste is an isolate, and given enough time and continued isolation each would be expected to differ from others due to differential chance fluctuations of the gene frequencies. The question is: What prevented them from achieving this status of closed genetic isolates? The answer must be sought in the social structure of the upper caste Bengalis. The author leaves the question to the social anthropologists. It is sufficient that such a question has arisen as a result of genetic approach towards the studies on castes.

The three upper castes totalled about 3 millions or roughly about 14 per cent of the Hindus in Bengal in the year 1931. The large number of genetical characters in which they are similar point to the fact that they must have at an earlier times shared the same gene pool, which was also probably shared by such lower castes as Namasudras and Mahisyas. The members of the latter two castes are both numerous and widespread together forming about 20 per cent of the Hindu population. The rest of the lower castes, presumably arising from the aboriginal tribal folk of the land, akin to the modern Santals, always kept a respectable distance between themselves and the higher castes, and exchange of genes between them was probably at a minimum. Among the lower castes the heterogeneity in ABO may reflect the fact that caste rules are and had been in the past more rigidly adhered to as compared to the upper castes. Moreover, it must be further stressed that Kulinism was absent among them.

Taken as whole, however, the difference between the higher and lower castes is very small indeed, judging simply from the slight though significant difference in the B gene frequency between the groups of castes. Further difference may exist but unless more genetic characters are investigated among them we cannot be sure. For the present we must assume on the basis of a somewhat lower incidence of the B gene that the upper castes are genetically differentiated from the lower castes. Nevertheless, the gene is found in both the groups of castes in relatively high frequency, and the probability that they had a common origin cannot be ignored. The small difference in the B gene frequency between the upper and lower castes is in fact hard to explain. There is no doubt that western influence is great among the upper castes, but that does not explain the present B gene frequency among them which is about 22 per cent as compared to 28 per cent among the lower castes. This might mean that while the lower castes have been composed almost wholly of the tribals who have turned Hindus, the higher castes have only been partially influenced by them and have more or less maintained the B gene frequency of the original western immigrants, in whom the gene frequency must have been somewhat lower than 22 per cent. This frequency might be assumed to have been round about 17 per cent as is observed in Persia (Mourant, 1958, p. 155). We mention this region because of its close linguistic affinity with India. Admittedly this is a far fetched explanation, but at the present state of our knowledge we can do no better till more complete genetic information is obtained of the communities not only of Bengal, but of other parts of India as well.

Part IV: *Bengalis compared with other populations in India*

Before we compare Bengalis with other populations in India, we must investigate the relationship between the Bengalis of West-Bengal (India) and those residing in the eastern part of Bengal, now called East Pakistan. Although politically, East Pakistan is a foreign country, still from the point of view of linguistic and other cultural matters the Bengalis of that area are closely related to the Bengalis of India. There is, however, a marked difference in the professed religion of the people in the two areas. The East Pakistanis are predominantly Muslim while the Bengalis of India are predominantly Hindus. It is the consensus of opinion of most historians that almost all Pakistani Muslims are the decendants of Hindus in Bengal, converted to Islam during the period of Muslim rule in India. Thus for our present purpose we may consider the East Pakistanis as one with the Bengalis of India.

We have at our disposal the excellent samples collected by Boyd and Boyd (1954) from the Pakistani Bengalis and tested for A_1A_2 BO, MNS and Rh groups for comparison with the present sample. Two hundred and thirty six persons were tested for the A_1A_2 BO blood groups. The gene frequencies are as follows: $A_1 = 14.03$, $A_2 = 3.31$, $B = 23.09$, $O = 59.57$. These values closely confirm to those obtained in the pooled upper caste samples of Sen's (1960) study: $A_1 = 15.66$, $A_2 = 2.75$, $B = 20.70$, $O = 60.89$.

The authors tested 230 Pakistanis for the MNS system. Since

no samples from Bengal have been tested for Ss groups, we have
for purposes of comparison combined the MS and Ms on the one
hand and NS and Ns on the other into M and N respectively.
We get the following gene frequencies: M = 58.04, N = 41.96.
When we compare these frequencies with the total Bengali values:
M = 64.51, N = 35.49. We see that there is no very great differences between them.

Two hundred and thirty-six persons were tested for the various
Rh subgroups and the authors calculated the following chromosome
frequencies from the phenotypes:

	East Pakistanis	*Indian Bengalis*
	(Boyd & Boyd, 1954)	(Sen, 1960)
CDe	63.30	67.07
cDE	7.64	7.92
cde	17.07	16.11
Cde	6.49	3.41
cDe	3.87	5.50

We can see very clearly that the chromosome frequencies in
these two samples are very much alike, especially in the incidence
of the more frequent chromosomes.

From all these comparisons we conclude that from the point
of view of blood groups, the East Pakistani Bengalis are genetically
similar to their linguistic counterparts from India.

Table 8 contains the ABO gene frequencies of the populations
of the respective States. These are mean values corrected for the
size of the samples. All samples are from non-tribal populations
and mostly have been taken from the excellent compilation of the
ABO data from all over the world by Mourant, (1958). The Bengal
data is the combined value of the upper caste and the lower caste
Hindus as shown in tables 4 and 5 respectively. Only castes that
inhabit the gangetic plains of Uttar Pradesh, have been considered
to represent the State. Other details of samples are shown in the
table .

It will be seen from these mean values that of the three gene
frequencies q and r are the most variable while p varies within a
small range.

When the B gene frequency alone is compared we notice that the
Bengalis with their higher B show a marked difference from the
populations of Madhya Pradesh, Maharashtra, Madras and Kerala.

TABLE NO. 8

*Comparison of the mean ABO gene frequencies in
non-tribal populations of some of the states of India*

States	No. tested	Gene frequencies		
		p	q	r
Assam	2,000	18.61	23.67	57.72
Bengal	3,282	17.41	24.17	58.45
Uttar Pradesh (Plains)	2,180	18.22	25.23	56.55
Punjab	4,248	18.44	23.18	58.38
Rajasthan	711	17.40	24.82	57.78
Gujerat	2,173	19.55	25.34	55.11
Maharashtra (Maratha)	2,512	21.30	17.76	60.94
Madhyapradesh (Brahmins)	695	19.00	17.76	63.25
Madras	2,644	14.68	21.81	63.50
Kerala (Nayar, Malayali, Izhavan)	513	19.25	11.67	69.08

The populations in the three latter states are further differentiated from the Bengalis in respect of a higher proportion of the O gene.

On the other hand the Bengali blood groups (ABO) are very similar to those observed in the states of U.P., Punjab, Gujarat, Rajasthan and Assam. The Bengalis together with the populations in these states inhabit a wide stretch of land running from the eastern border of India to her western border, a distance of more than two thousand miles. The similarity in their ABO frequency probably denotes a common origin. Further, throughout the area q is almost uniformly the highest value being found among the populations in Utter Pradesh and Gujarat. Thus Bengalis cannot be said to be distinguished by a higher B gene frequency than other populations in the north and there is therefore no justification for describing Bengal as the focus for the dispersal of this gene.

The essential similarity in the populations of Northern India is further stressed by the similarity in the Rh chromosome frequencies of the Bengalis and the Sikhs of Punjab. It is regrettable that tests of Rh groups have not been done in the populations of Uttar Pradesh, lying as it is between Punjab and Bengal, but it may be predicted that future investigations will not in all probability reveal any striking differences between the Bengalis and the Sikhs on the one hand and the populations of Uttar Pradesh on the other.

Mention has been made of the difference between the Bengalis and the populations of Maharashtra, Madhya Pradesh, Madras and Kerala, with regard to their ABO frequencies. However, the difference extends also to other serologic systems where they have been studied. Thus, while a similar M gene frequency is observed between the Marathi-speaking and the Bengali-speaking populations, the two are very different in the frequency of their P-negative phenotypes. The Madras populations are different from the Bengalis not only in that they have a lower B and a higher O gene frequency but also in the non-secretor frequency, though not in a very marked degree.

The existing blood group data does not give us a valid clue to the direction of the movements of the Bengalis, for the ABO frequencies do not show any clearcut gradient from the west to the east of India. In the present context the frequency of the haemoglobin variants may perhaps prove to be of some importance. We know that the Gujeratis, the Punjabis and the Bengalis, all have HbD in more or less equally low incidence. However, HbE is found only among the Bengalis and presumably not among the Punjabis. If we can place any weight on a gene present in such low frequency, the simultaneous presence of HbD and HbE in Bengal would mean that the direction must have been from the west to the east rather than from Bengal to the west, for under the later condition to Sikhs also would have shown the HbE, which, as far as is known, is absent among them.

Part V: *Some Comparisons between Bengali Brahmins and Kayasthas with those from other parts of India*

From very early times, probably even prior to the 5th and 6th centuries A.D. numerous Brahmins from practically all over India came to Bengal and settled there. Similarly there is evidence to show that at that early period, and also later, Bengali Brahmins emigrated to other parts of India (Roy. 1954). Brahmins are ubiquitous in India, but there are only a few adequate samples from them. The ABO frequencies of these are listed below

It will be seen from the table that the Brahmins of Bengal are similar to those of U.P. and Gujarat. The common features among them are the q above 20 per cent and r below 60 per cent. But the Brahmins of Bengal are very different from those of Bombay. In the latter area, the Brahmins are distinguished by a lower frequency of q and a higher one of r. It is needless to say that the U.P. and the Gujarat Brahmins are also differentiated from the same

State	No. tested	Gene frequencies		
		p	q	r
Bengal	726	17.04	23.36	59.60
U.P.	203	20.70	22.28	57.02
Gujarat	213	21.44	21.47	57.09
Maharashtra	904	17.85	15.73	66.42

caste in Bombay, exactly in the same way as the Bengal Brahmins are differentiated from the latter.

The differences and similarities between the Bengal Brahmins and those in other parts of India mentioned above, are of the same order as was noticed when the mean values of the general populations in the above mentioned areas were compared previously.

Besides the differences between the Bombay and Bengal Brahmins in their ABO frequencies, there are also marked differences in their P group frequencies. Thus, the P-ive phenotype among the former is 18.70 per cent while that of the latter is much higher, 47.53 per cent. Among the similarities between the two groups of Brahmins are the same high M gene and low A_2 gene frequencies. In spite of these similarities, the difference in the ABO gene and P group frequencies observed between the Bombay and Bengal castes, separates them genetically.

Unfortunately we cannot compare the Brahmins from Bengal with those from the Dravidian-speaking areas because of the lack of data from the latter. There is only one sample of 50 individuals of Brahmins from Madras, which shows a somewhat different frequency of the ABO genes from those of Bengal.

The Kayastha caste is not found among the Dravidian speaking peoples of the south. They are mainly found among the Aryan speaking societies of the North and West India. Besides Bengal, Kayastha samples are available from U.P. and Bombay only. The ABO frequencies of these caste samples are shown below:

Province	No. tested	Gene frequencies		
		p	q	r
Bengal	1075	17.00	22.87	60.14
U.P.	111	17.03	24.94	58.03
Bombay	300	21.93	20.10	57.98

It would appear from this table that the Bengali Kayasthas differ but slightly from those of U.P., but the difference between the former and those from Bombay is considerable, though not so much as was observed between the Brahmins of these two areas with respect to the ABO frequencies.

The A_2 and M gene and D-negative and P-negative phenotype frequencies of the Kayasthas of Bombay and Bengal are shown below:

TABLE NO. 11

	A_2	D-ive	M	P-ive
Bengal (Sen, 1960)	1.56	5.26	62.11	49.75
Bombay (Sanghvi and Khanolkar 1950)	6.63	10.00	57.75	24.59

We see from this table that the two sets of Kayasthas differ greatly again in the P-ive frequencies, while the difference in the other frequencies is not of a high order. In general then, as in the Brahmin samples, so in the Kayastha samples, we observe evidence of genetic separations.

We conclude from this comparative study that the upper castes of Bombay and those of Bengal could not have been recruited from the same source. The same may or may not be true for the upper castes of the north Indian populations. Apparently judging from the similarities in ABO gene frequencies, the upper castes of Bengal, U.P. and Gujarat seem to belong to the same original stock, but so long as other genetic systems are not investigated it would be premature to be dogmatic about it, for a great difference in the frequency of a single system would separate two populations even if other systems show considerable similarities.

Part VI: *Bengalis Compared with Populations Outside India*

Bengal is situated on the western fringe of the great land mass inhabited by the Mongoloid race. In order to look into the problem of the origin of the Bengalis, it may be worth while to compare them with these Mongoloids to the east or south east of Bengal. The countries to be compared are Burma, China, Indo-china,

Thailand, Malaya and Indonesia. The blood group data concerning the populations of these countries have been taken from Mourant (1954: 1958).

A_1A_2BO GROUPS

Most populations in East and South East Asia have ABO frequencies roughly comparable to those of the Bengalis. We find here and there samples that are aberrant in nature; for example one of the samples from Burma consisting of 100 observations showed no individuals belonging to group A (Eickstedt, 1958).

Most Chinese, Siamese and Indonesians lack the A_2 gene altogether, but the Burmese have the gene at a relatively higher frequency. The Mongoloids, therefore, appear to be distinct from the Bengalis from this point of view. The relatively higher frequency of the gene among the Burmese can best be explained as contributed by the populations of Bengal. Wherever the ABO subgroups have been investigated in India among the non-tribal populations, A_2 genes have always been found to be present but in variable quantities. We may thus conclude that the Bengalis show the distinctly Western pattern of A_1A_2BO frequencies rather than the eastern Mongoloid pattern.

MNS GROUPS

Broadly speaking, the M gene occurs with an equally high frequency among the Bengalis and the Sough East Asiatic Mongoloids in question, though as it is natural in this wide area, there are some populations like the Siamese, who show a somewhat lower frequency of the gene. However, when the Ss genes are also considered, the difference between the Bengalis and the S. E. Asiatic Mongoloids becomes very apparent. Boyd and Boyd tested the Pakistani Bengalis with anti-S serum together with anti-M and anti-N. The MN data has been presented and discussed earlier. He found that the MS and NS chromosomes are almost equally frequent in the population. In contrast to this we find that among the Chinese and the Malay the NS chromosomes occur much more frequently than the MS chromosome.

P GROUPS

The frequency of P-ive phenotypes among the Mongoloids (Chinese and Malays) varies widely from 21 to 28 per cent among the Malays to 67 to 73 per cent among the Chinese. The Bengali frequency of 49.33 per cent (Sen, 1960), therefore, falls well within this wide variation. It may be mentioned here that the European frequency of P-ive is much lower than that of the Bengalis (and Marathis). A mixture of a Chinese type and a European type would very well explain the intermediate position of the Bengalis in the P group frequency.

RH GROUPS

One of the most important differences between the Bengalis and the Mongoloids is the almost total lack of the D-ive phenotypes among the latter as compared to the relatively high proportion among the former. Data are available of only the Chinese and the Burmese, of which the latter completely lacks the phenotype, whereas in the former the frequency is much less than 1 per cent.

In the detailed sub-groups of the Rh system, the Chinese show a very much higher frequency of the cDE chromosome than the Bengalis. On the other hand the distribution of the Rh positive and negative phenotypes and that of the Rh sub-groups of the Bengalis are wholly Western in pattern, though the D-ive are somewhat lower than is observed in most Western countries.

KELL GROUPS

These Chinese and the Malays show a complete lack of the Kellive phenotype as against 7.76 per cent frequency among the Bengalis (Sen, 1960). This frequency also is typically west European.

HAEMOGLOBIN VARIANTS

Mourant's table on the distribution of the sickle cell trait (1954) gives the data of a small series of Chinese tested in Jamaica, and an even smaller sample (n. 30) of 'Mongoloids' tested in Brazil. Both these show the absence of sickle cell trait among the respective subjects. On this basis we cannot say very much about the incidence of the trait among the Mongoloids of the South East Asiatic countries, but we might presume that it is at least rare if not absent among them. We are on the other hand fairly certain that the trait is absent in Bengal at least among the upper caste populations (no information is available about the frequency of the trait among the lower caste Bengalis). On the other hand the haemoglobin variant E is very frequent in some Mongoloid populations in East and Southeast Asia. Thus Lehmann et al (1959) observed 15.6 per cent of the Burmans carrying the trait, while Na-Nakron et al (1956) recorded 13.6 per cent of HbE among the Siamese. The Indonesians are said to carry the trait at a lower frequency (2.9 per cent). Thus we see that the Bengalis with about 2.7 per cent of the trait carriers fall naturally within the Mongoloid influence from this point of view. Moreover, the peripheral lower frequency of the trait among the Bengalis and the Indonesians contrasting with high frequency in the central zone of Burma and Siam indicates that the latter two areas probably constituted the focal area for the distribution of the trait.

In addition to HbE, the Bengalis possess HbD which is absent among the Mongoloids so far studied. However, the frequency of the latter among the Bengalis is very low, so that its absence among the Mongoloids would probably not constitute a serious barrier to the hypothesis of Mongoloid influence on the Bengalis.

Our examination has shown that the Bengalis and the Mongoloids show differences with respect to the Rh MNS and Kell groups. In these respects the Bengalis clearly show Western affinities. We may also place the presence of HbD in this category. The presence of HbE among the Bengalis is the only character that links them with the Mongoloids in the east. Medium frequency of the P groups among the former is characteristically intermediate between that of the western Caucasoid and the eastern Mongoloid.

With these facts before us we are led to conclude that the Bengalis are largely of Western extraction with the Mongoloid element forming a minor factor in the population. Similarity in the ABO blood groups between the local Santal population and the Bengalis also points to a third element which may have contributed to the make-up of the latter, although more blood group systems should be studied before the tribal legacy of the Bengalis may be substantiated.

Part VI: *Physical Anthropology of Bengalis on the Basis of Anthropometric and Serologic Studies*

. It is an old usage among anthropologists to describe a group by putting on record the mean values of various dimensions of individuals in the group and sometimes also appending with these the standard deviation and probable error of such means. When later on the principles of population genetics were applied to man, it became easy to estimate the gene frequencies of those characters whose genetics proved to be quite simple. In as much as the change in the gene frequency of the populations is held to be the prime cause behind both macro- and micro-evolution, the method was thought to be superior to that involving dimensions of the body which is still not amenable to simple genetic analysis. However, both the approaches suffer from a lack of understanding of selective processes acting on individual characters chosen for study.

In spite of their limitations for taxonomic purposes, the morphological methods have one very important advantage over genetic characters. This comprises the body of fossil material, which can be measured, but obviously at the present stage of our knowledge, no gene frequency estimates can be calculated. Oliver and Howells (1957) in the introductory part of their paper on the physical anthropology of a number of populations in Bougainville, also emphasised the importance of the continued use of the metric method. They remarked: "... however, traits of continuous variation (such as underlie the familiar anthropological measurements of form) are doubtless determined by several loci, and may be polygenic in the proper sense yet these traits constitute a whole field of variations in size and shape, furthermore involving modification by environment as well as the relationship and differentiation of populations, in short, all the processes of micro-evolution. It should also be noted that this normal morphology is traditionally the central field not only of physical anthropology but of zoology and palaeontology as well."

With these remarks in mind, it seems to be an ideal procedure to include both the genetical and morphological methods when describing a population and when comparisons are made between populations. An attempt will be made in the following pages, therefore, to compare the conclusions arrived at independently by both the morphological and serological methods on the relationship between the caste groups of Bengal and also between them and the populations outside India, in order to present a possible explanation of the origin of Bengalis.

Intercaste Relationship

The most comprehensive anthropometric survey of the Bengalis in recent years was carried out by Majumdar & Rao (1958). Majumdar measured 3240 individuals consisting of 68 social groups. However, out of these, only 12 social groups could be used for analysis by Rao, his co-author. This is because the rest of the social groups were inadequately represented in his samples. The samples from the castes and communities dealt with by Majumdar were taken from all over undivided Bengal and from a number of different districts.

The D^2 statistic was then computed to show intergroup relationship. This method takes into consideration the degree of similarity and dissimilarity between the samples, depending on twelve characters for which measurements were taken. The inter-sample distance was the sum total of these differences and similarities. It will be seen that blood group data are available only for seven out of the twelve caste samples for which anthropometric measurements are available. We shall therefore, confine ourselves to the relationships of these caste samples only. With the help of D^2 statistic the authors came to the following conclusions.

(1) There are no distinct clusters in the groups chosen for study. There are, however, a large number of small clusters in the form of a chain of consecutive clusters, themselves being linked by a common group or groups. For instance, Brahmin, Kayastha and Vaidya form one cluster. However, Muslims are found to be very closely related to the Vaidyas, and therefore, may also be linked to this cluster. In one of the clusters we find Muslims, Kayasthas and Vaidyas, but these having close affinities with the cluster including Muslims, Kayasthas and Namasudras. In another cluster we find Muslims, Namasudra, Brahmin and Kayastha closely interlinked.

(2) Another striking feature of the material under study is the clustering of the groups more on the basis of the region to which they belong than on caste or religion. For instance, the three groups of Brahmin, Kayastha, and Muslim of Dacca form a cluster, so also Muslim and Namasudra of the same place with Muslim in the neighbouring district of Mymensing, and Kayastha of Barisal with the Muslims in the continuous districts of Barisal, Nadia and Burdwan.

Among the Muslim groups the physical resemblance appear to be broadly related to the nearness of the districts to which they belong.

The groups Vaidya, Brahmin and Kayastha with individuals represented from a wider region consisting of a number of districts are remarkably close together, again supporting strong regional affinities. Thus, the D^2 between the Brahmins in districts other than Dacca and Brahmin of Dacca is 0.93 and between Kayasthas outside Barisal and in Barisal is 1.26 all of which are greater than the average D^2 within the clusters Brahmin and Kayastha of other districts and Brahmin, Kayastha and Muslim of Dacca.

Further evidence of regional difference in the metrical characters of castes can be shown from the Namasudras, who show clear differences between those residing in Dacca and those residing elsewhere. The group closest to Namasudra of Dacca is the Muslim Brahmin, Kayastha and Vaidya occupy a position further from the Namasudra than the Muslim. The distance between the Namasudra and the upper castes is due almost entirely to the smaller dimension of the head and body of the former. Among the Brahmin, Kayastha and Vaidya, affinities seems to be more on the regional basis than on caste. Thus the Kayastha of Dacca is close to the Brahmin of Dacca rather than to the Kayastha of Barisal and of other districts.

(3) All these comparisons go to show the heterogeneity among single castes in Bengal which is independent of any subcaste differences. Analysis of the Muslim data also clearly go to show the heterogeneity among them on the basis of their domicile. The affinities between the Muslim groups from various districts appear to be related, as in the Hindu castes, to the proximity of the districts in which they live.

In comparing the blood group and other serological findings with those arrived at by anthropometry, we are at once faced with a serious lack of blood group and other serological data for the Bengali populations. As against twelve characters on which the anthropometric results are based, we have only one character, the ABO system for most of the castes, tribes and communities. The present work of the author has to some extent endeavoured to fill up the gap by taking into consideration other serological characters but it must be noted again that it refers largely to the upper caste peoples only. Moreover, the existing data cannot be arranged according to the places of origin of the subjects, for more samples do not include this information. Under the circumstances we must make the best use of the available data, though certainly this will not carry us very far.

For instance we cannot test adequately the very interesting finding of Rao of the existence of regional variation of the castes. There is, however, a suggestion of such variation between the Brahmins tested by Sen (1954) in South Bengal and those tested by others in Calcutta and elsewhere. But it must be noted that no such variation is noticeable among the Kayasthas of these separate regions. This conclusion is, of course, based only on the ABO data. Regional differentiation of the Kayasthas might be demonstrated if additional genetic characters were investigated.

The small values of D^2 between the upper castes clearly go to show a very close connection between them. This confirms similar findings on the basis of a number of blood group characteristics, as the present work has shown. However, the slight deviation of the Vaidyas from the other two higher castes is not evident from the anthropometric data.

There is some difference between the Namasudra and the upper castes which does not show in the ABO data. We have seen earlier that the difference here is mainly in the size of the body. Since it depends at least partially on nutrition the smaller body size of the poorer Namasudras may be due to this factor. Under these circumstances the ABO data and the anthropometric data would point toward the similarities in the genetic make-up of these two groups of castes.

Another important point raised by the analysis of Rao is the affinity of the Muslim with the non-Muslim groups belonging to the same region. Rao further conjectures that the Muslim converts came not only from the lower castes, tribes and other peasant communities but also from higher Hindu castes. While we have no such data for regional comparisons, the series of data provided by Boyd and Boyd (1954) already referred to, among the Pakistani Bengali Muslims compares favourably with the data belonging to the upper castes collected by the present author.

A comparative assessment, involving both anthropometric and serological characters between the upper and lower castes in order to find their relationships, is difficult to make. We have earlier dealt with the ABO data of a number of lower castes other than the Namasudra. Unfortunately, adequate anthropometric samples of lower castes are not available for the Rishi and the Sankhari. These differ from the upper castes chiefly in a very small reduction of face breadth and a small increase of the head length. The D^2 value between the Rishi and the Sankhari is fairly high, so that physical difference between them also is considerable. Corresponding separation between these two caste groups is also shown to exist in ABO blood groups, the B gene frequencies being 30.44 per cent for the Rishi and 23.58 per cent for the Sankhari. These figures also show that while the Rishi is separate from the upper castes in ABO frequencies which conform to the finding of metric investigation, the Sankhari, in having a similar blood group frequency to those of the upper castes, do not conform to the metric findings. It is thus obvious that in this case the blood group and metric findings are not consistent. Again, this might be due to the paucity of data.

The Rishi and the Sankhari do not exhaust the list of lower castes in Bengal, but as metric data on the rest of them are lacking, we cannot investigate how far the interpretation of the relationship between the upper castes and the lower castes arrived at on the basis of serological data earlier will conform to the findings of metric investigations. The need of the hour is to launch a project similar to that initiated by Sanghvi (1953) where selected castes were serologically tested as well as measured according to the anthropometric tradition.

Finally, we have to consider the anthropometrists' conclusions about the origin of the Bengalis. There are two current views on this subject both based upon the shape of the head. These are stated below:

(1) According to the recent anthropometric survey of undivided Bengal (Majumdar and Rao, 1953) the variability of the cephalic index among all Bengali castes and communities was not very great. The range was observed to lie between 71.75 and 78.86, indicating dolichomesocephaly as the characteristic of the population as a whole. On the other hand, Bihar and U.P. contain populations, who are predominantly dolichocephalic (Chatterjee, 1934, Mahalanobis et al., 1949). One other centre of high values of the cephalic index is in Gujarat (Majumdar, 1950) situated on the western coast of India. This distribution of the cephalic index in India, and the undoubted western origin of the Bengali language as part of the indo-European family of languages, led Chanda (1916) and Guha (1931) to postulate western migration to explain the high cephalic index of Bengal, linking it in some way or other with the populations of Gujerat. Whether these broad-headed peoples came earlier than the long-headed ones as typified in U.P. or *vice versa*, is really beside the point for our purpose, for whatever is the situation, the main point is that the immigration came from the west.

(2) There is another school of opinion that views the mesocephaly as due to Mongoloid influence coming from the north and the east (Risley, 1912; Keith, 1936). Keith believes that the high cephalic index of the Bengalis is part of the great area of brachycephaly

which extends to most parts of the north and the east. Linguistically, some of the populations like the Mundas, the Hos and the Santals, who are Protoaustraloid or Veddid in their physical make up, speak a language which allies them with the Mongoloid Khasis of Assam, and other Eastern and Southeastern populations. This language has been classed as Monkhmer of the great Austric family. Haddon reports that some of the Santals and the Hos he has seen show 'often reminiscence of Mongoloid traits' (Haddon, 1934, p. 108) though in a rather vague way. In addition to these, there are a large number of people, of frankly Mongoloid appearance, who live especially in the northern hilly regions of Eastern Bengal. That both the Proteaustraloid group and the Mongoloids, have exerted some influence on the non-tribal population of Bengal, cannot be denied. However, no definite Mongoloid features can be discerned in the majority of the Bengalis, especially in the higher caste people of Western Bengal.

Our conclusion, arrived at on the basis of serology alone, regarding the relationship of the Bengalis with the populations outside India, as stated before, is that the Bengalis are largely of Western extraction with the Mongoloid element forming a minor factor in the population. It is evident from this conclusion that if we ascribe any value to the haemoglobin variants for tracing physical relationships, neither of the two views stated above purporting to explain the origin of the Bengalis is alone sufficient. On the other hand, serological evidence strongly suggests a judicious synthesis of the two opposing view-points.

REFERENCES

BOYD, W. C. and Lyle G. BOYD, 1954, *Amer. Jour. Phys. Anthrop.*, N. S. 12, 393-405.

BUCHI, E. C., 1953, *Bull. Deptt. Anthrop. India*, 2, No. 1, 49-54.

CHANDRA Rama Prasad 1916, *Indo Aryan Race*, Part I, Rajshahi.

CHATTERJEE, B. K., 1934, Quoted from *Race Elements in Bengal*, D. N. Majumdar and C. R. Rao, 1958, Calcutta.

CHATTERJEE, J. B., Sushila SWARUP, S. K. GHOSH and R. N. ROY, 1957, *Bull. Cal. Trop. Med.*, 5, No. 4, 159.

CHOWDHURY, A., 1936, *Man in India*, 16, 16-26.

EICKSTEDT, Egon Von, 1958, In A. E. Mourant, et al., *The ABO blood groups*, Blackwell, P. 134.

GREVAL, S. D. S., 1951, *Blood Groups*, Thacker's Press & Directories Ltd

Calcutta (quoted from Buchi, 1954, *Anthropologist*, 1, No. 1, 3-9).

GREVAL, S. D. S., S. N. CHANDA, and L. S. F. WOODHEAD., 1939, *Ind. J. Med. Res.*, 26, 1041-54.

GREVAL, S. D. S. and S. N. CHAND, 1940, *Ind. J. Med. Res.*, 27, 1109-16.

GUHA, B. S., 1931, *Census of India*, Vol. I, Part III, Ethnographical.

HADDON, A. C., 1924, *The Race of Man*, Cambridge.

KEITH, A. 1936, *Man*, 36, 28-30.

LEHMANN, H., 1959, *Brit. Med. Bull.* 15, No. 1, 40-46.

MACFARLANE, J. W. E., 1958, *J. Genetics*, 36, 223-37.

1940, *J. Asiat. Soc. Beng.*, 5. 71-80.

MACFARLANE, J. W. E., and S. S. SARKAR, 1941, *Am. J. Phys. Anthrop.* 28, 397-410

MAHALANOBIS, P. C., D. N. MAJUMDAR, and C. R. RAO, 1949, *Sankhya*, 9, 90-324.

MAJUMDAR, D. N. and C. R. RAO, 1958, *Sankhya*, 19, Parts 3 and 4.

MOURANT, A. E., 1954, *The Distribution of Human Blood groups*. Oxford.

MOURANT, A. E., Ada C. KOPEC and K. DOMANIEWSKA-SOLEZAK, 1958, *The ABO Blood Groups*, Oxford.

Na-NAKRON. S., V. MINNICH and A. I. CHERNOFF, 1956, *J. Lab. Clin. Med.* 46, 490.

OLIVER, DOUGLAS L., and HOWELLS, W. W., 1957, *Am. Anthrop.* 59, 965-978

RISLEY, H. H., 1912, *People of India*, Calcutta.

ROY, N. R., 1954, *Bangalir Itahasa*, Calcutta.

SANGHVI, L. D., 1953, *Am. J. Phys. Anthrop.* N.S. 11, 384-404.

SANGHVI, L. D. and V. R. KHANOLKAR, 1950, *Am. Engenics*, 15, 52-64.

SEN, D. K., 1954, *Man in India*, 34, 50-60.

1960, *Jour. Roy. Anth. Inst.*, 90, 161-72.

VENKATARAMAN, K. V., 1950, Quoted from Mourant (1954 p. 379)

10

THE BLOOD GROUPS AND HAEMOGLOBIN
OF THE MALAYALIS

G. W. G. BIRD, ELIZABETH W. IKIN,
A. E. MOURANT AND H. LEHMANN

THE MALAYALIS are the people who speak the Malayalam language: they inhabit the State of Kerala, South-west India. They comprise a number of Hindu castes, in addition to Muslims and Christians.

The Namboodaris constitute the highest caste and are Brahmins: they were the landlords of Kerala and the hereditary priests of certain temples. The women marry only within their own community. The men also take wives from the ruling families (Thamborans, Thambans and Thirumulpadus) and the Nairs, but the children of these marriages take the caste of their mothers. The Nairs were formerly the feudal lords of Kerala. They are divided into many sub-castes. Marriage is mainly within the community but Nair women may marry Namboodaris, Thambans or Thirumulpadus. The Ezavas are believed to have originated from Ceylon. Since castes other than those already mentioned are hardly represented among the persons tested they will not be described here.

Christians comprise Roman Catholics, Orthodox Syrian Catholics and Orthodox Syrian Yakobites. The original Christian community is an old one, said to have been founded by St. Thomas. Some Christian families, presumed to be descended from Namboodaris, do not eat meat.

Blood samples were obtained from 190 Malayalis, comprising officers and other ranks on the staff of the Armed Forces Medical College, Poona, and students of the College. Refrigerated samples were sent by air to London and tested at the Blood Group Reference Laboratory, and duplicate specimens were tested at Poona.

Tests were carried out by standard methods for the antigens A_1, A_2, B, M, N, S, C, c, D, E and e in London, and for all these antigens, except S, in Poona. The results of these tests, which were identical in both places, are shown in Tables I-IV together with gene frequencies calculated from them. As no significant differences in pheno type frequencies were found between persons of different castes and religions, these were all combined for purposes of gene frequency calculations, but those who wish to do so can perform separate calculations by using the data given in Table I.

The haemoglobin present in each of the specimens was examined at St. Bartholomew's Hospital, London, by means of paper electrophoresis, but no abnormal haemoglobins were found.

Discussion

Data on blood group frequencies in India are now very extensive and no attempt will be made here to cite references to all the numerous papers which we have consulted. Most of the data, with full references, are to be found in the works of Mourant (1954) and Mourant, Kopeé and Domaniewska-Sobczak (1958).

In comparing the Malayalis with other South Indian populations the ABO groups give more detailed information than those of the other systems, since so many more populations have been tested, belonging both to the settled Hindu community and to numerous tribes of varying degrees of civilisation. The Malayalis fit well into the framework of the Hindus of South India, differing from most of them chiefly in having a rather lower frequency of B and a higher one of O. In this they show some resemblance to the Sinhalese, according to most series of observations on the latter. Ayer and Mummurthi (1953), however, find a somewhat higher B frequency for Malayalam speakers (of Madras province), which would bring the Malayalis rather nearer to the Tamils of Ceylon and South India, while Macfarlane (1938), for lower caste Malayalis of Cochin, finds higher A and lower B frequencies than we do. The total combined data of these three workers yield frequencies not differing greatly from our own.

The MNS frequencies of the Malayalis are typical of India as a whole, the main difference from the average being a raised frequency of Ms (and of M as a whole), all other chromosome frequencies in the Malayalis being slightly lower than the Indian average. For the more southerly parts of India, and for Ceylon, full MNS data are available only for tribal peoples, and among these the Paniyans most closely resemble the Malayalis in this particular respect (though differing very widely in ABO frequencies). Considering only the simple MN groups, the field available for comparison is somewhat wider. There is very little difference from the frequencies in "South Indians" (Rao, 1952). The Malayali frequencies are somewhat closer to those found in the Sinhalese than in the Tamils of Ceylon (Wickremasinghe, 1961), and there is some resemblance also to the Irulas, Todas and Paniyans among the tribal peoples.

The Rh frequencies of the Malayalis fit well into the Indian picture and agree closely with those found for South India by Venkata-ramiah and Krishna Rao (1953). They show no close resemblance to those of any of the south Indian tribal peoples or of the Veddahs (Wickremasinghe, Mourant, Ikin and Lehmann, 1961), but resemble those of the other peoples of Ceylon, the closest resemblance being that to the Muslims, and next, that to the Tamils (Wickremasinghe, 1961).

The absence of abnormal haemoglobins differentiates the Malayalis clearly from the Veddahs who have a high frequency of haemoglobin E, and from many of the tribal peoples of south India who have haemoglobin S, sometimes with a high frequency. The settled peoples of India, on the other hand, never show more than a very low frequency of abnormal haemoglobins.

The Malayalis may thus be said to resemble, in their blood group frequencies, the other peoples of South India, especially the Tamils, and also the Sinhalese; they are perhaps slightly nearer to the latter.

Though the Ezavas, like the Veddahs, appear, from the small sample examined, to have a very low frequency of A and a moderately high one of B, a consideration of their MNS and Rh groups gives no indication whatever of a special connection with Ceylon. It is, however, possible that tests on larger numbers of Ezavas would lead to more definite conclusions regarding their possible origin in Ceylon.

TABLE I

THE BLOOD GROUPS OF 190 MALAYALIS CLASSIFIED
ACCORDING TO CASTE OR RELIGION

Phenotype	Nairs	Christians	Ezavas	Others	Total
O	43	26	22	2	93
A₁	15	15	5	0	35
A₂	2	4	1	1	8
B	22	11	14	1	48
A₁B	2	3	1	0	6
A₂B	0	0	0	0	0
MMS	17	15	8	1	41
MsMs	25	16	15	1	57
MNS	14	12	12	1	39
MsNs	20	10	7	0	37
NNS	1	3	0	0	4
NsNs	7	3	1	1	12
CCDee	33	23	11	2	69
CcDee	32	22	19	1	74
CcDEe	8	4	4	1	17
ccDEe	3	3	4	0	10
ccDee	2	0	0	0	2
Ccddee	0	1	1	0	2
ccddee	6	6	4	0	16
Total	84	59	43	4	190

TABLE II

THE A_1A_2BO BLOOD GROUPS OF THE MALAYALIS

Phenotype	Number Observed	Frequency Observed	Frequency Expected	Number Expected
O	93	0.4895	0.4990	94.81
A_1	35	0.1842	0.1811	34·41
A_2	8	0.0421	0.0348	6.61
B	48	0.2526	0.2421	46.00
A_1B	6	0.0316	0.0355	6.74
A_2B	0	0.0000	0.0075	1.42
Total	190	1.0000	1.0000	189.99

GENE FREQUENCIES

p_1	0·1149
p_2	0·0242
q	0·1545
r	0·7064
Total	1.0000

TABLE III

THE MNS BLOOD GROUPS OF THE MALAYALIS

Phenotype	Number Observed	Frequency Observed	Frequency Expected	Number Expected
MMS	41	0.2158	0.2591	49.23
MsMs	57	0.3000	0.2533	48.13
MNS	39	0.2053	0·1646	31.27
MsNs	37	0.1947	0.2422	46.02
NNS	4	0.0210	0.0242	4.60
NsNs	12	0.0631	0.0566	10.75
Total	190	0.9999	1.0000	190.00

CHROMOSOME FREQUENCIES

MS	0.2068
Ms	0.5090
NS	0.0463
Ns	0.2379
Total	1.0000

TABLE IV

THE Rh BLOOD GROUPS OF THE MALAYALIS

Phenotype	Number Observed	Frequency Observed	Frequency Expected	Number Expected
CCDee	69	0.3632	0.3692	70.15
CCddee	0	0.0000	0.0003	0.06
CcDEe	17	0.0895	0.0863	16.40
CcDee	74	0.3895	0.3799	72.18
Ccddee	2	0.0105	0.0105	2.00
ccDEE	0	0.0000	0.0050	0.95
ccDEe	10	0.0526	0.0456	8.66
ccDee	2	0.0105	0.0114	2.17
ccddee	16	0.0842	0.0917	17.42
Total	190	1.0000	0.9999	189.99

CHROMOSOME FREQUENCIES

CDe	(R_1)	0.5906
Cde	(r')	0.0173
cDE	(R_2)	0.0710
cDe	(R_0)	0.0183
cde	(r)	0.3028
Total		1.0000

REFERENCES

AYER, A. A. and C. MUMMURTHI, 1953, 'Distribution of O, A, B and AB blood groups in the major South Indian communities', *J. Anat. Soc. India,* 2, 6-12 (and personal communication 1957).

MACFARLANE, EILEEN, W. E., 1938, 'Blood group distribution in India, with special reference to Bengal', *J. Genet.*, 36, 225-37.

MOURANT, A. E., 1954, *The Distribution of the Human Blood Groups.* Blackwell, Oxford.

MOURANT, A. E., ADA C. KOPEC and Kazimiera DOMANIEWSKA-SOBCZAK, 1958, *The ABO Blood Groups*: *Comprehensive Tables and Maps of World Distribution.* Blackwell, Oxford.

RAO, A. K., 1952, 'Blood Group characteristics in South Indians', *Current Science*, 21, 188.

VENKATARAMIAH, C. and A. KRISHNA RAO, 1953, 'Rh sub-groups in South Indians', *Current Science*, 22, 365-66.

WICKREMASINGHE, R. L., 1961, Personal communication.

WICKREMASINGHE, R. L., Elizabeth W. IKIN, A. E., MOURANT, and H. LEHMANN., 1961, 'The blood groups and haemoglobins of the Veddahs' (unpublished).

11

DERMATOGLYPHICS IN INDIA

S. S. SARKAR

IN AN earlier publication (Sarkar, 1954) a preliminary review of the dermatoglyphic data of some aborigines was made on the then available material. Since then some notable advances in this branch of study have been made. Rife (1953, 1954) in a series of studies has paved the way for the understanding of the ethnic affinities. He has also made out a good case of the pleiotropic genes in order to explain the similarities of dermatoglyphic patterns. In a recent paper Rife (1958) has emphasised the need for reform in dermatoglyphics so that they are fully suited for genetic studies, they being originally designed for anatomical ones.

In India, dermatoglyphics as propounded by Wilder, Cummins, Midlo and others, have not been so well tried so as to suggest any modification of the system already in vogue. There are just a few data on the different caste groups. In recent years some data have been collected from among the different aborigines of this country under the auspices of the Department of Anthropology, University of Calcutta and in the present study our remarks will be confined to the various aboriginal peoples of this country. This does not mean that there is no room for improvement on the diagnostic system already in practice. A clear definition of the various patterns of the palm is primarily called for. It appears that there are too many approximations in the diagnosis of a pattern. The confusion can be seen in the case of a single palm line, known as the simian crease, which has so far, been the subject of many studies (Sarkar, 1961).

An anthropologist in this country is very much confronted by the enormous variations in genetic characters like blood groups, finger or palm prints within the same ethnic strain, whose homogeneity is almost apparent in the morphological and anthropometric characters. It may, to some extent, be due to mixing up the data of the two sexes together in genetic studies like blood groups or dermatoglyphics, which an anthropologist hardly does.

Genetic explanations, like drift, selection, etc., in blood groups and dermatoglyphics are difficult to be reconciled in the morphological characters of physical anthropology. Dermatoglyphics, in view of their anatomical basis, are somewhat akin to anthropometry and many correlations are not known. It is not known, whether the *processus unguicularis* of the terminal phalanx is in anyway related to the various types of finger print patterns. Morphologically the radial fingers have flat tips, while the ulnar fingers are rounded and vaulted ones. The relationship of the different finger print patterns with the above morphological differences in the finger tips is not well known. How far the transversality of the papillary ridges is related with the torsion of the whole hand is also unknown.

Sex differences in dermatoglyphics have not always been taken into account. Bonnevie (1924) pointed it out in respect of Kubo's Korean data and Dankmeijer (1938) was of opinion that sex differences in finger prints is of the nature of sex difference in stature. The nature of sex difference in dermatoglyphics is not fully known.

It is also useful from the genetic standpoint. Walker (1941) reported of a sex linked recessive radial loop pattern on the II finger. Radial loops occur in a lower frequency among women than men. I am not aware of any investigation in which the above point has been enquired in larger detail. Among some aboriginal tribes, like the Kadar, Urali, Pahira, males show a higher frequency of whorls over loops, while females that of loops over whorls (Table 1). The Oraon, however, do not show such a sex divergence and the same is seen among the gypsy-like Lambadis of Central India.

The II interdigital pattern, also appears to show a large amount of sexual variation. Some of the Australoid tribes, mentioned above, show 1-2 per cent of this pattern, but it is absent in the two female groups (Kadar and Urali of Kerala). The Juang males (Table 2), on the other hand, show no patterns on the II interdigital, while a small sample of 17 female Juangs show 3.33 per cent of this pattern. These variations need study on sex basis. A study of the Paniyan women (Table 1) is urgently required to assess the highest male II interdigital frequency of 19.45 per cent.

Recent studies in physical anthropology and linguistics indicate that India had an autochthonous population of the Australoid ethnic strain—a strain, which is very much evident in the aboriginal populations of South India, and among other castes as well. Above this basic strain, the Indo-Aryans entered India between 1200-1000

B.C. from the west. And there appears to have entered from the east another ethnic element with Mongoloid affinities, represented by the speakers of the Mon-Khmer (Munda) language. There are other smaller ethnic waves, which we may not take into account here. The above three ethnic types are almost clear from the morphological and anthropometric points of view. The same is not clear from blood groups, even when a few more systems besides the ABO are utilised.

Dermatoglyphic studies, however, indicate certain changes in the relative ratio of the different patterns, which is difficult to explain without further work, but a part of it can probably be attributed to hybridisation.

The aboriginal tribes of India offer a unique field for the study of hybridisation, without which again genetic variations are not well understood. These are no doubt, effects of inbreeding, isolation, genetic drift, selection and such other processes. The Australoid and the Mundari-speaking peoples have undergone some amount of intermixture with one another, as is evident in certain regions of Bihar, Orissa and Madhya Pradesh. Each of the above two ethnic types has therefore been divided into two groups; (a) one showing a higher concentration of the original ethnic strain, and, (b) the other showing evidences of diverse strains, which following Hooton (1958) has been called "interbreeds."

Table 1 shows the frequencies of the various dermatoglyphic patterns of the Australoids of the two sexes. When they are compared with the Australoid interbreeds, for which there is unfortunately only one female sample, the change in the average values may be noted. Tables 2 and 3 show the same for the other ethnic types, the Mundari and the Mongoloids, the latter being mostly from Assam. The Mongoloid and the Mundari appear to stand close to one another in respect of finger prints than either of them to the Australoids. This evidence is confirmed by anthropometry and morphology. Sexual difference appears to be the greatest of all in the Australoid and the least of all in the Mongoloid. It appears to be greater than ethnic difference. Among the Australoid interbreeds sex difference is further apparent, particularly in the frequency of whorls and arches. The Mundari interbreeds show further increase of this difference in all the patterns.

In respect of the main line formulae the three ethnic types appear to differ from one another, but the choice of only three formulae out of the many in each population is not probably a safe procedure.

Rife (1953, 1954) has shown very well the ethnic variations in the palmar patterns. Compared with finger prints, palm patterns show much lesser sex variations and this is seen in the II and the III interdigitals, while the Mundari show much lesser sexual variation than the former. The Mundari interbreeds show the greatest sexual variation in respect of the III and IV interdigitals. We have unfortunately no data on the Mongoloid palm patterns and the percentages given in Table 4 are those of the Bhotia. The ethnic variation is very well seen in respect of the thenar/I interdigital. The Mongoloid vary widely in respect of the hypothenar and the IV interdigital patterns from both the Australoid and the Mundari. Between the latter two ethnic types the Australoid males are characterised by a higher frequency of all the palmar patterns than the Mundari males but the two female groups appear to stand close to one another than their male counterparts.

TABLE 1

| | | | Finger | | | | | | | Palm | | | | | | | |
| | | | Loops | | | | | | | | | | | | | | |
Serial No.	Peoples	No.	Whorl	Radial	Ulnar	Total	Arch	P.I. Index	The-nar/I	II	III	IV	Hypo-thenar	11.9 7.—5.	9.7 5.—	7.5 5.—	Authors
									Australoid Tribes (Male)								
1.	Kadar	80	59.38	2.57	37.53	40.10	0.52	15.88	24.52	1.20	18.86	57.86	23.27	13.21	19.50	40.25	Chakravartti, 1959.
2.	Oraon	107	57.18	1.28	40.17	41.45	1.37	15.53	13.48	8.39	28.12	58.59	30.48	18.86	22.64	23.72	Chakravartti (unpublished).
3.	Urali	60	53.49	1.02	45.49	46.51	—	15.35	21.01	1.68	21.84	50.42	32.77	20.17	12.61	40.34	Chatterjee et al 1960.
4.	Paniyan	33	55.95	4.85	35.57	40.42	3.63	15.23	30.57	19.45	55.57	66.67	16.66	47.72	5.56	11.11	Sarkar 1954.
5.	Pahira	33	55.95	4.85	35.57	40.42	3.63	15.23	16.67	6.06	28.78	39.39	28.79	24.24	28.78	12.12	Chakravartti 1959.
6.	Nayadi	—	—	—	—	—	—	—	21.74	2.17	52.17	52.17	34.78	34.78	15.22	17.39	Chakravartti, 1958.
7.	Adiyan	20	52.26	1.51	41.21	42.72	5.03	14.72	—	—	—	—	—	—	—	—	Sarkar 1954.
	Average		55.70	2.68	39.26	41.94	2.36	15.32	21.33	6.50	34.22	52.75	27.79	26.50	17.39	24.16	
									(Mixed)								
1.	Kurmi mahato	53	51.53	0.96	45.22	46.18	2.29	14.38	7.61	7.61	50.00	65.70	24.76	31.42	17.14	19.09	Chakravartti, 1960.
2.	Bhil	90	43.20	2.90	50.30	53.20	3.20	13.96	13.96	—	—	—	—	—	—	—	Biswas, 1957.
3.	Lambadi	51	38.11	3.14	53.04	56.18	5.70	13.24	—	—	—	—	—	—	—	—	Gupta (Unpublished)
4.	Vettu Kurumba	22	32.41	2.31	58.80	61.11	6.48	12.59	—	—	—	—	—	—	—	—	Sarkar, 1954.
	Average		41.31	2.33	51.84	54.17	4.42	13.54									
									Australoid Tribes (Female)								
1.	Kadar	65	47.72	1.52	50.25	51.77	0.51	14.72	24.80	—	13.88	60.47	26.35	10.85	17.83	51.94	Chakravartti, 1959.
2.	Oraon	93	54.51	1.27	41.00	42.27	3.23	15.13	14.67	6.63	38.61	52.89	40.38	27.27	12.30	26.53	Chakravartti (Unpublished).
3.	Urali	24	44.30	0.84	53.59	54.43	1.27	14.13	16.67	—	20.83	56.25	22.91	14.58	22.92	47.92	Chatterjee et al 1960.
4.	Pahira	21	43.32	3.34	51.90	55.24	1.44	14.18	14.29	2.38	16.66	21.43	45.24	16.67	30.95	9.53	Chakravartti 1959.
5.	Nayadi	—	—	—	—	—	—	—	20.69	1.72	41.38	49.99	12.07	31.03	24.14	20.69	,,
	Average		47.46	1.74	49.19	50.93	1.61	14.59	18.22	2.15	26.27	48.21	29.39	20.08	21.63	31.32	
									(Mixed)								
	Lambadi	54	30.24	1.67	60.48	62.15	7.61	12.26									

TABLE 2

Mundari Tribes (Male)

Serial No.	Peoples	No.	Whorl	Radial	Ulnar	Total	Arch	P.I. Index	Thenar/I	II	III	IV	Hypo-thenar	11.9 7.—	9.7 5.—	7.5 —	Authors
1.	Santal	62	52.51	2.10	43.78	45.88	1.61	15.09	13.01	6.50	26.82	56.10	24.39	—	11.38	33.33	Chakravartti (Unpublished).
2.	Munda	112	49.65	2.50	45.88	48.38	1.96	14.76	12.49	5.36	30.80	44.64	25.90	—	12.94	27.23	,, ,,
3.	Baiga	30	48.95	1.40	47.22	48.62	2.43	14.65	—	5.93	28.81	50.37	25.14	—	11.66	30.28	Dutta (Unpublished).
	Average		50.37	2.00	45.63	47.63	2.00	14.83	12.75	5.93	28.81	50.37	25.15	—	11.66	30.28	
1.	Juang	74	42.00	1.64	55.00	56.64	1.36	14.06	11.20	—	25.86	63.80	18.96	12.93	28.44	32.00	Sarkar et al, 1957
2.	Sabara	54	42.42	0.94	54.95	55.89	1.69	14.07	25.00	8.65	37.50	51.92	23.08	22.12	16.35	27.89	,, ,,
	Average		42.21	1.29	54.98	56.27	1.53	14.07	18.20	4.33	31.68	57.86	21.02	17.53	22.39	29.95	
	**Mundari (Female)**																
1.	Santal	61	48.52	2.13	45.25	47.38	4.10	14.44	25.62	7.44	31.41	52.89	23.96	25.62	14.05	31.40	Chakravartti (Unpublished).
2.	Munda	101	38.60	2.18	55.06	57.24	4.16	13.44	11.00	2.00	32.50	52.00	31.00	24.00	13.50	29.50	,, ,,
	Average		43.56	2.15	50.16	52.31	4.13	13.99	18.31	4.72	31.96	52.45	27.48	24.81	13.78	30.45	
1.	Juang	17	38.82	—	57.66	57.66	3.52	13.62	26.67	3.33	33.33	73.33	33.33	13.34	10.00	43.34	Sarkar et al., 1957
2.	Sabara	9	24.72	1.12	66.30	67.42	7.86	11.68	12.50	12.50	12.50	87.50	13.45	6.25	43.75	43.75	,, ,,
	Average		31.77	0.56	61.98	62.54	2.69	12.60	19.59	7.92	22.92	80.42	23.39	9.80	26.88	43.55	

TABLE 3

MONGOLOID TRIBES—(Male)

Loops

Peoples	No.	Whorls	Radial	Ulnar	Total	Arches	P.I. Index	Authors
Hill Garo	76	50.76	0.93	46.55	47.48	1.74	14.90	Das, 1959
Plains Garo	94	47.96	1.39	47.57	48.96	2.98	14.48	,, ,,
Hajong	75	44.68	1.73	51.96	53.69	1.63	14.30	,, ,,
Kachari	109	54.66	0.55	42.86	43.41	1.84	15.27	,, ,,
Rajbansi	130	43.11	2.02	51.12	53.14	3.73	13.93	,, ,,
Rabha	295	50.66	1.55	46.24	47.79	1.55	14.94	,, ,,
Galong	152	46.00	2.07	49.92	51.99	2.00	14.40	Kumar
Bhotia	36	50.73	2.49	44.52	47.01	2.23	14.85	Tiwari, 1955
Rajis	62	46.55	3.41	48.58	51.99	1.46	14.51	,, ,,
Khasi	260	41.73	2.55	54.31	56.86	1.38	14.03	Das (unpublished)
Miri	100	49.29	1.61	48.00	49.61	0.90	14.81	Sharma ,,
Average		47.83	1.85	48.33	50.18	1.94	14.58	

(Female)

Peoples	No.	Whorls	Radial	Ulnar	Total	Arches	P.I. Index	Authors
Rabha	295	44.98	0.94	49.77	50.71	4.31	14.06	Das, 1959
Khashi	256	35.41	2.83	58.18	61.01	3.90	13.18	,, (unpublished)
Miri	58	44.42	1.37	52.63	54.00	1.56	14.28	Sharma ,,
Average		41.60	1.71	53.53	55.24	3.26	13.84	

REFERENCES

BISWAS, P. C., 1957, 'Finger Dermatoglyphics of the Bhils of Rajasthan', *The Anthropologist*, Vol. 4.

BONNEVIE, K., 1924, 'Studies on Papillary patterns on human fingers', *Journal of Genetics*, Vol. 15, pp. 1-111

CHAKRAVARTTI, M. R., 1958, 'Dermatoglyphics of the Nayadis and Paniyans of Madras', *Man in India*, Vol. 38, pp. 199-207.
Journal of Genetics, Vol. 15, pp.

1959, 'Dermatoglyphics of the Pahiras of the Dalma Hills', *Man In India*, Vol. 39, pp. 1-19.

1959, 'Dermatoglyphics: A Physical Survey of the Kadar of Kerala', Chap. V of *Mem.* No. 6, Department of Anthropology, Government of India, pp. 50-70..

1960, 'The Dermatoglyphics of the Kurmi Mahatos of Bihar', *Science and Culture*, Vol. 26. pp. 285-86.

CHATTERJEE, B. K., CHAKRABORTY, M. R., and GUPTA, P., 1960, 'Dermatoglyphics of the Uralis of Kerala', *Man In India*, Vol. 40. pp. 36-51.

DANKMEIJER, J., 1938, 'Some anthropological data on finger prints', *American Journal of Physical Anthropology*, Vol. 23, pp. 377-88.

DAS, B. M., 1959, 'Finger Prints of the Hajong', *Man In India*, Vol. 39, pp. 20-27.

HOOTON, E. A., 1958, *Up from the Ape*, New York,

RIFE, David C., 1953, 'Finger Prints as Criteria of Ethnic Relationship', *American Journal of Human Genetics*, Vol. 5, pp. 389-99.

1954, 'Dermatoglyphics as Ethnic Criteria', *American Journal of Human Genetics*, Vol. 6, pp. 319-27.

1958, 'Proposed Revisions in Classification of Palmar Dermatoglyphics', *The Anthropologist*, Vol. 5, pp. 17-18.

SARKAR, S. S., 1954, *The Aboriginal Races of India*, Calcutta,

1961, 'The Simian Crease', *Zts. Morph. Anth.*, Vol. 51, pp. 212-19.

SARKAR, S. S. and Banerjee, A. R., 1957, 'Finger Prints of Orissan Aborigines, *Man in India*, Vol. 37, pp. 182-91.

TIWARI, S. C., 1955, 'Finger dermatoglyphics in Rajis of Askote (U.P.)'. *The Anthropologist*, Vol. , pp. 51-54.

WALKER, J. F., 1941, 'A Sex linked recessive finger print pattern', *Journal of Heredity*, Vol. 32, pp. 279-80.

Social-Cultural Anthropology

12

SOCIAL ANTHROPOLOGY IN INDIA

S. C. Dube

I

ANTHROPOLOGY is a young discipline in India. Beginning in the latter half of the nineteenth century with the ethnographic compilation of traditions, customs, and beliefs of different tribes and castes in the various provinces of India, it has moved slowly to establish itself as an independent field of study and enquiry. Notwithstanding the fact of its having gained increasing academic acceptance over the years, its foundations are still somewhat insecure for it appears to be undecided both about its objectives and methods. Social anthropology as an articulate and independent branch of the science is perhaps only beginning to emerge now.

The earliest organized effort in the field was the compilation and publication of several volumes on tribes and castes, containing brief and often sketchy accounts of the divergent customs and practices of various groups. The orientation of these volumes was administrative rather than academic or scientific, for they were intended primarily to acquaint the administrator with the diversity of custom in the different segments of the country's population. Most of the material going into them was hurriedly compiled by minor officials who had little general education and no special training for the job. The editor-authors of these volumes permitted themselves some anthropological digressions, mostly in line with current trends, and offered conjectural hypotheses and theories regarding the origin, migration and ethnic affiliation of the different people, but by and large they did not deviate much from their main objective of producing compendia of information for the administrator.

The second phase in the development of the subject, characterised by detailed monographic studies of individual tribes mostly through personal observation and enquiry extending over a fairly long period, was also inspired by administrative needs. The all too fragmentary accounts of tribal people in the different tribes and castes volumes were found generally inadequate for the purpose of day-to-day administration of tribal areas and were often not very reliable. This inspired the administrators working in tribal areas to undertake detailed studies of tribal groups, and for this they received support and encouragement from the government. The monographs emerging from such effort, although they varied in quality, provided objective and systematic descriptions of tribal life and institutions. Presented according to the current formula they covered nearly all or at any rate most of the main branches of anthropological study; besides chapters on economy, material culture and technology, social organisation, life cycle, religion, and magic and witchcraft, they invariably included material on origin and migration, physical anthropology, language, folklore, customary law, and administrative problems.

In the earlier stages most of these compendia and studies were produced by British administrators. When Indians later entered the field, they accepted the earlier works as their model and produced comprehensive volumes on tribes and castes as well as single studies on individual tribes following the established pattern. The ranks of field anthropologists of this type were reinforced at this stage by some scholars from overseas, who came to India primarily for anthropological research and did most of their work independently without any direct association with the government of the day. Accounts of tribal life produced by them followed largely the traditional ethnographic model, but their academic interests and theoretical orientation were also unmistakably reflected in their writings.

Indological studies too provided some incentive and encouragement to studies of an anthropological nature. References in the classical texts to the tribal element in India's population were carefully examined. Religious cults and practices also were studied from this angle. Attempts were made to trace the origin of various Hindu social institutions, particularly the caste system, on the basis of scriptures and religious texts.

Acceptance of anthropology as an academic discipline in Indian universities was slow. Although a separate department of anthropology was started in the Calcutta University in 1920, to which the first university Chair in the subject was added later, other universities were not prompt in following the lead. Over the years short courses in anthropology were developed at different universities as a part of the curricula in economics, political science, philosophy and sociology. It took several years for the second full professorship in the subject to be instituted at the Lucknow University in 1950. Dr. Majumdar, in whose memory the present Volume of essays is being published, was appointed to this professorship

So far anthropology was thought of primarily as the study of tribal cultures. The accent was on many-sided and well-rounded descriptive studies that could preserve for posterity accounts of a way of life that was fast disintegrating and disappearing from the Indian scene. The field anthropologist was enjoined to record everything that he saw and heard. Conjectural history having fallen into disrepute, every kind of speculation was now discouraged. In fact theoretical considerations were taboo to the field anthropologist, who had to relegate his *theory*, if he found it irresistible, to a separate appendix quite apart from his *facts* embodied in the main body of the text. Social anthropology during this period was an inseparable part of cultural anthropology; the latter itself being a constituent of the wider discipline of general anthropology. A good anthropologist was essentially a 'general anthropologist' and a resourceful field worker. He avoided theory for the fear of being branded an "arm chair anthropologist", the worst ridicule that could be showered on anyone in the profession.

It is against this background that we have to understand the entry of Indian anthropology into the third phase of its development—a period of considerable quantitative advancement and some qualitative achievement.

This phase started almost soon after the attainment of national independence by India. During this period teaching of anthropology at the universities expanded rapidly. A number of new university departments were started and the existing ones were strengthened. During this phase some anthropologists courageously broke away from the tradition of ethnographic study of tribes. A new dimension was added to Indian anthropology when village communities were included among the subjects regarded as constituting legitimate fields of anthropological enquiry. Alongside the subject-matter, the approach to anthropological studies was also undergoing a significant change. There was a perceptible awareness of the wider theoretical implications of some of the problems being studied. The excessive concern with the study of single cultures was gradually being replaced by an anxiety to study wider social systems. This trend was encouraged by the field studies of a small band of theoretically sophisticated anthropologists from foreign universities. Senior Indian scholars visiting leading centres of anthropology abroad and younger anthropologists studying at major foreign universities also were stimulated by recent advances in theory and method. This stimulation found expression in their research endeavours at home. On the whole there has been an unprecedented spurt of activity, symbolising, as it were, the coming of age of anthropology in the country.

While the vigour and enthusiasm with which anthropological studies in the country are being pursued at present are to be welcomed, it is necessary at this critical stage in the development of the discipline to take stock of its major achievements and evaluate the trends that are in motion. It is my feeling that anthropology in India today is riding on a wave of artificial prosperity. At a time when an alarmingly large number of students are studying anthropology either independently or in conjunction with some cognate discipline, it is desirable to have a second look at our curricula and to evaluate our teaching methods. Do our university courses in anthropology have sufficient integration and sense of direction? Recent years have doubtless witnessed the publication of a number of major studies; it is now necessary to ensure the continuity of the process initiated by them. A tendency to pass on shoddy work to the publisher to exploit the market popularity of the subject is also unfortunately all too apparent. Some recent work has contributed toward bringing about greater conceptual clarity in our general thinking and research, but it has to be admitted that the growing popularity of theoretically-oriented research is also being abused by some in the profession. Extremely thin and low-calibre empirical work is often clothed in high-sounding but spurious concepts of almost no worth. Today more and more money is being made available for empirical work, much of which comes from sources interested in findings useful for policy formulation and action in the general area of planned change. This increases the responsibility of the anthropologist many-fold. It is perhaps time we assess our methods for their adequacy and effectiveness.

In this paper I am concerned mainly with the developments and contemporary trends in social anthropology in India. Reference was made so far to anthropology in general, because social anthropology in a rudimentary form existed within the larger framework of general anthropology for a long time without having a separate identity. The historical connexions notwithstanding, in the present state of high specialisation of the different branches of anthropology (i. e. physical anthropology, pre-history, linguistics, etc., besides social anthropology) one wonders how long the 'grand design' for the unified and total study of man can be maintained. The unity of the divergent disciplines encompassed within anthropology is already beginning to look artificial, and at advanced levels of study and research the relevance of insistence on their study together appears doubtful. Social anthropology has in the sense in which it is used here, greater kinship with sociology, history, philosophy and other social sciences. In fact I do not see any real distinction between social anthropology and sociology if the latter concerns itself with the study of social forms and processes by using direct and intensive methods of observation and investigation. Thus some of the observations made here will have as much relevance for sociology as for social anthropology.

II

Anthropology is now an accepted and established subject in the curricula of most Indian Universities.[1] Every year it attracts an increasing number of students, and with expanding job opportunities for graduates with anthropology degrees its popularity is likely to increase all the more.[2]

A review of university courses in anthropology brings out certain significant trends :

(i) In most universities there is a conscious effort to maintain the classical 'grand design' for the study of man; anthropology being thought of as a composite and unified study of man from the biological, historical, sociological, and psychological points of view.

(ii) Recent advances in theory and method, in anthropology as well as in other cognate disciplines, are sought to be fitted into this wider frame-work, without any radical alterations in its basic structure.

(iii) Conceptually and methodologically the teaching of anthropology has lagged behind the requirements of the developing research interests in the subject.

(iv) Training in methods of field research is, notwithstanding the theoretical recognition of its crucial significance, poorly developed at the university centres of anthropology.

Let there be no misunderstanging. I am not against a unified and integrated science of man, nor do I claim that any one part of anthropology is more important than the others. There is a good case for different university departments developing along their individual orientation and interest, emphasising one or the other branch of anthropology. I do wish to suggest, however, that the 'grand design' is being sustained more by nostalgia than by logic; accidental factors in the historical growth of the subject appear to have involved us emotionally to such a degree that at present we are unable to foresee clearly the natural and inevitable requirements for the growth of the individual constituents of anthropological studies. While it is desirable to work also for a unified science of man, it may be dangerous to overlook the high state of specialisation in the different branches of the subject. The so-called composite courses in the subject claim to lay equal or nearly equal emphasis on the different branches; physical anthropology (including human biology), prehistory, cultural anthropology and social anthropology are tied together in the university teaching of anthropology. There are two major objections to such an arrangement. First, the teaching of these independent branches is not sufficiently and imaginatively integrated; the student is often left wondering about their logical connexion. Secondly, the burden of the different branches put together is so much that it severely limits the possibilities of specialisation available to the student. As it is, even the most comprehensive courses in anthropology have not been able to give adequate representation, for practical reasons, to ethnology (culture history), linguistics, and folklore. It is time we think in terms of giving greater autonomy to the separate branches of the subject in the university curricula at the master's level.

The basic error in planning the university courses appears to lie in the confusion regarding the aims of university teaching of anthropology. It is necessary to make a clear distinction between the teaching of the subject as a part of liberal education and as professional training for an academic speciality. For the first degree the emphasis could be on teaching it largely as a part of liberal education; the different branches of the subject being imaginatively unified in the syllabi. The main focus here should be on the fundamentals and their implications rather than on a mass of technical detail. In other words, the philosophy of the subject should emerge clearly in the teaching at this stage; opportunities for specialisation should be deliberately restricted. At the master's level the emphasis would naturally change, for here we shall be preparing future entrants to the profession. Insistence on equal emphasis on the different branches of the subject at this level would appear to be meaningless. A common core course at a fairly general level may be understandable even at this stage, but beyond it the different branches should be left free to develop in association with cognate disciplines having greater logical relevance to them. Any one seeking to specialise in physical anthropology need not be burdened with a great deal of theoretical social anthropology, nor should a student preparing for a professional career in social anthropology be compulsorily required to work in unrelated fields such as serology and craniometry. Obstinacy in this regard will seriously limit the acquisition of the desired professional competence by the students in their chosen field of specialisation.

To add to the confusion, many university departments have been all too anxious to enlarge their already cumbersome courses by adding to them every conceivable new development in their own subject as well as in allied disciplines. Thus the student today has also to study little bits of culture and personality (including projective techniques), higher statistics, sociometry, small-group theory, and complicated theoretical constructs of the grand theorists. It is not suggested that the subject should deliberately insulate itself and refuse to explore new frontiers; the protest is against the curious patch-work on the traditional frame-work that is leading to the emergence of a crazy pattern which does not quite make sense for the integrated growth of the subject. A judicious selection of some of the more important recent developments in anthropology as well as in allied subjects can be included in the curricula, but this pre-supposes some radical changes in the present structure of the courses. While doing so it is necessary to be discriminating and selective in the choice of new items. There is something pathetic indeed in the present craze to grab indiscriminately everything that is the latest in fashions and fads. In the process, old masters are often sacrificed. For a student training for a possible career in social anthropology, I think, a close acquaintance with the writings of Durkheim and Weber and with the analytical studies of Firth and Evans-Pritchard is more essential than piece-meal erudition in a large number of unrelated fields such as personality psychology, statistics, and sociometry. It is necessary, therefore, to reexamine and reorganise the present university courses in anthropology with a view to bringing in them greater balance and sense of direction.

The shifting focus of research interests in anthropology also calls for suitable adjustments in the university curricula. Anthropology could afford (though at some cost) to be ahistorical when it was concerned primarily with the study of tribal cultures; the growing interest in the study of larger traditions and complex social systems makes it obligatory for the social anthropologist today to take cognisance of historical factors. A study of religion and its associated symbolism is also similarly necessary. Nor can the student of the Indian social system ignore the classical texts. On the other hand, any one interested in the study of a changing society, especially one committed to planned change, has of necessity to keep in touch with theoretical development in economics, politics, and public administration. The traditional framework within which social anthropology is taught today in Indian universities does not permit it to seek closer association with these subjects. A more rational and logical grouping of subjects, mainly in terms of research interest, thus appears indicated.

The problem of research methods will be discussed at some length later in this paper. In the context of university teaching, it is necessary to mention that the present arrangement is not conducive either to adequate theoretical preparation for fieldwork or for practical training in it. The multiplicity and diversity of subjects taught together leave little room for such preparation. Theoretical lectures on methodology help, but only to a limited extent. Few students have the opportunity or the encouragement to get to know the better analyses of particular societies intimately. Under heavy pressure from all sides field training is reduced to a ritual; the student having neither the time nor the patience to have a sustained orientation to the problems and methods in the field.

The results of this type of training are reflected in the nature and type of research undertaken by students prepared under this system. Nostalgia for the past traditions of the discipline thus appears to be coming in the way of the natural and logical growth of its

different branches that have in the meantime come of age and are
ready for a greater degree of autonomy.

III

Anthropological research in India was, until recently, confined
to the study of tribes and was geared largely to the needs of administration. Even when anthropology was recognised as a subject
suitable for research at the universities, it retained its descriptive
character. Theoretical analysis of the field data, often in a functional or culture-pattern frame of reference was at best superficial;
the primary strength of the contributions lay in their systematic
observation and description, some theoretical analysis being added
to them only as an after-thought. Notwithstanding the inadequacy
of theoretical analysis, this effort produced many dependable
monographs and established the tradition of sustained and systematic fieldwork.

A major weakness in most of the tribal studies was that they
described their units of observation in a biotic frame of reference.
Tribes were viewed often as independent units and described as
self-contained cultures, without adequate consideration of their
vital links with other tribes and the Hindu peasantry. Brief accounts
of the processes of acculturation and culture-change could hardly
do justice to this important aspect. Deliberate rejection of history
further came in the way of making affective analyses of the dynamics
of tribal societies. Insistence on itemised description of all or
most aspects of the culture of a group considerably limited the
scope for full and adequate study of particular aspects of social
structure. It is a pity that in our new found love for village studies
we are neglecting the study of tribes. With the better conceptual
methodological equipment at our disposal today, tribal studies
need to be revived. Some welcome departures in this field have
already appeared in print; the process has now to be consolidated
and strengthened.

Village studies, the current rage of Indian social anthropologists
and sociologists, inherited some of the traditions of tribal studies.
In the absence of a satisfactory model, the descriptive mode of the
tribal monographs had to be adopted by the students of individual
village communities. They were handling materials of infinitely
greater complexity and were studying units that had vital extensions

and ramifications in a wider region. These studies involved the analyses of several inter-locking sub-systems within the larger framework of a system. The problem of definition and delimitation of units were baffling. It is indeed heartening to note that the many conceptual and methodological challenges involved in studies of this type were recognised early and attempts were made to meet them at least part of the way. Village studies published in the course of the last ten years, most of them excellent by themselves, have highlighted a series of problems that have immediate relevance and urgency for the study of the Indian social system.

The urban dimension of Indian society is as yet poorly represented in studies by sociologists and social anthropologists. Studies in this area will present vexing problems of theory and method, necessitating imaginative but cautious experimentation. The points of interaction between the rural and urban sectors of life are so many and so significant even for the understanding of rural society that sociological studies of urban communities are essential. Being indispensable for the understanding of the Indian social system, such studies cannot be postponed indefinitely. The sooner we accept the challenge, the better it will be for developing an integrated study of Indian society. Statistically-oriented surveys of urban communities fall far short of the requirements of social anthropology. Penetrating and intimate studies, at least of certain segments of urban population, need to be taken up on a priority basis.

Studies of individual tribes, villages, and towns are important in themselves, but their value will be greatly enhanced if they also pave the way for our understanding of the wider social systems. This necessitates serious reexamination of our conceptual and analytical categories.

The problem of definitions acquires an added significance in this context. Even a simple but basic term like 'family' has been used to denote several different types of structural and non-structural units. Indiscriminate use of the term 'joint family' has contributed more to confusion than to clarity in the understanding of Indian society. 'Clan', 'gotra', and 'lineage' have also been used without due caution. But the climax is reached perhaps in the use of the term 'caste'. It is surprising indeed that a basic concept like caste has as yet remained so poorly defined and is still being used to denote a variety of meanings. Developing a consensus in regard to the use of these terms is an urgent necessity.

There have been some useful general studies of family, kin, and caste in India, but they had all to rely on extremely thin ethnographic data from some parts of the country. In consequence, almost all of them lack balance and fail to offer a systemtic and adequate picture of the particular aspect of the social system they choose to describe. Many of them offer provocative hypotheses and survey the available sources with competence, but the final outcome nevertheless remains unsatisfactory. This situation is not likely to improve until a series of representative village and urban communities are studied in different regions of India, with special reference to the different aspects of their social structure.

Studies of social structure themselves need reorientation. Anatomy of the structure of a number of societies has been excellently described, but most of these studies lack time perspective. Time and space determinants of the social structure do not appear to have been adequately analysed for most of the societies studied by social anthropologists or sociologists in India. In the absence of such studies it is doubtful if we can make meaningful and valid generalisations regarding the range and depth of changes in the fabric of the society.

The last decade has witnessed a definite conceptual progress in the study of Indian society. Some broad trends, such as *sanskritisation*, *universalisation*, and *parochialisation* have been identified on the basis of dependable fieldwork in certain areas. The Great Tradition-Little Tradition frame of reference provides a useful approach to the analysis and understanding of cultural processes in India. Being inter-related these concepts constitute a complex that can be considered together.

Writing elsewhere about them I have said, "While the broad framework provided by these concepts is simple and attractive, operationally they are not without inherent contradictions and difficulties. There is apparently no precise definition of Great or Little Traditions. To define the Great Tradition as the corpus of beliefs, rituals, and social patterns embodied in the sacred canonical literature does not take us very far. Even the clarification that it often emanates from the Little Traditions of the little communities and is abstracted and synthesised by the urban *literati*, does not help our understanding very substantially. It is difficult to reduce the inviolable central core of the more or less static ideas of a Great Tradition to a list of traits and complexes; nor is it easy to classify them, with any degree of precision, as universals, alternatives and specialities. The concept must also allow for a wide nebulous area covering ideas and institutions that are not accounted for by the sacred or near-sacred texts. This only adds to our difficulties in using the concept as an analytical tool. Where there are more than one Great or near-Great Traditions, each with its canonical texts and ethical codes, the situation becomes all the more confusing. In such a situation we have no criteria for determining the elements which could be said to be basic to the Great Tradition. Scriptures and sacred texts themselves often illustrate certain aspects of evolution and change in society and there is by no means unanimity among them. When conflicting ideal patterns are laid down by the sacred texts, and there is no universality in the acceptance of one in preference to the others, the efforts to find the Great Tradition-Little Tradition frame of reference does not allow proper scope for the consideration of the role and significance of regional, Western, and emergent national traditions, each of which is powerful in its own way. Some of these considerations would apply also to Srinivas' concept of *Sanskritisation*. In our study of Indian village communities, therefore, it may be useful to consider the contextual classical and local traditions, as well as the regional (culture-area), Western (ideological-technological), and emergent national (nativistic-reinterpretational adaptive) traditions" (Dube 1961, p. 122).

During the last few years these concepts have been discussed over and over again, but mostly at a superficial level. Attempts to test them by rigorous empirical methods in the field have been very few. Recent fieldwork suggests that the primarily ritual concept of *sanskritisation* can explain only a part of the contemporary cultural process in India and that simultaneous consideration of secular factors and trends is necessary for their adequate explanation. Srinivas, the author and leading exponent of the concept, has himself been one of the first to emphasise the desirability of studying also the process of *westernisation*. The constituents of the Great and Little Traditions, tested in some recent field-work, have also been found inadequate. They could definitely bear some amplification and augmentation. The merit of these concepts lies chiefly in the discussion they have initiated and in the suggestive leads they have thrown up for further research. One should regret, however, that the research inspired by them is proportionately inconsequential compared to the large volume of hair-splitting controversies raised by them.

Conceptual poverty of contemporary Indian social anthropology will become apparent to any one who is a witness to the still-birth of weak and ill-formed 'concepts' by the dozen at any professional convention. These pathetic efforts have elements both of tragedy and of comedy in them. The theorists-in-a-hurry appear to forget that good concepts can emerge only out of penetrating and sustained work, and that running after current fashions can, in the end, prove inj. ious not only to the subject but also to the scholarly reputation o. the individuals concerned.

To sum up, o. the credit side in research in social anthropology today we have some good work on contemporary village communities showing ar increasing theoretical awareness, a set of useful hypotheses and concepts, and a tendency—perceptible though not strong—towards focused work on specific aspects of social structure. On the debit side, mention can be made of the feeble interest in tribal studies, unpreparedness coupled with possible lack of interest in urban studies, significant gaps in knowledge about communities in a number of regions, and a tendency towards hit-and-run as well as get-rich-quick theoretical formulations. The artificial dichotomy between 'pure' and 'applied' research, and the availability of large funds only for the latter, is also coming in the way of developing systematic studies of the structure and organisation of society. It is not sufficiently realised that such studies alone can pave the way for fruitful applied research into the contemporary problems of society.

IV

The question of methods is inseparably connected with the areas and problems of research in social anthropology.

Research in the field can be viewed at two different levels. Some problems are amenable to investigation either by a single field-worker or by an individual anthropologist working with a very small number of assistants and interpreters. On the other hand, there are some problems that require large research teams. In either case intensive and intimate fieldwork is necessary.

In Indian social anthropology today there is unforunately a tendency to underrate the value of intensive individual fieldwork.

One may go it alone for his doctoral dissertation, but once established in academic positions the tendency for the scholars is to seek funds for 'projects' employing team assistance. The fresh entrant to the ranks of professional fieldworkers sees his seniors in action and draws his own inferences. The requirement of individual fieldwork, extending to a fairly long period, is viewed by him often as an imposition involving unnecessary hardships. The educative value and mental stimulation implicit in such an experience is neither emphasised nor recognised. Many fieldworkers, when they are forced to take up independent assignments of this type, seek short-cuts to getting results. What they achieve appears quite impressive on the surface, but one wonders how much the truth is vitiated in the process.

Having branched out into several unexplored fields, social anthropology today cannot entirely rule out research by large field teams. The extent of coverage and the penetrating depth required in certain fields makes it inevitable for a number of people to work together. Qualitative generalisations made by social anthropologists have often been questioned, and there is need to work on statistically adequate samples within the chosen universe. The rigorous criteria of reliability and validity demand more careful planning and greater depth in the research. Carefully chosen and thoughtfully trained teams can do so more effectively than single individuals. But the recent experience of team research raises more doubt than hope. Inter-disciplinary teams have often turned out in practice to be multi-disciplinary teams. In the absence of conceptual and technical integration many such projects represent nothing more than haphazard collection of data by a number of investigators, each struggling to complete his erratically assigned tasks. The busy director is rarely in a position to maintain close and continuous touch with the progress of work in the field, and comes into the picture invariably at the last stage when he is required to evolve some semblance of order out of the chaotic files for preparing a final report. Even the most elaborate statistical tables and impressive sociograms in such reports cannot hide the lack of feel for the field and the extreme thinness and uneven quality of data. The perspective for the interpretation of the data is bound to be distorted when analysis is based on materials lacking in coherence and integration. Organisation of research by bureaucratic methods and collection of data on assembly line techniques repre-

sents a most serious danger to the growth of true scholarly research.
The gains of such endeavours are doubtful all around. The findings
embodied in such hurriedly compiled reports are open to question;
their implications for action may even be dangerous. The investigator, working most of the time as a mercenary under great pressure,
is perhaps the worst loser in the bargain. Academic recognition
to his individual work is lost in obscure acknowledgment by the
director to several helpers, and to him personally the experience
is rarely positive and stimulating. What is worse, he also probably
loses faith in the honesty and integrity of field-research. The latent
possibilities of group research still remain largely unexplored.
Successful experiments in this field are not entirely lacking, but
their number is woefully small.

The social anthropologist was perhaps guilty of over-emphasising
the merits of his methods of fieldwork, which largely consisted
of participant-observation. Although under expert hands this
method has given excellent results, its uncritical use by some was
certainly open to doubt. The method was largely conditioned
and limited by the personal equations of the individual fieldworker.
Its drawbacks came in for some well-merited criticism. In reaction,
new methodological approaches were sought and some of the
techniques developed by sociology, psychology, and statistics
were adopted. While some methodological experimentation is
necessary and desirable and the acceptance of tools from sister-
disciplines is to be welcomed, the rejection of time-tested methods
and uncritical acceptance of every new technique can be dangerous.
This is what is happening in a great deal of anthropological and
sociological research in India. Instruments today are becoming
more important than the objective they seek to attain. Schedules
and questionnaires are slowly replacing careful observation and
patient interviewing. Framed after considerable exploratory work
and discriminatingly pre-tested, such instruments can be valuable
aids to research, but in practice they are hurriedly put together
without even a careful consideration of the variables entering
into the social situation that is being studied. Impatiently administered by inadequately trained investigators, these schedules often
provide the bulk of the materials on which some sociological
studies are based. Scaling techniques, much in vogue these days,
also suffer from the same defects. In some instruments of this
type even elementary precautions, such as avoidance of interviewer

and/or interviewee fatigue, are not kept in mind; closely printed thirty page schedules cannot be trusted to give reliable results, especially when they are administered in great haste. Wording of questions, structuring of response categories, and phrasing of probe questions also leave much to be desired. In the absence of systematic and integrated observation, the responses to schedules and questionnaires often distort the truth. Use of psychological tests and projective techniques, unsupported by close contacts and intimate fieldwork, can also yield undependable results.

No science can grow if it refuses to question its own methods and shows a willingness to experiment with new techniques. Social anthropology will have to be more careful in its sampling procedures, acquire greater statistical sophistication, and improve its techniques of observation and interviewing. Discriminating adaptation of some of the sociological and psychological techniques can also be a source of strength to it. But it is only against the background of systematic and careful observation that the results of investigation by these methods can be properly evaluated. Short-cuts invariably destroy the spirit of fieldwork. In our excessive love for new tools, we should not discard the time-tested methods that have aided us so well in the analysis and understanding of society.

V

The new tasks of social anthropology in India, as they emerge in much of contemporary research, necessitate careful thinking in regard to the future of the subject. While alternative approaches to the understanding of society should have full freedom to grow, there is a strong case for developing an articulate body of social anthropologists in the country. Faced by the danger of being relegated to a position of insignificance within the wider classical frame-work of general anthropology on the one hand and of being submerged in the currents and cross-currents of sociology on the other, social anthropology must press its claims for autonomy. The vitality that it has shown in recent years is indeed remarkable for a young discipline. With a more integrated sense of direction in its teaching, with careful assessment of the trends of its growth in the sphere of research, and with cautious avoidance of methodological confusions it can stabilise itself. The dangerous signs of a crisis within have to be recognised and remedied in time if the subject has to continue to progress towards its natural and logical goals.

NOTES

[1] There are at present 11 university departments of anthropology in the country; 7 with full professionships. Only one of these is designated as a Department of Social Anthropology. There are also 15 departments of sociology, many offering some courses that are broadly social anthropological in orientation. One of these departments may perhaps be better described as a leading centre for social anthropology. In two others also social anthropology is well represented.

[2] In one north Indian University alone some 1400 students recently offered a paper in anthropology at the M. A. examination.

REFERENCE

DUBE, S. C., 1961, 'The Study of Indian Village Communities', *Sociology, Social Research and Social Problems in India*, ed. by R. N. Saksena. Bombay.

13

THE SCOPE OF SOCIAL ANTHROPOLOGY IN THE STUDY OF INDIAN SOCIETY

F. G. BAILEY

The Prestige of Social Anthropology

A GENERATION ago the politically-minded intelligentsia of India held anthropology and some anthropologists in low repute, for during the debates about Partially Excluded Areas, the subject had become identified with the forces of conservatism.[1] For, it was implied (in that famous phrase about the anthropological 'zoo'), if the tribal peoples of India were to become assimilated with the rest of the population, what would be left for the anthropologist to study? Even ten years ago, when I was preparing for my first visit to India, I was warned by an Indian friend that anthropology was for 'natives' while sociology was for civilised people, and I would be wise to call myself a sociologist.

It is my impression that at the present time anthropologists in India, whether Indian or foreign, are considered an asset by the Administration and their books are read and their point of view considered even by their fellow-intellectuals in other disciplines. No research team is complete without someone to put the anthropological point of view, and no welfare organisation feels itself properly constituted unless it has someone carrying on social research for the purposes of planning or evaluation.

The object of this essay is, in a sense, to evaluate this social research by asking just where our competence lies. It is a mistake to think that the respect which we sometimes command from political scientists or historians or administrators is a respect for the elegance or the validity of our theoretical constructions: quite the contrary, for our theory is often dismissed as 'jargon' and they complain that we have lost the people in a smoke-screen of abstractions. Where we are held in respect, it is the respect and authority that invests a traveller returned from a foreign land: what we say about our own experiences is incontrovertible and those who have to take their information at secondhand are at a disadvantage. In a sense our work is valued because we have some information (our ideas are not in demand) to provide a hard core in the shaky foundations of social engineering. If peasants were interested and articulate, we would be out of a job.

Nevertheless, whatever the attitude of outsiders, our subject is not defined only by the fact that we search for information in places where other scholars do not care to go. Ours is a distinct discipline within social studies, because we ask different kinds of questons from those asked by other people, and there does exist a theoretical framework, which guides these questions. Without this framework we would be no different from any other traveller. My purpose, then, is to ask what special competence our techniques and our theoretical equipment provide for us, what types of problem in Indian society are tractable, and what are our limitations. I shall first try to say what social anthropology is, and in doing so I shall outline the development of the subject in India.

Descriptive and Analytic Studies

Social anthropologists themselves are quite clear about the differences between their own discipline and the other branches of anthropology. But the non-specialist may take his picture of the subject from the structure of some university departments, and it is necessary to make clear at once that in some places an anthropology department includes disciplines which have only the slightest practical connections, and no theoretical connections with one another. There can be little significant interchange of ideas between social anthropology on the one hand and such other disciplines as physical anthropology, prehistoric archaeology, or the description and classification of objects of material culture. My essay has nothing to say about these disciplines nor about their relevance to Indian society.

A less obvious difference is that between ethnography and social anthropology. The difference is usually said to be that ethnography is purely descriptive while social anthropology is analytic and concerned with problems. But this is not quite so: ethnography cannot be purely descriptive since, as has often been observed, there can be no statement which is not the answer to some question, and no 'plain facts' which do not presuppose some body of theory. The difference is rather one of degree. The ethnographer's concepts are no more than a means of conveying to his reader a picture of the society in which he is interested and its culture. For the social anthropologist the priorities are reversed: he is interested in that particular society only in so far as it helps him to understand a problem of general reference: for example, what happens to property-holding descent groups (like the Indian joint-family) which developed in an agrarian economy, when they are exposed to the forces of an expanding capitalist economy. The social anthropologist wants to understand how a society, or a segment within a society, works: the ethnographer is concerned to portray all he can of his chosen society.

These two different approaches to the study of Indian society can be found long before the professional anthropologists entered the field. On the one side were, for example, the compilers of the several Tribe and Caste series: on the analytical side were such men as Maine, Ibbetson, Senart, Bouglé and others whose principal concern was to find out how particular institutions worked. A similar division is to be found among the professional anthropologists, both in the period up to the end of the Second World War when mainly tribal peoples were studied, and since that time when more attention has been given to peasant societies. By and large, there has been, however, a gradual change in which the analytical approach has grown at the expense of attempts at comprehensive descriptive works. To some extent this change has been associated with the change in emphasis from tribal studies towards village studies, and it is likely to become more marked when we turn to more complex sectors of Indian society.

Ethnographic studies have their own value and demand particular skills and resources, but they are not the concern of this essay. I therefore now turn more closely to the definition of social anthropology, beginning with some remarks about the Indian village studies which marked the decade of the 1950s.

'Tribal' studies, 'Village' studies, and the Concept of Structure.

The phrase 'village studies' can have several meanings. First there is the division already made between descriptive and analytic studies: in some accounts the analytical content is low while there is a lot of description, in others the main concern is in solving problems about social control, or social stratification, or the function of religious institutions in a village. Other types of research, which concern units larger than a village—for example, the organisation of a particular caste—are not village studies, although the investigator may have spent all his time working in one or two villages, not merely as a matter of convenience, but as a necessity.

The decision to study village problems, or to answer questions about wider social units by the intensive study of one or two villages, is a break with the traditions of social study by anthropologists both in India and elsewhere. In India virtually all those few professional anthropologists who were at work before and during the war were concerned with tribes: their predecessors, who compiled the Tribe and Caste series for various parts of India, were likewise concerned with wider units. Even those few analytical writers of that period who wrote about villages—Maine is an example—did not base their conclusions on the careful study of one or two villages, but wrote about the village in general. Studies by social anthropologists in Africa were likewise concerned not with villages but with larger units, tribes, defined sometimes by social criteria and sometimes by cultural homogeneity.

Whether in India the pre-war concentration upon tribal peoples was an accident of the personal interests and inclinations of the few people in the field, or whether this interest can be traced to ideas of that period about the scope of anthropology or to the political situation in India, is a question which I shall not discuss here. But we can ask what prompted the break with this tradition in the years after the Second World War. There are two factors concerned in this.

The first is that this was a part of a widespread change in the interests of social anthropologists, a change which began before the war but which has only become significant since the war. This change is towards the study of peasant communities. Anthropology was no longer exclusively concerned with savages and primitive people, and there is no doubt that this change of outlook, coupled with a somewhat diplomatic stressing of the 'social' as against the 'anthropological' half of the phrase, is one element which has made social anthropology respectable in India. When anthropologists were studying communities not only in South and Middle America, but also in Canada, Japan, the United States and several countries in western Europe, there was no longer any reason for the people studied to feel that they were being classified with the naked savages of the Sudan or with the Australian blackfellow.

The second reason for concentrating upon villages comes from another and paradoxical source. The studies of truly primitive peoples had shown the value of intensive and resolute empiricism. It became accepted that for a study to be acceptable the investigator must learn the language of the people studied, he must live among them, he must spend at least a full year with them, and he must patiently follow through and unravel all the complicated networks of relationship which lay behind the events he observed from day to day. In order to do this, in a peasant society, the investigator must live in one place for a long time, and the only place in which he can live is a village.

But this is not the whole story. Those anthropologists who made intensive studies of tribes also lived a long time in one place, and this too would be a tribal village or hamlet. Why, then, did they feel justified in assuming that their material was good for the whole tribe, while those who later worked in non-tribal villages were much more cautious about assuming that their material had a general validity for people in a wider area? The first reason is that a tribal village, by definition, is both homogeneous within itself and with other villages: there is no caste stratification. The investigator is more quickly led out of the village to such larger groups as lineages and clans, because the tribal village is usually smaller and less complex than the non-tribal. The second reason why the investigator feels no embarrassment in generalising his findings is that the tribal villager is linked to a bounded universe of other tribal villages and this is the same for everyone: while in a caste village, the different castes have systems of inter-village relationship which vary in direction and extent. To some degree these can be mapped and we can talk loosely of the wider area of social relations in which the village is enmeshed, but this is far from being the simple operation that it is in a tribal area.

The difference between the two types of 'region' can be put in several ways. When we are dealing with a tribal region, then we can comprehend it by means of a single system of relationships and regard it as a single structure. This single structure is an abstract of all the different kinds of activities: for example, our description of the ritual activities which link the several villages of a tribal region, will be found to be inextricably bound up with political activities, and will probably be expressed in the idiom of kinship.

A single coherent set of values cover all the relevant fields of activity. All activities—ritual, political, kinship—have the same boundary since, in a sense, they are one unspecialised activity. This lack of specialisation can be put in another way: in the relationships between tribal villages, a man is dealing always with the same set of people, whatever the activity: he does not have one set of people with whom he interacts politically, and another with whom he interacts in ritual affairs, and so forth. These are multiple relationships: a single relationship carries many interests. Alternatively, we may say that there is a high degree of summation of roles.

If we make a study of a caste village, and so long as we isolate it in a manner to be discussed below, then broadly the same set of concepts will be found applicable. Within the caste system in a village—again speaking broadly—once again the different kinds of activity are woven together into one relationship: the dominant caste is dominant not only politically, but also economically and (to a lesser extent) ritually: equally a caste which is politically subordinate is also economically subordinate and its subordination is expressed in the rituals concerning pollution. Once again the different kinds of activity can be seen as one activity, and a boundary drawn around one will be a boundary for all of them. Once again, in other words, there is a high degree of summation of roles.[2] Once again, the system is dealing always with the same set of people.

But it is by no means the same picture when we come to deal with relationships which pass between one multi-caste village and another. In the field of caste and kinship the ties which bind the Weavers of Bisipara[3] to other Weavers run north and west of the village: analogous ties for the Ganjam Distillers of south and east: and the Ganjam Distillers in the south and east have nothing to do with the Weavers in the north and west. A similar statement could be made for other castes in the village. Again, if we consider the different forms of activity, the ties which link Bisipara economically with the outside world, do not coincide with ritual or political ties passing outside the village in the same neat way that they do for a tribal village. For each activity a partially different universe of people is involved. The relationships are not multiple but specialised and single-interest: there is a low degree of summation of roles. Finally we cannot fit any single structure over this larger field and pretend that it has an explanatory value.

The crucial point in this distinction, since we are discussing the scope of social anthropology, is that our conceptual framework can deal satisfactorily with the former type of social system—with structures—but has not yet found an explanatory framework to deal with the second type of social system. Indeed, we are not even justified in calling it a system, for we do not know that every part is linked with every other part: it is for this reason that the vaguer concept of a social 'field ' is used. In a structural analysis our explanation consists essentially of pointing out how the different types of activity fit on top of one another, and are consistent with one another, and how conflicts are contained and prevented from changing the structure. In a social field the different types of activity do not fit over one another, they may be more or less insulated from one another or they may contradict and bring about change.

In order to make the exposition simpler I shall adopt from the pairs of adjectives suggested 'simple' for the type of society in which structural analysis is possible, and 'complex' for the other type which I have so far called a social 'field'. In the next section I shall discuss some of the ways in which anthropologists have dealt with the complex society.

Structural Explanations and the Complex Society in India

A peasant village is one which is, by definition, connected with urban markets and with the world outside the village. Again, in India the villages of the countryside—and indeed the tribal areas—have been administered for a long time, and the life of the villagers is profoundly and increasingly affected not only by the regular Governmental activity of maintaining law and order and collecting revenue, but also by welfare activities. No social anthropologist could live in a village for a year and remain unaware of these factors. But to be aware of these activities, and to be able to build them satisfactorily into a theoretical framework, are two different things.

One solution has been to concentrate on spheres of activity in which outside elements—that is, elements from the complex society —could be ignored. Successful studies of the function of ritual and religion (Srinivas 1952), or of kinship and caste (Mayer 1960), have been made in this way. One reason why these studies are successful is that these kinds of activity have retained a high degree of social—but not, of course, cultural—autonomy, and are relatively unaffected by the Administration or by the presence of an expanding capitalist economy.

A second solution has taken note of outside influences, but has treated them as accidents intruding into the theoretically closed system under observation. If the society we are studying is unfortunate enough to suffer from a famine or a drought, we may note the effects of this upon the system of social relations, but we do not feel called upon to explain why the famine came about. If there is an explanation, then it belongs to another discipline, and so far as we are concerned, the drought is an accident. But events which originate in a *social* field outside the system under observation, can be treated in just the same way: a change in the prices in the national or world market for a crop which the village exports, the growth and propaganda of political parties, or the policies executed by the Administration can all be treated as accidents, whose effects in the village are to be noted, but whose antecedent causes can be left unexplored. This method of procedure gives rise to two questions. Firstly, what effect does it have upon our structural explanations of village society? Secondly, can the procedure be carried on indefinitely, or is there a point at which it no longer seems satisfactory?

The effect of this procedure is to erode the area of village behaviour covered by a structural explanation. In essence we set up an ideal—or, less cautiously, postulate an antecedent state of affairs—in which ritual, political and economic behaviour are shown to be consistent with one another: and that is the extent of our structural explanation. We then say that accidents of Government policy or of economic change in the complex society, have caused, for example, the economic status of untouchables, who are politically and ritually low in the village, to be high and therefore out of step with their political and ritual status (see Bailey 1957). There is no longer a summation of roles. Our analysis, then, does not stop at a demonstration of structural coherence, but goes on to show that this structure exists as an idea, or may have existed in the past, but is not a comprehensive explanation of social life in the village to-day. I used the word 'erode' because we are in effect taking note of the fact, in the example given, that untouchables now have relationships which go outside the village. These relationships are treated as accidents in our account, and the effect is that the area of relationships covered by our structural explanation is cut down.

This leads to my second question. Clearly the more the villagers are involved with the world outside, the less comprehensive and therefore the less satisfactory will become a structural explanation, in terms of coherence and equilibrium, of village life. Up to the present I think that rural India is for the most part very far from this stage. But the fact that this situation may come about, and that the trend is in that direction, is an argument in favour of seeing what is our competence for dealing with those 'accidents', that is, for studying the complex society.

Before I take up this question, I should make clear that the above argument applies not only to 'village studies' in the strict sense, but also to studies of wider units. Regional studies, of the type done in Kerala (Gough 1952 and Miller 1954 and 1955) and North India (Mayer 1960) have so far been studies of simple societies, and although both these studies do take account of the complex society outside, they treat outside elements as accidents and intrusions, and do not fit them into their structural explanations.

The Study of Complex Society in India

To discuss the competence of social anthropologists in studying complex society, one must examine the methods which they use. These methods are of two kinds, as I have implied throughout the essay: firstly techniques by which information is collected; secondly, the conceptual framework which directs both the collection of data and its analysis.

I said at the beginning of this essay that it is our technique of gathering information which commands respect from other disciplines. But this technique of gathering information is in one way closely connected with the method of interpretation. Broadly our technique is one that rests on patience, on a willingness to wait and watch and allow the material to soak into us rather than to take quick samples out of the pool, as in done in less intensive methods of social research. One can deal in this fashion only with a very small universe: furthermore the technique is best fitted to those simple societies, defined above, where the same set of people interact with one another in all the different fields of activity of which a society consists. It is only in this way that one can observe the interconnectedness of the different fields of activity, which is the essence of structural analysis.

To what extent is this method possible in studies of a complex society? Firstly the tradition of long and patient observation, the willingness to look for details and to let the patterns and ideas emerge out of what one sees and hears will clearly be as useful in the study of a complex society as it has been in the study of simpler societies. We can expect to produce the same down-to-earth and exact information.

But what will the information be about? What questions will we be trying to answer? In simpler societies we can answer by saying that we intend to describe the structure of the social unit under observation, or the way in which this structure is being changed by forces coming from outside. But we cannot claim to analyse the structure of the complex society because we cannot set a boundary to any feasible unit of observation (at least not the same kind of literal boundary as in primitive societies), and because the different sets of activities do not overlap to a significant degree, as they do in primitive societies.

One tentative solution to this problem is that, given the narrow universe of behaviour which our techniques of collecting information allow us to observe, we can select some discernible segment from within the complex society. There are many possibilities, which fall broadly into two categories.

Firstly one might select a locus of intensive activity, for example a factory, or, as I have done, a legislative assembly (Bailey 1959 and 1960b), or a political party, or a trade union or some form of association. Secondly, we may fasten upon particular roles, which we consider important—politician, civil servant, lawyer, teacher and so forth—and see what kind of relationships adhere to these roles, both with other people in the same role and with the public at large I suspect, but I am not sure, that in the end this distinction is a false one and that the study of, for example, a legislative assembly or a political party, will in fact turn out to be a study of the role relationships of politicians.

The reader will have noticed that these fields of enquiry are already occupied by other specialists. For example, political parties and assemblies have been studied by political scientists: economists have something to say about the working of trade unions or the running of factories. How, then, would our enquiry differ? The answer is not difficult and it takes us back to our studies of simpler societies, where a structural analysis pointed out the linking of

political relationships with economic, ritual and kinship relations-
ships. The specialists in other disciplines work to a high degree of
abstraction, and, until very recently, have held or treated as accidents
factors which intruded into their specialist field, equal or have dealt
with them in a very naive way. An economist knows that the behaviour of workers in factories is likely to be affected to some extent
by their family obligations, their political associations, their religious
beliefs, and so forth: but for the most part economists have considered
the worker purely as a worker. Our contribution, I would suggest,
is to put these enquiries back into the social matrix from which
the specialist disciplines have abstracted them. This is precisely
the reason why our information is valued by economic planners
and others, who, by the nature of their discipline, must plan for
'economic man', whom they know in fact to be three parts
'social man'.

In short, in our research into complex sectors of society, we
have to behave as if in fact our chosen sector were a simple society.
We have to ask to what degree are apparently specialised single-
interest relationships in fact multiple relationships, and, secondly—
and this is a different thing—to what extent do the different single-
interest relationships, which are linked through the role relationship
under observation, affect one another. For example, to what extent
is the politician's behaviour influenced by ties of caste or kinship?

Nevertheless, we can never hope to arrive at the rounded and
complete picture which a structural description of a simple society
gives. There is no single structural framework to fit over a complex
society. The different kinds of activity—political, economic, or
religious—do not have the same common boundary. But they do
overlap with one another, and it is in this area of overlap that
the possibility of our making a significant contribution to the
understanding of complex society exists.

Conclusion

I have traced the study of Indian society by social anthropologists
through three stages: first the study of isolable wholes, such as
the village or the tribe, and these are equilibrium studies; secondly
the study of change in these societies, following on the intrusion
of factors from the complex society outside; thirdly, studies within
the complex societies itself. I think that this is the way our discipline

will evolve, but this does not mean that these are three stages, each one being completed or outdated when the next comes into existence. All three can go on together. It is, for example, quite clear that the last word has not been said about traditional Indian society and about the caste system. But it is also true that we do not need to have heard the last word on subjects like these before we go on to investigate, where we can, sectors within the complex society. As yet, social anthropologists in India have scarcely entered this last field.

NOTES

[1] I refer, for example to the debate between Ghurye (1943) and Elwin (1943).

[2] A clear exposition of the significance of this phrase will be found in Nadel (1957).

[3] Bisipara is described in Bailey (1957 and 1960a). In the latter book, some points concerning structural analysis, made briefly in this essay, are more fully discussed.

REFERENCES

BAILEY, F. G., 1957, *Caste and the Economic Frontier*. Manchester.
  1959, 'Politics in Orissa', nine articles in *The Economic Weekly*, Aug.-Nov.
  1960a, *Tribe, Caste and Nation*. Manchester.
  1960b, 'Traditional Society and Representation', *The European Journal of Sociology*, Vol. 1, No. 1.
ELWIN, V., 1943, *The Aboriginals*. Bombay.
GHURYE, G. S., 1943, *The Aborigines—'So-called'—and their Future*. Poona.
GOUGH, E. K., 1952, 'Changing Kinship Usages in the setting of Political and Economic change among the Nayars of Malabar,' *Journal of the Royal Anthrop. Institute*, Vol. 82, Pt. I.
MAYER, A. C., 1960, *Caste and Kinship in Central India*. London.
MILLER, E. J., 1954, 'Caste and Territory in Malabar', the *American Anthropologist*, Vol. 56, No. 3.
  1955, 'Village Structure in North Kerala' in *India's Villages* ed., by M. N. Srinivas.
NADEL, S. F., 1957, *The Theory of Social Structure*. London.
SRINIVAS, M. N., 1952, *Religion and Society among the Coorgs of South India*. London.
  1955, (Ed) *India's Villages*. Calcutta.

14

SYSTEM AND NETWORK : AN APPROACH TO THE STUDY OF POLITICAL PROCESS IN DEWAS

ADRIAN C. MAYER

IT IS fitting that a contribution to a volume honouring the late Professor D. N. Majumdar should consider an aspect of the changing nature of social anthropological studies in India. Concerned with problems of tribal analysis and acculturation before the Second World War, later concentrating on the 'village study', and finally developing into research in urban communities, Professor Majumdar's work was more than any other scholar's in the forefront of the expansion of interest in the subject over the past quarter century.

With these changes have come problems of method and theory. One of these is the way in which anthropological techniques can be used in the study of peasant and urban India. The titles of most of the first post-war books—*Village India, Indian Village, India's Villages*[1]—might suggest that villages were being studied as isolable systems. Such an approach would have received support, not only from the 'village republic' theory of Indian rural structure, but also from a tradition of socio-economic surveys centred on single villages.[2]

But a glance through these volumes is enough to show that the outside is often discussed. It may enter into the consideration of social and economic change, or the degree to which the village can retain its identity, or the relation between the culture of the village and the civilisation of which it forms a part. At no point was there, in fact, any assertion by anthropologists in India that the village was a complete social isolate. Even in accounts which deal for the most part with a single village, there is mention of external agencies of change, and of the existence of inter-village kin ties and mechanisms of social control.

Nevertheless, it was considered possible to take the village as an *isolate for study*, seeing other influences as external to the village system. This view stemmed partly from the demands of anthropological techniques, which required a small population which could be intensively studied by personal observation, and partly from the village's key place in the social system, through the inter-dependences of its economic system, the administrative pattern which for long made the village the unit of statutory authority and, of course, the groups stemming from the basic fact of co-residence.

Post-war research made it clear, however, that the village could not be studied as an isolate, and that outside influences should be discussed as parts of a wider system, rather than as external factors impinging on the village. The next step was therefore towards the study of problems, rather than of village systems. It may be no coincidence that, in much recently published work, caste is the major item in the title and a major problem, and that the word village disappears entirely.[3] Ideally, the village enters such studies merely as one of several contexts of research. But the difficulty still remains of how to reconcile the nature of such problems with the limitations of anthropological technique. For the problems demand a wide-ranging study—of kinship organisation, or an economic system—which covers a large area; but the technique restricts the number of people to be observed, preferably in the fairly limited area in which personal contacts can be maintained.

A possible answer to the dilemma lies in teamwork, in which several workers can deal with the same problem over a large area. This has not yet been attempted in India, where teams have only worked in single villages.[4] The other answer seems to lie in the technique of the 'village-outward' type of study. This consists of studying the population of a single village in its intra-village *and* inter-village activities, and in then trying to abstract the structure of those activities reaching outside the village. The advantages of this approach are first, that it deals with a limited and manageable number of people, whose ties are observable in interaction either in the village or outside it; and second, since observation is by definition limited to those activities in which villagers themselves are actors, the ties with the outside are also thereby limited.

The ramifications of extra-village linkages can run on almost indefinitely unless they are bounded by this sort of limitation. As it is, kin ties with other villages are followed insofar as they can be observed through the behaviour of guests coming to the village at weddings, etc., and of the villagers when they go outside as guests. Economic links are traced to moneylenders and crop brokers in the town, religious links to places of pilgrimage, and so on. To study any problem adequately on this basis poses difficulties of 'being everywhere at once'. But then, so does study of a single village, or even of a single household.

The village-outward type of study tries to maintain the holistic and microcosmic approach; but it is the central problem, not the village, to which the material is related. Further research problems may, of course, stem from the initial concerns of the study. For example, when investigating inter-caste commensal relations of Malwi villagers, it became apparent that these varied from village to village between the same castes (Mayer 1960, p. 49). An important problem regarding the degree of cultural and structural homogeneity in the area was thereby raised. Again, a study of social control within the Malwi subcastes brought in the role of local councils, and called forth a correlation of the type of case dealt with, and the scale of the council which dealt with it (*ibid.* p. 260 seq.). These problems may be of a different kind from those to be considered in a purely village-outward study, and might have to be dealt with in an even wider-ranging study.

The village-outward kind of study stimulates an attempt to distinguish different fields of interaction in various frames of reference (economic, political etc.). Such fields comprise those populations which are, or have possibilities of, interacting with any central person or number of persons. Thus, one can isolate an individual's field, a village subcaste population's or indeed a village's field. The last two would be the fields of interaction of the people comprised by the village subcaste group or the village at the time of research. I have tried to show elsewhere that members of Malwi subcastes in a locality form kindreds of cooperation and kindreds of recognition, the latter comprising populations within which marriage can take place without enquiries as to credentials of membership[5] (*ibid.* p. 4 ect.). Each individual has his own kindreds of cooperation and recognition, which vary over time with births and deaths as well as with his own decisions about those with whom he will cooperate. In addition the kindreds of all the subcaste members in a single village can be at least conceptually combined to form a village subcaste's kindred of recognition or co-operation. I have called these the individual's and the subcaste group's kinship regions, since it is within this area that there is interaction as regards kinship rights and obligations.

It is clear that this sort of region is quite different from the cultural region or culture area, insofar as the former is a structural concept. Further, the cultural region would in normal cases embrace a much larger territory than the structural region—in this instance, it might comprise 'Malwa', some ten times as large as the kinship regions of the Malwi village studied. Nevertheless, the villagers both recognise an area in which there is marriage and sometimes ascribe to it certain common cultural features, such as dialect. In some cases, then, the kinship region may be seen as a cultural 'micro-region'. But even though this coincidence of the two kinds of region may exist, they are morphologically quite distinct. Because the use of the word 'region' for both may lead to confusion, I think it may be wise to call the structural region a 'field of interaction'. There are thus fields of individual, subcaste and village kinship, and also economic, political and other fields.

It must be realised that there is a wide variety of interaction included in such fields. In the economic field, for example, there are ties between people and the craftsmen of nearby villages, and ties between kin in different villages. These ties form a single strand in the complex relations which bind these people, since socio-religious duties also exist in each case. By contrast there is the link with the grain broker or the moneylender in the town. Here the tie is simply one of economic transaction; the Malwi crop broker is never, to my knowledge, invited to his clients' weddings, for instance. Again, in the field of social control, there is the complex link between members of a subcaste council, who are at the same time kinsmen; and there is the simple link between villager and judge in an urban court. Both kinds of relationship contribute to the individual's or the subcaste group's field of interaction and both are regular and enforced by legal or social mechanisms of control. But they exist in different universes of action and of moral values.

The use of the concept of field is an attempt to solve the problem of studying a complex society, in which there is no single system which subsumes all of a village population's social relations. It is an attempt to distinguish the actual and potential ties of the villagers with the outside in various frames of reference. The extent of a field is imprecise, and depends on individual decision, but even if another term is thought better, the study of rural India seems to demand a concept of this kind. The term 'kindred' is admirable for caste and kinship analysis; but for other subjects it must be replaced by a term of similar connotation.

Can this concept be used in other contexts, besides that of the village-outward study? And can the village-outward approach itself be followed at other levels? An answer is suggested by recent research in the direction of a 'town-outward' study.[6]

In such a study, the problems of scale and technique enter with renewed vigour. Clearly a 'town study' in isolation could mean no more than a 'village study'. Yet, to follow all activities out of even a small town, in the same way as out of a village, would be an impossible task. The solution can only be to focus research on a relatively small area of activity. Work is thereby concentrated on the few hundred people who lead in this activity; and a similar research pattern is created as in the village, though on a narrower front. The 'outward' ties are then seen to be with fellow townsmen as well as with people of other places. In this case, the aim has been to study political process in Dewas, the headquarters of the District of the same name.

By political process I mean here the acquisition and use of power directed towards government. I use the term 'government' rather than 'internal cooperation' (Schapera 1956, p. 218) because I want to make it clear that I am considering a sector of the national political and administrative structure. It could otherwise be maintained that the study should embrace the political aspects of all associations in the town—i.e. those of subcaste organisations. Subcaste councils can, and should, be studied in political terms; but in this study they may be considered only insofar as they influence activities in the wider governmental sphere, and the bases of power of the individuals having major roles in this sphere.

Dewas is a town of some 35,000 people situated 22 miles from Indore and 95 miles from Bhopal, the commercial and political capitals of the State of Madhya Pradesh. Formerly divided into the capitals of the States of Dewas Senior and Dewas Junior, the town has now been merged into a single Municipality, and contains the administrative offices of the Dewas District. This comprises an area of 2,376 sq. miles, having in 1951 a population of 345,306 souls; it is divided into five administrative units (*tehsil*) all save the Dewas *tehsil* having as headquarters a market town of between 1500 and 7000 people.

Political activities can be divided by the observer into two classes, though in practice these often merge. First there are those activities which take place in one of three systems; the municipal, the rural and the legislative. They include running for an elective office, and taking part in the work of the body to which election is made. Second, there are those activities which are not co-ordinated systematically. These frequently include efforts to gain power in one of the systems, by recruiting support on caste, kinship or other grounds. All three systems have their locus in Dewas, and can be studied with a town-outward approach.

Dewas is served by a Municipality of 16 elected members and four aldermen. Councillors have powers to raise money by various forms of local taxation, of which octroi yields the major amount. They also have the responsibility for managing the town's water supply, roads, sanitation etc., of controlling the erection of buildings, and of developing facilities in the Municipal area. For this they are able to raise loans from the State Government in addition to the normal revenue, which is at present in the neighbourhood of Rs. 400,000.[7]

Political activity within the Municipal system has from the first been lively. Passing from a post-Independence Congress majority to a large Praja Socialist (PSP) majority after elections in 1954, the town elected an equal number of PSP and Congress Councillors in 1957. The chairman, and his casting vote, was chosen by lot each year, and the more important Municipal meetings which I attended in 1960 were hard-fought affairs. It is noteworthy that neither side was able to detach the crucial single vote from its opponent until the end of 1960, when a PSP Councillor defected to give Congress a slender majority. The system shows intense activity, and a strong party organisation. In addition, there have been rivalries within each party, sometimes because individuals have wished for more power within the system (e.g. to have the party's nomination for the Municipal Chairmanship or Vice-chairmanship).

Dewas is also at the apex of the system of rural government. The District's villages are grouped into 208 Village Committees, whose members are elected by adult suffrage. The Village Committees of each *tehsil* select one of their members to sit on a Central Committee, meeting at the *tehsil* headquarters (i.e. in Dewas for Dewas *tehsil*). The Central Committees in turn send three representatives to the District Committee, which meets in Dewas. Village Committees raise funds through local taxes and use these for the maintenance and development of village services.[8] Most of the projects they undertake, however, are paid for by Government grants, given with matching contributions from villagers in cash or labour.

Grants are distributed both through the District administration, and through the blocks of the Community Development Ministry. In each case, officials are advised in committee by representatives from the District and Central Committees respectively, as well as by other prominent non-officials, mostly men of political influence. Central and District Committees have few funds of their own to distribute. But the power of their leaders is great, because they speak for the countryside, and because they are seen as the channels through which Government money is obtained. Officials must to some extent heed their advice on how to allocate the large sums at their disposal,[9] or the co-operation of the villagers tends to stop. There has been considerable rivalry over the elections of Central and District Committee chairmen, some of it on a political party basis. This rivalry has also spread to wherever there are positions of power which these rural leaders can capture. An example would be the Board of the Dewas Central Cooperative Bank, with its Rs. 5,200,000 of working capital.

Finally, Dewas has been in a double-member constituency electing representatives to the State Legislative Assembly (MLA) and to the Lok Sabha in Delhi (MP). The constituency has always elected Congress MLAs, the town tending to be more fervently Congress than the country-side, where sentiments for the Jan Sangh are strong in parts. There has been competition for the Congress ticket, of course; and on one occasion a disappointed contender stood as a Congress Independent. The MLAs have an important position in Dewas, both as leaders of the party, and as arbitrators in political and other disputes and as spokesmen for the public with the administration.

These three contexts of political activity form systems, since there are definite rules of procedure, and any action in one part affects the pattern of power in the other parts. Though only the Municipal system is confined to Dewas town, the main activities of the two others take place there. The MLAs as well as the Municipal Councillors are townsmen, and the leaders of the District Committee can almost be counted as Dewas inhabitants, since their duties encourage them to spend the greater part of the time in Dewas, with only occasional journeys home to see to the management of their farms. It is, in fact, possible to see the three systems at work by staying in Dewas, only going outside with the leaders who live there.

Though activity in these systems is ruled by statutory procedures, the actors are products of and participants in a wider struggle for the power to control the systems. Part of this struggle takes place in contexts provided by the systems themselves—*e.g.* the rivalry to control committees, or to win an election. Part occurs outside, both in political parties and in the society which sustains them. Specifically political contexts are provided by those national political parties having branches in Dewas—that is, the Congress, Praja Socialist, Jan Sangh, Communist and Swatantra parties.

Each party consists of a small core of active workers, a penumbra of interested people, who are active on such occasions as elections, and an outer fringe of nominal members. In this, Dewas parties differ little from parties anywhere. The total Congress membership is 868 in Dewas town and 3,790 in the District. That of the Jan Sangh is known to be considerably less, though figures are not available; other parties do not have more than two or three hundred members in all. Each party has an internal structure of elected committees and office bearers.[10] In the smaller ones, the District and the Dewas town committees coincide; but the Congress and Jan Sangh both have committees, at least on paper, at the sub-District level,[11] whose representatives join certain *ex officio* members, such as the MLA, on the District Committee. Congress has most of its leaders in Dewas town, whereas the Jan Sangh's leadership is dispersed in three *tehsils*. The political parties now contest almost every position within the three systems. The legislative and municipal elections have long been party matters; but recently party rivalry has spread in the rural system until it encompasses the Central Committees and even some of the Village Committees.

To describe the ways in which parties gather support is outside the scope of this paper.[12] But, apart from recruitment through the party's programmes, they are ways by which social groups are invested with a political dimension. The caste, the kin-group, the locality, the trade union are all tapped to gather support. So are individual obligations of an economic or social nature, or long-standing friendships. Some of these stem from the days of the Maharajas, whose political structures were dismantled at the time of the merger of the States. It is in the manipulation of these relationships that the politician shows his skill; and it is a measure of this skill to be able to turn his own place in society, and his personal characteristics, to good advantage. For a man works for his own, as well as his party's, advantage. Not only does his skill enable him to win victory for himself and his party in elections within the three systems; it is also used in politics within the party, in elections to party posts. It would be an exceptional party with no differences among its members. Rivalry for positions of responsibility in Dewas parties has at times been intense, and has reflected on the party's public standing. In such rivalries, social backgrounds and the contacts leaders may have with politicians outside the District— in Indore, Bhopal and elsewhere—are important. So is the power held in the three systems; for power overflows from one context to another, in the total political situation.

I have given a very general picture of political activities in the District. Its outlines could be duplicated in many parts of India and abroad, for the influence of social contacts, and the manipulation of personal rivalries are common political features. It has been given to show how a town-outward study can distinguish fields of interaction in the same way as can a village-outward study. For all the activities I have described can be approached in this way.

We have seen that an individual acts in a political frame of reference at two levels—that of the systematic political organisation and that of the unstructured social contacts which are invested with political content. The latter are only unsystematic in the political frame of reference, of course. In their own frames of reference they may be equally systematic—i.e. the caste system, the kinship system.

To put it differently, the political acts of the individual occur in one or more of three fields. First, he may act as the member of a primary group, such as the Dewas Congress Working Committee, or the Dewas Municipality, in which there is face-to-face contact. His behaviour here is part of a system, since his acts in a measure influence the subsequent behaviour of others in the group.

Second, he acts as a member of an extended group, which has a definite boundary but is not primary because the people in it are not all known to one another. Such a group would be the Dewas District Congress party, with its 3,790 members. This is again a systematic entity, since the actions of any member will influence the future of the group, however slightly.

Third, he acts as a component of what might, following Barnes, be called a network (Barnes, 1954). This is a social field, the units of which 'do not make up a larger social whole; they are not surrounded by a common boundary (Bott 1957, pp. 58-9). Both Barnes and Bott distinguish between the 'total network' and the parts of it composed of kin, neighbours, and friends (Bott 1957, pp. 93-94, Barnes 1954, p. 43). I would go slightly further, and suggest a distinction of different networks according to these different frames of reference all being parts of the total network.

For the individual in Dewas, the political network comprises, in addition to the first two fields, those relations which can at least potentially be used for political purposes, even though some connections with the object of contact may be through some other activity. That is, I see every individual's total network of relations stretching away from him along political, economic, kinship and other lines. A interacts with B politically; B interacts with C as a friend; C interacts with D as a kinsman, and so forth. Of all these people, A may know only B personally, and not C and D; and B may only know A and C, and not D. A may be able to enlist C's aid in a political matter (e.g. an election). He may either do so directly, or by contacting C through B's good offices,[13] or through B's influence on C quite unknown to him. C may then spontaneously influence D. All these men will comprise A's political network at that time, their links abstracted from the totality of uncoordinated and often temporary relationships. The network overflows into different categories of institutionalised behaviour; that is, the individual makes use of links through say, the kinship system[14]—but these are not systematically used in this frame of reference.

From the individual's point of view, these three fields mean a difference between face-to-face co-operation (or rivalry) of a systematic kind: potential co-operation of this kind: and potential or actual interaction of a politically uncoordinated kind. The first two are based on the local group and its sanctions and procedures, the last on *ad hoc* interaction due to mutual political interests or rivalries.

That this distinction of fields of interaction is not confined to the political frame of reference is seen if we compare it with the situation in the kinship frame of reference. It will be recalled that I distinguished the kindred of co-operation and the kindred of recognition for villagers. These, I suggest, correspond to the first two of the political fields. The first concerns actually co-operating kin, and the second those with whom there is the possibility of cooperation within a local population capable of enforcing internal normative behaviour. Beyond the kindred of recognition there is an 'attenuation' (Mayer 1960, p. 272) into the total formal subcaste membership. By this I mean that kin ties, if contracted, are not subject to any local mechanism of enforcement. This stage corresponds to the political network, which is also a field of potential relations of an uncoordinated kind. Beyond it, the subcaste is a bounded unit; the network within it is not bounded, however, but is rather a residual context of interaction, just as is the political network.[15]

So far, I have been writing from the viewpoint of the individual. But it is at least theoretically possible to apply fields of these three kinds to a small group, or even to all the politically-minded men of a town, just as one can see kinship fields in terms of a village subcaste group or a whole village. Thus we can move to the framework for a town-outward study of political activity.

What is to be gained by this approach? In the first place, it provides us with a justifiable way of opening up our focus of research. Through a town-outward study, we can break away from the idea of the village as a unit, and the rural as the main focus of research, and yet not be presented with an indefinite number of relationships, since the fields of interaction are bounded by the relations of a limited number of people—i.e. the few hundred men and women who form the permanently politically active population.[16]

In the second place, the approach lends itself to comparative research. What sort of people, and what parties, can count on the largest fields of interaction? What is the relation of these political fields to caste, community or occupation? Can networks be distinguished as 'close knit' and 'loose knit' (Bott 1957, p. 59)[17] and can this variation be correlated with party or context?

Clearly, such questions are not easy to answer: but, in considering them, we may widen the scope of social anthropology in India in fruitful ways.

NOTES

[1] Marriott (1955), Dube (1955) and Srinivas (1955) respectively.
[2] A good list of these works is contained in Marriott (1960 pp. 67-75).
[3] i.e. Dumont (1957), Bailey (1960), and Mayer (1960).
[4] e.g. the work of teams directed by Professors Dube, Majumdar and Opler.

I understand that Professor Dube has been conducting precisely this kind of coordinated extended research in villages near Saugor, but no results have yet been published.

[5] Cf. Firth (1956): 42 seq. for a somewhat similar classification.

[6] This field work was carried out between January 1960 and April 1961, through a study leave most generously granted me by the School of Oriental and African Studies, University of London.

[7] The full list of powers and duties is set forth in the Madhya Bharat Municipalities Act (No. 1 of 1954) under which the Municipality operates.

[8] The working of the rural system is contained in the Madhya Bharat Panchayat Act (No. 58 of 1949) and its amendments.

[9] Approximately Rs. 1,200,000, for the District administration, and some Rs. 1,750,000 for the Dewas *tehsil* development block during the two Five-Year Plans.

[10] The Swatantra Party, as the newest of all, had not yet elected on..cers by the start of 1961.

[11] Congress has several local committee in a constituency, each covering a total population of 20,000. Each of these committees sends a representative to the District Committee. The Jan Sangh's structure is one of a committee covering the whole of each constituency (though there are two in a double-member constituency); under them are local committees elected by the population going to a single polling station.

[12] See a forthcoming article, entitled 'Municipal Elections: a Central Indian Case Study' in C. H. Philips ed. *Indian Politics and Society* for an account of elections in Dewas Municipality.

[13] See the similar role of the 'connecting relative' (Bott (1957), p. 140).

[14] Cf. the concept of 'bridge-action' (Bailey (1960), pp. 251 seq.).

[15] The network is only unbounded here *within the kinship frame of reference*, Logically it is impossible to have an unbounded total network in a finite population. This may make the network an unsatisfactory concept for some. But within specific frames of reference, it, or a similar concept is valuable for analysis.

[16] Elections present a special difficulty, for at these times the politically active population increases enormously. Hence, some sort of samples must be taken at these times.

[17] Similarly Barnes talks of the 'mesh' (1954, p. 44).

REFERENCES

BAILEY, F. G., 1960, *Tribe, Caste and Nation*. Manchester.

BARNES, J. A., 1954, 'Class and Committee in a Norwegian Island Parish', *Human Re ations*, VII, 1, pp. 39-58.

BOTT, E., 1957, *Family and Social Network*. London.

DUBE, S C., 1955, *Indian Village*. London.

DUMONT, L., 1957, *Une Sous-Caste de l'Inde du Sud*. Paris.

FIRTH, R. ed., 1956, *Two Studies of Kinship in London*. L.S.E. Monog. on Soc. Anthrop. No. 15. London.

MARRIOTT, McK. ed., 1955, *Village India*. Chicago.

1960, *Caste Ranking and Community Structure in Five Regions of India and Pakistan*. Deccan Coll. Monog, 23. Poona.

MAYER, A. C., 1960, *Caste and Kinship in Central India*. London.

SCHAPERA, I., 1956, *Government and Politics in Tribal Societies*. London.

SRINIVAS, M. N. ed., 1955, *India's Villages*. Calcutta.

15

MORAL CONCEPTS IN THREE HIMALAYAN SOCIETIES[1]

CHRISTOPH VON FÜRER-HAIMENDORF

THE STUDY of value systems and ethical concepts has so far received less emphasis in anthropological research than the analysis of social and political structures. This is all the more regrettable as there are few spheres of human relations in which the differences between ethnic groups are as fundamental and significant as they can be in the sphere of moral ideas. An understanding of the ideology of a society is one of the most important keys to the interpretation of social conduct, and a description of a social system remains incomplete unless it accounts for the motives which determine the actions and moral choices of individuals. When we investigate the moral system of a society other than our own we are not concerned with the question what actions are right or wrong by absolute standards, but we want to find out in what manner the members of this society in question evaluate human actions. In other words we are concerned with descriptive and not with normative ethics.

In the present contribution to this volume in memory of Professor D. N. Majumdar, one of India's most eminent anthropologists and a friend of mine of many years standing, I propose to analyse the moral concepts and values of three Himalayan societies, of which I have personal experience. The unifying bond between the selected populations is their geographic location in the Himalayan region extending between the plains of India and the highlands of Tibet. The Daflas, who represent a pre-literate tribal society, inhabit the middle ranges of the Assam Himalayas; the Chetris, who form a constituent element of a Hindu caste-society, live in country of similar altitude in Nepal, and the Buddhist Sherpas dwell in the high region on the frontier between Eastern Nepal and Tibet.

Daflas

Until recently the Dafla tribesmen remained entirely outside the orbit of the great historic civilisations of both India and Tibet. From the latter they were separated by the Himalayan main range, and from Assam by a belt of rugged hills too steep for cultivation and largely covered by rain forest. At the time when I came to know them they were not yet subjected to outside interference and it is only since 1945 that they have been drawn into the sphere of Indian political influence. The following description of their social system, conduct and moral concepts relates to the time before this influence became effective, and though I use the ethnographic presence, I do not wish to imply that raiding, kidnapping and slavery continue to be practised in areas under Indian administration.

A few ethnographic notes may set the scene for the argument which is to follow. The Daflas are a population of Mongoloid race and Tibeto-Burman language, extending over a large part of the Subansiri Division, NEFA. Their settlements, situated at altitudes of between 3,000 and 6,000 feet, are loosely scattered over the hills, and all Daflas are organised in exogamous patrilineal clans which are grouped in phratries. Apart from regulating marriage, the clans do not function as social units; there is no mechanism for securing co-operation of clan members, who may and indeed often do oppose each other in war and blood-feuds.

The only firmly integrated social and political unit is the household which usually comprises several primary families and in some cases consists of as many as sixty or seventy members. All these persons live in one long-house, which is an unpartitioned hall with a line of fire-places down the centre. Each primary family lives round its own fire-place, cultivates its own field, and owns its own granary which stands close to the communal long-house. The owner of the long-house is the head of the 'household' and his authority is unquestioned by its inmates. Four or five such long-houses may form a settlement, or there may be up to thirty long-houses grouped on one village-site, standing not in streets but in twos and threes, dispersed over hill slopes of different levels. Such a settlement is not a closely knit social and political unit. Households may join and leave at will, and in some areas there is a continuous movement of people from one settlement to the other. There is no one man, and no council of household-heads, to wield authority over all the householders. No one has by virtue of his position any influence over his neighbours, and it is for this reason that the settlement lacks an organisation which might enable it to function as a corporate unit. Feuds and wars are usually not between village and village, but between joint-family and joint-family. It is quite a common occurrence that one or two houses in a village are raided and burnt, and the inhabitants killed or carried off captive, while the other households remain unharmed and make no attempt to help the victims.

The first question relevant in our context is how social controls and laws, based on concepts of right and wrong, operate in such an atmosphere of instability and insecurity. In Dafla society there is outside the household no individual or group of privileged individuals possessing the authority to impose sanctions, enforce conformance with custom or redress the grievances of the victims of violence. Yet, there are certain conventions which regulate the conduct of feuds, of negotiations and finally of peace-settlements, and these conventions are generally recognised, even though there is no authority above the parties in the dispute which could enforce their observance or punish their breach.

Let us take a concrete case which will demonstrate Dafla custom regarding disputes and their settlement:

A, living in Talo village arranges to buy from B, living in Jorum village, a string of valuable Tibetan beads for two mithan (*bos frontalis*). He pays one mithan at once, receives the beads and promises to pay the second mithan after a few months. But he delays payment, either because he regrets the bargain or because a mithan he expected to receive with a bride-price or in some other way was not forthcoming.

B, the seller of the beads, reminds A, several times of the debt, but without success.

What steps can B take in order to realize his debt?

There is no village or tribal council he can appeal to, and the other people of A's village cannot be held liable for the debt. If B belongs to a kin-group much weaker than that of A he will probably do nothing, but will nurse his grievance and pass it on to his son, who may find an opportunity of pressing the claim. But if A and B are of approximately equal status, B will embark on an act of self-help. He will watch for a chance of catching one of A's mithan grazing in the forest, and take the animal to his village. And he is quite likely to take a mithan of greater value than the one due to him, or even a cow with a calf.

In this act, which resembles an Ifugao practice described by Barton as 'illegal confiscation', (1919, pp. 86, 100-07) B has acted according to custom, and all his kinsmen and friends will uphold the righteousness of his case. But A has lost face, and will feel aggrieved. To have one's cattle captured is almost as bad as having a kinsman kidnapped, and A is likely to seek revenge. B will probably have sent the attached mithan and all his other mithan into the safe-keeping of friends in another valley, and thus A cannot retaliate in kind. B knowing that he is himself in for trouble, will also be particularly careful not to expose his person. If A is determined to avenge the capture of his cattle and regain his prestige, he may wait for an opportunity to kidnap a member of B's household, or one of his close kinsmen. Such an opportunity may arise when B's kinsmen are on a fishing expedition, fetching thatching grass from a lonely slope or visiting a neighbouring village. The capture usually takes the form of an ambush: surprise and the number of attackers make resistance difficult. People are seldom killed in resisting capture, and once disarmed there is little chance of escape; the captive is taken to his captor's village and his leg is inserted in a large hollow log. But he is not badly treated and it is a point of honour that prisoners should be well fed.

When the quarrel reaches the stage at which a kinsman or dependent has been seized, a new situation has arisen and the next steps follow a more or less customary course. The captor has no interest in keeping the kidnapping secret and when the relatives hear of the capture of their kinsman they are under a moral obligation to arrange for his release. This obligation falls primarily to the head of the household to which the captive belongs, but if, as in our case, the captive does not belong to B's household, B will be held responsible to indemnify the captive's household for the expenses involved in the release.

The captive's kinsmen then commission a man of their own settlement, who is on good terms with A, to act as mediator. While engaged as mediator, his person is sacrosanct and he goes to A's house to discuss terms. Once the negotiator has embarked on his mission everybody knows that a ransom will be paid. Only the amount of the ransom is at issue, and this is determined by several factors. Most important is the status of the captive, but the reason for the capture has also to be taken into account. In our case A had only to revenge the theft of a mithan, but in more complicated cases a ransom may have to cover greater losses, and the release may even be made conditional on the payment of compensation for a kinsman slain in the distant past.

In the concrete case under discussion there are two possibilities. A and B may both be tired of the quarrel and A will not only agree to release the captive against a reasonable ransom—say one mithan and a few cloths and minor valuables—but A and B may afterwards meet and negotiate a general settlement of their differences including the original debt and the injuries suffered by both sides in having their cattle and kinsmen captured. Such a settlement concluded between the two parties is their own affair and no higher authority is concerned with it.

The other alternative is that A extracts from B's party a very high ransom—say three to four mithan— and that B is not prepared for a settlement on those terms and, while paying the ransom in order to effect his kinsmans release, bides his time until he can take revenge. He has now an added grievance, for the quarrel began with A's refusal to pay a freely contracted debt, and the exaction of an exorbitant ransom adds to the injury. If B does nothing to restore the balance, he acquires a reputation of being weak and ineffective, and may be cheated in other trade-deals.

Yet there exists no tribal authority to which he can appeal. Everybody may agree that he has been wronged, but nobody will make any move to redress the wrong unless B takes another step of forceful self-help. If he can count on the support of a number of powerful kinsmen, he may decide to raid A's house, not necessarily with the intent to kill, but in order to revenge himself and to obtain captives whose release he will make conditional on A's paying indemnity for all past injuries.

The organisation of the raid requires some capital outlay, for warriors joining in—and any young warrior may enlist for such an adventure—must be feasted before they set out. They also expect some minor share in the loot, but they do not share the responsibility for the raid. They are considered merely hired mercenaries, and the organiser of the raid—who often does not take an active part— is held responsible for their deeds.

Raids organised by one man and directed against a single household are frequent, and most Daflas have been involved in several raids, both as victims and attackers. Indeed these private raids do not seem to fall easily into the category of war, but are in many cases more in the nature of an extreme form of self-help supported by force.

It is difficult to draw a line between a raid which is but the last phase in a long drawn out dispute over property, and predatory raiding the only aim of which is the capture of slaves and the looting of property. Some such raids appear to be unprovoked but the organisers usually put forward some story of an old grievance, inherited perhaps from the generation of father or grandfather.

There is no individual or group that can either punish a breach of custom or act as judge or tribunal in a dispute. Self-help is the only course open to the injured party, and the weak man has no redress but to put himself under the protection of a powerful person, who may find it to his own advantage to gain a new dependent. Such protection involves, almost invariably, entrance into the protector's house, and thus effacement of the protegé's social individuality.

Although there is no *administration of justice* in any sense of the word, questions of right and wrong are continuously discussed in the course of a dispute. In the mind of the Dafla there is a great difference between "justified retaliation" and "unprovoked robbery", and when hostile parties meet to discuss the settlement of a feud, both harp on details of custom, each trying to prove that their own actions were justified and those of their opponents were a breach of custom.

There are certain customs which we might almost describe as laws but even their breach does not set in action a legal machinery. It is generally recognised, for example, that a man sheltering another man's runaway slave should either restore him to his owner, or, if unwilling to do so, pay the owner the slave's market price. If he takes neither of these two courses, the slave-owner is deemed justified in recouping his loss by an act of self-help. He may attach one of the offender's mithan or kidnap a member of his family. But unless he takes action himself, nobody will do anything about this breach of custom. Yet, there are certain limits to repeated breaches of custom. If a man makes too many enemies they are likely to combine in an act of revenge, and his persistent defiance of accepted standards of behaviour may alienate his kinsmen and friends whose help he would require for retaliatory action.

Resort to force and even warfare in the settlement of conflicts is, of course, a feature of many societies, and the peculiar situation in

Dafla society is due to the unusual smallness of the in-group. As the joint-family inhabiting one long-house is the only real in-group, most economic and social contacts are between autonomous and independent bodies; *i.e.* they are not subject to a rule of law, but can ultimately only be resolved by compromise or war.

In trying to discover the ideology underlying a social order which leaves the individual largely to fend for himself, and does not provide for a tribal authority to restrain the powerful and protect the weak, we must consider whether in the mind of the Dafla there is any consistent assessment of conduct as good or bad. At first glance it would appear that Dafla ideology can be summed up by the phrase 'might is right', but closer consideration leads us to the view that even though the powerful and wealthy man, capable of hiring warriors to intimidate and crush his enemies, may get away with riding roughshod over the interests of others, his acts of violence are by no means regarded as right. One has only to listen to a Dafla complaining of the injuries and injustice done to himself or his close kin, to know that in describing the high-handedness of his adversaries he is appealing to a sense of moral values he presumes his listener will share with him. By accusing his enemies of treachery, breach of promise, outright lies, unprovoked aggression, theft, adultery, or similar acts, he manifests his conviction that the person to whom he addresses his complaints will be moved to indignation, *i.e.* show a response expressing a moral judgement similar to that of the complainant. The fact that there is no independent tribunal capable of translating such indignation and the assessment of an act as unjust into punitive action, is indicative only of the absence of legal sanctions in the narrow sense, but not of the absence of any generally accepted standard of right and wrong.

The fact, for instance, that the person in the position of a go-between is treated as sacrosanct by all parties involved in a feud proves the existence of a code of behaviour which even the most high-handed and powerful will hesitate to infringe. Another example of the acceptance of certain standards is the rule that captives and prisoners of war held to ransom ought to be well treated and, above all, well fed. A deviation from this expected conduct arouses indignation and is detrimental to a man's prestige.

Even more positive a proof of the recognition of binding moral obligations is the invocation of a god of oaths on the occasion of a peace-pact. This god, Potor-Met, is begged to avenge any breach of the pact, and it is believed that whosoever did not abide by the solemn promise to abstain from further violence would be stricken by disaster. While a pact concluded between former adversaries is thus reinforced by an appeal to a supernatural power, there is otherwise no suggestion that the gods and spirits are normally concerned with the moral conduct of human beings. Offerings and sacrifices are tendered in propitiation of deities believed to have afflicted people with illness, but never in atonement of wrong conduct. In the endless debates over past events which accompany all negotiations regarding the release of prisoners, payment of compensation and the settlement of feuds there is never any hint of a sense of guilt or sin in relation to deeds of violence or acts of treachery. While a man may readily admit that by killing a person— particularly if the act was unprovoked—he inflicted an injury on the dead person's kinsmen and may even agree to reconcile them by the payment of compensation, he is not conscious of having offended against an impersonal moral order. Consequently there is no sense of guilt, and the matter is closed as soon as the slain person's kinsmen accept the valuables or cattle offered in compensation.

In cases of adultery, too, it is the likelihood of adverse social consequences, namely the revenge of the deceived husband, and not the reluctance to infringe a moral code which may induce a man or woman to discontinue an unlawful association. A deed which escapes the notice of society is apparently never a cause of scruples or remorse on the part of its perpetrator.

Consistent with this lack of any sense of guilt or sin are the Daflas' eschatological beliefs. On their way to the Land of the Dead the departed have to pass a deity who acts as the gate-keeper of the nether world and subjects the new arrivals to an interrogation regarding their record in life. Those who can point to successful raids, the capture of prisoners, the acquisition of many wives and slaves, and other symbols of worldly success are received with honour, whereas little notice is taken of the meek and peaceful who have led an inconspicuous life. According to the beliefs of one of the Dafla tribes the guardian of the Land of the Dead shows, however, some concern for the veracity of the departed. If they answer his questions truthfully, whatever their deeds may have been, he sends them along a straight and easy path to the Land of the Dead.

But if they lie to him, he scrutinises the palms of their hands, rebukes for having lied and sends them along a different road.

The final destination of the departed, however, depends solely on the manner of their death, and not on their record in this life. Those who died a violent death are believed to go to a place different from the ordinary Land of the Dead, but there is no concept of two contrasting worlds beyond comparable to the idea of heaven and hell.

If one compares the Daflas' approach to human relations with that of another Himalayan hill-people, the Buddhist Sherpas, one is struck by this total absence for the feelings and dignity of other human beings. No Dafla has any scruples to capture and —if they are not ransomed—sell as slaves men and women born free and as members of families of good status, no one considers the feelings of a person kidnapped to serve as security for the unpaid debt of a kinsman, and no one feels compassion for children torn from their parents. They are pawns in a game of raids and counter-raids, and their emotions and sufferings are not even taken into account. One of my closest Dafla friends, an intelligent and gay person, told me that if his wife were ever unfaithful, he would kill her lover, roast some of his flesh, and force the adulterous woman to eat of it. But he would neither kill nor divorce his wife, for would this not involve the loss of the large bride-price he had paid for her?

Such harshness, characteristic of Dafla attitudes, is by no means the outcome of puritanical condemnation of adultery, but is the product of anger and wounded personal pride. There is, in the hard world of these tribes, no room for sentimentality and a spirit of forgiveness; everyone is always ready to take up arms in the defence of his interests.

A breach of custom may bring about massive retribution at the hands of those immediately concerned, but it does not affect the offender's social or ritual status. There is no idea of an automatic loss of status or any concept of pollution, either confined to the offender or contagious and transmissible to those with whom he maintains social contacts. As long as a man can get away with violence and the disregard of customary conduct, he retains his position in society and there is even admiration for the strong man and successful organiser of raids. On gentleness and compassion there is no premium either in this or in the next world.

One may well wonder how a society can actually hold together, if there is no provision for preventing or at least limiting the encroachment of the powerful on the rights of the weaker members, either by legal sanctions or by a moral code which arouses spontaneously a sense of guilt in offenders against the legitimate interests of their fellow-tribesmen.

The answer is probably that Dafla society is in an equilibrium only where groups of approximately equal strength face each other and self-interest prevents their members from resorting to violence and aggression. Where forces are not equally matched, the situation is fluid, and there is little security of life and property. There are no generally accepted moral injunctions which would deflect the powerful from enriching themselves at the expense of weaker members of the tribe, and the history of most clans and settlements illustrates the ruthless way in which groups on the crest of a wave of martial success have whittled down neighbouring communities until clans, once populous and prosperous, were reduced to isolated families living as dependants in the houses of rising clans.

The trend to self-aggrandisement pursued regardless of the rights and the welfare of others is consistent with the Dafla world-view according to which material success, achieved at whatever the cost to others, provides not only gratification in this world, but perpetuates itself automatically in the Land of the Dead. For the world beyond is to the Dafla a reflection and continuation of this world, and the aims of all conduct is hence of necessity "this worldly", and tribal morality lacks the "other-worldly" incentives of the ideologies of the two societies discussed in the following sections.

Chetris

Though inhabiting mountain country not unlike the habitat of the Daflas, the Chetris of Nepal evince a cultural pattern totally different from that of the tribal populations of the Assam hills. They speak Nepali, an Aryan tongue, and conform in physical features to the so-called Mediterranean type widely prevalent in Northern India. Their status in the Hindu caste-hierarchy of Nepal is inferior only to that of Brahmans and the royal Thakuri caste.[2] Together with the far less numerous Thakuris they constituted the ruling class of Nepal from the time of the Gurkha conquest in 1768 until the end of the rule of the Rana family in 1951. During this period the values of Chetri society were those of the state of Nepal.

As members of a hierarchically ordered caste-society the Chetris are in daily contact with castes and ethnic groups different in status, traditions and patterns of living, and it is against the background of a multi-ethnic caste society, that we must view the ideology underlying the moral concepts and conduct of the members of a high Hindu caste such as the Chetris. In its basic premises this ideology conforms to the tenets of orthodox Hinduism. Human life on this earth is considered a phase in a process extending over a sequence of existences, and as it is believed that in the same way as conduct in past lives determines a person's status in this existence, so achievements or failings in this life will influence his or her fate in future reincarnations. 'Right' or 'wrong' conduct involves thus not only social approval or disapproval, but extends in its effects to a level beyond an individual's life in present day society. Closely linked with the idea of reincarnation is the belief in the possibility of building up a store of *merit*, a store which is increased by every virtuous action and decreased by every sinful act.

The very idea of *merit* as an effect of morally positive conduct, distinguishes Chetri ideology from that of such tribes as the Daflas described above. For in Chetri ideology human behaviour is motivated at least partly by aims other than material success and a favourable status for the individual. While in Dafla belief gratification and success in this life produce a repetition of like experiences in the next, Chetris believe on the contrary that abstention and and sacrifice in this life create the basis for gratification in a life beyond death.

The primary means of acquiring merit are prayer, participation in ritual performances, pilgrimages, the giving of alms to the poor and donations to Brahmans and temples. All these are considered acts productive of the merit which will ensure rebirth in a higher form and thus a happy fate in the next life. Merit is lost, on the other hand, by evil conduct, i.e. such actions as the neglect of religious duties, the breach of caste-rules, untruthfulness, and above all such supreme sins as the killing of a Brahman or a cow.

The evaluation of conduct in interpersonal relations is mainly legalistic. There is no premium on spontaneous warmth and kindness, nor an expressive injunction not to offend the feelings or encroach on the interests of others. Chetris insist primarily on the rigid observation of caste-rules, and their supreme preoccupation is the avoidance of pollution which might adversely affect their social status. Their ideal is the man who lives strictly according to the rules of his caste and never undertakes any action which endangers the purity of his status. Chetris judge a person's virtue mainly by the strictness with which he complies with the rules regulating the conduct appropriate to his caste-status. They see the individual not so much as an independent agent, whose conduct must depend on the promptings of his own conscience, but as a member of a tightly organised community whose every action affects not only his own status within that community but even the status of those closest to him. For the wrong conduct of one individual can have a chain-effect on the others. By incurring pollution he in turn pollutes the innocent members of his household, or even kinsmen or friends who, ignorant of his fall in ritual status, have partaken of a meal which he offered. The pollution, which follows certain offences against caste-rules, such as social contact with low-caste persons, is automatic and contagious. Whereas 'sin', resulting in a loss of merit, may be a matter for the individual's conscience, the social effects of many forms of sin are the concern of the whole kin-group.

Ever anxious about the preservation of his own status, the Chetri tends to be extremely critical of any deviation from the narrow path of orthodox behaviour on the part of other caste-members. He is quick to boycott those whom he suspects or knows to have violated the rules of their caste. Parents will disown a daughter guilty of a pre-marital love affair and it is unthinkable that an illegitimate child might be brought up by the mother's family. The same unbending attitude is taken towards an erring wife. A Chetri husband, even if personally inclined to forgive a temporary unfaithfulness cannot do so, because of the pressure of public opinion which prescribes that a faithless wife must be divorced or unceremoniously evicted.

While there is an injunction to dispense charity to Brahmans and to the poor, there is little compassion with the weak and the erring. The average Chetri's attitude to interpersonal relations is puritanical and even the relations between father and son, or husband and wife, are formal and hedged in by numerous interdictions. There is not much room for spontaneousness and warmth, and emotional relationships are confined to a narrow circle of close kinsmen. Very little latitude is left to the ethical choices and reasoning of the individual, for the behaviour appropriate to members of the

Chetri caste is narrowly circumscribed. There is a strong authoritarian element in Chetri ethics, and this expresses itself in several ways. The authority of the caste rules is supposed to be accepted unquestioningly and conformity with the laws of society is valued for its own sake. The justification for the various prescriptions of the caste rules is neither sought in any intellectual argument nor traced to the command of divine beings, but it is seen merely in the prevailing tradition. Another symptom of the authoritarian trend is the attribution of ethical competence to comparatively few members of the society. The presumption of ethical incompetence in a young child, common to all human societies, extends far into manhood in Chetri families, for adult sons, unless explicitly separated from their father, are expected to abide by his wishes and commands. The early separation of sons, however, is viewed unfavourably by public opinion, which strongly supports the continuation of paternal authority until the father's death.

The discipline this system imposes on the younger members of society is very great, and there is little doubt that obedience to their elders whether given willingly or reluctantly, is a much more powerful motivation of ethical conduct than any thought of acquiring supernatural merit by virtuous actions. Women, moreover, are subject to the authority of man throughout their lives, for when they marry the place of the father is being taken by their husbands, to whom they owe unconditional obedience.

A sense of responsibility towards the members of his family and kin group is instilled into the Chetri from an early age, for deviant behaviour is thought to harm not only the living members, liable to contagious pollution, but may affect even the deceased ancestors.

There is a belief that although a person's acquired merit may help him to go to heaven (*svarga*), he is not secure there, for any of his descendants up to seven generations can, by a serious offence, throw all his departed ancestors into hell (*narka*). Acts supposed to propel a man's ancestors into hell may appear to a Western observer as comparatively trivial. Thus marrying with full wedding rites a girl who had already been formally betrothed and whose first match had been broken off after the completion of the *swayambar* rite, is considered so unpropitious an act that even those of the bridegroom's kinsmen who had already reached heaven may have to leave it and go down to hell.

It is therefore considered preferable to attain *mukta*, liberation from rebirth, rather than to experience for a limited period the joys of heaven, where one is exposed to the risk of expulsion due to an offence committed by a distant descendant.

There are other examples for the collective responsibility of a kin-group in relation not only to society, but to a supernatural order. The Chetris believe that the lineage of those failing to observe death-pollution for agnatic kinsmen of certain degrees of consanguinity will become extinct or completely impoverished. Supernatural sanctions thus reinforce the pressure of public opinion.

The supernatural sanctions upholding Chetri morality, however, must not be equated with those enforcing ethical conduct in theistic systems. They are comparable rather to the automatic and impersonal ill effects believed to follow the breaking of a taboo in certain primitive societies. For the gods of the Hindu pantheon as well as the clan- and family-deities are imagined as capable of rendering man assistance and protection, but they are not specifically considered as upholders or originators of the moral code. Sins are not thought of as offences against the will of any particular deity, but as offences against the inner order of the world and human society. The worship of gods, no doubt, increases a person's merit and in the final reckoning this may be set against any sins committed, but the motivation is to balance bad by good actions rather than to obtain forgiveness of sins.

The Chetris share the general Hindu idea of the relativity of ethical conduct. Actions permissible for members of one caste are wrong for those of another, and there is consequently not one generally applicable moral code, but there are many variations adjusted to the conditions of the individual castes.

Righteousness in the eyes of the Hindu is not compliance with a moral code universal to humanity or even the whole of Hindu society, but it is above all the observance of caste rules. What is thought morally right for the man or woman of low caste may be deemed wrong for Chetris or Brahmans. As far as occupational codes, marriage laws, kinship behaviour, rules of interdining and diet, and manners of worship are concerned, each caste is a law to itself. The man of high caste moreover is indifferent to the behaviour of those of inferior status as long as they do not encroach on his privileges, but he grows indignant if a member of his own group should be found to debase himself by adopting low caste habits in such matters as diet and association. The person guilty of such an offence will first be warned and asked to seek purification, but if unwilling to conform to caste-custom he will be excluded from commensality and social intercourse. A serious lapse from the standards can never be remedied, but places the perpetrator irretrievably among the people of low caste.

Great importance is accorded to all matters relating to the eating of ritually relevant food, of which boiled rice is the most essential. To share in a meal including boiled rice signifies that the diners consider themselves of equal status, and the high caste man who eats such a meal in the company of a person of lower status loses thereby temporarily his own high status, and must undergo a purification rite before he can be readmitted to commensality with members of his own caste-group. Anyone who inadvertently eats food cooked or served by such a person before the required purification rite has been performed, becomes subject to the same pollution and also needs to be purified. An offence against the rules of commensality is therefore in some respects more serious than a ritually neutral crime such as theft, because the man who allows himself to be polluted by contact with a low caste person becomes a danger to those with whom he consorts. While the thief robs his victim of a material possession, the polluted man who hides his offence may rob his kinsmen and friends of their purity and caste status, and put them to the trouble of undergoing expensive purification rites.

In the evaluation of sex relations high caste Hindu morality takes an ambivalent stand. Sexual congress with an untouchable pollutes the high caste partner, and places him or her into the category of untouchables. According to the strict legalistic view a man guilty of this offence cannot be purified, but I have heard it said that in cases when the offender acted in genuine ignorance of his partner's caste status, purification was possible. A woman, however, who has had sexual relations with a man of low caste—whether aware of his status or not—can never regain her status. Chetri society is inexorable in disowning her, and treating her as permanently contaminated. Both she and her lover can be hauled before a criminal court, in which case they are sentenced to a term of imprisonment—usually 3 years for the woman and 12 years for the man—but this is rarely done, for high caste families prefer to hush up such a case and allow the couple to escape and leave the locality rather than give rise to a scandal and the suspicion that they were themselves polluted by contact with the offender before her crime was discovered.

The attitude to inter-caste unions is relative. What is an offence and a cause for excommunication in the case of a woman is permitted to a man. Conversely a lower caste woman can to some extent be assimilated into a high caste household, while there is no possibility of accepting as son-in-law a man of substantially inferior caste status.

The distinction between two types of inter-caste unions is only one aspect of the specifically Hindu concept of the relativity of values and the acceptance of different moral codes for different persons or different segments of society. This acceptance makes possible the co-existence of an attitude of extreme intolerance regarding any deviant behaviour on the part of the members of one's own in-group and great tolerance in regard to the conduct of members of other castes. Isolated by the social distance which exists *ab initio* between different castes, the Hindu views the behaviour of those below and above him with indifference. He takes it for granted that they observe customs different from his own, and such divergence seems to him neither shocking nor even undesirable, but inherent in the divine world order, which provides for the division of humanity into groups of different status and value.

A universal ethical code applicable to all human beings is clearly incompatible with such a supposition, for individual actions are not considered good or bad *per se*, but are evaluated according to the status of the agent as well as of the other persons concerned. There is no one way of conduct which is valid for all men, but everyone has to behave according to the rules of his caste, and—as an old Sanskrit saying tells us—"it is better to do the work of one's own caste inadequately, than to perform the work of another caste well."

The Hindu's indifference to the doings of men of other castes is not to be mistaken for a spirit of tolerance springing from sympathy and understanding. Love and compassion for one's fellow men, a quality we find developed to a high degree among the Buddhist people of Nepal, is not one of the characteristic features of Hindu social philosophy. No doubt, there may be high caste Hindus of gentle and generous nature, but their ethical code does not prescribe an attitude of personal interest and sympathy for persons standing outside the narrow circle of kinsmen and caste-fellows.

The Chetri thus feels no obligations towards members of castes other than his own, except of course, towards his Brahman family priest, and such Brahmans as he may employ for the performance of domestic rites or for worship at the shrines or temples visited in the course of pilgrimages.

In an analysis of the motivation of ethical conduct among Chetris, we must distinguish between actions prescribed or prohibited by specific caste rules and subject to strong social sanctions, and actions counselled or discounselled by a more general moral code but not enforced by the authorities of caste or state. Among the former are all those actions which relate to the maintenance or loss of ritual purity, while the latter, which alone have some general validity for members of all castes, relate to the accumulation or decrease of religious merit. Every action which renders a person subject to pollution and the loss of caste status belongs to the first category. Its prohibition is mandatory and the sanction by which it is enforced is excommunication. Actions such as lying and cheating, which offend against a moral code applying not to one particular caste but to society in general, are believed to diminish the offender's store of merit, but do not bring about immediate retribution in the shape of excommunication or other punitive measures taken by the offender's fellow caste men.

Under certain circumstances the two categories of offences can be purposely made to coincide: a Brahman, for instance, who has committed a capital offence, but on account of his priestly status cannot be executed, will be forcibly polluted in order to remove him for all time from caste-society. His head will be shaven, he will be forced to eat pork—a meat prohibited to high caste Hindus—his sacred thread will be broken, and untouchables will be made to lead him through the streets and to announce at every cross-roads the nature of his crime. Such a person can never regain his caste-status; not because he has committed a crime, but because in punishment of this crime he has been irremediably polluted. The automatic social sanctions of a caste offence such as eating pork and being touched by untouchables, are here employed to punish offences such as murder or political treason, which by themselves do not automatically result in excommunication.

We may now pause to compare the moral concepts of the Hindu Chetris with those of the Dafla tribesmen. Common to both societies is the view that actions which disrupt social harmony and bring about an unfavourable reaction on the part of other members of the society are 'wrong' and must be avoided. This attitude to morality is known as prudential, and is prevalent in many less advanced societies. Both Chetri and Dafla morality contains moreover some elements of conventionalism, in the sense that most moral prescriptions are justified by reference to the customs and traditions of the tribal society or the caste and not by reference to any supernatural legislator or moral order of universal validity. Either system of morality is concerned mainly with the relations between the members of the in-group, while the attitude towards members of other groups is indifference in the case of the Chetris, and indifference alternating with hostility in that of the Daflas.

The differences between the two systems, however, are greater than the similarities. The most important difference is the Hindu concept of pollution as the automatic ill-effect of a wide range of actions contrary to caste-rules. The Daflas have no comparable concept. While among the Chetris a person's action may cause him to be polluted long before his offence has come to the notice of the community, the adverse effects of wrong-doing in Dafla society flow exclusively from the reaction of society and the undetected breach of custom remains without any retribution.

Excommunication as punishment or as a means of enforcing conformity has no place among the sanctions wielded by Dafla society. In the form used by Chetris it is peculiar to Hindu society, which equates the status of being outcasted with the status of pollution.

Absent from Dafla ideology is the concept of religious merit as well as the concept of sin. The whole idea that moral conduct in this life determines an individual's fate in his next existence is foreign to the thinking of this tribe, and it is this idea which distinguishes the ideology of the Chetris from the 'this-worldly' utilitarianism of the tribal ideologies. With the belief in reincarnation, and the associated beliefs in the effects of merit and sin on the modes of reincarnation, Chetri ideas enter a sphere of thought in which the individual conscience and the sense of responsibility to a supernatural order begin to function independently from the social pressure of public opinion. I have said earlier, that compared to the rigid conformity enforced by caste-rules and the fear of social sanctions prevailing in Hindu society the quest for individual merit, plays a comparatively small part in determining behaviour, but it is the beginning of a motivation of moral conduct entirely different from that operating in Dafla society, and we shall see presently how this motivation assumes a dominant role in the ideology of the Buddhist Sherpas.

Sherpas

The third of the Himalayan societies I have chosen for this comparative analysis of ideological systems are the Sherpas of the highlands of Eastern Nepal. The caste Hindus of the Nepal Valley look upon the Sherpas and other populations of Tibetan stock as crude mountain folk of very low social status, but this self-satisfied assessment is largely due to their ignorance of the Sherpas' cultural attainments. These become apparent to any one who enters their villages and houses, or visits Sherpa monasteries replete with works of art unequalled by any achievement in the aesthetic field that such high Hindu castes as Chetris and Thakuris can boast of. Sherpa culture is basically an offshoot of Tibetan culture, and groups of Sherpas are found scattered over a wide area of Eastern Nepal, but their main concentration is in the regions of Khumbu, Pharak and Solu, where Sherpas form a compact population firmly rooted in their traditional culture.

The Sherpas' religious beliefs and practices are those of Tibetan Buddhism, and although there are great differences in sophistication between the more learned monks and lamas on the one side and the ordinary villagers on the other, the basic religious and ideological concepts are common to all members of Sherpa society. Both laity and clerics think of the desired end-state, towards the attainment of which all moral actions are directed, in the terms of Buddhist philosophy, and the difference between the two classes lies more in the means employed to attain it than in their concept of the nature of the ultimate human goal.

An analysis of Sherpa moral concepts begins most conveniently with the examination of the idea of *sonam*, 'religious merit', which corresponds roughly to the concept of merit prevalent among such Hindu populations as the Chetris. Sherpas believe that every act of virtue (*gewa*) adds to an individual's store of *sonam*, whereas every morally negative action or sin (*digba*) decreases this store. Addition and subtraction of *sonam* is thought of in more or less mechanical terms. Throughout a man's or woman's life, good and bad deeds make their marks on the person's record-sheet, and this process is imagined as the action of two anthropomorphic beings, believed to be born with every individual and sitting invisibly on his right and left shoulder. The former, known as *lhen-cig-kye-wai-lha*, is the person's good genius who marks every deed of virtue with a white mark, while the latter, known as *lhen-cig-kye-wai-dre*, is his evil genius, who strives to lead a man along a downward path and marks every sin with a black sign.

At a man's death the account is made and the balance of white or black marks determines his fate in the next world. It is therefore everybody's endeavour to accumulate as much *sonam* as possible, and to avoid as much as possible actions likely to diminish the stored up merit. Moral prescriptions may thus be seen as a guide to the acquisition of *sonam*, and the acts they enjoin are teleological in character. But while they are as purpose-directed as the prescriptions of conduct in the ideologies of many less sophisticated tribal societies, the desired end-state of Sherpa ideology is not this-worldly but clearly transcendental. There is no promise of well-being and prosperity in this life as the result of *sonam*-gaining actions, but the promise of bliss or release in the world beyond.

Closely linked with the idea of rewards and retributions in the world beyond is the concept of reincarnation. This concept, basic to much of Hindu religious thought, is not peculiar to the Sherpas or even to Tibetans in general, but unlike Hindus the Buddhist Sherpas and Tibetans give social recognition to the belief in the reincarnation of individual persons and reincarnate lamas play a vital rôle in the religious system. Persons who have gained so much *sonam* that they would be entitled to the final release, or in Sherpa words to the entry into *Devachen*, a kind of superparadise beyond the world of the six spheres, may return as reincarnate lamas to the position they held in their former life, and as they are supposed to retain all the knowledge gained in previous lives, they are attributed with a degree of sanctity far exceeding that of even the most devout person in his first life.

Morally positive acts, which add to a person's *sonam* include conduct ranging from the building of religious monuments and in small acts of kindness to animals. Unlike monotheistic religions, such as Christianity, the Sherpas' Buddhist ideology does not provide a motive for moral acts comparable to such ideas as the "love of God" or "obedience to the commands of God." Though the one supreme motive for leading a good life is in Sherpa eyes the wish to acquire *sonam*, this motive is not directly linked with a belief in a personal deity to whom man is responsible for his behaviour. Similarly 'sin' is in the Sherpa's mind not an act which offends any particular deity, but an offence against a moral order existing independently of any of the gods the Sherpas worship.

The nature of behaviour believed to produce *sonam* can be understood, however, from a list of acts described as meritorious by my Sherpa informants. Sherpas are usually not very systematic in enumerating such acts, but here I have grouped them into three main categories: religious and ritual acts, acts in relation to persons, and acts in relation to animals.

All prayer and the recitation of sacred scriptures fall into the first category. It is meritorious to read and recite any of the sacred books, as well as to pay others to recite them. Thus the 108 volumes of the Kangyur kept in a village-temple are annually recited by lamas paid from a fund which the villagers raise by public subscription. All those subscribing derive merit from this reading of the scriptures, and there are many occasions when individuals or groups may commission recitations of that type. Different from the mere reciting of scriptures, is the performance of rites which, in addition to the recitation of the appropriate liturgical texts, involve the presentation of food offerings and butter lamps, and the playing of musical instruments. Such rites too may be commissioned by individuals, who either derive *sonam* personally from the performance, or can direct the *sonam* produced to the assistance of a deceased relative.

Turning of prayer wheels, circumambulation of temples and religious monuments, and above all the construction of such monuments, are all productive of *sonam*. The Sherpa country is full of *mani*-walls, bearing stone tablets with engravings of the sacred formula *om mani padme hum*, and of rock inscriptions containing this and other sacred formulae. The *sonam* produced by their construction or carving goes to the person who paid for the work, and not to the workmen or the artisans. Monks will sometimes carve rock inscriptions on speculation, and then "sell" them to whoever wishes to acquire the *sonam* created by the carving.

The second category of meritorious acts includes all those involving interpersonal relations. All kinds of charity produce *sonam*. Gifts to lamas, whether they are in need of them or not, as well as alms to the poor result in the gain of *sonam* by the giver. It is particularly meritorious to feed those lacking food, and to clothe those inadequately dressed. Acts which indirectly benefit others, such as the building of bridges or rest-houses, fall also within this category. On the occasion of religious festivals wealthy people distribute food and drink in the expectation of gaining *sonam*.

It is considered meritorious to act as peace-maker. Many quarrels are settled by persons without official status, who far from deriving any profit from their activities in the interest of social harmony, incur considerable expense in providing the drink necessary to bring the parties together. What they gain is *sonam* and social approval. It is significant that Sherpas admire a skilful mediator and man of peace more than a "strong" man. Their ideal is not the heroic personality, but the wise, restrained and mild man.

This emphasis on the virtue of mildness is particularly apparent in the Sherpas' attitude to animals. Acts of kindness to animals are a source of *sonam*, and I was told specifically that a person about to hit a dog or a cat which has stolen meat or butter, may pause and let the animal get away with its ill-gotten gains for the sake of acquiring *sonam*.

These examples of *sonam*-producing actions reflect the type of conduct considered ideal for laymen. The members of monastic communities have additional means of acquiring *sonam*, not the least important of which is the voluntary renunciation of sex and family life.

The injunctions of a moral code are usually matched by corresponding interdictions, and one might well assume that the actions regarded by the Sherpas as 'sin' can also be divided into three major categories. It seems, however, that at least in the consciousness of the majority of Sherpas—and I have no material on the attitude of the more sophisticated and learned clerics—there is no concept of a 'sin' outside the sphere of interpersonal relations and the relations of man to other animate beings. In other words, the wide range of religious and ritual acts producing *sonam* is not matched by sins relating to purely religious and ritual realities and not involving other human beings. The Sherpa layman is not conscious of a possibility of committing 'sin' by offending any of the numerous divinities he worships and it would seem that even a neglect of their cult is interpreted as foregoing an opportunity of acquiring *sonam* rather than as a breach of the moral code. In the case of monks and nuns the position is different in so far as a violation of their vows of chastity is clearly described as sin. For them sexual congress is sinful quite irrespective of the status of the other partner, and their action is hence not judged on the basis of rules regulating inter-personal relations. The monk who consorts with an unmarried woman sins only because he breaks his vow of celibacy, and his partner sins because she causes him to sin. Were he not bound by his vow, sexual relations between the two persons concerned would be considered morally neutral.

The problem arises therefore whether the behaviour of the un-chaste monk is wrong, simply because it violates an undertaking freely contracted, or whether it is sin because it offends any higher power. The question posed in this form can probably not be answered, because Sherpas view morality not in relation to any personal legislator and upholder of a moral code, but against the background of an impersonal moral order. And according to this order the breach of a vow is 'sin' irrespective of whether any harm is done to another person.

The vast majority of 'sins', however, relate to interpersonal behaviour, and result in particular from any infringement of the rights or dignity of another person. The way in which Sherpas view such infringements is demonstrated by the following list of sins enumerated spontaneously by one of my lay informants:

1. All quarrelling is sin.
2. To steal is sin.
3. To cheat in trade is sin.
4. To talk ill of someone behind his back is sin, particularly if what one tells about him is not true.
5. To kill any living creature is sin. If someone kills a cat he commits so great a sin, that he cannot make up for it even by burning as many butter lamps as the cat had hair on its body. To kill yak and sheep is sin even for the butchers, but not for those who buy the meat.
6. To have sexual relations with another person's spouse is sin.
7. To have sexual relations with a nun is sin, because the man involved contributes to the sin committed by the nun.
8. To threaten children or make them cry is sin whatever the reason.

9. To marry a girl who is unwilling is sin both for the husband and for her parents who arranged for the marriage.
10. To hit any animals is sin.
11. To fell trees is sin, though on occasion it is inevitable; even to pluck flowers is sin, and it is sinful to set fire to the forest.
12. For a monk it is sin to drink too much and get intoxicated.
13. To cause a spirit long associated with a locality to be driven out is sin for the person who commissions the exorcising, but not for the lama who executes it.

This list, though by no means systematic, is illuminating in so far as it reflects the ideas which arise in a Sherpa's mind when he thinks about sin. A more complete list, compiled from the statements of all my informants, would cover several pages, but without substantially adding to our understanding of what Sherpas consider wrong and morally reprehensible. There are many actions, which though socially undesirable, do not fall within the category of sin. Moral and social evaluations do not by any means coincide. Thus it is sin to have sexual relations with a nun, but for the man concerned this offence has no adverse social consequences. On the other hand, it is *not* sin for an unmarried man to sleep with an unmarried girl of inferior—mildly untouchable—status, but persistence in the relationsip deprives a man of his own superior status, and he sinks to that of the girl concerned. While it is sin to marry an unwilling girl and even graver sin to impose on such a woman sexual relations, no adverse social consequences result from such an arranged marriage, except of course the likelihood of its early break up.

The consideration shown for a girl's wishes reflects the exceptionally high regard for the dignity and independence of the individual personality. Any action encroaching forcibly on this independence is considered sin. Respect for the independence of the individual is expressed also in the attitude to those known to have committed sins. Their actions are held to be their own affair, and no public notice is taken of what is recognized as a violation of the moral code. In the village of Khumjung there were an ex-monk and an ex-nun, who lived as man and wife. Though my informants were unanimous in describing the violation of their vows of celibacy as sinful, they said that this was a matter of no concern to the villagers. The offending couple might suffer in the next world, but there was no reason why the neighbours should object. Indeed there were no signs of any cold shouldering of such or similar couples by other members of the village community.

This attitude brings out the difference between 'sins', which result in a diminishment of the offender's store of *sonam* and may expose him to retribution in the next world, and civic offences, which may not reduce a person's *sonam*, but affect the interests of the community and are therefore punished by the elected village-officials. Such morally neutral but socially reprehensible acts are violations of the rules regulating the use of grazing grounds or of publicly owned forest reserves. The Sherpas' attitude in these matters is perhaps comparable to a European's view of parking offences or the evasion of customs duty, which only those with the most tender conscience will regard as sins.

The whole sphere of sexual behaviour, which in Hindu morality is rigidly controlled by numerous interdictions, is according to Sherpa ideology only partly subject to ethical ordinances. Basic to the Sherpas' attitude to sex is the view that sexual relations between those bound neither by marriage ties nor monastic vows are morally neutral. Sexual intercourse of such persons is neither considered 'sin' nor is it socially disapproved of. Even a girl already formally betrothed may sleep with unmarried men other than her fiançé, and such behaviour arouses no unfavourable comment. The pregnancy of an unmarried woman may be an economic embarrassment, but does not subject her to either social or supernatural sanctions.

Neither a sense of 'sin' nor a sense of 'shame' attaches to premarital sexual relations, and even extra-marital relations do not provoke severe condemnation on the part of society. No doubt adultery is considered 'sin', but it is a sin far less serious than say the killing of a cat, and its detection does not expose those concerned to strong social disapproval. Even the deceived spouse can be placated by a small payment or perhaps only the presentation of a bottle of beer or liquor offered together with the offender's apology.

There is no feeling that adultery offends any supernatural being or exposes the perpetrators or even the whole community to any specific danger. The idea widespread among Indian populations that certain breaches of the moral code draw disaster upon the heads of the offenders as well as upon the community to which they belong finds no echo among the Sherpas.

In sharp contrast to the tolerant attitude toward lapses in marital fidelity, is the uncompromising condemnation of clan-incest. Sexual congress between members of the same clan, irrespective of their marital status, is considered a crime and my Sherpa informants were unanimous in the affirmation that a couple guilty of such incest would not be tolerated in the village. None of them remembered a concrete case, but they thought that in the event of a case occurring the offenders would be bound and delivered to the Government court for trial. In the absence of concrete instances, I omitted to inquire whether incest is considered a sin as well as an offence against society, but none of my informants mentioned it when enumerating the various types of sinful behaviour.

Indeed there are some indications that transgressions of the moral code which incur retributions in the world beyond are not considered subject to social sanctions, whereas morally neutral but socially undesirable behaviour may have to be checked by secular punishments. Just as Evans-Pritchard found among the Nuer tribes that sins do not arouse indignation (1956, p. 189), the Sherpas are not indignant about adultery or the killing of animals, punished no doubt in the next world, but reserve their indignation for such acts as the flaunting of an order of the village-assembly or a breach of the custom of clan-exogamy.

We may then conclude that certain actions, such as incest, are prohibited, because they arouse social disapproval, while others are interdicted and considered 'sin' because they result in a loss of *sonam* and possibly punishment in the world beyond. The idea, that an infringement of the moral code or tribal custom may entail immediate retribution in the form of sickness or other disaster is not a part of Sherpa belief.

Sickness and other misfortune is often attributed to ghosts, house-deities and evil spirits, who have been offended by the actions of the persons concerned. But the actions which cause offence are usually trivial and lacking in ethical aspects. In order to avert the spirits' unwanted attention and cure the sickness, it is necessary to placate them with offerings, but the question of avoiding morally negative acts is usually not involved.

The idea of contagious pollution, which occupies a position of cardinal importance in Hindu social ideology, is virtually absent among Sherpas. There is no suggestion that a grave sin or social offence could debase the ritual and social status of the perpetrator to such an extent that contact with him or her would spread the corruption to persons unconnected and innocent of the original offence.

The Sherpas, who believe that every human action will find its own reward in the world beyond, do not think of immoral behaviour in terms of change or loss of status. The locus of all sanctions imposed on those who sin lies outside the human sphere, and a man's kinsmen and co-villagers do not arrogate to themselves the right to forestall this transcendental judgement.

Another vital feature of Sherpa ideology is the equation of knowledge and virtue. The greater a lama's learning, the greater is his claim to sanctity, for Sherpas believe that an intellectual grasp of the true doctrine will normally result in virtuous behaviour. They emphasise, however, that in relation to the eternal order a pure heart is more important than all knowledge of scriptures and the lavish performance of rites and ceremonies. The most elaborate and costly rites do not serve any purpose if performed for the benefit of those lacking purity of heart, the most essential of all qualifications for the gain of *sonam*. This purity of heart manifests itself in charity and kindliness towards all living beings, and it is the charitable, mild and tolerant person whom Sherpas admire. Even wealth is conducive of social prestige mainly when it is given away in charity or spent on religious works. Not the possession, but the generous disposal of riches is an object of admiration and social approval.

There is a certain analogy between the approved disposal of wealth and the ideal use of an accumulation of *sonam*. While a rich man is expected to distribute on such occasions as a funeral feast for a deceased parent or wife large portions of his wealth to lamas and the general population, a saintly lama possessing a store of *sonam* which would enable him to attain the paradise of Devachen may forego the immediate attainment of bliss, and place his *sonam*, wisdom and own personality at the disposal of humanity by consenting to be reincarnated. The free and joyous employment of resources, material in the one and spiritual in the other case, for the benefit of others, characterises the ideal attitude to fellow human beings, and it is this model attitude which accounts for so many aspects of Sherpa social behaviour.

A comparison of the moral concepts of the Sherpas with those of the Chetris leads us to the conclusion that Sherpa ideas are not a necessary concomitant of the doctrine of *karma*. While the concept of *sonam* is similar to what the Chetris and other Hindus of Nepal understand under religious merit, the way in which these similar concepts influence social conduct is different in each of the two societies.

Both Sherpas and Chetris believe that the balance between a man's virtuous and sinful acts determines his fate in the next life, and that by the performance of virtuous deeds he can build up a store of merit. The difference in the ideologies of the two peoples lies, however, in the definition of what is meritorious conduct. Whereas the Chetris judge a person's virtue mainly by the strictness with which he complies with the rules regulating the conduct appropriate to his caste-status, and see him primarily in the role of a member of a tightly structured community, Sherpas see the individual as an independent agent, responsible for his virtuous and sinful acts to an impersonal, supernatural order, but not answerable for these acts to the members of his community, unless of course another person's material interests are affected.

The area of agreement between Sherpa and Chetris morality relates mainly to the belief in the meritorious character of prayer, ritual performances, the giving of alms to the poor and of donations to priests—lamas in the former case and Brahmans in the latter. Both Sherpas and Hindus believe in the effectiveness of pilgrimages to secure a happier fate in the life beyond.

Basic differences appear, however, in the attitude to interpersonal relations. Foremost in the Sherpas' mind is the injunction to treat all other human beings, irrespective of their race and caste, with kindness and with consideration for their personal dignity. Theirs is a moral code of universal validity. It does not evaluate actions according to the status of the agent or of the person which they affect, but recognises standards applicable, at least in theory, to the whole of humanity. Assuming a general brotherhood of man, Sherpa morality also encourages hospitality, conviviality and a general atmosphere of warmth in social relations. These qualities determine relations within the Sherpa community no less than those with members of other ethnic groups. While the social life of Hindu castes is strictly exclusive, Sherpas readily admit strangers to their houses and take a pride in entertaining them hospitably. Even inter-marriage with outsiders is not frowned upon and there are several cases of men of other castes settling in Sherpa villages and becoming assimilated to the Sherpa way of life. An ideology which does not discriminate between different sections of humanity and presupposes the universal validity of the Buddhist doctrine permits such an acceptance of strangers, which to the high caste Hindu would be unimaginable.

Another basic distinction between Chetri and Sherpa ethics is the attitude to what we might call the striving for spiritual perfection. Among the Chetris, prayer, attendance of religious rites, and the giving of alms to the poor or to Brahmans are approved of as means of acquiring merit. But their pursuit rarely occupies a central position in a person's activities, and their claim on time and resources competes with the claims of family and kin-group. Only some very old people devote the greater part of their time to religious practices. No doubt, any Hindu can become a *sanyasi*, leave the society of his caste-fellows, and follow a solitary path of renunciation. But such a course is rare and hardly meets with social approval. It is almost considered as a kind of escapism and the *sanyasi* may reach personal perfection, but does not work for the spiritual benefit of his society.

The Sherpa, by contrast, has the choice of two socially approved ways of achieving spiritual perfection and increasing his store of merit. He can remain within the society and acquire merit by religious practices, the study of scriptures, charity and kindness to all animate beings, or he can renounce all worldly ambitions, join a monastic community, and devote himself as a celibate monk exclusively to the pursuit of the religious life. But even in doing so, he does not cut himself off from either his family or the Sherpa community as a whole, but on the contrary gains an honoured position and is believed to work by his religious practices and the attainment of wisdom and saintliness for the well being of the community at large.

The choice of the monastic life is therefore in no way a kind of escapism. The young monk does not escape the obligations of society in the same way as the Hindu *sanyasi*, but on the contrary accepts greater obligations not only in his own interest but also to serve the interests of his society and indeed the whole of humanity. Great emphasis is laid on the merits of learning, which is virtually equated with sanctity, the assumption being that a proper knowledge of the true doctrine must inevitably lead to virtuous conduct and saintliness. It is partly for this reason that the Sherpa has so high an esteem for the life of study led by lamas and particularly by the inmates of monasteries.

From the serene life of study and meditation in a Sherpa monastery it is a far cry to the turbulent and insecure existence of warring Dafla tribesmen only a few hundred miles distant. The ideologies underlying the two ways of life are also miles apart. In the centre of Dafla efforts and ambitions stands the individual's self-interest in its most materialistic, 'this-worldly' sense. Moral precepts do little more than indicate a course of action which should steer the individual past harmful clashes with the self-interest of other individuals. The very fact of perpetual feuding, raids and war is symptomatic of the inadequacy of their motivation. Neither expectation of reward nor fear of punishment in an after-life act as restraint on the self-seeking drives of individuals, and generosity and kindliness towards weaker members of the society—though in practice sometimes forthcoming—are not prescribed or even councelled in any generally valid moral code.

Among the high Hindu castes of Nepal the interest of the caste-group and within it a small group of related families replaces the interest of the individual as the dominant motivation determining social morality. The interests and inclinations of the individual are unhesitatingly sacrificed when the interests and above all the ritual status of the caste-group appear to be at stake. Conformity with caste-custom is considered good in itself and is the supreme aim towards which all moral prescriptions are directed. There is recognition of a supernatural order, and compliance with its tenets is considered a duty. But social and legal sanctions enforce compliance so severely, that there remains little scope for the promptings of the individual's conscience. Fear of the punishments which society might inflict on the offender against its rules is more powerful an incentive to conformity than any thought of personal responsibility *vis-à-vis* a supernatural order.

Yet, there is in Hindu ideology as found among Chetris and other castes of Nepal, an awareness of the lasting merit man can gain for himself if he ignores self-interest and the inducements of immediate gratification and acts in accordance with the demands of piety and transcendental values. But this awareness, which is inseparable from the doctrine of *karma*, is largely overlaid by the continuous anxiety to satisfy the demands of caste and kin-group, and to avoid actions which might be detrimental to one's status within the society.

In the ideology of the Buddhist Sherpas, on the other hand, the awareness of the inestimable value of virtue and wisdom, and of the necessity to strive for spiritual perfection, stands first and foremost. The interests of society are secondary to the interests of the individual in relation to the supernatural order. But whereas the Dafla believes in serving his self-interest by ruthless self-assertion, the Sherpa knows that in the long run self-interest is served best by the practice of charity and self-sacrifice inspired by love and compassion for all animate beings. And even though the harmony and equilibrium of society as a whole is not as conscious an aim of human conduct as in a Hindu caste society, the spirit of kindliness, tolerance and compassion encouraged in the individual confers immeasurable benefits on social relations, which are far more relaxed and harmonious than among Hindu castes, where conduct is regulated by rigid rules. Even greater, however, is the benefit this spirit confers on the individual, who appears invested with a human dignity such as has developed neither in the amorphous tribal society of the Daflas nor in the tightly structured society of Hindu castes.

NOTES

[1] The fieldwork on which the major part of this paper is based was greatly facilitated by a grant from the Wenner-Gren Foundation for Anthropological Research.

[2] For a description of the caste-society of Nepal see von Fürer-Haimendorf (1960): 12-32.

REFERENCES

BARTON, R. F., 1919, *Ifugao Law. University of California Publications in American Archaeology and Ethnology*, Vol. XV.

EVANS-PRITCHARD, E. E., 1956, *Nuer Religion*. Oxford.

VON FURER-HAIMENDORF, C., 1960, 'Caste in the multi-ethnic society of Nepal' in *Contributions to Indian Sociology*, No. IV.

16

ROLE VARIATION IN CASTE RELATIONS

David G. Mandelbaum

In his study of the village called Mohana, Professor Majumdar gave us a valuable record of the relationship among the several caste groups. He described the roles taken by members of each group in the organisation of village life. In several places he mentions certain regular variations in these roles (Majumdar, 1958a, pp. 78, 304-305); in this paper we consider some of these regular variations as they may be seen in the perspective of caste organisation in India generally. The term here used for an endogamous group in a local caste hierarchy is *jati*; this usage may avoid some of the difficulties which attend the terms caste and subcaste. The present paper is part of a larger work which is currently under preparation.

In the network of relations among people of different *jatis*, each person's social position is broadly defined by the status of his *jati*. His *jati*-status identifies and classifies him; it marks out a range of potential and of proscribed inter-relations with others. Within that broadly defined range, there are more specific prescriptions for conduct. Each person is classified by sex and age as well as by *jati*. The relations of a woman—of any *jati*—tend to be more restricted than are those appropriate for a man. The behaviour of young children is usually more permissively regarded than is that of adults.

Appropriate role-behaviour varies also according to the context of action. A role is the set of expectations applied to a person of a particular social position, and role-behaviour is the action which flows from these expectations. (cf. Gross et al. 1958, p. 67). These expectations differ according to various situations. For example, in the context of work in the fields, men may permit themselves freer relations and contacts than they do in the household or on ritual occasions. During certain ceremonies there is a relaxation of some taboos, while at other ceremonies there is an intensification of ritual precaution. In the context of visits to town there is often more latitude in social relations than would be countenanced in the home village.

In each of these contexts a man shifts his own role-behaviour and his role-expectations of others; he rephrases (if only slightly) his conduct *vis-a-vis* those of other *jatis*. This is also done in situations which do not recur with as much regularity as do the occasions of work, of ceremonies, of visits to town. Guring emergencies and while on a pilgrimage a villager may shift his role-behaviour from that which would be proper, say, at a village feast.

Similar variations occur in relations within a *jati* and within a family as well as among *jatis*. The definition of role according to sex applies to all social units and situations. Not only are there different tasks for women than for men (cf. Dube 1955a, pp. 170-172), but also different expectations of ritual stringency.

Women generally are expected to be more stringent about keeping ritual distances than are men, and they tend to be particularly mindful of this in relations with villagers of different *jati*. Thus, to take an example from a village of West Bengal, Brahman women "observe ritual purity more particularly than men and the community behaves accordingly". Brahman men may eat food especially prepared for them as an act of merit in houses of higher non-Brahmans. Brahman women do not dine out this way and, in general live within a more restricted social radius than do Brahman men. (Sarma 1955, p. 172).

So it is also in Rampura, Mysore. ". . . while the men of equal castes may eat food cooked by each other, women do not do so. Thus the Peasant and Shepherd men eat food cooked by each other, but their women do not" (Srinivas 1955, p. 20). Stricter conduct for women applies also in the lowest *jatis*. Among the Balahis, weavers of western Madhya Pradesh, "it is the woman who is most conservative and observes the old caste rules and regulations to the letter" (Fuchs 1950, p. 171).

The same conclusions were reached from a questionnaire given in 1952-53 to 121 men and 152 women in 13 villages of Eastern U.P. The respondents were selected from eight groups, ranging from Brahman to Chamar and were asked about their attitudes towards relations with people of *jatis* other than their own in such matters as intermarriage, interdining, making friends. "A vast difference exists between the attitudes of men and women of every group. The women are much more conservative in every field than the men." (Guha and Kaul 1953, p. 31.) Village women are not only more fastidious about the niceties of *jati* standards but the transgression of *jati* rules by a woman usually brings a more severe reaction than does a similar violation done by a man.

This stringency figures in the marriage pattern called hypergamy. Formal hypergamy does not occur everywhere in India but where it is known, a groom may take his bride from a social group which is somewhat lower in social rating than is his own. A woman may not do so; she must marry a man of equal or of higher rating. A man, when he marries, can afford to descend a bit in the social scale without loss of rank; a woman cannot. This principle is widely observed in making marriage alliances. Where it is a formal part of marriage arrangements, it has important consequences for *jati* organisation. We take up this matter of *jati* structure here because it arises from the difference in status, within a *jati*, between men and women.

The principle is propounded in several scriptural sources. Marriage between a man of higher position and a woman of lower is called *anuloma* ("with the hair"), and is, within certain limits, approved. The reverse case, of a woman marrying beneath her position, is called *pratiloma*, against the grain ("against the hair") and is strongly disapproved. (Hutton 1946, pp. 48, 128-130; Majumdar 1958b, pp. 254-255; Ghurye 1950, p. 56; also see Bouglé 1908, pp. 122-126.)

The groups which may be linked through hypergamous marriages are of different kinds. In some *jatis*, families or lineages are so delineated. More commonly, hypergamy is used in marriage arrangements among social units within a *jati*, such as clans, or village-circles, or regional sections.

The history of some of the princely dynasties, especially among Rajputs, shows a pattern of hypergamous alliances for ruling families (Karve 1953, p. 142). The usual kind of Rajput hypergamy is among clans, which are classified and ranked in a complex fashion. There are four major sets of clans, named after the Sun, Moon, Fire, and Serpents; the sets are generally ranked in that order (with some question about the relative ranking of Serpents and Fire sets) for purposes of hypergamy.

A Rajput clan often is associated with a geographic region and there is a concomitant rating by region. People of Rajput identity are found in a belt from Rajputana to Bihar and ". . . the status of Rajput clans, whatever origin (the Sun, Moon, or Fire) they may claim, becomes lower and lower the more easterly their region. . .

the clans in Rajputana thus stand above all Rajputs in the rest of India. The rough rule for marriage is given in the saying 'the girl from the East, the boy from the West.'" (Karve, 1953, p. 143.) While a Rajput man, and especially a ruler, can theoretically marry into a clan far lower than his, in practice hypergamous marriages are made mainly between clans which are not far apart in the clan ratings, as these are understood by the families contracting the alliance. (There may be much the same difference of opinion about the relative ranking of Rajput clans in a locality as there is about the relative rating of some of the jatis in the caste system of that locality.)

Hypergamous marriages are also common among the clans of the Marathas of Western India. These clans too, are arranged in ranked sets. The highest, most exclusive set includes the smallest number of clans; a clansman of this set may take a wife from any of the other sets down to the one which is lowest in position and which includes the greatest number of clans. Dr. Irawati Karve depicts this clan arrangement by five concentric circles (1953, p. 158). The innermost, smallest circle represents the set of "the five clans": a woman of one of these clans can be married only to a man of one of the other four clans of the same set. Next larger and next lower is the set of "the seven clans." Their women may be married to men from one of the five clans or from any of the seven clans except their own. Largest and most inclusive is the set of "ninety six clans." Their women may marry into any of the other sets. Their men can take brides only from their own set since there are no lower clans in the *jati* and they will not be given brides from a higher set.

Another kind of hypergamy inside a *jati* is by village-circles, as occurs among the Pātidārs of Charottār (Kaira District) in Central Gujerat, who are the dominant land-owning cultivators there. "These circles are arranged in a hierarchy such that Six Villages at the top of Charottār Pātidārs will take brides from any other village if the father is able to pay a substantial dowry but they refuse to give their daughters outside the Six Villages." (Pocock 1957, p. 21.) This hierarchy is not as clearly demarcated as that depicted for Maratha clans because another Pātidār village-circle, Twenty-Six Villages, also prohibits the marriage of any of their daughters outside their circle. Yet a father of this circle who marries his daughter to a Patidar from one of the Six Villages incurs only a light fine and gains some prestige. The fine presumably assuages their claim to topmost rank. The prestige accrues from the fact that they view an alliance with Six Villages as no real come-down.

Pātidār husband and wife must come from different villages. Many North Indian *jatis* observe village exogamy, and in some places all the *jatis* of a village follow the same pattern of ranking other villages.

This occurs in Kishan Garhi (Aligarh District, U.P.). If a Kishan Garhi man—of any *jati*—has taken a wife from village X, then that village is deemed an inferior one for marriage alliances by all of Kishan Garhi. No father in Kishan Garhi will give his daughter in marriage to a man of village X. In this area, the northern villages are generally regarded as the superior and brides at marriage usually go north to the groom's village.[1] Martial relationships are formally one-sided and unbalanced: the boy's side is the high and demanding side, while the girl's side is the low and giving side." (Marriott 1955, p. 176.) Hypergamy is here built into every marriage arrangement. By definition, the village from which the bride comes is inferior, for purposes of marriage arrangements, to the villages into which she is married. Hypergamy is compulsory in marriage alliance.

A common form of hypergamy is that among ranked sections within a *jati*. These sections are not localised in particular village-circles nor are they only sets of clans; they are descent groups which are rated according to a combination of attributes. Thus the Rarhi Brahmans of Bengal are divided into four ranked sections, of which the Kulin is the highest. (The term "Kulin" is used widely for the highest unit in any ranking having to do with hypergamy.) A woman of the Kulin section may marry only a Kulin man, while Kulin man may marry into one of the lower sections. (Bhattacharya 1896, p. 38; Risley 1915, pp. 163-171; Hutton 1946, p. 47; Majumdar 1958a, p. 337.)

Hypergamous arrangements among the sections of certain Brahman *jatis* are very complex. A table listing forty-six sections of the Kanyakubja Brahmans of eastern Uttar Pradesh is presented by Sharma as an illustrative and not a complete list. Each of these forty-six sections is characterised by a unique combination of attributes, such as *Upadhi* (surname), *gotra* (clan), grade (one of four categories), *Assami* (a famous person in the genealogical line), residence (traditional locality), and *biswas* (an evaluative number). (Sharma 1956, pp. 24-25).

A most interesting form of hypergamy was followed by the Nayars, people of Malabar whose descent and family arrangements were strongly matrilineal. The marital arrangements among the Nayars of the kingdom of Calicut, up to the end of the nineteenth century, have been described by Kathleen Gough. A girl went through a marriage-like ceremony before her puberty. After the newly-wed couple spent three days of seclusion they were promptly divorced. Thenceforth the girl continued to live in her mother's household and she would typically have several consorts, either concurrently or *seriatim*. But she could have sexual relations only with a man of equal or higher rank than herself.

When she became pregnant, one or more men of such rank had to give gifts to the midwife who would attend her at childbirth, thus acknowledging possible paternity of the child. The child was then a true Nayar, belonging to his mother's matrilineal lineage and *jati*. If no man of proper status did so, it could be assumed that she had relations with a man of lower rank. The Nayar woman might then be outcaste and even sold into slavery. (Gough ms. n.d., pp. 12-14.)

Nayars were classed into four main ranked groupings, the royal and chiefly lineages, five different sections of Temple Servants, five of Commoner Nayars, and three of Temple Menials. Sexual alliances among the lower three groupings followed a regular hypergamous pattern, Nayar Commoner women could consort with Temple Servant men, Commoner men with Temple Menial women. But royal and chiefly men had relations only with Commoner women, not with women of either Temple grouping. Within the temples, the Temple Servants could go where other Nayars, even of royal lineage, were debarred. In other contexts, those of ruling rank preceded the Temple Servants.

No alliances were made between a couple from two different sections within the Temple Servant bracket because these two disputed for precedence. A union between a man of one and a woman of another Temple Servant section would be an admission that the man's section was higher. The same was true among the three Sections of Temple Menials. The five sections of Commoner Nayars were ranked in a serial, hypergamous order.

Capping the hypergamous ladder were the local Namboodari Brahmans whose men could have alliances with a Nayar woman of any status. At the other end of the local social scale, below the lowest Nayar *jatis*, were the "polluting" *jatis* of the locality; there was a sharp cleavage between them and all Nayars. No Nayar or Namboodari man could have any kind of intimacy with women below this line. (*ibid.*, pp. 3-10; also see Thurston 1909, vol. 5, pp. 300- 303; Aiyappan 1955, p. 124.)

Jati structure among the Nayars was unique in that the functions of *pater* and *genitor* were relatively peripheral to family organisation. Mrs. Karve tells how she once was taking blood samples in a household of Kshatriya (Chiefly) Nayars. After taking samples from all but one old man who was looking on, she told one of the sons of the family that she wanted to get a blood sample from the old man too. The answer was, "You may if you like, but he is not one of us. He is our Nambudri father." The old man had come into the wealthy Nayar household as a Namboodari younger son, and stayed on, spending much of his time in the household but never part of that family. (Karve 1953, p. 260.)

With the father of a family so relegated, Nayar family and *jati* organisation was different from any other in India. In some ways, the specialised Nayar Sections were like *jatis* elsewhere in India; they were named, hereditary, ranked groups, each of which had traditional occupational specialisation within a local system. But endogamy among Nayars included an unusually large number of specialised subgroups because of their liberal version of hypergamy.

Nayar hypergamy came to fulfil several purposes. For the patrilineal Namboodari Brahmans, as Gough points out, it made possible an ideal form of primogeniture in which only eldest sons were married to women of their own *jati* and perpetuated their families while younger sons helped perpetuate those of Nayars. Rivalries between the most powerful Brahman lineages and the Nayar rulers were eased by the alliances between Brahman younger sons and women of the chiefly families, unions which were seen as mutually advantageous to the partners and to their households. Nayar political organisation was strengthened by the alliances between Ruler men and Commoner women, also viewed as mutually beneficial. Such ties between Nayars of different ranks cemented the loyalties of the woman's kin to their kinswoman's consort and lessened any possibility of the alignment of one Nayar bloc against another. Nayars were thus differentiated into *jati*-like groups, but also gained an internal unity from their unusually broad hypergamy. (Gough n.d., pp. 25-30.)

The more usual practice of hypergamy, among subdivisions that more clearly belong to a single *jati*, also permits the differentiation of groups according to ritual practice, power, and rank, yet maintains a certain unity among the parts which are hypergamously differentiated.

Hypergamy may be initiated by families which are rising in social rank, in recent decades the rise is through education. By 1915 there was a *jati* of farmers and fishermen, called Pods, in the region of Calcutta, some of whom had acquired enough Western education to become professional men and government officials. These educated men, feeling themselves superior to the other Pods, refused to give their daughters in marriage to Pod families in which the *jati's* traditional calling was practised, although they would still take brides from them for their sons. In reporting this development, Risley predicted that the development of hypergamy within the *jati* would be followed by a complete severance and by the formation of a new *jati* of educated Pods. (Risley 1915, pp. 164-165.)

Occasionally an ambitious family may even succeed in marrying a daughter into another *jati* of higher rank. In such cases each *jati* remains an endogamous unit in the sense that the normal and usual marriage alliance is within the *jati*, but there is acceptance of some special instances of marriage across *jati* lines. (cf. Russell and Hira Lal 1916, vol. 1, p. 28.) There was hypergamy between *jatis* in Malabar to the extent that a Namboodari Brahman man would sometimes perform the ritual part of the groom in the prepuberty "marriage" rite of a Nayar girl of very high rank. But this marriage was dissolved after three days and subsequent relations between the couple did not publicly concern their respective households but only entailed whatever mutual affection and sexual relations which the two might choose to have.

The same marriage principle applies widely in village India; a woman is under greater stringency about the lower rank of her spouse than is a man. Formal hypergamy is found where there are ranked groupings within a *jati*; in such cases *jati* endogamy is not fully reciprocal but is qualified by considerations of the rank and sex of each marriage partner.

Hypergamy may be optional, as it is among Rajput and Maratha clan groupings, or it may be compulsory as it is in Kishan Garhi. The children of a hypergamous marriage, in these patrilineal instances, have the father's superior rank. Formal hypergamy entails consensus between the contracting families that one side is inferior to the other. Contradictory accounts of the patterning of hypergamy are often a result of differing views as to which groups are inferior. (cf. Dumont and Pocock 1957, p. 58, and Pocock 1954, p. 197.)

Whatever disagreements there may be about the relative ratings of groups within a *jati*, there is total agreement that a woman must marry a man of a social position equal or superior to her own while a man take a wife of somewhat inferior rank. Even in a *jati* which is not formally differentiated into ranked sections a similar procedure is followed in arranging a marriage. It is usually easier for a man of esteemed family to marry a girl of humbler (but perhaps newly-rich) family than it is for a family of high repute but needy circumstances to marry a daughter into a newly affluent family.

In any kind of hypergamous marriage, the bride and her kin gain by their alliance with the long-term ritual superiority which the groom and his kin provide. But a certain reciprocity is also involved. The groom and his family frequently stand to gain something in addition to the person of the bride, mainly from such relatively short-term advantages as her special beauty or her family's wealth. A common motive in an ambitious villager and the hallmark of his success, is to marry his daughter (or granddaughter) into a family suitably higher than her own. Thus, the variation in status between the men and the women of a *jati* have far-reaching consequences—for individual motivation as well as for *jati* organisation. There are other important and regular variations in social position within a *jati* which lead to varying kinds of role-behaviour.

Age is one such variable. Toddlers are usually considered to be much less affected by polluting influences than are older children or adults. Since they have as yet little in the way of social personality their social relations can scarcely be curtailed by pollution. Their activities are not much hedged about with ritual precautions. When they begin to wear clothes, children become more liable to ritual defilement. As for caste restrictions among the school age children of Mohana, D. N. Majumdar observed, "As far as eating and drinking go the restrictions are the same with them, otherwise there is free mixing of the children of all castes, for children are children, and they love to romp and play together, no matter to which caste they belong. In the school, children of all castes sit together on the same benches." (1958a, pp. 78-79.) In the Sanskritic tradition, a Brahman boy is not fully a Brahman until he undergoes the ceremony of investiture of the sacred thread. Before that he is not held responsible for role-behaviour appropriate to his *jati* station, and in scripture is considered to be of Sudra status. (Stevenson 1920, p. 27.)

Among some Brahmans, the full role-behaviour appropriate for a *jati* member is expected of a man only after he marries and has a child. Thus there are four Brahman *jatis* of Telangana whose young people interdine but their elders do not. "Younger people of Vaidiki and the Niyogi castes can eat with the Nambu and the Aradhya, but they will stop doing so as soon as they become adults and have children." (Dube 1955b, p. 184.)

In differing contexts of action, suitable role adjustments are permitted or required. When many people must work together quickly in order to harvest a crop, some of the usual avoidances may be slighted. In Sarola Kasar village (Ahmednagar District, Bombay State) for example, the very low ranking Mahars are hired as agricultural labourers and work side by side with workers of higher rank; ". . . in the course of their daily work they inevitably touch each other constantly and think nothing of it." When it is time for the midday meal, the Mahars eat apart from the others "but in the afternoon the gang of labourers fall in and recommence work together without any scruples as to untouchability. . . No doubt, there are a few orthodox labourers who try to shun the Mahar labourers, but nobody takes any notice and it has no perceptible effect." (Jagalpure and Kale 1938, pp. 393-394.)

In the context of certain ceremonies, a villager rephrases the role-behaviour appropriate to his *jati*. During the more solemn holy days, villagers of all *jatis* are especially careful to keep themselves free of defilement or, if ritually contaminated, to cleanse themselves with greater alacrity and intensity than on ordinary days.

During the euphoric celebration of *Holi*, some of the ordinary taboos of touch and trespass may be broken wholesale. Coloured powder or water or dust may be thrown at anyone at all. There is jostling and intermingling of a kind not tolerated in the village on other occasions. Women of the highest *jatis* may hear men of low rank bandy remarks about them that would be insufferably rude on other occasions, but on *Holi* have to be taken as part of the fun of the festival. An old man may be teased by allusions to the escapades of his youth; a wealthy, powerful man may be taunetd with jeers about his miserliness. (Gupte 1919, pp. 88-93; Lall 1933, pp. 44-55.)

But only for the duration of the holiday and only in certain ways is this unfettered behaviour allowed. The "unrestrained" merry-making of a saturnalian occasion goes on within well understood bounds of restraint. Even in the context of *Holi*, considerations of position and of ritual are not absent. Nowadays a cabinet minister may be squirted with coloured water on *Holi*; photographs of the drenched dignitary accepting the common touch may be published in newspapers throughout the land. But the youths who douse him do not treat him just as they would any old man who had come around the corner of a hamlet lane. So it is also in a village, when the wealthy headman appears in the street on *Holi* morning. The roisterers may not spare him from the *Holi* anointment, but they also temper their jokes and jostling in deference to his rank and power.

The same kind of role-shift, similarly kept within well understood limits, is exemplified in Rampur village near Delhi where the women on *Holi* beat their men relatives with sticks. While a woman may make so bold, on that occasion, as to strike her husband's elder brother, she must not go so far as to hit her father-in-law. (Lewis 1956, p. 187.) Social regulations are relaxed on that day but the fundamentals of social order are by no means totally abandoned, even for the day. *Holi* does not everywhere provide an occasion for relaxation or removal of social distances. In Mohana, as Majumdar describes the *Holi* celebration, caste distinctions are observed in all phases of the festivity. (1958a, pp. 259-263.)

When a villager goes into town, whether on a holiday or ordinary weekday, he is apt to be somewhat less meticulous about keeping his physical and social distance from those of lower *jati* than he is in the village. Buses and trains are often crowded and there is no room to spare on them for polite spacing. At pilgrimage centres, fairs, markets, and latterly in cinemas, there is inevitably some rubbing together of people of different social position. Niceties of spatial intervals cannot be observed in these contexts; a man must revise village-role expectations a bit when he comes to town. When he returns, he can give himself a ritual wash and then take on his usual *jati*-role and its spatial precautions again. Those who are troubled by such shifting, simply do not go to town very often.

Army service demands similar glossing over of the *jati*-roles appropriate in one's home village. This was true even in those units of the Indian army which were made up of men from similar *jatis.* In recent decades there has been much more commingling of *jatis* within military units. The recruit quickly learns to lay aside, while he is in the army, certain of his expectations concerning relations among *jatis*; the discharged veteran returns home and usually takes them up again.

Where there is a special, sanctioned relation between two people, as occurs in those localities where a man and a woman may formally adopt each other as brother and sister, ordinary *jati* roles may be modified in the relationship between the two. For example, in Gaon village (Poona district, Bombay) a man and a woman can adopt each other as brother and sister by taking token instruction from the same *guru*, religious teacher. (Orenstein 1957, pp. 36-37.) The two may be of the same *jati*, "but we very frequently find the relationship existing between people of different but nearly equal castes. And in a surprising number of cases there are *guru* brother-*guru* sister relationships between individuals in castes far distant from one another in the hierarchy; for example, a Temple Priest man and a Scavenger woman." Rank differences between the two are then mitigated, in some part, by the adoptive relationship of brother and sister, a relation which, throughout India, is an especially warm and supportive bond.

Such ties of fictional kinship across *jati* lines are not common. But special modifications of *jati*-roles to suit particular needs and situations are frequently made. An example of such shift from usual role-behaviour is given in an incident noted by M. N. Srinivas in Rampura village, Mysore. There the Brahman priest of the Rama temple "is accorded every respect by the village headman who is a peasant (Okkaliga) by caste." But the priest is dependent on the wealthy headman in mundane matters. Hence when the priest became worried about the further education of his son, which meant sending the boy to Mysore City and required money, he took the matter up with the headman and then with the headman's mother, "an old matriarch of seventy-odd years." For all that she is a woman, an old widow and of lower ritual rank than is the priest, she is also a forceful person and not without influence over her son and in the village. Hence the priest addressed her by the respectful term for mother, as one of her *jati* would, and sought her advice in a deferential manner.

Although the priest was acting as a supplicant and a dependent, "the headman and his mother knew they were dealing not with an ordinary peasant, but with a Brahmin and a priest at that . . . . Helping any poor man confers spiritual merit, but more merit would accrue when the poor man is also a Brahmin and a priest." (Srinivas 1954, p. 363.) The ritual eminence of the priest was muted in this episode, but it was not entirely disregarded. The priest in the role of deferential dependent is given special consideration. Such modifications are constantly made, whenever role-prescriptions do not quite fit the requirements of a special situation. In general, a person tends to interpret his *jati*-role more strictly in the context of hearth and home, in matters of eating, marriage and worship, than he does in the context of field and of town, in matters of labour, play or travel.

Each villager is expected, by his kin and neighbours, to act in accord with the roles which are considered appropriate for his *jati*. In certain matters, the *jati* role-definitions are specific and apply to all *jati* members alike; each person of any *jati* must observe those taboos of touch, taste and marriage which characterise his group. But in other areas of social relations, the villager's definition of *jati*-role is a broad directive which allows for the kinds of variation we have mentioned—those of age and sex, of situation and occasion, of special bonds and considerations.

NOTES

[1] In the Ganges-Jumna valleys, upstream is the superior direction in marriage alliances. This is north in the region of Kishan Garhi; it is west after the Ganges changes the main direction of flow.

REFERENCES

AIYAPPAN, A., 1955, 'Symposium on Caste and Joint Family', *Sociological Bulletin* 4: 117-122. Indian Sociological Society, Bombay.

BHATTACHARYA, Jogendra Nath, 1896, *Hindu Castes and Sects*: *An Exposition of the Origin of the Hindu Caste System and the Bearing of the Sects towards each other and towards other Religious Systems*. Calcutta, Thacker, Spink and Co.

BOUGLÉ, C., 1908, 'Essais sur le régime des castes.' *Travaux de L'Année Sociologique*. Paris, Libraries Felix Alcan et Guillaumin Reunies.

DUBE, S. C., 1955a, *Indian Village*. Ithaca, Cornell University Press.

1955b, 'Ranking of Castes in Telangana Villages,' *The Eastern Anthropologist* 8:182-190.

DUMONT, Louis and D. POCOCK eds., 1957, *Contributions to Indian*

Sociology. No. 1. Paris-The Hague, Mouton and Co.

FUCHS, Stephen, 1950, *The Children of Hari, A Study of the Nimar Balahis in the Central Provinces of India.* Vienna, Verlag Herold.

GOUGH, Kathleen, n.d., *Hypergamy in Malabar.* (ms. Typescript).

GHURYE, G. S., 1950, *Caste and Class in India.* Bombay, The Popular Book Depot.

GUHA, U. and M. N. KAUL, 1953, 'A Group Distance Study of the Castes of U.P.', *Bulletin of the Department of Anthropology,* Government of India, Vol. 2, No. 2:11-32. Calcutta.

GUPTE, B. A., 1919, *Hindu Holidays and Ceremonials.* Calcutta, Thacker, Spink and Co. (2d. ed. rev).

GROSS, N., W. S. MASON and A. W. McEACHERN, 1958, *Exploration in Role Analysis: Studies of the School Superintendency Role.* New York, John Wiley and Sons Inc. London, Chapman and Hall Ltd.

HUTTON, J. H., 1946, *Caste in India: Its Nature, Function, and Origins.* Cambridge University Press.

JAGALPURE, L. B. and K. D. KALE, 1938, *Sarola Kasar: Study of a Deccan Village in the Famine Zone.* Amednagar, L. B. Jagalpure.

KARVE, Mrs. Irawati, 1953, *Kinship Organization in India.* Deccan College Monograph Series S:11. Poona, Deccan College Post-Graduate and Research Institute.

LALL, R. Manohar, 1933, *Among the Hindus.* Cawnpore, Minerva Press.

LEWIS, Oscar, 1956, 'The Festival Cycle in a North Indian Jat Village.' *Proceedings of the American Philosophical Society* 100: 168-196.

MAJUMDAR, D. N., 1958a, *Caste and Communication in an Indian Village.* Bombay, Asia Publishing House.

1958b, *Races and Cultures of India.* Bombay, Asia Publishing House.

MARRIOTT, McKim, 1955, 'Little Communities in an Indigenous Civilization', *Village India: Studies in the Little Community,* McKim Marriott ed. Chicago, University of Chicago Press.

ORENSTEIN, Henry, 1957, Caste, Leadership and Social Change in a Bombay Village. Unpublished Dissertation. Dept. of Anthropology, University of California.

POCOCK, D., 1954, 'The Hypergamy of the Patidars.' In *Professor Ghurye Felicitation Volume,* K. M. Kapadia ed. Bombay, Popular Book Depot.

1957, 'Inclusion and Exclusion: A Process in the Caste System of Gujerat.' *Southwestern Journal of Anthropology,* 13: 19-31. Albuquerque, New Mexico.

RISLEY, Herbert H., 1915, *The People of India.* 2d ed. London, W. Thacker Co.

RUSSELL, R. V. and RAI BAHADUR HIRA LAL, 1916, *The Tribes and Castes of the Central Provinces of India.* Vol. 1. London, Macmillan and Co. Ltd.

SARMA, Jyotirmoyee, 1955, 'A Village in West Bengal', *India's Villages.* pp. 161-179. West Bengal Govt. Press.

SHARMA, K. N., 1956, 'Hypergamy in Theory and Practice', *The Journal of Research,* 3: 18-32.

SRINIVAS, M. N., 1954, 'Varna and Caste.' In *A. R. Wadia, Essays in Philosophy Presented in his Honour.* Bangalore.

1955, 'The Social System of a Mysore Village', *Village India: Studies in the Little Community*, McKim Marriott ed., University of Chicago Press.

STEVENSON, Mrs., Sinclair, 1920, *The Rites of the Twice-Born*. Oxford, University Press.

THURSTON, EDGAR, 1909, *Castes and Tribes of Southern India*. Madras, Government Press.

17

INDIA AS A CULTURAL REGION

Irawati Karve

WORK AS an anthropologist involves asking certain questions, trying to find answers and seeing if they fit in a general framework. Sometimes the answers modify the framework. It has been my attempt to find a rough framework into which different parts and people of India could be fitted in, in such a way that certain expectations arise and certain types of investigations are called for as soon as one finds oneself in a particular region or among a particular group. The scheme itself is never a complete or a detailed scheme providing all explanations. As stated, it is rough but concrete enough to allow examination of it or of a social situation in terms of it and which gets continuously more defined as well as modified as knowledge increases. The investigation about kinship organisation (Karve 1953) was such an attempt, but while work on particular aspects of a culture goes on there is also a rough picture of the whole culture.[1] It would not be possible to give an overall picture in a small space but an attempt is made here to present a framework which concerns certain very concrete things about people in India. I started work as an anthropologist with a very vague idea about India as a cultural region. I cannot say that my ideas have reached any great definiteness even now, but I am presenting them in the hope that such a presentation will evoke an examination by co-workers and that the framework will consequently become defined and modified.

As a land-mass India presents certain well marked peculiarities. It is surrounded by the sea on the west, south and east of the southern part. To the north it is bounded by the Himalayan ranges. India lies a little apart from the great overland trade routes between the ancient Middle East and China. Its sea-coast is rather distant from Africa, though along the western coast fishing vessels can go all the way up to the Persian gulf. Towards the south-east and east the land is much nearer across the Bay of Bengal and towards the south-east the way opens to the island world of Indonesia and to the pacific coast of South-East-Asia. The north-west is arid and semi-desert while to the north-east are dense tropical jungles and mighty rivers. These features have remained so at least for the last five or six thousand years, except for minor changes. The western semi-desert seems to have become more arid and a lot of forest has been destroyed by agricultural people.

Indian frontiers have never been impenetrable but they have afforded a certain type of isolation to people. When people came into India they could not keep up easy communications with the land they came from. They became isolated and became natives of the new land.[2] While not presenting insurmountable barriers for ingress or egress, the boundaries were (1) difficult for passing and (2) a little away from the main corridors of migration and trade. The result of these two features was that while new influences and new people entered India, they had time to settle down and become native. The 'new' entered India also comparatively late. In a way India represents almost a peripheral position with regard to certain cultural features. A few examples should suffice. As far back as in the palaeolithic age the first phases of Sohan culture have been interpreted by Movius to be the westernmost phase of a widespread Sino-Burmese palaeolithic era. The Indian neolithic has been interpreted by the same author as the western most extention of a neolithic culture which originated and flowered in Burma, Indo-China and Cambodia. Thus India played apparently a peripheral role to eastern Asia.

As regards the palaeolithic hand-axe culture also, it is felt that the very first crude phases are absent in India. The Acheulian type of core implements and flakes represent a phase which seems to be more advanced as compared to those found in Europe and Africa. In this respect also India seems to have received the old stone age cultures later than Eurafrica.

The new stone age with its implements does not seem to have reached India at all from the west. What did reach India was the Chalcolithic phase represented by two types: (1) the city cultures and (2) a cruder chalcolithic people with fine weapons but not dwellers of the cities.

The art of writing also got established in India at a date much later than the Middle East countries. In later historical times people came into India and became Indians losing their connection with whatever country they came from. This peculiar role of India must be borne in mind when considering Indian cultures. The main entrances to India, which have been well-known in history are:

(1) The north-western passage,
(2) the north-eastern passage,
(3) the western sea-coast.

The north-western passage admitted peoples whose record in Indian literature started from the Vedic Aryans and went on to the Moghuls without any considerable break. The Indus civilization which predates the coming of the Vedic Aryans had a very great extent. It spread from the northern border of the Punjab upto Kathiawar in the South and from Sind in the west to Western U.P. in the east. This civilisation had a script which remains undeciphered. The north-eastern passage, from the point of view of Indian people and culture is equally important. The earliest people to come to India seem to belong to a stock which is linguistically represented by scattered folks from the pacific coast to the centre of India today. It is possible that these people were spread much further west than they are found today.

There is a curious cluster of names ending in -*nga* like Anga, Vanga and Kalinga belonging to countries at the mouth of the river Ganga (another name ending in -*nga*) which might belong to these ancient people or to some later Mongoloid stock as similar place and river names are found right up into China.

The same corridor of migration admitted Mongoloid people who spread through Assam into Burma and represent the Tibeto-Burman stock. The same stock has penetrated into India along the whole Tibeto-Indian frontier including the central Himalayas.

The western sea-coast has admitted into India the Arabs, the Portuguese, French and the English. The peculiarity of all these people is that in spite of the vast distances, they kept up communication with the land of their origin. Recently discovered Roman pottery in all excavations speaks of great trade with the Mediterranean world. Apparently this trade went back to the days of ancient Egypt and Babylonia, but people coming into India via this route before the Arabs have not left any record except two legends.

(1) The Syrian Christians of Kerala claim that they were converted to Christianity by the first disciples of Christ.

(2) The Bene Israelite community of the west coast claims to have come into India long before the Arabs.

The eastern and southern portions of the seaboard have land masses very near them, namely Burma, Malaya, Indonesia, Ceylon. The names like Burma, Andaman, Java, Ceylon, Laccadive, and Maldive are definitely of Sanskritic origin. The whole of this coast has a recorded history of people going out of India into the nearby lands, but any record of peoples coming in either from these nearby lands or from the more distant Pacific Islands is not known. The word *Malai* for mountains in South India and for the land of Malaya might mean an older pre-Sanskritic connection. The word for green coconut in Malyalam also seems to belong to the Malayan language. The people of the island world of the Pacific and the Indian Ocean were skilled and adventurous sea-farers who went as far as Madagascar. They could not have missed India, but India has not preserved any legends of people coming from those countries.

When one speaks of different folk and racial elements in India today, one puts together in a big class quite different people and calls them "tribals". The author would like to make a distinction between the tribals, which rests on their regional distribution as also on physical and cultural traits. The western tribals seem to be hunters and gatherers to a large extent and possess very much smaller heads than the western agricultural population. The eastern tribals, on the other hand, seem to be practising primitive agriculture side by side with hunting and gathering and have head circumferences comparable with the agricultural populations of the east.

In this context it must be remembered that the neolithic age came to India from the east. The east did not domesticate cattle for agricultural purposes or for milk. The neolithic complex of the east is therefore not bound up with animal husbandry as that of the west. Cultivation of small patches by clearing of forest was apparently the mode of cultivation of the neolithic people of the east. The burning of forest and the dibbling stick and the hoe were enough to yield crops like rice and small millets *e.g.* panicum (see Grigson 1949, p. 134). Such a culture can support quite large populations and quite high civilisations. In India even today quite a number of rice producing areas have no bullock carts, though buffaloes and cattle are used for ploughing rice fields.

Harking back to the prehistoric record, comparatively few ancient skeletons have been found in India. A series of chalcolithic finds of pot-burials were made during the last five years along the banks of the Godavari and recently (March 1961) at Chandoli near Poona. These skeletal remains are not yet fully described. They have been worked on by (Miss) Erhardt, and (Mrs.) Karve and recently Shri Gulati and Shri Malhotra have been associated with the work. Physically they seem to be people of medium height, dolicho-cephalic, with rather broad noses and slight prognathy. Culturally they were people possessed of metal and stone implements, the former especially reminding one by shape of those found in Europe and Persia and seem to belong to the Indo-Aryan people. They seem to have occupied the river valleys of the western part of central India and Maharashtra before the Shatavahana Kings. Carbon dating of the remains of cereals seems to suggest a date between 1000 to 1500 B.C. (see Sankalia and others 1960, p. 67) which agrees well with the eruption of the Indo-Aryans into the sourthern coun-tries from the eastern Mediterranean to India. The skeletal remains do not, however, agree with the imagined Indo-Aryans who are supposed to have been orthognaths and narrow-nosed. These river basin people must have a part in the composition of the Indian population of today. The other important skeletal finds are confined to north Gujarat. Culturally the people belong to the mesolithic stage and seem to have been relying on hunting and gathering. These also are dolicho-cephalic people with slight pro-gnathy and extremely broad noses. They appear to be of middle height with rather slender bones of the legs. Among the animals they hunted was the rhinoceros. This shows that north Gujarat in those days had more bush and more water. These hunting folks also must have been taken up in the population of India. Unlike the chalcolithic people who might have represented the coming in of Aryans, no known folk-movements can be connected with these north Gujarat hunters. They may have belonged to an age from anywhere between 5,000 to 10,000 B.C. The circumference of their heads is comparable with the modern agricultural folk and therefore they cannot be easily connected with the tribal people of western India. Whether they have any connection with the eastern primitives (not belonging to the neolithic age) cannot be ascertain-ed. They might represent the westernmost thrust of the eastern primitives. This however is purely conjectural.

This is all we know for the present of people dwelling in India in the near past and in the distant past. The story does not help us to understand the present distribution of people and races of India because archaeological excavation is yet very meagre' in relation to the vastness of the country. Linguistic evidence points to four major partners in Indian culture. The eastern Himalayan regions upto Manipur and Lushai Hills have been recently dominated by the Tibeto-Burman people. Among these as broken groups sit a more ancient people who can be traced in small groups along the eastern coastal hills to the south of the Godavari. One small isolated group is found in Central India. These are people who speak languages belonging to the Mundari and Khasi language families. The whole of North India from the Punjab to Assam and from the cis-Himalayan regions including Kashmir upto the middle and upper reaches respectively of the Godavari and Krishna speak languages belonging to the Sanskritic family. A point which is of importance is the penetration of this group deep into the south upto Mangalore along the western coastal strip. If one looks at a linguistic map of India one can see that the Sanskritic languages extend further south in the western half than in the eastern half. This fact connects itself with the extent of the fourth linguistic group viz. the Dravidians. The whole of South India upto the middle reaches of the Krishna (except the western thrust along the coast of the Marathi- and Konkani-speaking people) and Godavari and along the eastern sea-board almost upto the river Vamshadhara, with some penetrations even more northwards, is solidly Dravidian. The point of interest to note here is the northward extension of the Dravidian speaking people right upto the river Ganges in the hilly tracts and jungles of eastern India. While the Dravidian people of the south are non-tribal, farming folk, the people of the northward extension are counted among the tribals.

A third significant point to note is that in the whole half of western India all the tribal people ranging from the Bhils in Rajputana to the Mala Vedan and Irula of the Travancore high ranges speak a language belonging to the surrounding non-tribal people, or easily understandable dialects of that language or akin to that language. As against this the eastern region, north of the Godavari is such that the tribals speak languages belonging to three distinct families, viz. Mundari, Dravidian and Tibeto-Burman. This linguistic distribution can be interpreted in terms of (i) geographical factors like

open corridors of migration or regions of isolation and retreat, and
(ii) historical factors about the spread and the intensity of domina-
tion of different cultural groups.

There are a number of well-established routes between north
and south, and east and west. Once the immigrant tribes were in
the Punjab, they spread into India, as history shows, by two routes.
One was the ancient route of the Aryans eastwards along the
northern banks of the Ganges. The second was the route leading
south either along the Indus or through Rajputana and Gujarat
down the west coast or up the Ghats into the heart of the peninsula.
Other routes were from Delhi through Central India and the Burhanpur gap southwards. Through the western path came the chalcolithic people, the later Kshatrapas and many other tribes. After
coming to the south of Gujarat, these folks went up the mountains
and spread over what is now western Maharashtra, eastern Andhra
and Karnatak. The present day Marathas and many other castes
of Maharashtra, Karnatak and the Reddis of eastern Andhra present
so many similarities as regards head form, nose form, etc., that they
seem to belong to some wave of immigration coming via Gujarat.
The same path led in historical times the Chalukya Kings of Karnatak into Gujarat from south to north. Kathiawad, a little away from
this route, has proved to be an area of colonisation and retreat
for northern people. Kathiawad myth and legend speak of kings
and people travelling between it and Sind. One such tribe which
apparently grazed cattle from Kathiawad to Sind was the Ayar or
Ahir of Kathiawad. It may be remembered that the Yadavas,
retreating before the conquering Jarasandha and his allies found
refuge in Kathiawad under the leadership of Krishna. The central
route over the Tapi at Burhanpur was used in historical times by
northern conquerors like Allauddin Khilji and by southerners like
Bajirao Peshwa to go northwards. In Maharashtra a number of
people, who have come but recently through central India or Gujarat,
are spread on both sides of the Burhanpur gap, *e.g.* the Leva, the
Bhil, and the Maheshwari trading community.

Another way from north to south is through the Bheda Ghat
at Jabbalpur. From Burhanpur to Jabbalpur the Marathi- and
Hindi-speaking people have crossed the Narmada and Tapi. In
Mahabharata, in the story of Nala and Damayanti, the former
seems to have shown to Damayanti this ancient road, which from
Burhanpur leads on the one hand to the south and on the other

into Berar, the home of Damayanti's father. This conjecture is strengthened by the mention of the river Payushni (modern Tapi) which Nala is supposed to be pointing out to her.

The fourth corridor of migration within India is from the Bank of the Ganges via the Chhattisgadh plain deep into the Godavari forest. This appears to be the ancient route taken by Rama and Sita in their journey to the Godavari. This is also the route taken by the southern Dravidian people to go northward and by the Mundari-speaking people to go to the south.

I conjecture that at some time just before or after the Christian era some cattle-breeding pastoral people pushed their way southward and deep into the plateau of Karnatak and parts of eastern Andhra. My investigation (see Karve 1951) has shown that Maharashtra population becomes longer headed from west to east. The same can be said about Andhra, while the Karnatak plateau population including the stretch from north Karnatak to Coorg is meso- to brachy-cephalic. While in Maharashtra meso-cephalic and dolicho-cephalic communities are found on the coast, in Karnatak the coastal Kannada-speaking people are dolicho-cephalic and the meso-cephalic community is represented by the Konkani-speaking Saraswat Brahmins. The majority of the rest of the Dravidian-speaking India is dolicho-cephalic. Unlike western Maharashtra, the Karnatak plateau has populations which are, with only a few exceptions, meso- to sub-brachy-cephalic. The southern Kannada-speaking region is a conquest by the Kannada language over what was Tulu area. Jenu Kuruba, Betta Kuruba and some coastal untouchables (Ager and Mukri) seem to represent a different physical strain. It appears that the people who speak Kannada in what was the heart of ancient Kannada Kingdoms (Bijapur, Bagalkot, Badami and the valley of Ghataprabha) must have replaced some older population. From this centre the Kannadas seem to have spread southwards, westwards and a little eastwards. If this hypothesis, that they represent a migration from the north is correct, then they must have taken up the language of the region in which they settled down as conquerors.[3] Before pushing southwards, whatever were the tribes which populated Karnatak must have picked up a considerable amount of Prakrit vocabulary. That is perhaps the reason why the Kannada language has such a large number of words of Sanskritic origin. Before the Kannadas spread westwards, the western coast was ruled over by Kadamba Kings, who employed the Saraswats and whose inscriptions are in Sanskrit. This shows that the whole of the western coast upto Mangalore was open for penetration to people coming from the north, from the east and also from the south. The penetration from the south is marked by the people who call themselves Bant and Nadavara. The Bant are still matrilineal; Nadavaras apparently were so formerly.[4]

Turning to the conditions in modern Andhra the Reddis, at least some part of them, represent the thrust of the meso-cephals as would appear from Dr. Guha's work. They, however, do not represent older Andhra people, whose centre of consolidation seems to be along the eastern seaboard and inland between Rajamahendry on the Godavari and Guntur on the Krishna. While the river Godavari happens to be the centre of Marathi culture in its upper and middle reaches, it represents the northern tribal boundary from a little eastward of Nanded almost upto Rajamahendry, for the Andhra people. Even today on both banks of the Godavari in this stretch live forest tribes like Gond, Naikpod and others. Konda-reddi (mountain Reddi), who are also described as tribal people, seem to be late arrivals from the south into these parts. Northwards from Rajamahendry are tribal people speaking Mundari languages as also Dravidian languages and the tribal belt reaches almost to the Gangetic plain in a north south stretch. One of the most numer-ous of these tribal people are the Gonds. East of them are the Kondhs. The Gonds are spread over three linguistic region today, viz., Andhra, Maharashtra and Orissa. In the 12th and the 13th centuries they had powerful kingdoms. North and slightly to the east is another Dravidian-speaking tribe called the Oraons. In the south, the Dravidian-speaking peoples seem to have pushed and split a more ancient Mundari-speaking people namely the Saoras and Bondos. In the north, the Gonds seem to have given a push northwards to the Oraons, who and the Gonds together seem to have pushed and split the Mundari-speaking people like Santhals, Mundas and Juangs to the east, and the Korkus to the west. It appears as if the push of the Karnatak people from the west and the Andhra people from the east displaced an older population which could not penetrate southwards as the land was already occupied by Telugu and Tamil-speaking advanced people. They therefore pushed northwards into the region of retreat of the ancient Mundari-speaking people, who were slowly receding before the eastward push of the many tribes who came through the north-western passage into India.

This hypothesis raises many questions: (i) the relationship between the Oraon, Gondi and Kondh languages on the one hand and the literary Dravidian languages on the other; (ii) the origin and affinity of the Dravidian languages themselves. This second question needs further elucidation.

Many attempts have been made to find out affinities outside India to the Dravidian languages. Some have tried to connect them to the Hungarian or the Finnish languages. Some have tried to prove that the ancient people of the city states of the Indus (Mohenjodaro and Harappa) were Dravidian and that the language on their seals is more or less like Tamil. None of these attempts have found general acceptance among linguists and the Dravidian languages remain as unconnected with any other languages as before. There is one exception to this and that is the Brauhi language spoken by some people in Baluchistan. The little bit of Brauhi which is known shows it to be a modern Dravidian language. The existence of Brauhi far north has led to a hypothesis, generally accepted, that the Dravidian-speaking people came into India from somewhere north through the north-western gate. They occupied once the whole of northern India and were driven southwards to their present habital by the Aryans who came later. This hypothesis does not seem to be borne out by the known facts of history. However unhistorical the Indian people might be, they have recorded every now and then, names of people they have met or fought with. The Vedic and Sanskritic records contain names of people like Dasa or Dasyu, but the word Dravida occurs rather late and does not place a person so mentioned in the Gangetic plain. The Dravidian-speaking people found today in the eastern Gangetic plain, as my hypothesis above suggests, appear to have occupied this region in late historical times. Dravidian records begin much later than the Sanskritic one, but they reveal two things: (i) the Dravidians seem to be as much a conquering people as the northern Aryans; (ii) unlike the northern Aryans they were sea-farers from the very first. The sea-faring activities are well described in their earliest literature and also in the early inscriptions from Amaravati. Even today the sea-fishing as far north along the eastern coast as Puri is in the hands of Dravidian-speaking fishermen. Brauhi therefore can be explained also as the language spoken by a group of people who during their sea-faring reached that part of the world. There is no doubt at all about south India having received new people. The meso-cephalic people from the north have already been mentioned above. The megalithic graves found mostly in south India also tell of a new people with iron implements and weapons. The meso-cephals, inasmuch as they speak three different languages in the three regions where they are found, cannot be the original speakers of the Dravidian languages. The people of the megalithic graves, though obviously a dominant people, appear also to be so late that they could not have brought the Dravidian languages to India. While the other three partners to Indian culture have linguistic affinities outside India, the Dravidians upto date do not seem to have any.

As regards other cultural features, kinship organisation of the north, leaving the cis-Himalayan regions, is patrilineal and patrilocal with a taboo on marriages of kin. There is also a taboo on marriages of people living in one and the same village. In most of Dravidian India, the prevalent kinship organisation is also patrilineal and patrilocal, but marriages with kin of two types are allowed and quite 50 per cent of the marriages seem to take place within the village. They allow cross-cousin marriage both ways as also the marriage of a man with his elder sister's daughter. There is a taboo on marriage with a younger sister's daughter. Matrilineal households are also found in a part of the Dravidian region (South-Western tip of the peninsula). This cultural fact, together with the existence of masked dances suggests a connection with south-east Asia and the Oceanic world. To me, there appears to be another fact which might give support to this suggestion. When the Singhalese Chronicle of Ceylon opens, the Singhalese Kings are shown to be either fighting or contracting marriages with the Tamil Kingly houses. The Tamilian occupation of the north-eastern region of Ceylon seems to be part of the same colonisation by the same people of the south-eastern part of India. This might mean that the Tamil-speaking people came from somewhere in the South-east to India to colonise simultaneously the north-eastern part of Ceylon and the south eastern part of India. From here they spread westward and northward.

The picture that I have in mind is of land-wandering hordes from the north coming into India and maritime people coming a little earlier or later from the south-eastern tip. They met in India two types of people: (i) hunters and gatherers who apparently were spread from the southwest upto the western part of central India and (ii) a more advanced people doing a little agriculture without the help of cattle in the south-east, north-east and westwards, perhaps right upto the Punjab. Most of these people were absorbed by the new comers but some remained isolated or escaped into the more inaccessible jungle tracts. These are the tribal people of today.

India divides itself into two broad cultural regions, very roughly on two sides of a line drawn from Bengal to Karnatak. To the north of this line are people who cultivate millets and wheat, use the plough, and the method is of broadcast cultivation. These people grind their food-grains dry and make the flour into a dough later. They also use a knife for purposes of cutting. In this mode of cutting the knife-hand moves up and down while the thing to be cut remains stationary below the cutter. These people also use foot-wear and have sanskritic names for leather footwear as also for the caste of leather workers. They like to cook their food-stuffs with ghee (clarified butter). To the south of this line the people are mainly rice-growers, where now though the plough is used, it is not an essential implement for the rice fields. The most important item in rice cultivation is the transplantation of seedlings and putting them in their new place by hand. Again, the grinding implements in these parts are a flat stone below with a cylindrical stone above worked in the way of American Indian mano and matate. Grain is first soaked in water and then ground so that the very act of grinding gives the "dough". The cutting implement is a slightly curved blade which is held in place by the foot or fixed to a wooden board on which the person sits. The object to be cut is held in the two fists and moved up and down while the cutter remains stationary. The name for this implement is definitely non-Sanskritic and appears to be Dravidian. The Dravidian-speaking people of the south used not to wear, until quite recently, any footwear. The words used for footwear like *Sapata* seem to be of Portuguese import. The name of leather-working castes are of Sanskritic origin. Maharashtra, Gujarat, Bengal and parts of Orissa share both northern and southern traits in different proportions.

These differences can be further augmented by such facts like the prevalent use of pottery in northern India for fetching or drinking water and of metal containers in the south. But one need not go into them as the differences are not so widespread in other items as in those enumerated above.

A reference has already been made to the sea-faring and fishing activities of the Dravidian-speaking people of the eastern coast. On the western coast of Gujarat and Maharashtra there are also very large fishing communities who however seem to be racially different from the eastern fishermen. Measurements of the fishing people near Bombay show them to be a meso-cephalic people often times having extremely fine, small noses and fine lips. In Maharashtra, the position is confused because the word *Koli* is applied to the western fisher-folk as also to an extremely widespread semi-tribal people who live in the mountainous regions of Maharashtra. These inland people are physically and culturally very different from the west-coast fisher-folk, but practise fishing in the inland mountain streams whenever fishing is available. They also ply river craft wherever rivers are navigable. I feel that the name *Koli* denotes that these tribal folk belong to the extremely widespread Kol tribes and that later on the name was transferred to the west-coast fisher folk. It may be noted here that plying of river craft as well as fishing apparently were the activities of non-Aryan people. The literary record is quite consistent in this particular respect. In Ṛgveda there is a hymn which is supposed to have been sung by a sage (*Rgveda*, 3.33) to drive the bullocks of Bharata through a northern river. It shows that the Aryans apparently made their cattle ford the mountain streams. In *Mahabharata* Shantanu married a girl who was obviously very dark (Kali Satyavati, Adi-parvan, 1.90.51; 1.99.21) who plied a boat over the Ganges and whose father was called the King of Dasas. In *Ramayana* when Rama crossed the Ganges to go southwards the boat was plied by an aborigine. As late as about 4th century A.D., when Kalidasa is supposed to have lived, he sang about the greatness of King Raghu by saying that the eastern rivers which were crossed by boats became for him easily fordable. (*Raghuvamsha*, 4.31). Later on the Buddhist literature records extensive sea-faring activities from eastern harbours. Thus the traditions of using boats was definitely non-Aryan. Equally definitely it was Dravidian on the east coast. But whether all the people mentioned in old literature as plying boats were Dravidians or some were non-Dravidian people is worth investigating. People engaged in water-transport and fishing have always been quite distinct from the semi-nomadic pastoral people who came into India via the northwestern passage. This distinction appears to have been perpetuated through the caste system and there is always a little rivalry, if not antagonism, between the fishing and farming folks as seen in western India.

The suggestions put forward in this paper embody a sort of a provisional picture about the kind of culture complex India is and the kind of questions which I have tried to investigate. I have written them out so that the experience of other anthropologists in field might bring forth comments to clarify and wherever necessary to modify this picture.

NOTES

[1] The author is working at present on another aspect of the Hindu culture and hopes to present the scheme in a short time.

[2] There have been notable exceptions to this. Kushans had an empire extending over parts of Asia, north of India also. The Afghans have kept up a continuous connection on both sides of the Khyber pass and the British were in touch with their native land across the waters.

[3] A legend which records similar things about Maharashtra is follows: some Shatavahana king, apparently a very early one, did not know Sanskrit and was laughed at by one of his queens. He is then supposed to have patronised the Prakrit languages and the Prakrit poet Gunadhya.

[4] This information was given to me personally by many families while I was doing anthropological work there about 10 years ago.

REFERENCES

GRIGSON, W. V., 1949, *The Maria Gonds of Bastar*. Oxford Uni. Press.
KARVE, Irawati, and DANDEKAR, V. M., 1951, *Anthropometric Measurements of Maharashtra*, Deccan College, Poona.
    1953, *Kinship Organization in India*. Poona, Deccan College.
SUBBARAO, B., 1958, *Personality of India*. Baroda, M.S. University of Baroda.
SAKALIA, H. D., DEO, ANSARI, ERHARDT, *From History to Prehistory*, Poona, 1960.

18

ON TERMS OF KINSHIP AND SOCIAL RELATIONSHIP

K. P. CHATTOPADHYAY

IN THIS preliminary note, only certain salient facts about the earlier study of kinship will be set out. A more detailed paper of the nature of a monograph surveying the entire ground will be published later.

The great pioneer of cultural anthropology, Henry Morgan, was impressed by certain features of the kinship terms collected together, from his own work and that of others. It was evident that there were different types of kinship terminology and they were linked to societies with different social rules. The influence of the theory of evolution of man and animals was being felt in the social sciences, and Morgan put forward his theory of evolution of human society on the basis of his knowledge of cultural data in his time. Since marriage as an institution, and family life have profound influence in shaping social attitudes and terminology, Morgan postulated different forms of marriage for his different stages of society. Since the means of food getting and of satisfying hunger are equally important, and later on the more developed arts and crafts, Morgan postulated different social stages of "savagery" and "barbarism" at different levels of material culture. With these levels he linked different forms of marriage. In his study of kinship terms, Morgan selected as the most important, the sexual life regulating function in the institution of marriage. That other factors like common residence and common food supply or its equivalent common economic right might also be equally potent in their influence on kinship terms was overlooked by him. Morgan (1877) tried to support his hypothesis of an early universal stage of brother-sister mating by (a) the Hawaiian kinship terms and (b) the fact that the highest kind of chiefs there have this mating practice in marriage. The usual criticism levelled against Morgan for this use of the particular data is that the level of culture is not primeval (in the sense of very primitive) but on the contrary is highly advanced. A better phrasing of the criticism would have been that Morgan did not furnish any evidence regarding the process by which an institution which had allegedly developed in a very primeval condition of life associated with his lowest level of "savagery" had managed to survive among the aristocracy in Hawaii when their material culture had progressed upwards to a much higher level. Rivers, although he did not accept Morgan's hypothesis of different levels of savagery and barbarism and the associated forms of marriage, nevertheless agreed that kinship terms resulting from earlier social conditions survived even when the older conditions had changed and the particular institution that influenced the terminology had disappeared. He compared the kinship terms that survived, to fossil remains of extinct forms of life. Rivers suggested further that kinship terms which had once been distinguished and formed part of a complex system of kinship terminology tended to change to a simpler type due to social changes. He pointed out that in the Torres Straits Island the distinction between father's sister and mothers's sister was becoming obsolete. Kinsfolk formerly distinguished by separate terms had come to be denoted by the same term. Since a term had ceased to be distinguished, presumably when the discriminating function had disappeared, clearly the comparison to a fossil did not hold. In actuality Rivers and the earlier workers did not point out from field work any example where proved changes had occurred in terminology but noted only likelihood of the same. It was not possible for them to do so in the absence of records among non-literate people. It was not also indicated in what circumstances the term survived in spite of change and when it did not; in other words what factor determined this kind of change.

A second point to be discussed is the nature of the limit of the functions which determine kinship terminology. Westermarck, for example, had ridiculed the suggestion that an isolated custom like the tying of a perineal band by a mother's brother could affect a term of kinship.

Rivers had sought to dispel the misconception that terminology of relationship depends solely upon forms of marriage. He states clearly in his monograph on Kinship (1913) that "marriage is only one of the social institutions which have moulded the terminology of relationship". He did not however fully realise the importance of the family and its affiliation to kinsfolk in the formation of the terminology in almost all systems of it. In fact he contrasted the effect of clan organisation and of the extended family in the two distinct types of terminology prevalent in certain areas in Oceania.

The importance of ascertaining whether any evidence of actual change was available led me to study the data available in our ancient literature and to collect the relevant terms in our modern Indian languages at the present time. The results are set out in my paper on "Kinship and Levirate in India[1]". The data demonstrate clearly how a kinship term for the husband's brothers changed with the restriction of levirate, formerly prevalent in the unrestricted form, later to the younger brothers alone of the deceased spouse. It was further pointed out in that paper that while junior levirate was still prevalent among many of the Hindu castes in Orissa, Bihar and Uttar Pradesh, the institution had disappeared in Bengal. But certain associated customs such as joking with a sexual tinge between eBW and HyB which are present in the leviration had survived in Bengal. It was evident therefore that along with survival of a secondary effect of the kinship function, the terminology depending on the earlier institution which was now obsolete had survived. The sexual joking relationship may not however be the only survival of this older custom. It is well known that where levirate is a preferential form of marriage as among many tribal folk in India, a deviation from it in the direction of marriage with some other person leads to payment of compensation to the deprived levir. In South India marriage with the mother's brother's daughter was an ancient custom. It had also been prevalent among some of the royal clans and Ksatriya tribes in Northern India. Thus the family of Kṛṣṇa of the line of Yadu, and Arjuna his sister Pṛtha's (= Kunti) son had practised it. Gautama Buddha's clan, the Sakyas, regularly intermarried with the Kolis on this basis. There were other Ksatriya groups of this period who followed this custom. But the custom disappeared completely in Northern India many centuries ago, and no trace of it, even in a secondary effect has remained among Hindus of Indo-Aryan speech in Northern India. Concurrently with it we find no trace of a kinship equation[2] based on MBD as we find in the Dravidian languages or the Marathi language. There in the South when a man cannot marry his MBD he is paid compensation. This MBD marriage is recognised as a preferential form of mating in these areas. The kinship equations have therefore persisted there as formed by marriage with MBD.

It was pointed out by me in another context that "a term of social relationship T may be looked upon as determined by functions relating to the family, clan and tribe separately or together. Representing these by "1", "c", and "t" respectively and considering "f" to denote function, we get $T = f(1, c, t)$. If in any particular case, the descriptive term or some associated known custom is found to give definite information or value regarding these unknowns a solution may be obtained" (Chattopodhyay 1927). The particular term studied in that paper and its significance was then discussed and it was shown that the tribe was excluded, and connection with the family was very definitely indicated. Now a function like $f(1, c, t)$ can be expanded into a first term which consists of the directly impinging functions of the relevant social group or groups. There will be however other terms of second and third order and more distant effect. In actual practice however, the more distant effects become negligible and may be ignored. To place them on the same level as the effects of the first order or the next will be unjustified. For convenience we may replace the two variables c and t by "s" to denote any social group other than the family of different types. For individuals or a cluster of individuals p and q, the formula was set out as (Tpq denoting the term of relationship of p to q) $Tpq = f(1, c, t,)$ which becomes now $f(1, s.)$ ...... (I). If a number of individuals (or clusters of such) a, b,.......... are denoted by the same term of relationship by an individual "p", we have $Tap = Tbp$. ..... etc....... From (I), we get, $f(1, s)\, ap = f(1, s)\, bp$ (II). ......(III).

Evidently, the individuals a, b,....are not necessarily identical kin of P. Hence the term identity for (II) would be illogical. They are however each an equation and this term is proper for use in description. The system of equations can however become kinship identities if T is independent of s and is a function of "1" alone. This can be checked by detailed information about function. If T does not change when "s" changes we can conclude that T does not depend on other groups but on "1" alone. For analysis of data on terms of relationship, the following formulation was found useful:

(a) If a number of genealogically related kin, such as a, b . . . and others m, n, . . . who are members of a social group, other than the kin group, are denoted by a common term and have a common function towards the user of the term, the origin of the custom or institution connected with it will be found in the social unit in which the persons included are all equivalent to one another for this purpose.

One more working formula may be considered in this connection. It may be termed the law of disappearance of kinship correspondence.

(b) When the terminology of kinship changes with changes in social organisation, the primary kinship identity or equation based on the earlier custom or institution disappears first, and the secondary identities or equations later on, those distantly affected last of all.

(c) So long as the secondary effects of a custom or institution persist and a tradition of the earlier existing custom or institution is retained in such effects, the kinship terms resulting from the institution do not change. When such secondary effects disappear, the kinship terms also alter.

An example illustrative of (b) and (c) has already been given earlier; some more illustrations in regard to (a), (b) and (c) are noted below.

Radcliffe-Brown in his work on the Andaman Islanders (1922) has noted that among these folk a village or settlement is socially a more or less self-sufficient unit. Here a girl receives a name in childhood, when she is born in a family. When she reaches puberty and the local community know that she is no longer a child without sexual maturity, she gets a special name by which she is then known. Her childhood name, which is her individual label is not used. The special name is of a flower of which the time of her first menstruation is the season; it is an appropriate symbolical name. After a girl's marriage, the community co-operate to help her and her husband. She lives with her husband in their individual hut but until a child is born, she does not socially come first with her husband. Thus if the husband goes on a journey involving absence of some days, he will on his return not greet his wife first by weeping over her, according to the convention prevalent, but will do so over a member of his family of birth, usually a blood relative. Only after that, he will greet his wife. But if there has been a child born, he will come first to his wife, sit on her lap and weep over her. Again, if a husband or wife dies before a child is born, the survivor according to Man (1932) is not the chief mourner. It is the family to which the dead person had belonged, his, or her "blood relatives" who function principally in the rites. The position changes with the birth of a child. We find also that until a child is born, the woman is known as the "wife of so and so." When a child is born, however, she gets back her individual name. In the community (settlement) she is now an individual who is a full member of her own family formed by marriage.

A similar illustration of the attitude of the community—not just psychological, but social, as reflected in social behaviour—showing itself in use of special social terms in case of death and mourning may also be noted. Death of a very young child did not affect the community. Only the parents mourned and the settlement was not affected. But in case of death of an adult, burial or platform disposal occurred away from the settlement. Also, the settlement itself was deserted until the period of mourning of several months was over. During this period, however, the people of the settlement as a whole did not observe mourning. All of them smeared themselves with clay on the death of an adult; but when this was washed away or dropped off in the course of a few days, no further mud coating was done. The near relatives like parents, grown up children, husband or wife, brothers and sisters go on using clay on the body and especially on the head. They also abstain from dancing, from use of certain kinds of clay paints, and from partaking of certain kinds of food.

A mourner is described as an *aka-odu* from the term *odu* or mourning clay. But neither the name of the deceased nor those of his near kin are mentioned by others during the period of mourning. Special terms are used for this purpose. Thus a person who has lost a parent is referred to or spoken to as *Bolok*; a person who has lost a brother or sister is termed *Ropuc*.

It is clear that a number of social relationship terms have in these cases been determined by social functions, and the group in question is that of the settlement. The terms are not kinship terms, although the persons affected are members of families. The equation $T = f(l, s)$ applies fully here. The clear-cut distinction that we find in these instances between terms of social relationship and those normally regarded as terms of kinship, is not however always so definite. In the Andamanese society itself, there are terms which apply specifically to the father and the mother, referring to their biological relationship to the child. These two terms are never used with reference to any other person. There is also a term for ego's own child. But there is also a term in South Andaman which refers to own children, as well as children of brother or of sister, or even of unrelated persons. In north Andaman there are terms for the father used for the father's brother or in fact any man of that generation. Radcliffe-Brown states that it applies to any "man older than himself or herself" but as persons of the same generation who are older have a different term, the reference seems to be as noted. There is a similar term for the mother and women of her generation. There are also expressions which denote younger brother and also younger men of the settlement; similarly elders of the same generation are distinguished. The feminine is formed by adding a suffix. The terms for husband and wife are however specific. It is a term like the word "consort" distinguished by prefixes to mean the husband and wife.

In an Andamanese settlement, children as they grow up (a) may be frequently adopted in another family and grow up there as their children; (b) go to live at adolescence in a dormitory with other adolescents, and the food collected by them by hunting goes in the main to the elders living in families in that settlement. (c) Even when living with parents in infancy, it is quite common for a child to be petted as well as nursed by persons other than parents. Radcliffe-Brown states that a woman in milk may even suckle the child of another woman at her breast. (d) An elder brother takes precedence over a younger and is expected to look after the latter who in his turn is expected to show due respect and deference to the senior. A younger man of the settlement is treated somewhat like a younger brother. Sisters also behave in similar fashion towards each other.

It is clear that the custom of adoption, of life in the dormitory and the general pattern of behaviour as noted, tends to blur the distinction between the family as a unit in these functions, and the settlement as a whole in relation to the same. This does not mean that family life is loose-knit; it is not so, but the settlement figures like a large family in many respects. Hence the extension of the terms already mentioned. They are not just courtesy terms.

Long ago Kroeber (1909) stated in the case of another people that "the use of such identical or similar terms for distinct relationships is due to a considerable similarity between relationships." He elaborated, referring to the Sioux terms, that "a woman's male cousin and her brother-in-law are alike in sex, are both of opposite sex from the speaker, are of the same generation as herself and are both collateral." He then refers to the colloquial habit in modern English of speaking of the brother-in-law as brother, and that it cannot imply "anything as to form of marriage" as such an interpretation, according to him, would imply brother and sister marriage. He concludes "terms of relationship reflect psychology not sociology." Ignoring the loose use by Kroeber, of the term "brother-in-law" which in English, for a woman speaker betokens two distinct relatives, the sister's husband, and the husband's brother, both of whom are related only by marriage it may be pointed out that these criticisms were fully met by Rivers (*op. cit.*). As he observed, "in social as in all other kinds of human activity, psychological factors must have an essential part. These psychological elements are however only concomitants of social processes." It is however evident that the psychological element may be the result of two kinds of resemblances—(a) a resemblance in characteristics which have no important functions associated with such resemblance, and (b) a resemblance in or associated with closely similar function. It is these latter which through constant expression in social behaviour fix the distinction and equation of the respective kinsfolk in the language to describe them, which is kinship terminology. Where there is a lack of function but a general resemblance in certain "characteristics" the term "classing" together will be misleading. It has in fact led to confusion and to many arguments due to the participants thinking of different things. In my study of kinship terms specially and also of social relationship terms, I have found it convenient to use the expression "lumping" in place of "classing" in such cases. An example is noted below.

In early Roman society, the patrilineal family, of an extended type was the most important unit. After it came the gens, or clan, a wider patrilineal group. The family was patriarchal, the head of it having absolute control over its members, which included wife, sons, unmarried daughters and grandsons among others. They were his heirs in case of intestacy. The married daughter belonged to another family (see Barreat 1811). The mother's family of birth was different and her married sister belonged to still another family. Relations on the father's side were important. His brother (FB) is *patruus;* the sister (FS) is *amita.* The mother's brother being a male had a definite status in his father's patriarchal family and hence he is described by reference to the male head of the mother's natal family, the mother's father who was termed *avus*. He could not be described as a relation of the mother who had now become agnatic kin of the father. The son of this head, the *avus*, was referred to by the diminitive *avunculus* to indicate his juniority to the *avus* in generation. The mother's sister had no such position like her brother, and went elsewhere on marriage and only her relation through the mother is casually indicated by use of the term *matertera*. She could not be referred to in terms of the *avus*, as she was, when grown up, a married woman who was a member of her husband's family of birth. The father's brother's son was of the same patriarchal group and is clearly distinguished by the descriptive expression *patrui filius* or *frater patruelis*. The father's sister's son was *amitae filius* or *amitinus*. But the son of the mother's brother and of the mother's sister are both *consobrinus*. In Low Latin, it became *cosinus* and the French and English terms "cousin" originated from it. Now the *cousins german* i.e. the children of two brothers were debarred in marriage. So the use of the term *frater* for *patrui filius* is in order. At one time, none of the children of brothers and sisters could marry, not even their children. But this rule was later relaxed. What is of interest is that the son of the father's brother is clearly described. He has been and is still of the same patriarchal family. The father's sister was a member of it but has now gone to another family by marriage. So her children are described and distinguished in term of herself. But the mother's brother and mother's sister have never been of this family. The mother's brother is referred to by a term mentioning the family head of their natal family; the sister of the mother is merely referred to as a relative through the mother. Their children are "lumped" together as "consobrinus." The term "cosinus" was therefore a term of "lumping" and not "classing" relatives.

Radcliffe-Brown (1941) has stated that the term "cousin" is applied to children of "uncle" and "aunt" and that the common term owes its origin as such to the fact that (in England, France and Germany) a man or woman inherits equally from father's brother, father's sister, mother's brother and mother's sister. The statement is incomplete and the rights are conditional. Such inheritance occurs, or used to occur a century ago from an aunt only when the woman dies or died intestate, without leaving behind her husband and/or child. For a man the child or the father, if alive, takes precedence (see Paterson

1865). The nature of the determinant postulated by Radcliffe-Brown is therefore not one which is absolute but which operates only in special circumstances. Is this an adequate kind of determinant? Among the Romans if a man died intestate, without children, his brothers and unmarried sisters inherited the property. Marriage of the sister later did not deprive her of her share. But the children of the brother and sister did not on account of the conditional right to inherit have a common term. This right was not therefore a strong determinant of terms. Among Santals, the brother's sons inherit in the absence of a man's son, even though there is a daughter (unless a bequest of some property in the life-time of the testator in the presence of agnates is arranged). But a son is Kora, a daughter is Kuṛi, while the son's son and the daughter's son are both goṛom Kora and the girl children of children are goṛom Kuṛi. A brother's son is also Kora and his son goṛom Kora. There is no distinction although rights to inherit differ. On the other hand, among north Indian Hindus, a daughter inherits in the absence of a son in preference to brother's son. The daughter's son is described as "born of daughter" and son's son as "born of son." Both are referred to as grandsons in common speech. The brother's son is "son of brother" and his son "born of son of brother" but is also referred to as a "grandson." The Roman and Hindu Indian data and the Santal data, suggest that a right to inherit indirectly only in certain conditions does not necessarily affect kinship terms. It is suggested that the lack of function that led to the children of the mother's brother and mother's sister being lumped as "consobrinus" led also to the children of the "patruus" and "amita" to be brought under the same category as the patriarchal character of the family was lost in Aryanised Western Europe. They were all lumped under the term "cousin." The father's brother had a specific position in the patriarchal family; when he lost his functional importance he was lumped with the other relative of the same degree, the mother's brother, who was in the Aryan language the "uncle." He was honoured in the primitive Teuton society which had been Aryanised. But this had no basis in law, and succession among these people was through males. When land came into individual ownership, brothers and their sons had priority over sisters and their children. Matriliny cannot however be put forward as the reason for the Latin term for mother's brother being used later as a general term of relatives of the previous generation. The term "aunt" and "tante" for the corresponding women relatives are derived from amita applied to the father's sister in Roman society, and are not derived from the Mother's sister matertera. Subsequently when the brothers as well as sisters in Western European society obtained equal rights, the use of the terms uncle and aunt for the brother and sister of parents, and of the term cousin for their children was perpetuated. Even so, cousins as well as uncles and aunts have no function in ordinary day to day social life. It is true cousins are marriageable; but there is no preferential mating. A mere permissive rule does not determine terminology. The husband of the father's sister as also of the mother's sister are also termed uncle. Similarly the father's brother's wife and the mother's brother's wife are aunts. It is true that it is explained, in case the exact nature of relationship is enquired, that they are "uncles by marriage" or "aunts by marriage." But they are not referred to by terms with the addition of in-law as for the brother and sister, and father and mother, of husband and wife. The terms uncle and aunt have been extended to these relatives by marriage because of the original lack of direct function of the genealogically related uncles and aunts. The use of these terms, it should be remembered, dates from a number of centuries past.

As a contrast to this type of kinship system with lack of differentiation of cousins may be noted the case of North Indian Indo-Aryan speaking Hindus and South Indian Hindus who are speakers of Dravidian languages. All cousins of first and second degree are definitely debarred in marriage in North India and some even more distantly related are thus excluded. They are all referred to by terms used for brother and sister. In the southern area, children of a brother and a sister are preferential mates and refer to each other by terms meaning "marriage mates." Parallel cousins are however tabooed in marriage; they are termed "brother" and "sister."

One important point has to be stressed here. It has already been noted that the expression f (l, s), can be expanded to an effective first term and to succeeding terms showing only attenuated trends of the first term, the strength of the same falling off rapidly after the second. For, the kinship and social relationship terms are affected only when there is frequent contact in the course of social (including family) life. The limits of frequent contact are usually set by the geographical limit of the settlement and the limit of integration of the social group in a given area and culture. For simple people at a very primitive level of material culture, with social cooperation limited only to close relatives, the contact will be effective for a small number of families. For people living in larger settlements with better material resources (for large settlements require better food supply, for example) the limits will be extended to a wider social group. If overflow of a settlement occurs due to over-population, and a daughter settlement is formed by some of these out-going families, but a close link is maintained with the older settlement, then the terms of kinship will be extended in certain respects to this area as well. They will now include a social relationship. As noted before, the degree of integration is an important factor in these cases. The unilateral stress that led to the formation of the clan and the use of kinship terms like "brother" extended to clansmen, and exogamy of clan are recognised examples of this widening of the sphere of kinship term and function in an integrated large social group. Where the integrating factors are not so strong or disappear, the limits of such extension should tend to shrink. Examples are available of such change. A more detailed discussion of this point is postponed to the more comprehensive study of this topic, mentioned at the beginning of this paper.

NOTES

[1] Chattopadhyay (1922). This was, I believe, the first study of documented change in kinship terms with function.

The abbrevations used in this paper are as follows: F *for* father, M *for* mother, Z *for* son, D *for* daughter, B *for* brother, S *for* sister, H *for* husband and W *for* wife. The letter 'e' indicates elder and the letter 'y' younger. Thus eBW stands for elder brother's wife.

[2] The term "kinship equation' has been used by me in my lectures to my students since 1924 in preference to "kinship identity". The reasons stated for this distinction, as elaborated then, are also noted in this paper.

REFERENCES

BARREAT, B., 1811, 'The Twelve Tables of Rome', *Introductory Discourse in the translation of Code Napoleon*. London.

CHATTOPADHYAY, K. P., 1922, 'Kinship and levirate in India', *Man*.
1927, 'Social Organisation of Satakarnis and Sungas', *Journal of the Asiatic Society of Bengal*.

KROEBER, A. L., 1909. 'Classificatory System of relationship', the *Journ. of the Royal Anthrop. Institute*, Vol. 39.

MAN, E. H., 1932, *On the Aboriginal Inhabitants of the Andaman Islands*. London.

MORGAN, L. H., 1877, *Ancient Society*. New York.

PATERSON, J., 1865, *A Compendium of England and Scotch Law*. London.

RADCLIFFE-BROWN, A. R., 1922, *The Andaman Islanders*. Cambridge.

1941, 'The Study of Kinship Systems', the *Jour. of the Royal Anthrop. Institute*, Vol. 71.

RIVERS, W. H., R., 1913, *Kinship and Social Organisation*. London.

19

ON CLASSIFICATION OF FAMILY STRUCTURES

RAMKRISHNA MUKHERJEE

Dimension: Kinship Composition

I

IN THE light of empirically observed variations in the composition of the "family" as a societal unit, the classification of family structures has been standardized for a long time and this has led to scheduled scheme/schemes of classification which are found in textbooks on social anthropology and sociology. They have also proved their usefulness to research workers in these two branches of social science. But with the ever-accumulating data in this respect from different societies, with the significant details of variation observed in recent times in a particular society in course of intensive investigations, as well as in consequence of conceptual refinements current in social anthropology and sociology these days, the previously scheduled classificatory scheme/schemes are proving to be increasingly inadequate. Frequently, therefore, social scientists are found now-a-days, especially in India, to evolve their own schemes of classification in relation to their study of specific societies. Also revision, elaboration, or rejection of one or more facets of the standardized schemes of family structure classification are being discussed among them.

Against this background, an attempt is being made by the writer to evolve a comprehensive scheme of classification of family-units by treating them as constituting a system of variation and, accordingly, by taking into account (or, at least, by keeping room for taking into account) all possible variations in intra-family relations in respective units. Apropos, in whichever way the "family" may be defined, since one feature of this societal entity remains constant as forming distinct *kingroups* differentiated from one another by one or more para-familial attributes like commensality, co-residence, etc., the classification of family structures may be based, primarily, on inter-family variations in the characteristics of kinship and affinal relations (shortly, kinship relations), provided the kinship terms can be interpreted as "egocentric" and not as "sociocentric." (Service 1960: 752-754).

Such a classificatory arrangement may be found useful to the examination of the family as a social institution. For, firstly, whatever may be the para-familial attributes and their interpretation and supplementary conditions necessary to define the "family" and demarcate the family-units, "the organized, purposeful system of human effort and achievement" (Malinowski 1944:51) depicted by the institution in question embodies certain rules and regulations of mutual privileges and obligations (of rights and duties) between respective family members. Secondly, while these rules and regulations may vary from one society to another or within the same society in the time perspective, they are invariably expressed through the kinship relations a family-unit is involved with. And, thirdly, even if some or all the kinship relations in a family-unit are putative (instead of being real), they do not qualitatively alter the situation under reference.

In the ultimate analysis, therefore, what is required is to record the specific features of each and every individual intra-family relation of kinship and affinity as contained in respect family-units. But the number of intra-family relations within the units may be many, and it is likely to be at the same time a largely variable quantity between the units. For, if n be the number of kins and affines contained in any family-unit, and if n for the group of family-units under analysis ranges between 4 and 10, say, the number of intra-family relations f to be examined for different family-units would vary from 6 to 45; f being equal to $\frac{n(n-1)}{2}$. Unless, therefore, the sample of family-units to be studied is very small indeed, it may not be feasible to classify them according to all the features each and every one of their intra-family relations depicts.

There is also the point, perhaps more important than the one above, that to enumerate *all possible* characteristics of kinship and affinal relations within the bounds of family-units is practically an impossible task. At any rate, researches into the family as a social institution has hardly come up to that stage yet. On either count, therefore, a scheme of classification may be so designed that it would incorporate within one or another of its dimensions all possible features of intra-family relations as have already been found to be distinctive or may be found to be worthy of consideration in the immediate future. So that, unless the features brought out in future require an altogether different classificatory scheme, all of them may be eventually located at specific positions within the scheme in operation through successive orders of classification.

Pursuantly, at the first stage of evolving a comprehensive classification of family structures, the intra-family relations may be grouped under a number of broad categories as appropriate to the study of the family as a social institution and as required for a particular course of analysis. For instance, in the light of the nature of privileges and obligations (or rights and duties) between respective family members, the relation of kinship or affinity between any two persons in a family-unit can be classified under one of the following five categories. Namely: (1) *conjugal*, between husband and wife; (2) *parental-filial* (shortly, *parental*) between father and/or mother, on the one hand, and son and/or daughter, on the other; (3) *sibling*, between brothers and/or sisters; (4) *lineal*, between those related by common descent from the same ancestor as traced through males and/or females, excluding those related by parental or sibling relation; and (5) *affinal*, between those related through the spouse of one or both of them. These categories, then, would represent distinct types of kinship or affinal relation; all, some, or only one, of which may be relevant to the formation of a particular family-unit.

It would be noticed that in current practice this aspect of inter-family variations is brought into account for the major classification of family structures, and the categories distinguished thereby are usually labelled as *family types*, viz. elementary family, joint family, etc. Now-a-days, however, for many societies these broad categories of family types are found to be inadequate, and so they are often revised or amplified in the light of the objective of a specific study. Sometimes, on the other hand, such intrinsic variations are ignored so as to "fit" the kinship composition of the family-units under examination with the standard categories. It may be useful, therfore, to consider the desired alterations or the required specifications within a logically consistent framework; so that the various classificatory arrangements attempted in present times in this context are eventually made uniform and become more precise and efficient.

What is required accordingly is a successively detailed examination of family-units in terms of who as kins and/or affines compose these units, what are the specific categories of intra-family relations they depict with reference to as fine a distinction drawn between them as necessary, etc. The kinship composition of family-units thus becomes a major dimension of family structure classification.

The same kind of kinship relation in a family-unit may vary by degrees, and such variations may have a significant bearing upon the operation of the family as a social institution. For example, there may be two family-units comprising an "uncle" from the paternal side in each; but the two "uncles" may be distinguished from each other as "father's brother" in one and as "father's father's brother's son" in the other. Such features of intra-family relations would also require examination for the classification of family structures; but they point to a different dimension, viz. the matrix formation of family-units, as has been indicated earlier (Mukherjee 1959 : 133-140).

Likewise, another dimension of family structure classification may deserve notice as dealing with inter-family variations due to the inner mechanism of family-units. Such as: (1) complexities in intra-family relations because of the presence of step-relationship within a family-unit, for example; (2) partial disintegration of intra-family relations within a unit because of the absence, in full or in part, of one or more of its constituent cohorts (as for example, a unit composed of "grandparents" and "grandchildren" only); etc. This dimension of family structure classification may be labelled as cohort composition of family-units; the term cohort being employed to group those family members among whom sexual relation exists, is permitted, or at least tolerated in society, in contradistinction to their relations with the remaining members of the unit. For the above and the allied characteristics of kinship and affinal relations in a family-unit evolve entirely, or at any rate essentially, out of the formation of cohorts in the process of its structural ramification; and, therefore, the number and the quantitative and qualitative composition of the cohorts as well as the fact of their presence or not in the unit while being involved in the formation of a family have significant bearings on the aspects of variation represented by this dimension.

Either of the above two dimensions of family structure classification, however, is beyond the scope of the present paper. It will deal with the dimension of kinship composition of family-units only.

II

For the identification of family types according to the broad categories of kinship and affinal relations the family-units are involved with, the role of the two categories labelled as "parental" and "lineal" is not doubted by the general run of social scientists. Also, in this respect, the role of the category labelled as "affinal" is implicitly accepted; although not stated explicitly for all cases, as will be pointed out in due course. And the decidedly ancillary role of the category labelled as "sibling" is, likewise, not commonly denied. Controversies, however, are there among sociologists as to the distinguishing properties of the category labelled as "conjugal" in connection with the formation of distinct family types according to the kinship composition of family-units.

For instance, to Ogburn and Nimkoff the basic condition for the formation of a family-unit is that it represents conjugal and/or parental relation, while to Murdock it is the simultaneous existence of conjugal and parental relations that is of decisive importance in defining a "family":

"When we think of a family we picture it as a more or less durable association of husband and wife with or without children, or of man or woman alone, with children." (Ogburn and Nimkoff 1953: 459)

"The family is a social group consisting of two or more adults of different sex who are married to one another, and of one or more children, own or adopted, of the married parents. It is to be distinguished alike from marriage, the social relationship uniting the parents of opposite sex, and from the household, the social group occupying a dwelling or other domicile. Hence, strictly speaking, a married but childless couple or a widowed or divorced parent with children may form a household but not a family." (Murdock et al 1950: 86).

Such viewpoints, however, tend to undermine somewhat the relevance of specific intra-family relations to the organization of a family-unity. For if a unit is composed of a cohort only, it does not indicate merely an inter-sex grouping provided with the privileges and rights of conjugal relation. It also indicates the *de juré* acceptance by the cohort of obligations and duties in regard to "setting up a family", viz. their potential responsibility towards children, own or adopted, who may eventually appear. Therefore, in terms of possible intra-family relations within a unit, there are valid reasons to consider only a childless couple as a variant of family structures.

Under the same terms of reference, it is equally important to differentiate a childless couple from a couple with children, for in the latter situation the acceptance of parental obligations and duties by the couple is established *de facto*. And, following logically, where the conjugal relation is cut short and the parental relation is impaired by half, the unit should neither be rejected as beyond the sphere of a family structure classification nor be equated to a childless couple or to a couple with children as classified according to *possible* (and not *existing*) intra-family relations in a unit.

Hence, for the classification of family structures according to the possible intra-family relations in the units, it may be considered justified to have a category of family-units which represent only one set of conjugal relation in each and no other intra-family relations.

When the above category represents a cohort which has not yet produced or adopted any child, it may be labelled as a *nascent family;* nascent because a full-fledged family with children has not yet been established but its potentiality is there.

Such a cohort-unit is, evidently, different from that which had produced or adopted children but they are not to be taken into account as components of the kingroup in question as they may have set up "family-units" of their own, or are dead, or have removed themselves in any other way from the kingroup under reference. Therefore, if this difference should be stressed, the latter type of cohort-units may be designated in terms of disintegration of an "elementary" family with the "parents" present and the "children" absent. Or, pursuing further the logic of such a classification, these cohort-units may be examined in the light of disintegration of family-units belonging to other family types as well.

Accordingly, in addition to locating the cohort-units in the dimension of kinship composition of family-units, the process of classification would bring in the other two dimensions of family structure classification. Alternatively, all types of cohort-units may be amalgamated under the label of *conjugal unit* irrespective of their previous background. For all of them represent only one set of conjugal relation each; and none of them give in their present composition any indication of other categories of kinship and affinal relation which may have disintegrated with respect to the kingroups under reference.[1]

Since cohort-units are seldom found in so large a number for any course of study as to make them amenable to classification in further details,[2] the category of conjugal unit may be adopted from purely operational considerations. But the possibility of a detailed classification, in case the obtained sample of cohort-units (for example) would permit the attempt, should be borne in mind; while the concept of nascent family should be regarded, schematically at any rate, to indicate a significant stage in the consideration of family structures in the dimension of kinship composition of family-units. For, by extension from a nascent family, that is, with the presence of unmarried children to a cohort, an *elementary family* is formed.

The definition of elementary family, as given above, would be found to differ in certain respects from some of those adopted currently. For instance, in *Notes and Querries on Anthropology* it is written (1954: 70):

"The elementary or simple family is a group consisting of a father and a mother and their children, whether they are living together or not."

Yet the distinction has been so drawn for two significant reasons. One, the unit distinguished as elementary family is involved with one set of parental relation, and may therefore be concerned with more than one father or mother, or both, provided these fathers and mothers form only one cohort and thus represent only one set of conjugal relation; for the polygamous family-units, formed by one or more cohorts, would not otherwise be distinguished properly, and an independent classification of family structures in the dimension of cohort composition of all family-units cannot be made satisfactorily. The other reason is that the unit cannot contain married "children" (whether or not the spouses of the "children" are dead or absent); for the sphere of kinship and affinal relations is then extended or intrinsically altered if more than one cohort is involved in the composition of a family-unit, leading it thereby to a false identification with a different family group, viz. the extended family, as will be indicated in due course.

The elementary family type is thus determined by its formation due to one set of conjugal plus one set of parental relation, with or without one set of sibling relation in addition.

Proceeding beyond one set of conjugal relation or the one-cohort family-units, the sphere of kinship and affinal relations within the unit is enlarged when it is involved with two or more cohorts. For it includes hereafter lineal and/or affinal relations in addition to more than one set of conjugal relation, with or without more than one set of parental and/or sibling relation. Such a unit is generally labelled as an *extended family*, the minimum condition for the existence of which is that at least two cohorts were involved (not necessarily present) in its formation.

While thus differentiating the family-units in terms of the distinct types of kinship and affinal relations they are involved with, a complementary societal unit may have to be brought under consideration which is not concerned with any one of them, including the conjugal relation; or, for that matter, with any intra-family relation at all. Yet from the negative aspect of kinship composition of a unit, it may deserve taken note of under certain circumstances. Such as the eventuality would arise when the terms of reference to the family as a societal unit, viz. the para-familial attributes employed for its identification, allow for the occurrence of one-member units in society along with the presence of family-units which must contain more than one person.

Thus, if the para-familial attributes employed to distinguish the family-units are co-residence and commensality (with or without supplementary conditions attached to them for purposes of precise identification of the units), in some situations a family-unit will equate to a household as these two para-familial attributes are the principal ones to distinguish one household from another. But in some other situations, another complimentary societal unit may emerge or may entirely hold the field; for a household may consist of, either way or simultaneously, one or more kingroups—one or more family-units and one or more such persons who are not related to any one therein as kin or affine.

In such a context as above, the complimentary societal unit

represented by an individual without any kin or affine (as for example, a servant in a "family", the unrelated boarders of a mess, etc.) may also have to be brought under examination during a course of study of family structures so as to indicate the peculiar position of such individuals in society in the light of its familial organization and operation of the family as a social institution. Therefore, whether or not this contingency exists in a specific instance, in the perspective of a comprehensive classification of family structures, such units should be included in an order of classification within the dimension of kinship composition, and may be labelled as *non-familial units* in order to differentiate them qualitatively from the family-units.[3]

Pursuantly, according to the possibility of none, one, or more than one set of conjugal relation in a unit, it can be classified as a non-familial unit, a not-extended family-unit, or an extended family-unit.

Thereafter, the non-familial units may be classified in terms of para-familial attributes, which of course do not come within the purview of the present discussion. But, in conjunction with the classificatory arrangement of the family-units, it may be found useful to note particularly their sex and marital status. For the former would have a bearing upon their non-familial existence *vis-a-vis* the operation of the family as a social institution because the relative position of males and females is not the same in many societies and/or in different societal strata; while the latter as unmarried, married but spouse absent, widowed, or divorced would indicate the potential and present role of these individuals in society in connection with its familial organization.

Of these two attributes of the non-familial units, their marital status should logically be considered in the dimension of cohort composition of family-units, as is evident from the categorization of marital status as above. Their sex, on the other hand, may be taken into account in the present dimension; for this attribute of an individual, whether or not he/she is a member of a family-unit, is implicit in the categorization of conjugal relation as well as in various terms of kinship and affinity employed to denote the kinship composition of a family-unit. Accordingly, under a relevant order of classification in the dimension of kinship composition of family-units, the non-familial units may be categorised as: (1) "male" non-familial unit and (2) "female" non-familial unit.[4]

As regards the family-units, they may be further classified in the light of specific types of intra-family relations they are involved with. Thus the not-extended family group was dichotomized into elementary or nascent/conjugal family types with reference to the respective units being involved with a set of parental relation in each one of them or not. Likewise, the extended families can be classified in terms of the lineal and/or affinal relations in them; for these two categories of intra-family relations represent their essential characteristics.

But the classification of the extended families accordingly appears to face an initial difficulty. Because within any such unit the possible sets of lineal or affinal relations may be many in number and variety, as any person in a society can have lineal and affinal relatives extending over a large and practically an indefinite sphere and any combination or selection of them for all the family members can be represented in a kingroup. Hence, the unit itself, or the family members *en bloc*, cannot give any pointer to its classification according to the nature of lineal and/or affinal relations among its constituents.

These two categories of intra-family relations, however, evolve out of the establishment of more than one set of conjugal relation in the family-units, involving them either in generational and/or lateral extension beyond those for one-cohort units or in the movement of persons belonging to more than one set of conjugal relation from one family-unit to another, or in both. Therefore, the extended family-units may be classified by examining the nature of lineal and/or affinal relations in them with respect to *any one* family member in each selected as the Ego, and in the light of a societal norm which governs the configuration of relevant extended family-units in these respects. For, as it will be demonstrated in due course, irrespective of the functional implications of such a norm, that is, by taking recourse to it as a mere tool for classification, it would be possible to ascertain the variety/varieties of lineal/affinal relations the extended families are vested with.

This method, however, raises a moot question at the outset. Namely: who should be the Ego of a family-unit out of all its members? The issue could, of course, be resolved according to a specific role devolving upon or assumed by a particular member of the family in the sacred or secular, economic or non-economic, organization of this societal unit; but such a solution may not be accepted universally. Also, for the same course of study, the specific role referred above may be different for examining the data from various perspectives.

Such as, the principal earner of a family-unit may be its suitable Ego when the perspective is the organization of family-units in terms of their economic activities, while the traditionally recognized "head" (*karta* in Indian joint families) may be the desired Ego for a family-unit if the perspective is the familial organization in terms of centralized authority in the units; and these respective roles may or may not be borne by the same person in each of the family-units under analysis.

Variability in the selection of the Ego has, therefore, to be taken as an inherent complication that may possibly occur when classifying the family-units. However, in whichever way the Ego may thus be selected for successive, supplementary, or independent studies, it should be noted that this variability will not affect the process of classification. As it can be demonstrated, it would imply, at the most, some parallel sets of analysis of a distinct group of extended family-units for their further categorization; while in some situations no additional analysis would be required, and in some others it would be possible to deduce the altered composition of the relevant family-units from certain secondary information collected and/or collated during the course of investigation and arrangement of the data preparatory to their analysis.

Hence, the question raised in connection with the selection of the Ego can be safely by-passed while constructing a model for the classification of family structures. What is required to note in this context is that the Ego-ship of family-units will have to be determined in one way or another; in the last resort, by selecting any one member of a family-unit as such at random.

In current practice, however, the need for thus selecting the Ego for the classification of extended family-units is not so explicitly stated, although its implicit acceptance is almost invariably demonstrated. For instance, to quote again from *Notes and Querries on Anthropology* (1954: 72):

"A group may be described as a *joint family* when two or more lineally related kinsfolk of the same sex, their spouse and offspring, occupy a single homestead and are jointly subject to the same authority or single head. The term *extended family* should be used for the dispersed form corresponding to a joint family."

Here, evidently, the distinction could not be drawn between the family-units labelled as "joint" and those labelled as "extended" unless one member in each of these units was regarded as its Ego. For, in accordance with the two attributes employed above in order to denote the nature of integration of the family members, if the Ego's lineage is patrilineal and the Ego is a male or an unmarried female, the members of a "joint family" can be no other person than those males and unmarried females who belong to the Ego's line of descent and succession and those married females who are wives of the relevant male members. And if the Ego is a married female, the membership of a "joint family" will be restricted to those males and unmarried females who belong to the Ego's husband's line of descent and succession and those married females who are wives of the respective male members. Likewise, if the societal norm of descent and succession is matrilineal, the same conditions as the above will hold good provided in the aforesaid formulation "male" is substituted by "female", "wife" by "husband", and *vice versa.*

So that the categorization of the 1+ cohort-constituent family-units under the suggested label "extended", in contradistinction to the label "joint", depends upon any variation found in the kinship composition of the units in question from their prescribed constitution; and whether or not any such variation is there can be brought to light only by examining the stipulated attributes of classification with reference to any one member of each of these units selected as its Ego.

If, however, instead of merely an implicit acceptance, the concept of Ego-ship was deliberately employed for the classification of 1+ cohort-constituent family-units, several family types distinguished from one another by significant characteristics of their kinship composition would be elicited. This will be demonstrated in the following pages; but, prior to that, it would be desirable, and probably also of intrinsic interest, to examine the merits of the recommended dichotomous classification of the 1+ cohort-constituent family-units as "joint" or "extended."

For, as stated in the definitions of the above two family types, the process of classification is based on two attributes of social organization; viz. (a) the lineage-affiliation of the members of a unit and (b) their place of residence. Therefore, when in terms of the stipulated definition of the "family" the two attributes are the same for all the individuals under reference, that is, all of them belong to the same lineage and they live together, the unit should be labelled as "joint family"; whereas the "extended family" type would comprise such corresponding units in which either or both the attributes differ, that is, (a) lineage-affiliation is not the same but co-residence is maintained, (b) lineage-affiliation is the same but co-residence is not maintained, or (c) lineage-affiliation is not the same and co-residence is not maintained.

The "extended family" type thus becomes a residual group of heterogenous characteristics, while the stipulation of the attribute of co-residence may even forbid the application of this process of classification to family-units defined and mutually distinguished as kingroups *in all possible ways*.

It is necessary, therefore, to withdraw the restriction of co-residence from a comprehensive scheme of classification of family structures in order to make the process of classification amenable to all possible definitions of the "family" as mutually distinct kingroups; and it is also necessary to bear in mind that the attribute of lineage-affiliation of the family members would, thereafter, distinguish the 1+ cohort-constituent family-units as "joint" or "extended" only if the societal norm is patrilineage or matrilineage. For if this societal norm refers to a different structural arrangement, viz. *double descent, indirect descent, sex-linked descent,* etc., the cohesiveness of the members of family-units in terms of their lineage-affiliation cannot be denoted precisely.

It may, of course, be argued that under such a situation there would be no point in examining the cohesiveness of the family members in terms of the attribute under consideration, as its defined characteristics in this case preclude such an examination. But, all the same, the fact remains that, as based on the attribute of lineage-affiliation of family-members, all these family-units also will have to be categorised as "extended" according to the stipulated definition of this family type; making it a mixed bag of kinship composition as, on the one hand, due to deviations from the specific characteristics of the relevant societal norm in some cases and as, on the other, due to these very specific characteristics of the relevant societal norm in some others.

Thus the group labelled as "extended family" in *Notes and Querries on Anthropology* remains of heterogenous consistency, and so its further categorization would be desirable. At the same time, for cogent reasons, any other process of classification advocated instead should not be inconsistent with those currently adopted; of which the one discussed above deserves particular attention. Therefore, under the circumstances, it may be justified to suggest such an attribute of classification as would successfully dovetail those in practice while furnishing the desired categorization of family-units concurrently. One such attribute may be the societal norm of "locality", instead of "lineage", with respect to the affiliation of individuals in a society to respective family-units.

For, in whichever way the "family" may be defined and the family-units identified as mutually distinct kingroups, marriage as a stable union of persons of two sexes remains as the pre-requisite to setting up a "family" or in extending an existing one; and this institution involves in virtually all societies the post-marriage movement of the bride or the bridegroom, or of both, from his/her or of the couple's pre-marital residence. Accordingly, customary norms have developed in societies in terms of which either the bridegroom or the bride or both should move to the residence of kins or affines of these persons or they should form a new residence of their own. Hence, where the norm specifies a new residence or that of a definite kin or affine, as is found in the large majority of societies, the "legitimate" kinship composition of the extended family-units can be precisely enumerated. Also where the selection of the residence of the kins or affines of the bride and the bridegroom is a random proposition, a specific designation can be given to the extended family-units thus formed in those societies.

Rarely, of course, deviations are found in this respect; and neither the bride nor the bridegroom moves from respective natal "locality"; as reported to have been the custom for the Nayars of India or the Ashantis of Africa, for instance. But there, again, the structure of the family organization in terms of the specific characteristics of the societal norm of locality can be strictly specified.

So that, even though the attribute of co-residence may not be relevant to the general scheme of classification of family structures for reasons mentioned before, in terms of the societal norm of locality the possibly varied kinship composition of family-units can be precisely stated; and on that basis each and every family-unit in all societies may be classified, although the process of classification would be particularly relevant to the more than one cohort-constituent family-units.

Therefore, even if it is found to be appropriate only schematically, and not as depicting the actual situation because co-residence may not be an attribute employed for identifying the family-units, the norm of locality would give a more comprehensive classification of the 1+ cohort-constituent family-units than the norm of lineage can; while, as will be shown below, such a classification will simultaneously take into account their classification as "joint" or not in terms of the attribute of lineage as patrilineal or matrilineal. Hence, following the proposed arrangement, the usual classification of the "extended families" will not be disturbed in any way.

Incidentally, there is the point that in the light of the norm of locality the kinship composition of family-units may indicate specific features of family organization in particular societies. Therefore, if the extended families, which are directly concerned with such an organization, can be precisely classified according to the norm of locality, they will indicate the cohesiveness of the family members from an important aspect of family organization in society.

Additionally, this classificatory arrangement will bring out such characteristics of the family-units as may be of significant sociological interest. For instance, while examining the institutional characteristics of the family as conforming to or deviating from a societal norm, the attribute of locality is likely to have much more relevance these days than that of lineage. Because, in the unit-composition of family, deviations from the former are frequently observed in many societies these days, while violation of the latter is seldom met with.

Admittedly, variations in the line of descent and succession among family-units may occur in some societies, and especially in those where the societal norm or the traditional usage used to be a line of descent and succession other than patrilineal and which is gradually changing to patriliny. Evidence is there to show that in some such societies where everyone had previously traced the descent matrilineally or bilaterally, some individuals (whatever may be their relative number in respective societies) are now reckoning their descent and succession patrilineally, and this change is not resented in the *milieu* (Eggan 1960: 37, 61, 85, 91, 92, &c.).

The upshot is that in such societies family-units may be found which are entirely patrilineal/matrilineal or bilateral. Accordingly, a distinct order of classification of family structures in terms of lineage-affiliation of the members of family-units may be called for under special circumstances.[5]

But it is equally true that, in general, the societal norm of lineage suffers seldom from any deviation. For it usually has several very serious economic and spiritual implications in society; such as the devolution of family property. Therefore, this rarely variable attribute need not form the basis for a classification of the extended families in societies at large.

Contrariwise, if it is borne in mind that (a) the respective configurations of "joint family" according to patrilineage and matrilineage can also be obtained in terms of the societal norm of locality while with respect to other types of lineage the classification cannot be pursued satisfactorily or at all, and (b) the phenomenon of finding such members in family-units as do not correspond to the norm of locality of that society has become and is becoming so frequent these days that in the light of possible and probable variants to the "normal" family types, the term family is now frequently referred, operationally at any rate, to a co-resident and commensal kingroup,[6] the argument in favour of selecting the norm of locality instead of that of lineage affiliation for the classification of the extended family-units becomes very forceful.

To consider, hence, the attribute of locality for the classification of family structures, the following seven types have been brought under examination as found in Murdock's *Social Structure*, and the eighth as illustrated by the peculiar organization of the Nayars' *taravad*. Needless to say, others could also be considered in the light of still recent formulations of locality types (cf. Barnes 1960: 850-866, &c.). But, as it will be evident in course of the present discussion, they can be treated in the same way as shown for these eight types.

For two of them represent the permanent post-marriage movement of the consort/consorts of a particular sex (patrilocal and matrilocal); two others the permanent post-marriage movement of the consorts of both sexes (neolocal and avunculocal); one the post-marriage movement of one sex at a time in either of the two specific phases of residential change in their family life (matri-patrilocal); two of the remaining ones the post-marriage movement of either sex as succeedingly temporary measures or permanently with respect to a bride or a bridegroom (bilocal and alternating); and the last one no post-mairiage movement of either sex, as with respect to the Nayar *taravad* (natolocal). Thus the eight cases may be regarded as sufficiently complicated to provide the *modus operandi* for similarly classifying the extended family-units according to any other norm of locality.

Apropos, the eight types of locality are enumerated below:

(1) *Neolocal* = a new residence altogether set up by a member or cohort of the unit, which does not belong to any other family member and these kinsfolk have no *customary right* to live there.

(2) *Patrilocal* = male ancestral house for the males and unmarried females, and husband's male ancestral house for the married females.

(3) *Matrilocal* = female ancestral house for the females and unmarried males, and wife's female ancestral house for married males.

(4) *Avunculocal* = father's mother's brother's house for the unmarried males and females, mother's brother's house for the married males, and husband's mother's brother's house for the married females.

(5) *Matri-patrilocal* = "patrilocal" residence for the unmarried males and females, wife's mother's house for the newly-married males and mother's house for the newly-married females for one year or until the birth of the first child, and then as "patrilocal" residence for the married males and females.

(6) *Bilocal* = either "patrilocal" or "matrilocal" residence for the family members.

(7) *Alternating* = sometimes "patrilocal" and sometimes "matrilocal" residence for the family members under specific clauses.

(8) *Natolocal* (*taravad*) = mother's residence for all family members irrespective of their sex and marital status.

Of these, the definition of neolocal residence as a societal norm may appear as too categorical. But it should be borne in mind that if any family member is vested with customary right to a particular place of residence, neolocal residence cannot be maintained as a consistent phenomenon in society. For it will eventually lead to a norm of locality defined by the customary right to the place of residence of several kinship constituents of relevant family-units. Therefore, with respect to extended family-units, neolocal residence as a specific societal norm becomes an illogical proposition; while the non-familial units or the not-extended family-units can logically conform to it.

Quite contrary to the societal norm of neolocal residence, bilocal or alternating norm of residence connotes a situation in which any kin or affine of a person can be a legitimate member of his/her family-unit. Under these two norms of locality, therefore, the extended families may assume a character which was best described by Rivers as *kindred*; a term which may be retained in order to denote a variant of the extended family against two specific norms of locality (Rivers 1932: 16).

As regards the other six norms of locality, with respect to each one of them the "legitimate" members of a family-unit can be specifically denoted. This statement, again, may appear as dogmatic. But it can be easily seen that if these norms are consistently observed, they cannot but strictly delimit the sphere of kinship composition of the family-units. Therefore, with reference to these norms of locality, the possible coverage of family-units in terms of their kinship composition can be specified exactly.

For this purpose, a phrase *kinship constituent* may be coined in order to classify the family members according to their kinship or affinal relations with the Ego of the Unit. So that an enumeration of the legitimate kinship constituents to a family-unit may denote its kinship composition with respect to a specific norm of locality while avoiding the complications arising from the varying kinship and affinal relations the legitimate family members may have mutually within the unit. Apropos, the legitimate kinship composition of family-units under different norms of locality are given by the following formulae which incorporate all possible kinship notation-series depicting the prescribed kinship constituents of family-units under respective norms.

The formulae have been prepared under the following conditions:

(1) The kinship notation-series are composed of the occurrence, repetition, or rejection of the following kinship notations; viz. F for father, M for mother, B for brother, S for sister, Z for son, D for daughter, H for husband, and W for wife.

(2) Where a notation has to be qualified by the marital status of the kinship constituent concerned, the following subscripts have

been employed; viz. u for unmarried, m for married, w for widowed, d for divorced, and s for separated.

(3) In order that all relevant kinship notation-series with respect to the Ego can be constructed, the kinship notations have been primarily classified within brackets, showing thereby the distinct components of the formulae. The sequential order of the components in the formulae must be maintained for the enumeration of the kinship constituents under different norms of locality.

(4) If under a particular norm of locality a specific component of the relevant formula is obligatory for the enumeration of legitimate kinship constituents, it has been mentioned in the appropriate place. Otherwise, the components of the formulae, except the first one in each of them, may be present in toto, in part, or may not be present at all, in order to depict the notation-series of the legitimate kinship constituents under respective norms.

(5) The first component of each formula is obligatory; for it gives, as required: (a) the Ego's (E) sex as male ($\triangle$) or female (O), and his/her marital status; and (b) the notation of Ego's immediate relative through whom the other legitimate constituents of the family may have to be traced.

(6) In all components, dots . . . after a notation indicate that in a notation-series it may occur any number of times consecutively; strokes / between notations indicate that they may occur in combination or separately even without the presence of some of them; and commas , between notations indicate that they may occur only once and not in any combination.

In addition to the above conditions, it should be noted that complications may arise if divorced or separated persons are found to be the Ego or members of extended families or involved in the presence of some family members traced through them (such as their progeny—all or some and young or adult). For custom and/or law may vary from one society to another as to whether they should be regarded as members of a particular extended family or not. Such as, should a divorced or separated Hindu woman be considered as a legitimate member of her father's patrilineal-patrilocal extended family? Therefore, the presence of such persons in a unit as its legitimate members or not will have to be decided in accordance with respective social usages, and cannot be indicated in any general formula. The problem, however, may not seriously affect the usefulness of the formulae given below. For in any society the number of persons living as divorced or separated, or being involved as such in the composition of family-units, are few; and of them those concerned with extended families are fewer.

Subject to the aforesaid limitation, the general formulae to ascertain the legitimate constituents of family-units under respective norms of locality are as follows:

1. Neolocal: $(E_u F/M, E_{mwds})$ (H, W, Z_u, D_u),
   where $E = E_\triangle H/E_o W$, $F = EFH/EMH$,
   $M = EFW/EMW$,
   $B_u = EFZ_u/EMZ_u$, and
   $S_u = EFD_u/EMD_u$.

2. Patrilocal: $(E_{\triangle, o_u}, E_{o_{mw}} H)$ (F . . . /B/Z . . .)
   (also
   patrilineal) (M. W, S_u, D_u).

3. Matrilocal: $(E_{\triangle_u, o}, E_{\triangle_{mw}} W)$ (M . . . /S/D . . .)
   (also
   matrilineal) (F, H, B_u, Z_u).

4. Avunculocal: $(E_u F, E_{\triangle_{mwds}}, E_{o_{mw}} H)$ (M) (M . . . /S/D . . .)
   (B_{mwds}, Z_{mwds}) (W, Z_u, D_u),

   where, unless the notation-series contains only the first component, one of the last two components must occur in it; but the fourth cannot occur without the second.

5. Matri-patrilocal: (I) If the Ego is a permanent member of the unit, and is not living temporarily as a newly-married person:

   $(E_{\triangle, o_u}, E_{o_{mw}} H)$ (F . . . /B/Z . . .)
   (M, W, S, D) (H);
   or

   (II) If the Ego is a temporary member of the unit as a newly-married person:

   $(E_{\triangle_{mw}} W, E_{o_{mw}})$ (F . . . /B) (Z . . . /D)
   (M, W, S) (H),

   where the second component must occur if the third is to occur in a notation-series.

6. Natolocal   (E) (M) (M . . . /S/D . . .) (B, Z),
  (*Taravad*):   where the second component is obligatory for the fourth; so that, (i) $E_{\triangle/o}B=$
EMZ, (ii) $E_oZ=EMDZ$, (iii) $E_oD=EMDD$,
and so on.

From the above formulae it is seen that under any norm of
locality (except natolocal) the one-cohort family-units would
represent "normal" family types as nascent/conjugal or elementary; whereas the 1+ cohort-constituent family-units may represent the "normal" joint family type or deviants from the "norm"
because of the presence of some such relatives of the Ego in them
who should not be there as their prescribed constituents.

As regards the exception, it is obviously due to the peculiar
family organization among the Nayars; resulting from natolocal
residence. Hence this would not affect the process of classification
in any way. For the nascent/conjugal or a "complete" elementary
family (in the sense that the parental relation is represented by
both "father" and "mother") among these people may be interpreted as formed with "extra" kins/affines of the Ego, viz. the
male or female consort/consorts of the cohort, as for other
deviants from the "norm" with respect to natolocal or other forms
of locality.

Therefore, in order to distinguish the family-units with constituent "extra" kins and/or affines in terms of the societal norm of
locality (and/or lineage as patrilineal or matrilineal) from those
which are formed with the "legitimate" constituents only in this
respect, the former may be labelled as *family complex*.

The distinction thus drawn is manifest if a family-unit is schematically considered as composed of only the first or both of the
following components. The first is the *stock* to which the Ego
obviously belongs in view of the reasons for selecting him/her as
such for the family-unit, and also those who with respect to the
Ego can claim to be its legitimate constituents in terms of the
norm of locality and/or one of the two specified lineages. The second
component, which may or may not be present in a family-unit,
may then be called *adhesions*. For it includes all those "extra" kins
or affines of the Ego who are present in the unit but as schematically
"grafted" on to its stock have deflected it from forming a "normal"
family type in terms of the attribute under reference.

Pursuantly, a family-unit composed of the stock only will be one of the nascent/conjugal, elementary, or joint type; while that composed of the stock and adhesions will be a family complex.

Among the Nayars, of course, the nascent/conjugal type of the stock is ruled out by the very nature of their norm of locality; and, for the same reason, the elementary type of stock among them can only comprise either a "mother" and her unmarried "children" or a number of unmarried siblings. Either of these two forms of organization of the stock would thus correspond to the "incomplete" elementary type (with the "father" absent or the "parents" absent) for other norms of locality, as can be deduced while examining the family-units in the dimension of their cohort-composition from the partial or full disintegration of the "parent" cohort in this way. But as only they would conform to the legitimate forms of family organization among the Nayars according to their norm of locality, the elementary type of stock among them would naturally mean only such kinship composition.

So that, for all societies the above categorization of the family-units will give their precise identification in terms of the attribute of locality and/or patrilineage of matrilineage; while it will not be affected by the variablity in the selection of the Ego, although the selection is necessary for the process of classification. The omnibus category of the "extended family" according to the previously discussed dichotomy of the 1+ cohort-constituent family-units may thus be avoided for those societies where the norm is not patrilineage or matrilineage; while the category of family complex would not be contrary to the distinction made as "joint" or not for those societies where the norm is partilineage or matrilineage.

The classification of family-units, as elicited above, may have a significant bearing on studies of the family in specific societies. For the bulk of the Indian people, for instance, the importance of examining the kinship composition of the family-units in such details is obvious. Because although the patrilineal-patrilocal joint family system is regarded as the traditional norm among them, in their society/societies it is not at all uncommon to find nascent/conjugal, elementary, or joint family-units (and even the Ego alone) with agnates like widowed daughters and/or sisters to the man/men of the stock. Since such persons (with or without their children) could not be, or probably were not, provided for in their husbands' kingroups.

Similarly, it is not infrequently found in India that a family-unit contains such "extra" affinal-agnatic kinsfolk as are from the side of the "wife/wives" of the man/men of the stock; as for example, the presence of wife's brother, father's brother's wife's sister, etc., to the Ego in a Hindu or Moslem family of patrilineal-patrilocal stock. And equally likely it is to find "extra" agnatic-affinal kinsfolk in such a family-unit; as for example, sister's husband, mothers brothers wife, etc., to the Ego.

Hence, whether or not the resulting peculiar composition of the family-units illustrated above is due to the disintegration (temporary or permanent) of some family-units (usually of the joint variety) but not the growth of new ones instead, for a structural-functional analysis of the family as a social institution a classification of the family-units as nascent/conjugal, elementary, or joint, or as family complex, may be of some significant importance.

Furthermore, it may be worth bearing in mind that in societies where a non-obligatory custom may lead to the incorporation of "extra" kinsfolk in some but not all the family-units of, say, patrilocal or matrilocal stock, this form of classification receives added importance. For instance, it was often found in the wealthy families of Bengal, though rare now-a-days, that following the custom of *gharjamai* the sons-in-law lived in the fathers-in-law's families and thus formed the patrilineal-patrilocal joint family complex with "extra" agnatic-affinal kinsfolk grafted on to the stock of these units. Also when *kulinism* was prevalent in Bengal (up to the last century), it was not uncommon to find families of well-to-do Brahmins with married daughters and their children residing with the patrilocal stock and the *kulin* husbands visiting these grass-windows for short periods during their regular round of the fathers-in law's homes.

Likewise, in special situations as among the Nayars, it may be desirable to elicit the extent to which the organization of *taravad* is maintained; and this may be done from the relative number of family complexes found in society at any point of time or in course of an investigation in the longitudinal perspective.

For intra-society studies, therefore, the category of family complex may be regarded as worthy of taken note of.

For inter-society studies, however, this category, as such, suffers from a limitation. For, as pointed out earlier, in the case of the Nayars (or others with a similar type of locality) it may include also one-cohort family-units instead of only the 1+ cohort-constituent family-units as for the societies following other norms of locality. Further classification of this category is therefore indicated.

Moreover, this process of classification would be useful not only for such special situations as described above. For in other societies also, as corresponding to other norms of locality, it may be of significant sociological interest to elicit the deviants from the "norm" with respect to the distinct family types whose "normality" has been affected thereby; instead of merely classifying the 1+ cohort-constituent family-units as "joint" or not on account of the fact that deviations have been noticed in some of them in the light of the attribute under consideration.

For example, after stating that "nuclear" family with neolocal residence is the predominant characteristics of "American Family" today, Parsons noted: "It is of course not uncommon to find a surviving parent of one or the other spouse, or even a sibling or cousin of one of them residing with the family, but this is both statistically secondary, and it is clearly not felt to be the 'normal' arrangement" (Parsons 1956:10). In this context, therefore, it may be of significant sociological importance to identify how many American family-units are purely "nuclear", how many are "nuclear" but with one or the other of the above-mentioned adhesions, etc.; irrespective of the relative importance, numerically, of the categories of family structure classification thus being distinguished.

Also, as a corollary to the above, another situation may be taken into account. Namely, one social scientist may scrupulously consider a family-unit as representing the elementary type when it is composed of "parents"/"parent" and unmarried "child"/"children" only, while another may consider it as unnecessary hairsplitting to differentiate between a unit as above and another having, say, the widowed "sister" to the "father" as an additional family member. And still another social scientist may subscribe to either of the two views or differentiate similar units only when the adhesion is an affine like, say, "sister" to the "mother", as the norm for the society is patrilineage and patrilocality; and so on.

Thus, on account of their respective assumptions regarding the qualitative and quantitative significance of the nature of deviations from the "normal" types, the categorization of the family-units may suffer both objectively and subjectively. And the upshot would be, as is not uncommonly found from several studies, not only

diffused categorization of the family-units under their consideration, but also making the corresponding categories not strictly
comparable between their respective sets of data.

Hence, for inter-society studies, both in regard to the intrinsic
characteristcs of family organization in some societies as among
the Nayars and its overt variations as found in some others, the
family-units which are deviants from the "normal" family types
should, first, be clearly demarcated as family complexes; and, thereafter, the features of complication thus involved in their configuration should be distinguished, primarily, in accordance with the
kinship composition of their stocks.

The stock, however, as indicated earlier, can be characterized
by more than three types of its organization as nascent/conjugal,
elementary, or joint. For the concept of "extra" kins or affines
of the Ego incorporates the possibility of the Ego remaining in
the unit without any "legitimate" kin or affine. Under the circumstances, the Ego is unable to form such a sector of the unit as
may be labelled nascent/conjugal, elementary, or joint; and in
that situation he or she may be identified only as a "male" or a
"female" in order to distinguish him or her from the "extra" kins
or affines in the family-unit. Accordingly, the family complexes
with the stock represented by the Ego alone may be labelled as
"male" complex or "female" complex, respectively.[7]

Apropos, in consideration of (a) a comprehensive classification
of all units in terms of their kinship composition, (b) a logical
structural arrangement of all varieties of family-units that may
be found in societies, and (c) the sociological bearing such a classification may have as deviating from the societal norm of locality
and/or lineage as patrilineal or matrilineal, the first order of classification of family-units in the dimension of their kinship composition is proposed as follows[8]:

1. "Male" non-familial unit
2. "Female" non-familial unit
3. Nascent family/Conjugal unit
4. Elementary family
5. Joint family
6. "Male" family complex
7. "Female" family complex
8. Nascent/Conjugal family complex

9. Elementary family complex
10. Joint family complex
11. Kindred.

III

The order of classification detailed above may appear to be governed by the norm of locality in a society; and so it may be argued that if for a course of analysis of family structures this societal norm is not of intrinsic relevance, the utility of this classificatory order would suffer accordingly. It is necessary, therefore, to point out that irrespective of the role of this norm in society the proposed first order of classification would indicate precisely the kinds of lineal and affinal relations the stock of the extended families may possibly be vested with.

For instance, in a patrilocal "joint family" or in the stock of a patrilocal "joint family complex", these two types of intrafamily relations cannot go beyond those traced through "fathers" only as (great ... great) grandfather—(great ... great) grandchild, (great ... great) granduncle—(great ... great) grandnephew/grandniece, uncle—nephew/niece, cousins from the paternal side, and the corresponding "mothers", aunts and in-laws. Similarly, the kinds of lineal/affinal relations which may possibly be involved in the composition of family-units under other norms of locality or matrilineage can be precisely delimited.

So that even for those family-units which refer to such a norm of locality as may legitimately include all kinds of lineal/affinal relations (such as bilocal or "alternating"), the above order of classification may be employed, instead of classifying them as "kindred", in order to examine how many of them are involved with a particular set of lineal and affinal relations. The attempt, of course, would yield dividend provided there are reasons to believe from *a priori* considerations that although normatively the inclusion of all kinds of lineal and affinal relations in them is approved, in fact they are veering round to a particular set. But such a situation is not rarely indicated from preliminary investigations or pilot inquiries in appropriate societies.

The use made of the societal norm of locality and/or lineage for the classification of family-units thus does not condition the system of classification; on the other hand, it remains of distinct opera-

tional advantage. For, while deviants may not be rare, the probability density of family-units composed of the stock only according to the traditional norm of locality is high in almost all
societies.

The above classificatory order, however, brings to the forefront
a question regarding these deviants. Namely: what are the kinds
of lineal/affinal relations involved in family-units because of the
presence of adhesions in them? For the kinship affiliation of the
adhesions to the stock can vary indefinitely under any norm of
locality, and thus point to the presence of other kind(s) of lineal/
affinal relations in the units than those scheduled by the norm.
Such as, in a patrilocal "joint family complex", there may be a
"grandparent" as MF. and "uncle" as MB or FSH, an "aunt" as
FS or MBW, a "cousin" as MBZ or FSD, and so on with respect to
any one member of the stock. And such relations with respect to
one member of the stock may yield diverse kinds of lineal and
affinal relations in the unit with respect to its other members.

Therefore, further orders of classification of family-units in
the dimension of their kinship composition should be based on an
examination of the family complexes with respect to the kinship
characteristics of the adhesions in relation to the stock members as
well as among themselves.

In this respect, the first point to note may be the direction(s)
from which the adhesions have schematically grafted on to the
stock of the unit in question; the direction being determined
by the characteristic composition of the stock as resulting from
matrimonial alliance between family-units.

For marriage within the family being tabooed in virtually all
societies, the institution cannot but lead to the extension of the sphere
of kinship and affinal relations of the stock members of corresponding units with reference to specific points of their structural configuration. Therefore, as under respective norms of locality the family-
units evolve out of or extend with the process of post-marriage
movement of males and/or females in and out of corresponding
unit, and as even if the post-marriage movement of either sex is
against a specific form of locality the institution of marriage will,
in any case, lead to the structural ramification of relevant family-
units in ways specific to married males and married females, the
points of articulation of the adhesions to the stock of the unit in
question may be categorized according to the distinct sides of the

stock in which they are located in terms of post-marriage organization of the stock members.

Thus, to consider the six norms of locality cited as illustrative cases earlier, under patrilocal residence the males are scheduled to remain throughout their life in their families of orientation, while after marriage the females should move out of theirs to those of their husbands. Contrariwise, under matrilocal residence the females are scheduled to remain all their life in their families of orientation, while the males should move out of theirs to those of their wives after marriage. On the other hand, under neolocal, avunculocal or matri-patrilocal residence, both men and women are scheduled to move out of their families of orientation after marriage and are expected, according to respective norms of locality, to set up new families of the cohorts formed, or move permanently into the family-units of a specified lineal relative of the "husbands", or move temporarily into the family of orientation of the "wives". And, under natolocal residence as among the Nayars, even though neither the men nor the women are scheduled to move out of their families of orientation after marriage, the norm indicates that in the relevant society the families of orientation and procreation should be different for the males but not so for the females.

Hence, under any norm of locality, the stock of a family-unit may be schematically dichotomized into a stationery or moving "male"-side and of a stationery or moving "female"-side; so that the specific characteristics of the norm would then indicate whether for the males or for the females of respective societies the family of orientation should equate to or should not equate to the family of procreation. Thereafter, the adhesions, which "grafting" on to the stock of a unit have turned it into a family complex, can be distinguished as from the stock's: (1) "male"-side, (2) "female"-side, or (3) "male and female"-sides.

For where the males or the females have the same family-unit as the family of orientation and procreation and, correspondingly, the females or the males have not the same family-unit as the family of orientation and procreation, the adhesions may be characterised as from the "male"-side or the "female"-side of the stock, respectively. Such as: FS_w or D_m as the "male"-side and MB or WS as the "female"-side adhesions in a patrilocal family; FB or HS as the "male"-side and MB_w or Z_m as the "female"-side adhesions in a matrilocal family; BW or ZZ as the "male"-side and F or H as the "female"-side adhesions in a natolocal family (*taravad*); etc.

But where both the males *and* the females *have not* or *may not have* the same family-unit as the family of orientation and procreation, the adhesions will have to be characterised as from the "male"-side, "female"-side, or from the "male and female"-sides of the stock. Thus, under neolocal residence, the married male Ego's father, unmarried Ego's father's father, and married female Ego's husband's father are "male"-side adhesions; the married female Ego's father, unmarried Ego's mother's father, and married male Ego's wife's father are "female"-side adhesions; whereas, married Ego's married son or unmarried Ego's married brother are adhesions from both the "male and female"-sides of the stock, viz. of the cohort in question.

Similarly, the married sons and daughters to any stock member of an avunculocal family, or sons and daughters irrespective of their marital status to a temporary member (a married "daughter" or "son-in-law") in a matri-patrilocal family, are "male and female"-sides adhesions to the stock in question; while the stock members (including the newly-wed persons in a matri-patrilocal family) can have "male"-side or "female"-side adhesions, in addition. Such as: (1) male married Ego's father, sister's son's father's brother, etc., are the "male"-side adhesions and female married Ego's father, husband's mother's brother's wife's sister, etc., are the "female"-side adhesions in an avunculocal family; (2) married male Ego's father, his wife's sister's husband's mother, or married female Ego's husband's mother, etc., are the "male"-side adhesions and married male Ego's wife's mother's brother, wife's father's brother's wife's sister, or married female Ego's brother's wife's father, etc., are the "female"-side adhesions in a matri-patrilocal family, with the Ego residing temporarily in the unit as a newly-wed person; or (3) with the Ego a permanent member of the matri-patrilocal unit, the "male"-side and the "female"-side adhesions are determined in the same way as for patrilocal family but with the exception that the newly-wed "husbands" of the "sisters" and "daughters" in the family as well as these "sisters" and "daughters" are to be counted as stock members instead of as "male"-side adhesions.

The adhesions being thus categorized, the family complexes may be characterized according to the direction or directions from which a nascent/conjugal, elementary, or joint family, or the non-familial unit of the Ego alone, is transformed into a "complex"; and this may be of relevance to intra-society and inter-society studies of the family as a social institution. For, to mention one aspect of its usefulness, in the light of the societal norm of locality, the relative emphasis thus laid on the family of orientation (with or without additional appendages to them) of the stationery or moving males and/or females of the stock of the unit is worthy of examination.

As for example, that the two regions of undivided Bengal denoted by the people as East Bengal and West Bengal, are historically and culturally distinct irrespective of their further internal differences, is acknowledged by all social scientists. Therefore, with reference to the rural society of these two regions, it may be of significant importance to deduce from a preliminary analysis of data for 1946 that while in West Bengal 75, 23, and 2 per cents of the family complexes were formed by "male"-side, "female"-side and "male"-side plus "female"-side adhesions, respectively, the corresponding percentages for East Bengal were 68, 29, and 2 (Pakrashi 1959). Because such structural variations in family organization as found between these two regions of Bengal, or if noticed more strikingly in other societies, may be regarded as a pointer to focus the attention of social scientists on specific features of intra-family relations for a fuller appreciation of the functional implications of the family as a social institution in respective societies.[9]

Moreover, such a classification of the adhesions may be the first step in exploring the respective roles of different categories of bandhavas (viz, atmabandhu, pitṛbandhu, and matṛbandhu) to the patriarch or his male agnates in a Hindu family with respect to the inheritence of family or individual women's property, procurement of son to the family according to the custom of niyoga, etc. (Kane 1946: III, 753ff; Ganapati Sastri 1924: Part I, 89, 1.17; Part II, 16, III.2; 35, III.5; 39, III.6). And similar specific usefulness of the classification of adhesions as above in the aspect discussed here may be found for other societies.

Likewise, to consider another aspect of the usefulness of classifying the family complexes according to the above-mentioned categorization of the adhesions, whether or not under the neolocal, avunculocal and matri-patrilocal residence the formation of family complexes is mainly due to "male and female"-sides adhesion as against the "male"-side and/or "female"-side adhesions would be of specific relevance to note. For this may point out the changing characteristics of family organization in a society in transition from avunculocal or matri-patrilocal norm of residence, or the relative tenacity of some forms of intra-family relations therein in spite of neolocal residence being its norm (such as that of parental relation with the "parents" as the Ego of the family-units in question as against the "child" as the Ego).

Similarly, it may be useful to ascertain, or verify in case such a statement has been made on general considerations, whether changes in the kinship composition of family-units as contrary to the norm of locality is taking place in a society with respect to some particular facets of familial organization and in a particular direction only. For instance, it has been asserted that in Nayar families the male "head" of the *taravad* could retain his wife and children in the unit. In that case, the unit would form a "family complex" with the "male"—side adhesions only; a point worth recording and elaborating further in terms of other orders of classification in the dimension of kinship composition of family-units, as proposed later, in order to establish the importance and coverage of this form of variation in family organization in Nayar society.

Other usefulness of this form of classification of the family complexes may be found in course of specific studies in particular societies, especially if it is borne in mind that objective conditions are persuading the social scientists these days to define family (operationally, at any rate) as a co-resident and commensal king-roup. In any case, and irrespective of the intrinsic relevance of the societal norm of locality to the classification of family-units, it is important to point out here that the characterization of the family complexes as suggested above would indicate the first stage of locating what other kinds of lineal and affinal relations are involved in the units in question as are not already given by the characteristics of their stocks.

To ascertain, therefore, from his/her notation-series with respect to the Ego of a family-unit as to whether the adhesion is a "male"-side, "female"-side, or a "male and female"-sides adhesion, the following formulae have been prepared for the six norms of locality considered before. The formulae have been constructed under the same conditions as noted for the corresponding formulae for the stock members, but with the additional condition that any family member identified by this set of formulae cannot be the same as one who from the previous set would have been distinguished as a stock member.

Furthermore, in order that these formulae may serve the requisite purpose, they have been divided primarily into two distinct blocks by means of third brackets, and these two blocks have been placed in a chronological sequence. Subsequently, either of these blocks have been divided into a number of components by means of first brackets, and these components also have been placed in a chronological order. Additionally, the last component of the first block has been overlined for some formulae, as its representation was found obligatory under certain norms of locality in order to denote a particular category of adhesion; and the first component of the second block has invariably been considered as obligatory for all the formulae under all norms of locality.

As a result, the first block of the formulae would indicate the trunk of the family tree of the unit in question, as obtained from the conditional expansion of the kinship notations within its components; and thus locate those stock members with respect to whom a particular category of adhesions may graft on to the stock of the unit. Thereafter, the first component of the second block would point out those kinship notations of which any one appended to the notation-series of any one stock member represented by the first block would give the notation-series of an adhesion of the stated category with respect to the Ego of the unit.

As, however, the notation-series with the Ego of the unit of all possible adhesions of a stated category cannot be exhausted by the first component of the second block, but as at the same time the representation of this component is imperative to the formation of this particular category of adhesions to the stock of the unit, subsequent component(s) of the second block would provide the exact relationship of any adhesion of that category to the Ego in case the relationship is not fully stated by the first component only. For this purpose, ultimately any combination, repetition, or rejection of the kinship notations F, M, B, S, Z, D, H, and W may be required to be attached to that part of the notation-series of the adhesion concerned as made out of the first block and the preceding component(s) of the second block. Therefore, in the last component of the second block an omnibus notation K has been used to stand for any combination, repetition or rejection of the kinship notations F, M, B, S, Z, D, H, and W.

Thus designed, the formulae for the detection of "male"-side adhesions (a_m), "female"-side adhesions (a_f), and "male and female"-sides adhesions (a_{m+f}) in family-units under the six norms of locality considered before are as follows:

1. *Neolocal*

$$a_m - [(E_u F/M, E_{mwds}) (\overline{H})] [(F \text{ or } M, B_{mwds}, S_{mwds}) (H, W, Z_u, D_u) (K)]$$

$$a_f - [(E_u F/M, E_{mwds}) (\overline{W})] [(F \text{ or } M, B_{mwds}, S_{mwds}) (H, W, Z_u, D_u) (K)]$$

$$a_{m+f} - [(E_u F/M, E_{mwds}) (\overline{H/W})] [(Z_{mwds}, D_{mwds}) (Z \ldots /D \ldots) (H, W) (K)] ;$$

where, $E_{\triangle_{mwds}} H = E_{o_{mwds}}$ $H = E_{\triangle_{mwds}}$, $E_{o_{mwsd}} W =$ $E_{\triangle_{mwds}} W = E_{o_{mwds}}$, $FZ_u = MZ_u = B_u$, $FD_u = MD_u = S_u$; and in the second block the second component cannot exist without the first.

2. *Patrilocal*

$$a_m - [(E_{\triangle, o_u}, E_{o_{mw}} H) (F \ldots /B/Z \ldots)] [(S_{mw}, D_{mw}) (H) (K)]$$

$$a_f - [(E_{\triangle, o_u}, E_{o_{mw}} H) (F \ldots /B/Z \ldots) (\overline{M, W})] [(F, M, B, S) (K)]$$

$$a_{m+f} - \text{(Categoriaztion is not possible)}$$

3. *Matrilocal*

$$a_m - [(E_{\triangle_u}, o, E_{\triangle_{mw}} W) (M \ldots /S/D \ldots) (\overline{F, H})] [(F, M, B, S) (K)]$$

$$a_f - [(E_{\triangle_u}, o, E_{\triangle_{mw}} W) (M \ldots /S/D \ldots)] [(B_{mw}, Z_{mw}) (W) (K)]$$

$$a_{m+f} - \text{(categorization is not possible)}$$

4. *Avunculocal*

$$a_m - [(E_u F, E_{\triangle_{mwds}}, E_{o_{mw}} H) (M) (M \ldots /S/D \ldots) (B_{mwds}, Z_{mwds})] [(F \text{ or } M, S_{mw}) (H, W, Z_u, D_u) (K)]$$

a_f — $[(E_uF, E_{\triangle_{mwds}}, E_{o_{mw}} H) (M) (M.../S/D...) (B_{mwds},$
$Z_{mwds}) (\overline{W})] [(F \text{ or } M, B_{mwds}, S_{mw}) (H, W. Z_u, D_u) (K)]$

a_{m+f} — $[(E_uF, E_{\triangle_{mwds}}, E_{o_{mw}} H) (M) (M.../S/D...) (B_{mwds},$
$Z_{mwds}) (\overline{H/W})] [(Z_{mwds}, D_{mw}) (Z.../D...) (H, W) (K)]$

where, for all the three categories, the fourth component
of the first block cannot exist without the second component in the same block, and the second component of
the second block cannot exist without the first component
in that block.

5. *Matri-patrilocal*

(I) If the Ego is a permanent member of the unit, and is
not living temporarily as a newly-married person:

a_m — $[(E_{\triangle,o_u}, E_{o_{mw}} H) (F.../B/Z...) (S, D) (\overline{H})] [(F, M, B, S) (K)]$

a_f — $[(E_{\triangle,o_u}, E_{o_{mw}} H) (F.../B/Z...) (\overline{M, W})] [(F, M, B, S) (K)]$

a_{m+f} — $[(E_{\triangle,o_u}, E_{o_{mw}} H) (F.../B/Z...) (S, D) (\overline{H})] [(Z.../D...) (K)],$

where the third component of the first block is also
obligatory with the fourth component for the "male"-
side and the "male and female"-sides adhesions.

(II) If the Ego is a temporary member of the unit as a
newly-married person:

a_m — $[(E_{\triangle_{mw}} W, E_{o_{mw}}) (F.../B) (Z.../D) (S) (\overline{H})] [(K)]$

a_f — $[(E_{\triangle_{mw}} W, E_{o_{mw}}) (F.../B) (Z...) (\overline{M, W})] [(F, M, B, S) (K)]$

a_{m+f} — $[(E_{\triangle_{mw}} W, E_{o_{mw}}) (F.../B) (Z.../D) (S) (\overline{H})] [(Z.../D...) (K)]$

where, for all the three categories of adhesions, the
third component of the first block cannot exist without
the second component in that block, and for the "female"-
side adhesions the second or the third component of the
first block must exist.

6. *Natolocal*: (*Taravad*)

a_m — $[(E) (M) (M\ldots/S/D\ldots) \overline{(B, Z)}]\ [(W) (K)]$

a_f — $[(E) (M) (M\ldots/S) (D\ldots)]\ [(H) (F, M, B, S) (K)]$

a_{m+f} — (categorization is not possible)

where, both for a_m and a_f, the fourth component of the
first block cannot exist without the second component
of that block.

From the above formulae it should be evident that under any
norm of locality it would not be a difficult task to classify the
adhesions according to the above three categories from an examination of their kinship notation-series with respect to the Ego of the
unit in question. Thus, under patrilocal residence, any adhesion
presenting the notation S_{mw} or D_{mw} immediately after any combination, repetition or rejection of the notations F, B, and Z with respect
to a male or unmarried female Ego or the husband of a married
female Ego is a "male"-side adhesion, whether or not the notation-
series of the adhesion ends with the notation S_{mw} or D_{mw} or proceeds
to any length with all possible permutations and combinations of
the kinship notations subsequently. Likewise, under the same norm
of locality, any adhesion presenting the notation F, M, B, or S
immediately after M or W as the last notation for a stock member
but subsequent to the role of the notations F, B, and Z as described
above is a "female"-side adhesion, whether or not the notation-
series of the adhesion ends with the notation F, M, B or S, or
proceeds further as indicated above.

Similarly, under any other norm of locality, the adhesions of
the three categories can be sorted out from an examination of their
notation-series with the Ego. In fact, as it can be easily demonstrated, for different norms of locality simple rules can be laid out for the
detection and categorization of the adhesions as suggested above;
so that the operation can be performed mechanically by a person
with some general education but not necessarily trained as a
social scientist. Any complication in classifying the family-
units as discussed in the foregoing pages may not, therefore, be
apprehended.

Pursuantly, the second order of classification of family-units.

in the dimension of their kinship composition is proposed as follows:

1. Unit without adhesions
2. Unit with "male"-side adhesions only
3. Unit with "female"-side adhesions only
4. Unit with "male and female"-sides adhesions only
5. Unit with "male"-side adhesions and "female"-side adhesions
6. Unit with "male"-side adhesions and "male and female"-sides adhesions
7. Unit with "female"-side adhesions and "male and female"-side adhesions
8. Unit with "male"-side adhesions, "female"-side adhesions, and "male and female"-sides adhesions.

IV

While the kinship characteristics of the adhesions with respect to the stock members of a family complex are thus specified to an extent by the above classificatory order, and accordingly it gives the first approximation to what other kinds of lineal/affinal relations the unit is involved with than those indicated by the characteristics of the stock, its term of reference does not give any indication to the kinds of kinship relation involved between the adhesions. Namely, do the sets of adhesions categorized as the "male"-side, "female"-side, and "male and female"-sides adhesions represent only the scheduled kinds of intra-family relations among themselves as specified for the stock of the unit in question? And, if not, what other kinds of lineal/affinal relations do they represent within and between the sets?

To answer these questions, that is, to classify the family complexes in terms of their total ramification within the kinship structure of society, several other classificatory orders would evidently be required. But there is the point that too many characteristics of the adhesions may not be feasible to consider in view of the fact that the number of family complexes likely to be found in a society cannot be inordinately large. Therefore, a careful selection of the possible classificatory orders in this context is definitely indicated.

Apropos, the first consideration may be to note that the adhesions, categorized or not as the "male"-side, "female"-side, or the "male and female"-sides adhesions to the stock of a family complex, may refer to one or more points of articulation to the stock as a whole or to its respective facets of composition. For instance, in a patri-local society a family complex may contain simultaneously the Ego's widowed sister with her unmarried daughter, Ego's father's first sister with her husband and second widowed sister with her son, Ego's father's first brother's widowed daughter, Ego's father's second brother's widowed daughter with her son and married daughter, and perhaps also Ego's mother's brother and wife's mother.

In that case, in terms of the points of articulation there would be 6 distinct sets out of the 12 adhesions grafted on to the stock of the unit in question; one set of the first two adhesions with respect to the Ego, another set of the next four adhesions with respect to Ego's father, the third set of only one adhesion with respect to Ego's father's first brother, the fourth set of three adhesions with respect to Ego's father's second brother, and the fifth and the sixth set of only one adhesion in each with respect to Ego's mother and Ego's wife, respectively.

The enumeration of the points of articulation of the adhesions to the stock of a unit would thus give the initial indication of diverse kinds of lineal/affinal relations involved in a family complex because of variations in kinship relations between the adhesions; and this would be pointed out more precisely if these points are categorized beforehand in terms of the characteristics of the adhesions as from the "male"-side, "female"-side, or "male and female"-sides of the stock. Hence, another attribute of the adhesions which may be considered worthy of taken into account would be the complication effected by them in the kinship composition of a family complex as due to the number of sets they represent in terms of their points of articulation to the trunk of the family tree in question; the stock of the unit representing, evidently, the trunk.

These points of articulation can be enumerated easily from the first block of the above formulae to detect and categorize the adhesions in a unit by ascertaining the different stock members with respect to whom the adhesions have emerged in the unit. Thus, under patrilocal residence, the distinct stock members formed by any combination, repetition or rejection of the notations F, B and Z as are found to occur in the first block of the formula for "male"-side adhesions, and the distinct stock members found to occur for "female"-side adhesions by considering in addition to the notations F, B and Z the notations M and W (forming part of the first block of the corresponding formula as succeeding the previous ones), give in total the points of articulation of the adhesions to the stock of a family-unit. Such as in the case of the patrilocal family cited above the 6 distinct sets of adhesions are given as follows by the notation-series of the adhesions with respect to the Ego, with those notations overlined which indicate the formation of the different sets. Namely: $(\overline{ES}_w, \overline{ES}D_u)$, $(\overline{EFS}_1, \overline{EFS}_1H, \overline{EFS}_{2w}, \overline{EFS}_2Z)$, $(\overline{EFB}_1D_w)$, $(\overline{EFB}_2D_w, \overline{EFB}_2DZ, \overline{EFB}_2DD_m)$, $(\overline{EMB})$, and $(\overline{EWM})$.

Likewise, for other norms of locality also the distinct sets of adhesions can be ascertained by examining the notation-series of the adhesions with respect to the Ego in terms of variations within the first block of the laid out formulae. And it can be easily demonstrated that for all norms of locality the task can be accomplished mechanically by following some simple rules. So that, eventually, the adhesions contained in a family complex can be categorized as belonging to one, two, or a particular number of sets; viz., set a_1 for x number of adhesions, a_2 for y number, a_3 for z number, and so on, until the total number of the constituent adhesions in a unit is exhausted. Such as in the case of the patrilocal family cited above: $a_1=2$, $a_2=4$, $a_3=1$, $a_4=3$, $a_5=1$, and $a_6=1$; thereby, the six sets of adhesions $a_1 \ldots a_6$ accounting for the 12 adhesions contained in the unit.

As noted before, these sets of adhesions may be considered as such or as pertaining to different categories of adhesions. Thus, to refer again to the patrilocal family illustrated above, the 6 sets of adhesions it contains may be recorded directly as $(a_1 \ldots a_6)$ or the first four $(a_1 \ldots a_4)$ may be denoted as "male"-side adhesions= $(a_{m_1} \ldots a_{m_4})$ and the remaining two as "female"-side adhesions= a_{f_1} and a_{f_2} instead of as a_5 and a_6 for the previous arrangement. In the same way, for any family-unit under any norm of locality the sets of adhesions may be denoted as: $(a_{m_1} \ldots a_{m_x})$, $(a_{f_1} \ldots a_{f_y})$, and $(a_{(m+f)_1} \ldots a_{(m+f)_z})$.

Whether or not the sets of adhesions are thus additionally distinguished by the subscripts m, f, and (m+f), the highest value of a as obtained from its numeral subscripts for the unit as a whole or for different categories of adhesions would give the total number of the respective points of articulation to the trunk of the family tree in question. Either way, therefore, this figure may be denoted by α; so that, in case distinction is drawn in this value by the categories of adhesions as representing the characteristic facets of the trunk of the family tree, $\alpha = (\alpha_m + \alpha_f + \alpha_{(m+f)})$.

Hence, irrespective of the categorization of the adhesions as "male"-side adhesions, "female"-side adhesions, or "male and female"-sides adhesions, the variate α with its possible values ranging from 0 to any figure (with $\alpha_o, \alpha_{m_o}, \alpha_{f_o}, \alpha_{(m+f)_o}$ indicating the absence of adhesions from the unit as a whole or from the respective facets of its stock's composition) may be regarded as an independent course of categorization of family-units in terms of the kinship affiliation of the adhesions to their stock. The third order of classification of family-units in the dimension of their kinship composition is, therefore, proposed in terms of the varying values of α they represent.

V

Proceeding further, the variations in kinship relations between the adhesions would be more revealed if the sets of adhesions distinguished as above are subsequently or alternately categorized in terms of the distinct branches of the family tree they represent; these branches having forked out directly from a particular point of articulation with the trunk of the family tree in question. For, even among themselves, all the family members belonging to a set of adhesions as characterized above need not conform to only those kinds of lineal and affinal relations as dictated by their schematic affiliation to a particular norm of locality. So that, one aspect of such departures from the scheduled kinds of lineal/affinal relations can be registered, primarily, in this way.

To illustrate with reference to the patrilocal family-unit cited above, the set of adhesions categorized as a_1 is represented by ES_w and ESD_u who conform to the scheduled kinds of intra-family relations among themselves. But a_2 is represented by EFS_1 and EFS_1H as well as by EFS_2 and EFS_2Z; and these two sub-sets of adhesions refer to such kinds of lineal/affinal relations as do not conform to the scheduled ones with respect to themselves alone and irrespective of their relation to the stock members. Hence, whether or not such an eventuality has been registered in a family complex can be indicated by the number of branches the family tree is composed of as identical or in addition to its points of articulation. Such as in the above case the point of articulation a_1 consists of only one branch, while from a_2 two distinct branches have forked out.

To examine, accordingly, whether or not one or more branches has/have forked out of the trunk of the family tree under reference, either the last obligatory component of the first block or when that component is not obligatory the first component of the second block of the above formulae will have to be taken into account with respect to the notation-series of each and every adhesion of a family-unit with its Ego. For, under all norms of locality, the number of distinct individuals referred sequentially in the specified component by the notations with their subscripts can indicate the branches to the trunk of a family tree.

Thus, under patrilocal residence, the "male"-side adhesions formed by different ever-married sisters and daughters (S_{mw}, D_{mw}) with respect to relevant point or points of articulation to the stock of the unit denote different branches of the family tree; while the varying points of articulation of the "female"-side adhesions denote one branch each of the family tree, as with reference to different individuals denoted by M and W with their antecedents and subscripts in the first block of the formula the respective branches fork out of the trunk of the family tree. Therefore, the varying individuals denoted by the presence or not of S_{mw} and D_{mw} and their further distinguishing subscripts in the first component of the second block of the formula for the "male"-side adhesions plus α_f give the number of distinct branches to the patrilocal family-unit under reference. For instance, in the case of the patrilocal family cited before, the branches to the family tree are given as: $a_{m_1}=1$, $a_{m_2}=2$ (with reference to EFS_{1_m} and $E\bar{F}S_{2_w}$), $a_{m_3}=1$, $a_{m_4}=1$, and a_{f_1} and $a_{f_2}=2$; in all 7 branches.

In this way, with respect to any point of articulation a_i with the trunk of a family tree conforming to any norm of locality, the branches can be enumerated as, say, $a_i b_1$, $a_i b_2$, ... $a_i b_j$, ... $a_i b_n$; where j stands for any and n for the last chronologically denoted branch for any a. The value of n thus gives the total number of branches

formed at one point of articulation; and so, by noting $b_n = \beta$ for any a, the total number of branches to a family tree can be found as:
$$\left(\begin{array}{c} a = \alpha \\ \sum \beta \\ a = 1 \end{array} \right)$$

This value, represented by γ, say, will be zero when $\alpha = 0$ for a family-unit; otherwise, γ will be greater than or equal to α because each a must represent at least one branch of the family tree as a_1b_1, a_2b_1, etc. And this relation will hold equally good for γ_m, γ_f, and $\gamma_{(m+f)}$, in case the characteristic facets of the trunk of the family tree are severally brought under consideration and α is represented by α_m, α_f, and $\alpha_{(m+f)}$, respectively.

Hence $(\gamma - \alpha)$ will indicate whether or not more than one branch has forked out from one or more points of articulation with the trunk of the family tree; the latter being previously characterized or not as referring to the "male"-side, "female"-side, or the "male and female"-sides of the stock of the family-unit in question. And, in any case, irrespective of this characterization or even the consideration of the points of articulation by α, the value of γ as varying from 0 to any figure will point out whether the unit concerned is a "family complex" (when $\gamma > 0$); and, if so, how many branches to the trunk of the family tree it represents in terms of the grafting of adhesions to its stock. The fourth order of classification of family-units in the dimension of their kinship composition is, therefore, proposed in terms of the varying values of γ they represent.

VI

Another aspect of variation in kinship relations between the adhesions is with reference to the sub-branches formed successively to a particular branch; the branch constituting solely or partly a point of articulation with the trunk of the family tree. Such as the kinship constituents EFB_2D_w, EFB_2DZ, and EFB_2DD_m, belonging to the set of adhesions denoted as a_4 with reference to the patrilocal family-unit cited before, form one branch to the family tree; but of them the first two constitute the "stock" of the branch as articulating directly to the trunk of the family tree in question, while the third forms a sub-branch.

Like the formation of branches to a family tree, further distinction of the former also is thus based, schematically at any rate, on the societal norm of locality. The reason is obvious. Namely, since all the family members belonging to a set of adhesions need not form a legitimate unit by themselves in terms of the societal norm of locality and irrespective of the fact that they themselves are adhesions to another unit, under all norms of locality they may be distinguished according to the distinct branches and sub-branches they have formed to the family tree in question by cutting across the demarcation of family-units in this respect. For this would indicate the total range of coverage of distinct kinds of lineal/affinal relations contained in respective units.

Apropos, the type of variation in kinship relations within a family complex as under consideration affects also the nature of kinship relation of the adhesions to the stock members; and so it may be regarded as "interaction" between the previous two types of variation. For even though the stock of a family-unit may consist of only one branch, the sub-branches can be of any number (theoretically, at any rate). So that while the members representing all these sub-branches may not be present in the unit in question, those present may be drawing their relation to the branch under reference through several sub-branches. That is, the intervening sub-branches and/or the "stock" of the branch itself may merely form the link between the stock of the family-unit and the adhesion/adhesions concerned without themselves being represented in the unit as its constituents.

Thus, to take the case of an adhesion related to the Ego of a patrilocal family-unit as $ESHBWMSDD_w$, the relation of the adhesion to the stock of the unit is based primarily on $E\bar{S}_{mw}$; S_{mw} indicating the forking out of a branch to the family tree under reference. Thereafter, $ESHBW\bar{M}$ refers to the first sub-branching of the branch in question; while $ESHBWM\bar{S}_{mw}$ refers to the third sub-branching, as the second would be represented by $ESHBWM\bar{F}$ and from this sub-branch the next one of $ESHBWM\bar{S}_{mw}$ has forked out. Successively, $ESHBWMS\bar{D}_{mw}$ refers to the fourth sub-branching; and $ESHBWMSD\bar{D}_w$ to the fifth and the last sub-branching of the family tree with respect to the adhesion concerned. In other words, the adhesion related to the Ego of the unit as $ESHBWMSDD_w$ is linked to its stock through $(5+1)=6$ links; each one of them representing the stock of a family-unit in terms of the norm of locality.

Hence, whether or not the links are represented in the unit under examination by means of other specific adhesions, any adhesion would be found to register a definite *kinship distance* from the stock of the unit; the kinship distance being recorded by the degree of change in locality effected by the adhesions in order to belong to the unit under reference. For instance, in the case cited above, $ESHBWMSDD_w$ is an adhesion to the stock of a family-unit represented by $ESHBWMSDH=ESHBWMSDDF$, who in his turn is an adhesion to the stock of another family-unit represented by $ESHBWMSH=ESHBWMSDF$; and this person, again, is an adhesion to the stock of a third family-unit represented by $ESHBWMSF=ESHBWMF$. Proceeding further backwards, the person denoted by the notation-series $ESHBWMF$ with the Ego of the family-unit under examination is an adhesion to a fourth family-unit represented by $ESHBWMH=ESHBWF$, who in his turn is an adhesion to a fifth family-unit represented by $ESHBWH=ESHB=ESH=ES_m$; and this person is an adhesion to the sixth family-unit represented by E, that is, the family-unit under reference. Summarily, therefore, the kinship distance of the adhesion related to the Ego of a patrilocal family-unit as $ESHBWMSDD_w$ is of 6 degrees.

In this way, for each and every adhesion his/her kinship distance from the stock of the family-unit can be measured under any norm of locality; and for this purpose certain simple rules may be laid down with respect to the notation-series of the adhesions with the Ego of the family-unit, as obtained from the formulae presented earlier. Such as, under patrilocal residence, the kinship distance of an adhesion to the stock of the unit is given by the number of times S_{mw}, D_{mw} occur in his/her notation-series with the Ego plus the number of times M, W occur in that series as preceding other notation or notations.

So ascertained, the kinship distance of each and every member of a family-unit under any norm of locality may be recorded as d, with its values varying from 0 to any figure. Obviously, zero will be the value for all stock members of the unit under reference, while for the adhesions the value of d may be any from 1 upward. Of the values of the adhesions, again, 1 will indicate that these first order adhesions to the unit under reference refer directly to the stock of the family-units from which they have moved (schematically), while 2 will indicate that these second order adhesions refer to the first order adhesions as "adhesions" to their stocks. And, thus following chronologically, larger values for the adhesions as 3 and above will indicate that the further orders of adhesions refer to adhesions of successively later units in the same way.

In all, therefore, the kinship distances of the members of a family-unit from its stock will show its ramification by cutting across the demarcation of corresponding units in a society in terms of the norm of locality applicable to all of them; and thus will indicate the total coverage of different kinds of lineal/affinal relations by the unit. Hence, this characteristic of family-units in the dimension of their kinship composition may be represented by the maximum kinship distance recorded by the members of each unit; viz. δ, say, $= d_{max}$. for each and every family-unit under examination.

Like the variates α and γ, the variate δ also can be employed for the unit as a whole or for the respective facets of its trunk in relation to the grafting of adhesions to the stock of the family complex; namely, δ_m, δ_f, and $\delta_{(m+f)}$, where $\delta = [\delta_m/\delta_f/\delta_{(m+f)})]$ max. So that, whether or not the deviant structure of family-units in the dimension of their kinship composition is more marked with respect to a specific characteristic of their adhesions can be recorded directly. And, in any case, family-units classified by the values of δ ranging from 0 to any figure will indicate that: where $\delta = 0$, the unit has no adhesion; where $\delta = 1$, the ramification of the family complex within the kinship structure of the society is extremely restricted; and so on.

The fifth order of classification of family-units in the dimension of their kinship composition is, therefore, proposed in terms of the varying values of δ they represent.

VII

Continuing in this way, additional or alternative characteristics of the adhesions could also be considered for the classification of family-units in the dimension of their kinship composition. But if it is borne in mind that, firstly, too many characteristics of the adhesions may not be feasible to consider in view of the fact that the number of family complexes likely to be found in a society cannot be very many, and, secondly, those taken under consideration are likely to be of greater relevance to the characterization of the family complexes than others, further orders of classification of family-units in the dimension of their kinship composition may not be warranted.

Indeed, so few family-units are expected to be available for any course of analysis as have the values of α, γ, and δ greater than 1 after the distinction drawn in these variables as from the "male"-side, "female"-side, and "male and female"-sides of the stock of the units in question that if subsequent examination of their kinship composition is desired, further classification of the relevant family-units may defeat its own purpose. For, in that case, each and every such family-unit may have to be examined separately in order to ascertain what specific kinds of lineal/affinal relations they represent; as to group them accordingly in distinct categories of representable size would be virtually an impossible task.[10]

In this context, therefore, after classifying the family-units under analysis according to the first and the second order of classification proposed above, the succeeding third, fourth, and the fifth order would indicate whether or not such a contingency arises in course of a piece of research. Thereby the classification of family structures in the dimension of kinship composition of family-units would finally serve its purpose.

Further orders of classification of family-units in the dimension of their kinship composition need not, therefore, be discussed. For specific purposes, however, alternate or additional classificatory orders may be evolved within the prescribed framework, as it remains flexible enough to accommodate any and all such changes.

NOTES

[1] That any conjugal unit would thus present a "complete" structure is better realized if it is examined against a family-unit comprising, say, parents and widowed children. For, in the latter case, the disintegration of some sets of conjugal and affinal relations are indicated by the widowhood of the "children"

[2] For example, a sample survey of family structures in West Bengal (urban/. rural) in 1960-61 enumerated only 301 cohort-units out of the total of 4262 units in the sample. The survey conducted by the Indian Statistical Institute under the writer's guidance was sponsored by the Research Programmes Committee of the Planning Commission, Government of India.

[3] The sample survey referred to earlier brought out 736 non-familial units as compared to 3526 family-units in the sample; their proportion to the total units being as high as 33 per cent for the cities of Calcutta and Howrah, 20 per cent for the towns, and 9 per cent for the villages.

[4] Out of the 736 non-familial units in the previously mentioned sample, 597 were "male" non-familial units and 139 were "famale" non-familial units; with the proportion of "male" non-familial units to the total units varying sharply from 30 per cent in cities and 17 per cent in towns to 5 per cent in the villages. The corresponding percentage of "female" non-familial units remains practically the same in all areas as 3 per cent.

[5] Such an order of classification may be evolved by following the procedure shown in the following pages, or otherwise.

[6] See, for instance, Glick (1957: 1-4, 210-216, &c.). It may also be worthy of mention that while patrilineal-patrilocal joint family system is considered to be the norm in Bengal, from the previously mentioned survey 410 units or 30 per cent of the total of 1369 family-units involving more than one cohort in their formation were found as deviants from this norm; the family-units being identified by the attributes of co-residence and commensality.

[7] The 410 family complexes enumerated during the sample survey in West Bengal, as mentioned earlier, could thus be classified as: "male" family complex—20, "female" family complex—16, conjugal family complex—30, elementary family complex—174, and joint family complex—170.

[8] The categorization of family-units according to this order of classification may appear as too complicated in the light of (a) the conditional expansion of the formulae given earlier to detect the presence or absence of adhesions in the units, and (b) the scrutiny involved in categorizing the stock of the units in question as per the classificatory order. It can, however, be demonstrated that the task may be undertaken almost mechanically by a person of general education (of, say, the under-graduate level) without the intervention of a social scientist who is professedly in the know of things. Hence, operational difficulty may not be regarded as a bar to the application of this order of classification.

[9] For instance, the previously mentioned sample survey of West Bengal showed that at the time of interrogation 67 per cent of the family complexes in the rural areas were composed of the "male"-side adhesions only, 30 per cent of the "female"-side adhesions only, and the remaining 3 per cent of the "male"-side adhesions plus the "female"-side adhesions. A comparison of these figures for 1960-61 with those for 1946 may be of particular interest in view of: (1) changes in familial organization of the indigenous population of West Bengal during the intervening years, and/or (2) the specific characteristics of familial organization of the immigrant population from East Bengal after the establishment of East Pakistan in 1947.

[10] As for example, a cursory examination of the data collected by the previously mentioned survey of family structures in West Bengal in 1960-61 showed that even though 410 family complexes were recorded in the total sample of 4262 units (1) in no case the respective values of α, δ, and δ, exceeded 3, (2) $\alpha > 1$ occurred in 34 cases, (3) $\delta > 1$ occurred in 43 cases, and (4) $\delta > 1$ occurred in 54 cases.

REFERENCES

BARNES, J. A., 1960, 'Marriage and Residential Continuity', *Amer. Anthrop.* Vol. 62, No. 5.

EGGAN, Fred (ed.), 1960, *Social Anthropology of North American Tribes.* Illinois, Univer. of Chicago Press.

GLICK, Paul C., 1957, *American Families.* New York, John Wiley & Sons.

KANE, P. V., 1946, *History of Dharmashastra*, Vol. III, Poona, Bhandarkar Oriental Research Institute.

MALINOWSKI, B., 1944, *A Scientific Theory of Culture and Other Essays*: Chapel Hill, Univer. of N. Carolina Press.

MUKHERJEE, R., 1959, 'A Note on the Classification of Family Structures.' *Proceedings and Papers of the Regional Seminar on Techniques of Social Research*, Calcutta, UNESCO Research Centre.

MURDOCK, G. P., 1949, *Social Structure.* New York, Macmillan.

MURDOCK, G. P., *et al* 1950, *Outline of Cultural Materials.* Behaviour Science Outlines, Vol. I. New Haven, Human Relations Area Files, Inc.

OGBURN, W. F. and MEYER F. NIMKOFF, 1953, *A Handbook of Sociology.* London, Routledge and Kegan Paul.

PAKRASI, K., 1959, 'A Study of some aspects of the Types of Households and Family Organizations in Rural Bengal.' Paper read at the 4th All-India Sociological Conference held at Calcutta (30th Jan. to 1st Feb. 1959).

PARSONS, Talcott and Robert F. BALES, 1956, *Family: Socialization and Interaction Process.* London, Routledge and Kegan Paul.

RIVERS, W. H. R., 1932, *Social Organization.* London, Routledge and Kegan Paul.

Royal Anthrop. Institute of Gt. Britain and Ireland, The (pubs.) 1954, *Notes and Querries on Anthropology.* London, Routledge and Kegan Paul.

SASTRI, Ganapati, 1924, *The Arthashastra of Kautalya.* Trivandrum Sanskrit Series No. LXXIX. Trivandrum, Government Press.

SERVICE, Elman R., 1960, 'Kinship Terminology and Evolution,' *Amer. Anthrop.* Vol. 62, No. 5.

CONTRIBUTORS

ALLCHIN, BRIDGET

Dr Bridget Allchin (b. 1927; B.A. Cape Town, Ph.D. London) was formerly Lecturer in the Department of Extra-Mural Studies, University of London. She engaged in exploration and survey in Central India and the Deccan in 1951-52 and again in 1957-58. She is interested in comparative studies of the earlier prehistory of India, Southern Africa, Australia and South-East Asia.

Dr Allchin's publications include 'Microlithic Sites of Tinnevelly district, Madras State', *Ancient India*, 12, 1956 (with F. E. Zeuner); 'The Late Stone Age of Ceylon', *JRAI*, 88, 1958; and 'The Indian Middle Stone Age', Bulletin of Institute of Archaeology, 2, 1959. Her book *The Stone Tipped Arrow: A comparative study of the Late Stone Age Cultures of the tropical regions of the Old World* is now in press.

ALLCHIN, FRANK RAYMOND

Dr Raymond Allchin (b. 1923; M.A. Cambridge, Ph.D. London) is University Lecturer in Indian Studies (Art and Archaeology) at the University of Cambridge. He has conducted exploration in many parts of India and excavations in Raichur and Mahbhubnagar districts (1951-52 and 1957-8). His chief interests include studies of the neolithic culture of Karnataka, problems of the later pre-historic and early historic periods in the Ganges Valley and Central India, and the early historic culture sequence of W. Pakistan and Afghanistan.

Among Dr Allchin's publications, mention may be made of *Piklihal Excavations* (Hyderabad, 1961); *Utnur Excavations* (Hyderabad, 1961); and 'The Neolithic Stone Industry of the North Karnataka Region', *BSOAS*, XIX, 2, 1957. A work on the Deccan Ash Mounds is now in press.

BAILEY, F. G.

Dr Bailey (b. 1924; M.A. Oxon., Ph.D. Manchester) is Reader in Asian Studies at the School of Oriental and African Studies, University of London. He has made field trips to Orissa in 1952-54, 1955 and 1959. His major theoretical interests are the study of social change and political sociology.

Dr Bailey has published many papers, and two books, viz. *Caste and Economic Frontier* (Manchester, 1957) and *Tribe, Caste and Nation* (Manchester, 1960).

BIRD, Lt. Col. GEORGE WILLIAM GREGORY

Dr Bird (b. 1916; Ph.D. (Med.) London) is in charge of the Blood Transfusion Department, Armed Forces Medical College, Poona, and acts as adviser on blood transfusion problems to the Indian Armed Forces. His chief research interests are the anthropological, biochemical, clinical, forensic, genetic, haematological and serological aspects of human blood.

Dr Bird's publications relevant to Indian anthropology include: 'The ABO Blood Groups of Kumaonis', *Curr. Sci.*, 24, 162, 1954; 'A Third Example of Haemoglobin D', *Trans. Roy. Soc. Trop. Med. Hyg.*, 49, 399, 1955; 'Haemoglobin E in Asia', *J. Physio.*, 130, 56, 1955; 'Haemoglobin D in India', *Brit. Med. J.*, i, 514, 1956; and 'The Blood Groups and Haemoglobins of the Sikhs', *Heredity*, 10, 425, 1956.

CHATTOPADHYAY, KSHITISH PRASAD

Mr. Chattopadhyay (b. 1897, M.Sc. Cambridge) had his early training in Physics and went to Cambridge for advanced studies in that subject, but later changed to research work in anthropology. He has taught anthropology at the University of Calcutta since 1924, where he has been Professor and Head of the Department of Anthropology since 1937. He is a Fellow of the National Institute of Sciences (India). He has done field work among the Korku (Melghat), the Khasi (Maphlong) and the Santal. His interests include rural and urban surveys and biometry.

Mr. Chattopadhyay's publications include 'An essay on the History of Newar Culture', *Jour. of the Asiatic Soc. of Bengal*, N.S., XIX, 1923; 'Contact of Peoples as Affecting marriage Rules', Presidential Address, Indian Science Congress, Anthropology Section, 1931; *Report on Santals in Bengal* (Calcutta University, 1947); and 'Santal sibs', *National Inst. of Sciences of India*, Vol. 23, B, Nos. 1-2, 1957.

DUBE, SHYAMA CHARAN

Dr Dube (b. 1922, M.A., Ph.D. Nagpur), Professor of Anthropology at the University of Sagar, is at present working as Director of Research, Central Institute of Study and Research in Community Development, Government of India. He was Visiting Professor of Anthropology and Far Eastern Studies at Cornell University in 1955-56. He has done field-work in Madhya Pradesh, Andhra, Western Uttar Pradesh and Rajasthan. His chief research interest is the study of social structure and social change in Indian village communities

Dr Dube's major publications are *The Kamar* (Lucknow, 1950), *Indian Village* (London, 1955) and *India's Changing Villages: Human Factors in Community Development* (London, 1958).

FÜRER-HAIMENDORF, CHRISTOPH VON

Dr von Furer-Haimendorf (b. 1909; Ph.D. Vienna) is Professor of Asian Anthropology at the School of Oriental and African Studies, University of London. He was awarded the Rivers Memorial Medal, for anthropological fieldwork, in 1949. He has done fieldwork in the Naga and the Abor Hills, Assam (1936-37), Hyderabad-Deccan (1939-43, 1945-49), Orissa (1941, N.E. Frontier, India (1944-45), South India (1953) and Nepal (1953, 1957-58). While in Hyderabad he was adviser to H.E.H. the Nizam's Government for Tribal and Backward Classes (1945-49). His chief research interests are: comparative social and religious institutions, social stratification and inter-ethnic relations in India.

Dr von Fürer-Haimendorf's chief publications include *The Naked Nagas* (London, 1939); *The Chenchus* (London, 1943); *The Reddis of the Bison Hills* (London, 1945); *The Raj Gonds of Adilabad* (London, 1948); and *Himalayan Barbary* (London, 1955).

GATES, REGINALD RUGGLES

Dr Gates (b. 1882; Ph.D. Chicago, D.Sc. London), formerly Professor of Botany at the King's College, University of London, 1921-42, is Emeritus Professor, University of London, and a Fellow of the Royal Society. In the course of his investigations of races in India, he has studied the Muria Gonds, Kurumbas, Todas, Kotas, Birhors, Asurs and other peoples. His investigations have carried him into America, Africa, Australia, New Guinea, Japan and other places.

Dr Gates' major publications are *Heredity in Man* (London, 1929); *Human Genetics*, 2 Vols. (New York, 1946); *Human Ancestry* (Harvard, 1948); and *Negro Family Pedigrees* (Phila., 1949).

IKIN, ELIZABETH W.

Miss Ikin (b. 1914; B.Sc. London) is Senior Scientific Officer, Blood Group Reference Laboratory, Medical Research Council, London. She has visited the Andaman Islands (1953) for blood group studies.

Miss Ikin's publications include 'The Rh and MNS blood groups of some students from India', *Am. J. Phys. Anthrop.*, n.s. 7, 553-58, 1949; 'Study of Andamanese Negritos', in *Trans. Roy. Soc. Trop. Med. Hyg.*, 48, 12-15, 1953; 'The Blood Groups and Haemoglobins of the Sikhs', *Heredity*, 10, 425-29, 1956; and 'The Blood Groups of the Gorkhas of Nepal', *Am. J. Phys. Anthrop.*, n.s. 15, 163-69, 1957.

KARVÈ, IRAWATI (Mrs.)

Dr Karvé (b. 1905; M.A. Bombay, Ph.D. Berlin) is Professor of Anthropology and Sociology, Deccan College Post-Graduate and Research Institute, Poona. She presided over the Anthropology Section of the Indian Science Congress in 1939. Her research interests are: Racial composition of the Indian population; place names; kinship organization in India, origin of caste; and the sociological study of rural and urban communities.

Dr Karvé is the author of many research papers, and two books viz, *Kinship Organization in India* (Poona, 1953) and *Hindu Society: An Interpretation* (Poona, 1961).

LEHMANN, HERMAN

Dr Lehmann (b. 1910; M.D. Basle, Ph.D. Cambridge, Sc.D. Cambridge) is Reader in Chemical Pathology in the University of London and Associate

Chemical Pathologist, St. Bartholomew's Hospital, London. As an officer in the Royal Army Medical Corps he investigated iron deficiency anaemia in India in 1943-45. In 1952 he visited the Nilgiris and carried out blood-groups surveys and sickle-cell tests in South-Indian populations. Sickling in India was discovered on this occasion. He visited the Onge (Little Andamans) in 1954. Later in London he discovered Haemoglobins L and K in Indians living there, and Haemoglobins D and E in blood samples collected in India by Col. Bird. Dr Lehmann's chief research interest is in the study of the chemistry, pathology, and anthropological-genetical significance of abnormal haemoglobins.

Dr Lehmann's major publications include 'Why are the Red Cells the shape they are? The Evolution of the Human Red Cell' (with R. G. Huntsman), *Functions of the Blood* (London, 1961); 'The Haemoglobinopathies and Thalassemia' (with J. A. M. Ager), *The Metabolic Basis of Inherited Disease* (McGraw Hill, 1960); and 'Distribution of variations in Haemoglobin Synthesis', *Abnormal Haemoglobins* (Oxford, 1959).

MANDELBAUM, DAVID G.

Dr Mandelbaum (b. 1911; B.A. Northwestern Uni., Ph.D. Yale) is Professor of Anthropology at the University of California, Berkeley. He was Chairman of the Department of Anthropology at Berkeley during 1955-57. He has visited India for fieldwork several times (1937-38, 1943-44 (war service), 1949-50 and 1958).

Some of Dr Mandelbaum's publications on India are 'The Family in India', *The Family, and its Functions* ed. by R. N. Austen (New York, 1948); 'The World and World View of the Kotas', *Village India* ed. by Mckim Marriott (Chicago, 1955); 'Social Perception and Scriptural Theory in Indian Caste', *Culture and History* ed. by S. Diamond (Columbia, 1960); and 'Social Trends and Personal Pressures', *The Anthropology of Folk Religion* (Vintage Books, 1961). A major work entitled *The System of Caste in India* is in preparation.

MAYER, ADRIAN C.

Dr Mayer (b. 1922; Ph.D. London) is Lecturer in Asian Anthropology at the School of Oriental and African Studies, University of London. He has done fieldwork in Malabar (1950), Fiji (Indian peasants) (1950-51), Malwa, Central India (1954-55, 1956, 1960-61) and British Columbia (1959). His chief research interests are the study of peasant societies and social and political systems.

Dr Mayer's chief publications are *Land and Society in Malabar* (Bombay, 1952); *Caste and Kinship in Central India* (London, 1960); *A Report on the East Indian Community in Vancouver* (Uni. of Br. Columbia, 1959); and *Peasants in the Pacific: A Study of Fiji Indian Rural Society* (London, 1961).

MOURANT, ARTHUR ERNEST

Dr Mourant (b. 1904; D.Phil. Oxford, F.R.C.P., London) is Director of the Blood Group Reference Laboratory (Medical Research Council) at the Lister

Institute, London. He was awarded the Huxley Memorial Medal by the Royal Anthropological Institute in 1961. He visited India in 1960 to lecture and visit laboratories and research institutions at Calcutta, Bombay, New Delhi and Poona with the collaboration of W.H.O. His chief research interests are: Serology, genetics and the anthropological applications of blood groups.

Dr Mourant's major publications include *The Distribution of the Human Blood Groups* (Oxford, 1954) and *The ABO Blood Groups: Comprehensive Tables and Maps of World Distribution* (with Ada C. Kopec and Kazimiera Domaniewska) (Oxford, 1958).

MUKHERJEE, RAMKRISHNA

Dr Mukherjee (b. 1919; M.Sc. Calcutta, Ph.D. Cambridge) is Professor of Sociology at the Indian Statistical Institute, Calcutta. He was formerly Professor at the Humboldt University, Berlin. He has done fieldwork in Bengal, Bihar and Assam (India) among rural and tribal peoples, and in France (Breton peasantry), Sweden (Lapps), Turkey (peasantry) and Uganda (Acholis). His research interests include anthropometry, sociometry, research techniques, social change, Indian caste, and growth studies in socio-economic strata.

Dr Mukherjee's major publications are: *Six Villages of Bengal* (Calcutta, 1958); *The Dynamics of Rural Society* (Berlin, 1957); and *The Rise and Fall of East India Company* (Berlin, 1958). A major work on the classification of family structures is in preparation.

RAO, CALYAMPUDI RADHAKRISHNA

Dr Rao (b. 1920; M.A. Calcutta, Ph.D. Cambridge) is Professor and Head of the Division of Theoretical Research and Training at the Indian Statistical Institute, Calcutta. He is a Fellow of the National Institute of Sciences (India). During 1953-54 he was Visiting Research Professor of Mathematical Statistics at the University of Illinois, U.S.A. His research interests include the use of statistical methods in biometric research.

Dr Rao's publications include over 75 research papers, reports and several books including the following: *Advanced Statistical Methods in Biometric Research* (New York, 1952); and *Race Elements of Bengal* (with D. N. Majumdar) (Bombay, 1960).

SANKALIA, HASMUKH DHIRAJLAL

Dr Sankalia (b. 1908; M.A. Bombay, Ph.D. London) is Professor of Proto-Indian and Ancient Indian History, Deccan College Post-Graduate and Research Institute and Professor-in-charge of Ancient Indian Culture and Archaeology, University of Poona. He has conducted exploration and excavations in different parts of India with a view to bridge the gulf between Ancient History and Proto-History, and Proto-history and Pre-history.

Dr Sankalia's major publications include *University of Nalanda* (1934); *Archaeology of Gujarat* (1941); *Investigations into the Prehistoric Arachaeology of Gujarat* (1946); *Historical Geography and Cultural Ethnography of Gujarat* (1949); and *Indian Archaeology Today* (1962).

SARKAR, SASANKA SHEKHAR

Dr Sarkar (b. 1908; D.Sc. Calcutta) is Lecturer in the Department of Anthropology, University of Calcutta. He has presided over the Anthropology Section of the Indian Science Congress and is a Fellow of the National Institute of Sciences (India). His research interests include physical anthropology, human biology and human genetics.

Among Dr Sarkar's publications mention may be made of the following: *The Maler of the Rajmahal Hills* (Calcutta, 1938); *Aboriginal Races of India* (Calcutta, 1954); and 'Human skeletal remains from Brahmagiri', *Bull. Dept. of Anthrop.*, IX, 1, 1961.

SEN, DHARANI

Mr Sen (b. 1910; M.Sc. Calcutta) is Senior Lecturer in Anthropology and in-charge of the Pre-history Museum at the University of Calcutta. During 1952-53 he was Reader and acting Head of the Department of Anthropology at the University of Lucknow. He presided over the Anthropology and Archaeology Section of the Indian Science Congress in 1954. He is an Hony. member of the Instituto Italiano di Prehistoria e Protohistoria, Italy. He has been nominated a delegate to the International Science Congress of Prehistory and Protohistory, Rome (1962). He has done extensive field research in eastern India and Madhya Pradesh. His theoretical interests are interpretative archaeology and archaeological theory and his regional interests are eastern India and southeast Asia.

Mr. Sen has published over thirty research papers on Indian prehistory including the following: 'Lower Paleolithic Culture-Complex and Chronology in India', Presidential Address, 41st session of the Indian Science Congress, Anthropology Section; and 'Singhbhum Neolithic Typology', *Man in India*, 30, 1, 1950; (jointly with Uma Chaturvedi) 35, 4, 1955; 38, 3, 1958. A book *Excavations in Mayurbhanj* (Calcutta, 1948) was written jointly with Mr. N. K. Bose.

SEN, DILIP KUMAR

Dr Sen (b. 1921; M.Sc. Calcutta, Ph.D. London) is Lecturer in Anthropology at the University of Lucknow. His main research interests are in the serological studies of Indian populations, growth processes and demographic problems. He has studied blood groups among Bengalis living in Britain.

Among Dr Sen's papers mention may be made of 'Blood group investigations in the 24 Paraganas District (W. Bengal)', *Man in India*, 34, 1, 1954; 'Digital pattern frequency among two groups of criminal populations in U.P.', *The Eastern Anthropologist*, VIII, 2, 1955; 'Some Notes on the fertility of Jaunsari women', *The Eastern Anthropologist*, X, 1, 1956; and 'Blood group and Haemoglobin variants in some upper castes of Bengal', *Jour. of the Roy. Anthrop. Instt.*, 90, I, 1960.

SHAH, POPATLAL GOVINDLAL

Mr Shah (b. 1888; M.A. Bombay) has devoted a lifetime of dedicated service to the cause of anthropological research in Gujarat. A distinguished civil servant (Accountant General, Bombay, 1939 to 1943; Joint Secretary to the Government of Bombay, 1944 to 1946; Member of the Public Service Commission, Bombay and Saurashtra, 1947 to 1954), he cultivated a deep interest in anthropology, and not only sponsored research by professional anthropologists, but also engaged in it himself. His contributions to the subject led to his election as the President of the Gujarat Research Society.

Mr Shah has published many papers and is the author of three monographs including *The Dublas of Gujarat* (Delhi, 1958) and *Naikas-Naikdas: A Gujarat Tribe* (Bombay, 1959).

SUBBARAO, BENDAPUDI

Dr Subbarao (b. 1922; M.A. Lucknow, Ph.D. Bombay) is Professor and Head of the Department of Archaeology and Ancient Indian History at the M.S. University of Baroda. He has conducted exploration and excavation in Bellary (Mysore), Gujarat, Narbada Valley, Ranchi District and Kangra District. His research interests are studies in the pre- and proto-historic archaeology of India as a whole, with special reference to Western India.

Dr Subbarao's major publications are: *Stone Age Cultures of Bellary* (Poona, 1948); *Baroda through the Ages* (Baroda, 1953); The *Personality of India* (Baroda, 2nd ed. 1958); and *Excavations at Maheshwar-Navdatoli* (with Sankalia and Deo, Poona-Baroda, 1958).

EDITORS

Dr Madan and Mr. Śarana, both pupils of the late Professor Majumdar, are lecturers in the Department of Anthropology at the University of Lucknow.

Dr T. N. Madan (b. 1931; M.A. Lucknow, Ph.D. Austral. Nat. Univ.) has done fieldwork among the Brahmans of rural Kashmir and is engaged in writing a book on family and kinship among them. He is interested in the study of agnatic kinship systems generally and kinship among the Brahman communities of India in particular.

Dr Madan is co-author, with the late Professor D. N. Majumdar, of *An Introduction to Social Anthropology* (Bombay, 4th printing 1961). Among his papers mention may be made of '*Herath*: A religious ritual and its secular aspect', *Aspects of Religion in Indian Society* ed. by L. P. Vidyarthi (Meerut, 1961); 'Is the Brahmanic *Gotra* a grouping of kin?', *Southwestern Journal of Anthropology*, 18, 1, 1962; 'Indian Social Organization', *An Economic History of India* 1857-1956, ed. by V. B. Singh (Bombay, 1962); and 'The Joint Family: A Terminological Clarification', *Inter. Journ. of Comp. Socio.*, III, 2, 1962.

Mr Gopāla Śarana (b. 1935; M.A. Lucknow) has done field work among the Oraon of Chotanagpur; he studied their kinship system with special reference to fertility in 1958-60 when he was a Research Fellow of the National Institute of Sciences of India. Among his research interests mention may be made of the theoretical and methodological aspects of social anthropology.

He has published several papers including 'Radcliffe-Brown's contributions to kinship studies', *The Eastern Anthropologist*, X, 1, 1956; 'British social anthropology and its American Appraisal', *The Eastern Anthropologist*, XI, 2, 1957; 'A few comments on some of Radcliffe-Brown's basic concepts', *The Eastern Anthropologist*, XII, 2, 1959; and 'Professor Majumdar and anthropology of Indian religion', *Aspects of Religion in Indian Society* ed. by L. P. Vidyarthi (Meerut, 1961). An introductory Hindi book on prehistory, written jointly with the late Professor Majumdar, is now in press.

INDEX